ADVANCED PROGRAMMING TECHNIQUES

A Second Course
in Programming
Using FORTRAN

ADVANCED PROGRAMMING TECHNIQUES

A Second Course in Programming Using FORTRAN

CHARLES E. HUGHES
University of Tennessee

CHARLES P. PFLEEGER
University of Tennessee

LAWRENCE L. ROSE
Ohio State University

JOHN WILEY & SONS
New York
Santa Barbara
Chichester
Brisbane
Toronto

Library of Congress Cataloging in Publication Data:

Hughes, Charles Edward, 1943–
    Advanced Programming techniques.

    Includes Index.
    1. FORTRAN (Computer program language)
I. Pfleeger, Charles P., 1948–   joint author.
II. Rose, Lawrence L., joint author.   III.   Title.

QA76.73.F25H83   001.6'424   78-9009
ISBN 0–471–02611-5

Printed in the United States of America

10 9 8 7 6 5 4 3 2 1

PREFACE

This book is designed to cover material commonly presented in a second programming course. It includes the majority of topics currently being considered for inclusion in the second course of the revised ACM Curriculum '68 recommendations.

Our objective in writing this book was to bring together much of the material necessary for a novice programmer to mature into a professional or for a professional to grow. We do this by discussing topics and principles and then demonstrating the topics by means of extended examples. The examples show a variety of program development and documentation styles.

The programming language that we use to implement our algorithms is FORTRAN. We present specific details on the WATFIV dialect and on those dialects of 1966 ANS FORTRAN IV as implemented on the IBM 360-370 and the DEC-10 series machines. Where appropriate, we discuss changes to FORTRAN IV that have been made in the new ANS proposed standard, FORTRAN 77.

We have written this book to be usable both by students of computer science and by major computer users. No extraordinary sophistication is assumed of our readers. The only background we require is programming experience equivalent to having successfully completed a basic course in some procedure-oriented language, but this language need not be FORTRAN.

The material is organized into nine chapters and two appendices. Chapters 0 and 1 form the introduction. In Chapter 0 we discuss the portion of the FORTRAN language that is assumed in later chapters. The presentation is brief, serving as a review for those already having a basic knowledge of FORTRAN and as a primer for the reader who knows some other procedure-oriented language. In Chapter 1 we introduce topics of algorithm selection, program development, programming style, documentation standards, debugging techniques, and program maintenance.

In Chapters 2, 3, and 4 we present advanced features of the FORTRAN language. In Chapter 2 we discuss subprograms, with a particular emphasis on data-sharing techniques. In Chapter 3 we deal with character manipulation. In Chapter 4 we describe the organization and uses of tapes and disks; we then describe the FORTRAN statements for using these devices. In addition we introduce some relevant features of the IBM OS/360-370 and DEC-10 TOPS command languages.

v

Chapters 0 to 4 contain examples whose data structures are naturally represented through simple variables and arrays. In Chapter 5 we present techniques for representing and manipulating more complex data structures (linked lists, stacks, queues, and trees).

In Chapters 6, 7, and 8 we describe aspects of the environment—software and hardware—in which a user program runs. In Chapter 6 we discuss the representation of data within digital computers. We present elementary concepts of machine organization in Chapter 7. Finally, in Chapter 8, we discuss techniques for reducing the cost of program development, maintenance, and execution. Specifically, we introduce our readers to the notions of object decks, program relocation, loading, and overlay structures.

Appendix 1 lists and defines the function subprograms standardly built into most FORTRAN dialects. In Appendix 2 we summarize the features of FORTRAN 77 that differ from those of FORTRAN IV as presented in the main part of this text. There is a mark in the margin each time an item in the main text is complemented by a difference listed in the appendix.

The examples in this book intentionally exhibit a variety of styles. Several different techniques of algorithm development, program construction, and documentation are used. This is because we do not believe that there is one style that is universally superior to others; each style has its strengths and natural applications. We want each programmer to observe these styles, to note the appealing parts of each, and to develop a comfortable style.

We wish to acknowledge the many helpful suggestions offered by Al Davis, Bill Haynes, and Robert McGaffey, and by our three referees, J. Mack Adams, Frank Prosser, and Ben Shneiderman. We also wish to thank the many students who braved their way through the various versions of this text and whose criticisms have improved this edition. Finally, we wish to express our gratitude to Joyce Marlar, who skillfully typed much of the original manuscript. Of course, we are still solely responsible for any errors or omissions in this work.

The programs presented here were tested using the IBM 360 model 65 at The University of Tennessee Computing Center. In addition, several of them were tested on the DEC-10 KL processor at The University of Tennessee, and on the DEC-10 KA processor operated by The Ohio State University's Computer and Information Science Department.

Charles E. Hughes
Charles P. Pfleeger
Laurence L. Rose

CONTENTS

CHAPTER 0   Preliminaries

0.1 OVERVIEW

This book will help you to become a mature programmer. In it you will see examples of the tools and the techniques that experienced programmers use in solving their problems. We have chosen FORTRAN as the basis for our discussion, but much of what you will learn here also applies to other languages. We will describe many properties of computing, independent of the language being used.

As programmers mature, they develop "style," which means that they adopt certain habits of program structure, documentation, and coding. Chapter 1 is devoted to programming style, and we will also note points of good style throughout this text. In Chapters 2 to 4, you can learn about topics such as subprogram usage, character manipulation, and tape and disk I/O. In later chapters you will learn about the environment in which your program runs; we describe the internal representation of data, the structure of a digital computer, and the process of program execution.

Perhaps you have never learned FORTRAN, or your exposure to it occurred some time ago. This book has been designed for use by anyone with experience in some procedure-oriented language. If you know a language such as PL/I, ALGOL, PASCAL or COBOL, you should have no trouble learning FORTRAN. This preliminary chapter presents the material that you will need later. Even if you already know FORTRAN, we suggest that you read this chapter to refresh your memory and to guarantee that you know all of this background material. The description of each statement has been condensed to a block and shaded so that you can refer to it quickly.

In this text we describe FORTRAN as standardized by the American National Standards Institute in report X3.9-1966. A new standard has been proposed and appears to have achieved a favorable response; this new version is called FORTRAN 77. In places where the new form differs from the standard, we will mark that section of Chapter 0 with a vertical bar in the margin; you should refer to Appendix 2 for a description of the change.

Some features of FORTRAN depend on which computer and which compiler are being used. Some compilers accept part or all of standard FORTRAN, and some allow extensions to the standard. We will call each combination of a machine and a compiler a *dialect*. Many of our dialect-dependent examples are based on two widely used dialects: the IBM 360-370 computers under the WATFIV compiler, and the DEC-10 computer with the compiler FORTRAN-10.

0.2 BACKGROUND AND DEFINITIONS

0.2.1 Statement Form

A FORTRAN program consists of a series of statements; these statements appear in a fixed form on input records with at most one statement per record. Each statement looks like the punched card in Figure 0-1. Although the actual input medium could be something else, such as a line of a typewriter terminal or a record on a paper tape, we will speak as if the input comes from cards.

FIGURE 0-1 FORTRAN Statement Format

A *statement number* in FORTRAN is a number appearing anywhere in columns 1 to 5. A statement number is used on a statement that needs to be related to other statements in the program. On most FORTRAN statements, the number may be omitted.

The *body* of a statement is punched in columns 7 to 72. Blanks are ignored in the statement body (except within character data, to be described shortly); this implies that the body need not begin exactly at column 7, and that blanks may be inserted as desired to improve readability.

If the body of one statement is too long to fit on a single card, the statement may be continued by punching any character, except a blank or zero, in the *continuation field* (column 6) of the next card, and continuing the statement in columns 7 to 72 of this new card. Additional continuations may be made by punching a nonblank character in column 6 of succeeding cards. A maximum of 20 cards (19 continuations) is allowed for any one statement.

Columns 73 to 80 are reserved for a *sequence number*, although this may be omitted. (For some input forms other than cards, this field does not exist, or it may be filled in for you.) On large programs it is a good idea to punch numbers in this field to help you sort the input deck if it should be dropped.

Column 1 is used to identify *comments*. Any card with the letter C in column 1 is taken as a comment and is ignored by the compiler. Comments are used to identify a program, to separate a program into logical segments, or to explain a particular segment of a program.

0.2.2 Data Types

FORTRAN data items are stored in words of a fixed size. A word of storage consists of a fixed number of binary digits (0's and 1's) called *bits*. The IBM 360-370 uses a word size of 32 bits; the DEC-10 has a word size of 36 bits. A word may contain one or more data items, depending on the type of the data; on some machines multiple words are used to hold a single data item. The first four data types in FORTRAN that we will discuss are integer, real, logical and character.

Integer data items are whole numbers, that is, numbers with no fractional part. An *integer constant* is a series of one or more decimal digits, optionally preceded by a + or − sign. Examples of integer constants are +2, −9695, and 800000 .

Real data items may have a fractional part. There are two forms for a *real constant*: first, a series of digits containing a decimal point; and second, a series of digits, perhaps containing a decimal point, followed by the letter E and an integer constant. Both forms may be preceded by an optional + or − sign. Examples of real constants are: 1., +3.1416, −.483695 and +0.428E2, −369E6, and 1.0E−4 . The constants in the latter group are in "scientific notation"; the value after the "E" is the power of 10 by which the first value is to be multiplied. Thus the last three examples are equivalent to 42.8, −369000000., and .0001 . Scientific notation is commonly used to express very large and very small numbers.

Logical data items have either the value true or false; constants for these values are .TRUE. and .FALSE., respectively.

A character data item is a series of letters, digits, symbols, and blanks. A *character string constant* has the form nHconstant, where n is an unsigned integer constant indicating the length of (number of characters in) the character string, and the constant is the next n characters after the letter H. Examples of this form are 5HCPP01 and 11HCAN'T SPELL . An alternate form for character constants acceptable to many compilers is to enclose the character string in apostrophes. Within such a constant, the character "apostrophe" is represented by two successive apostrophes. Two examples of this kind are 'IBM OS/360' and 'ISN''T BAD' . The handling of character data is described in Chapter 3; for now we will use character strings only to label output.

The range of values for these types of data items depends on the word size of the computer being used. In Figure 0-2 we present the ranges accepted by several common computers. An integer range of n digits means that all n-digit integers may be represented on the machine. The real range is the limit of the magnitude of a real value; however, only the indicated number of digits of precision are maintained. The number of characters per word relates to the storing of character data and will be explained more fully in Chapter 3.

Computer type	Integer Range (digits)	Real Range	Real Precision (digits)	Characters per word
Burroughs 6700	12	10^{-46}–10^{+69}	11	8
CDC 6000-7000	18	10^{-293}–10^{+322}	15	10
DEC-10	10	10^{-38}–10^{+38}	8	5
IBM 360-370	9	10^{-78}–10^{+75}	7	4
UNIVAC 1108-1110	10	10^{-38}–10^{+38}	8	6
XEROX SIGMA 5-7	9	10^{-78}–10^{+75}	7	4

FIGURE 0-2 Basic Data Modes

Variables in FORTRAN may be of integer, real, or logical mode. (FORTRAN 77, WATFIV, and many other dialects allow a character mode, also.) The mode of a variable does not change during the execution of a program.

A FORTRAN *variable name* is a sequence of up to 6 letters or digits, the first of which must be a letter. Thus TOTAL, I, SUMOFX, and COL72 are legal variable names. A FORTRAN variable name may represent a simple variable, an array element, or an array name. A *simple variable* represents a unique value and is associated with a single word in storage.

Each *array element* likewise represents a single value in storage. Array elements are denoted in FORTRAN by enclosing the subscript(s) in a pair of parentheses following the name. Arrays may have up to three dimensions, but some compilers allow more. If ROWSUM is a one-dimensional array (also called a vector) of 10 elements, then the sixth element is denoted as ROWSUM(6). Subscripts must be integer-valued and less than or equal to the defined maximum size of the array. In FORTRAN each array begins with the element having subscript "1"; negative or zero subscript values are illegal. Thus if I is a simple integer variable then ROWSUM(I), ROWSUM(I+2), ROWSUM(3*I+15), etc., are legal references to vector ROWSUM, as long as the evaluation of each expression results in a subscript value not less than 1, and not greater than the number of elements in the array. The allowable complexity of subscript expressions depends on the compiler being used; some compilers allow nothing more complicated than a constant times a variable plus or minus a constant, while others allow any integer expression. You should determine what restrictions, if any, are imposed by your compiler.

An *array name* is associated with a group of contiguous words (one for each element of the array). FORTRAN stores array elements in *column-major order*. This means elements of the first column are stored, from the first row through the last row, then the second column follows, etc. Figure 0-3 shows possible storage of simple variables I, J, KOUNT, MAX, the 4 element vector TOP and the 3 by 2 array SUM.

I
J
TOP (1)
TOP (2)
TOP (3)
TOP (4)
KOUNT
SUM (1, 1)
SUM (2, 1)
SUM (3, 1)
SUM (1, 2)
SUM (2, 2)
SUM (3, 2)
MAX

FIGURE 0-3 FORTRAN Storage Allocation

When an array element reference appears in a program, the subscripts are evaluated and the single word of storage associated with that element of the array is accessed. This association is performed through the use of a storage mapping function and the symbol table. A *symbol table* is a table of symbols (variable names) used in the program, along with the address of the first word of storage associated with each symbol.

A *storage mapping function* is a formula to compute which word is associated with a given array element. Recall that in FORTRAN each array is stored as a block of contiguous words, and that arrays are stored in column-major order. Thus A(K) is stored (K-1) words after A(1). For a two-dimensional array, in order to locate a particular element, we must determine how many columns precede the one containing the desired element, and then determine how many elements in this column precede the desired element. If X is an M by N array, then the location of element X(I,J), relative to the beginning of array X, is

$$\mathrm{loc}[X(I,J)] = (J-1)*M + (I-1)$$

That is, the location of element X(I,J) equals the number of words occupied by the columns preceding column J (J-1 columns of length M), plus the number of words occupied by the elements of column J preceding row I (I-1 elements).

The storage of multidimensional arrays is by the first dimension (i.e., with the first subscript varying fastest), then by the second dimension, etc. For example, elements of the 2 by 3 by 2 array Y would be stored in the following order: Y(1,1,1), Y(2,1,1), Y(1,2,1), Y(2,2,1), Y(1,3,1), Y(2,3,1), Y(1,1,2), Y(2,1,2), Y(1,2,2), Y(2,2,2), Y(1,3,2), Y(2,3,2). In allocating storage, FORTRAN uses the declared size of an array to determine how many contiguous words of storage to set aside. Neither the number of dimensions nor the maximum size of an array dimension may change during the execution of a FORTRAN program. This is because FORTRAN uses a *static allocation* strategy in that the storage locations for arrays or simple variables are set aside before execution and do not change during execution of the program.

0.2.3 Operators

There are three categories of operators in FORTRAN: arithmetic, logical, and relational. Arithmetic operators are used in computations with integer or real values. The arithmetic operators are shown in Figure 0-4.

operator	meaning
**	exponentiation
+,-	plus, negation
*,/	multiplication, division
+,-	addition, subtraction

FIGURE 0-4   Arithmetic Operators

Exponentiation (**) means "raising to a power" (e.g. X**2 means X squared, or X raised to the power 2). The plus and negation operators (also called unary plus and unary minus) indicate the sign of a value (e.g., +3.75 or -2) or the negation of a value (e.g., -A). The four common arithmetic operators (*/+-) should be familiar.

The relational operators, shown in Figure 0-5, are used to compare two values, which may be variables or constants or expressions. These operators can test for the following conditions.

operator	meaning
.LT.	less than
.LE.	less than or equal
.GT.	greater than
.GE.	greater than or equal
.EQ.	equal
.NE.	not equal

FIGURE 0-5   Relational Operators

Each of the symbols is 4 characters long; the periods are a required part of the representation.

There are also three logical operators, which are listed in Figure 0-6. These operators are used to create complex logical expressions.

operator	meaning
.NOT.	logical negation
.AND.	logical and
.OR.	logical or

FIGURE 0-6 Logical Operators

The first of these negates the value of a single logical expression; the latter two join two logical expressions into one compound logical expression.

0.2.4 Expressions

There are two different types of FORTRAN expressions: arithmetic expressions and logical expressions. An *arithmetic expression* may be:

1. A integer or real constant.
2. An integer or real variable.
3. Two arithmetic expressions joined by an arithmetic operator.
4. An arithmetic expression enclosed in parentheses.
5. An arithmetic expression preceded by a + or - sign.

   Note, however, that two arithmetic operators may not be adjacent in a FORTRAN expression, so that "A times negative 10" must be coded as A*(-10).

Arithmetic expressions are written in a notation similar to that of mathematics. Parentheses are used to control the order of evaluation of terms in the expression as well as to denote array subscripts. An expression may consist of all real variables and constants, all integer operands, or a combination of real and integer. A single mode arithmetic expression (all integer or all real) is evaluated entirely in that mode. However, expressions with both integer and real terms (called *mixed-mode expressions*) yield real results; any time a real term appears as one of two values to be combined in a subexpression, that subexpression is evaluated in real mode.

In FORTRAN the placement of parentheses and the precedence of operators control the interpretation of expressions. The following four rules define the order in which arithmetic expressions are evaluated.

1. Quantities within parentheses must be evaluated before they can be combined with any other quantities outside the parentheses.
2. Operations within an arithmetic expression are performed according to their precedence: **, then plus and negation, then * and /, and last + and -. This precedence is the same order in which the operators are listed in Figure 0-4.

3. Arithmetic expressions having two operators (except exponentiation) of the same level of precedence are evaluated as if the operations were performed left to right.
4. Expressions involving two successive exponentiations (for example A**B**C) should be parenthesized to show order of evaluation, since the order is not standard among FORTRAN compilers.

Examples: Assume J = 7 (integer) I = 5 (integer) X(6) = 3. (real)

	expression	value	mode
(a)	I * 3.1	15.5	real
(b)	I - X(J-1)	2.0	real
(c)	I + J/2*5	20	integer
(d)	-X(I+1)**2/2	-4.5	real
(e)	(X(6)+1.0)*4.0	16.0	real

Examples a and b show mixed-mode expressions; hence their results are of real mode. In example c the division and multiplication are of higher precedence than the addition, so they are performed first, left to right by rules 2 and 3: 7/2 = 3,   3*5 = 15,   5+15 = 20,   which is the final result. Notice that the quotient of two integers is also an integer, and that any remainder is thus lost. We say the remainder is *truncated* as a result of the integer division; thus 7/2 is 3. In example d the exponentiation has highest precedence, followed by negation and finally division. Our result is equivalent to   (-(3.**2))/ 2 = -4.5 . Example e shows the use of parentheses to change the order of evaluation: here + is performed before *, producing (3.+1.)*4. or 4.*4. = 16.
    In addition to arithmetic expressions, logical expressions can also be constructed in FORTRAN. A *logical expression* may be:

1. A logical constant.
2. A logical variable.
3. Two arithmetic expressions separated by a relational operator.
4. A logical expression enclosed in parentheses.
5. A logical expression preceded by the logical operator .NOT. .
6. Two logical expressions separated by the logical operator .AND. or .OR. .

Logical expressions are evaluated in the following order.

1. Portions of the expression enclosed in parentheses are evaluated before portions outside parentheses.
2. Any arithmetic expression in the logical expression is evaluated first.
3. Expressions involving the six relational operators are evaluated next.

4. Finally, the logical operators are applied left to right in order of their precedence: .NOT., then .AND., then .OR. . (This is the same order in which the operators are listed in Figure 0-6.)

Examples: Assume that logical variables ON and A have values .TRUE. and .FALSE., respectively, and that integer I has the value 5 .

	expression	value
(a)	I .LT. 5	.FALSE.
(b)	ON .AND. .NOT. A	.TRUE.
(c)	A .OR. (I .GE. 3) .AND. ON	.TRUE.

In example a, I is not less than 5; hence the result is .FALSE. . Since rule 4 above states that .NOT. is applied before .AND., in example b, the first term evaluated is .NOT. A, which is .TRUE. . Then .AND. is applied to ON and (.NOT. A), yielding .TRUE. . In example c, rule 1 indicates that (I.GE.3) is to be evaluated first; this result is .TRUE. . (Even without the parentheses, this term would be the first evaluated, because of rule 3.) Then by rule 4, we apply .AND. to (I.GE.3) and ON, which is .TRUE. . Finally we apply .OR. between A and the previous result (.TRUE.); this produces the final value of .TRUE. .

0.2.5 Notation

We are now ready to introduce the basic statements of the FORTRAN language. In our descriptions of the statements, any upper case letters or marks of punctuation must be coded exactly as shown. The *italicized* terms are to be replaced with items as the terms direct. Any optional portions of a statement are surrounded by brackets; the brackets are not coded, and the portion enclosed by brackets may be omitted from the statement. For example, the notation

[*label*] IF (*logex*) *stmt*

indicates that the statement may have a *label*, and that it must consist of the word IF followed by a *logex* in parentheses, followed by a *stmt*. The terms *label*, *logex* and *stmt* are explained later in the statement block.

Except within character strings, blanks are ignored by the FORTRAN compiler. Thus blanks may be inserted anywhere within a FORTRAN statement to improve readability. We advise you to make liberal use of blanks, much the same as you would in other forms of written communication.

0.3 NONEXECUTABLE STATEMENTS

Most statements in a FORTRAN program are *executable*, meaning that they are converted to machine language and cause machine action as the program is executed. Other statements of FORTRAN are *nonexecutable*. This means that they are not translated into machine commands to be performed during execution; nonexecutable statements provide information that the compiler uses during the translation process. In this section, the nonexecutable statements of FORTRAN are defined.

0.3.1 Specification Statements

The first class of nonexecutable statements are the specification statements. These control the type, size, initial value and placement of variables within a program. Nonexecutable statements that will be described in this chapter are the DIMENSION, REAL, INTEGER, LOGICAL, IMPLICIT and DATA statements. The EQUIVALENCE statement is discussed in Chapter 1, and COMMON and statement functions are described in Chapter 2. These statements must all appear at the top of a program (or subprogram—to be discussed in Section 0.7) since they affect the manner in which the compiler interprets the executable statements that follow.

At the beginning of a FORTRAN program it is necessary to declare the maximum value of each subscript of the arrays used in the program. If the *dimension* of a variable is not explicitly declared, the variable is assumed to be simple (unsubscripted). The dimension of an array may not change during the execution of a program. One way to declare the size of an array is with the DIMENSION statement.

DIMENSION *list*

where   *list* is a sequence of subscripted variables separated by commas

Example   DIMENSION X(10), SUM(2,3), TOP(5)

Effect   This sets aside 10 words for vector X, 6 words (2*3) for array SUM, and 5 words for vector TOP.

Notes   1. More than one DIMENSION statement may appear in a program.
2. The number of dimensions allowed for an array is compiler dependent.
3. Subscripts must be integer constants and represent the maximum value allowed for each dimension.
4. Each array name must be unique.

As we have seen, variables may be of integer, real, or logical mode. This mode must be declared to the FORTRAN compiler so that it can interpret the bit pattern stored in the word associated with a variable. If the programmer does not declare the mode of a variable, the compiler assigns mode according to the first character of the variable name. The following three statements are used to declare mode explicitly in FORTRAN.

REAL *varlist*
INTEGER *varlist*
LOGICAL *varlist*

where   *varlist* is a list of simple variables, array names, and function names, separated by commas. (Some dialects permit mode statements to contain dimension information also. In this case *varlist* may also contain subscripted variables with the subscripts denoting the dimensions.)

Example   REAL X, KOUNT, ROW(6)

Effect   This declares X, KOUNT, and ROW to be of real mode; it also declares ROW to be a vector of dimension 6.

Notes   1. More than one REAL, INTEGER or LOGICAL statement is permitted in a program.
   2. A variable may appear in only one mode statement.
   3. Subscripts must be integer constants and represent the maximum value allowed for each dimension.
   4. If the dimension of an array is given on a mode statement, that array may not also appear on a DIMENSION statement. However, the array name can appear without subscripts on a mode statement, and the dimension may then be given on a DIMENSION statement.
   5. These statements are nonexecutable and must precede all executable statements in a program.
   6. *Default*: if a variable does not appear in a mode statement its mode is determined by the first character of the variable name: variables beginning with I through N default to integer mode; all others default to real mode.

Another means of declaring the mode of variables is by the IMPLICIT statement, although the statement is not acceptable in some dialects. This statement indicates a mode and a range of letters. In the absence of other declarations, all variables whose names begin with a letter in the range will be of the indicated

type. The implicit typing may be overridden for individual variables by the
REAL, INTEGER or LOGICAL statements. The IMPLICIT statement has the following
form.

> IMPLICIT *mode* (*range1* [, *range2*, etc.])
>
> where   *mode* is either REAL, INTEGER or LOGICAL
>   each *range* is either a single letter or a pair of letters separated by
>   a dash.
>
> Example   IMPLICIT INTEGER (C-D, H-K, Z)
>
> Effect   Any variables that begin with C, D, H, I, J, K or Z will default to
>   integer mode.
>
> Notes   1. The IMPLICIT statement must precede any other specification state-
>   ments in a program.
>   2. The default modes based on initial letters may be changed for
>   specific variables with the individual mode statements, REAL, INTE-
>   GER and LOGICAL.
>   3. Use of the IMPLICIT statement extends the range of default first
>   letters. In the above example variables beginning with letters
>   L, M or N will also be integers by default because of the standard
>   I through N default.

Normally, when a storage location is assigned to a variable, the value
currently in that location is unknown, and hence the variable is considered
undefined by the programmer. However, we may define the initial value assigned to a variable through the use of a DATA statement.

> DATA *varlist1 / values1 /* [, *varlist2 / values2 /*, etc.]
>
> where   each *varlist* is a list of simple variables and array elements; some
>   compilers also permit array names in the list
>   *values* are the constant value(s), separated by commas, to be initially
>   assigned to the variables in the preceding *varlist*. The notation
>   n*value, for some integer constant *n*, denotes *n* repetitions
>   of the value
>
> Example   INTEGER TOP, K, L
>   REAL X(3,2), Y(10,20)
>   DATA TOP/5/, X/3*1./, 3*10./, K, L/0, 1/, Y(5,2)/13/

Effect   This initializes variable TOP to value 5; the elements of array X to values 1., 1., 1., 10., 10., 10.; variables K and L to 0 and 1, respectively; and element Y(5,2) to 13.

Notes   1. If an array name is specified, it implies all elements of the array.
2. There must be a one-to-one correspondence between the elements in each *varlist*, and the constants in the following *values* list.
3. The variables and their values correspond left to right. For an array name, the values are assigned to the individual elements of the array in storage (column-major) order.
4. The mode of each variable and its associated initial value must match, except a character constant may be assigned to a variable of any mode.
5. This statement must follow all dimension or mode statements in a program.
6. This statement provides an initial value prior to execution. Once the value of a variable is changed, it cannot be reset by use of a DATA statement.
7. More than one DATA statement is permitted.
8. *Default*: any variable not in a DATA statement has an unpredictable initial value.

Some FORTRAN compilers allow data initialization to be included in a mode statement. When this occurs we can declare mode, dimension, and initial value of variables with one statement. For example,

```
INTEGER I/0/, LIST(5,2)/5*0, 5*1/
```

declares I and LIST to be of integer mode, I a simple variable of initial value 0, LIST a 5 by 2 array whose first column is initialized to zero and whose second column is initialized to one.

0.3.2 The END Statement

The END statement marks the completion of a main program or subprogram definition. It is the single word END and must physically be the last statement of a program definition.

END

where   nothing else appears in the record

Example   END

Effect   Terminate compilation of this main program or subprogram.

Notes   1. Only one END statement is allowed per main program or subprogram.
         2. This must be the last statement of each main program or subprogram definition.
         3. This is nonexecutable; it may not be labeled.

This completes our review of some of the basic nonexecutable statements of FORTRAN. The FORMAT statement will be discussed in Section 0.5.4, and other nonexecutable statements will be discussed in later chapters. We will now define the executable statements of FORTRAN. We first look at how to assign values to variables and how to perform input and output; then, in Section 0.6, we describe local control of execution in FORTRAN. Finally, in Section 0.7, we examine FORTRAN subprograms.

0.4   THE ASSIGNMENT STATEMENT

The *assignment statement* replaces the value of a variable with the value of some expression. The FORTRAN statement A = B directs that the current value of B be placed in the storage location for A. It should be interpreted as "assign the present value of B to A," instead of "A equals B." Thus the sequence of FORTRAN statements

```
A = 5
B = 8
A = B
```

results in both A and B being equal to the constant 8. The old value of A (5 in this case) is lost. The assignment statement has the following form.

   [label]   avarname = arex
                  or
   [label]   lvarname = logex

where   label is a statement number
        avarname is an integer or real simple variable or array element
        lvarname is a logical simple variable or array element
        arex is an arithmetic expression
        logex is a logical expression

Example
```
10 KOUNT = 2.7 * (I-1)
   LIST(3) = LIST(3) + 1
20 ON = LIST(I) .LT. KOUNT
   VALUE = LIST(KOUNT)**I / 2 - LIST(I)
30 LIST(2*I-1) = LIST(KOUNT-2) * LIST(I)
```

Effect   For each assignment statement evaluate the expression on the right side of the equal sign and and assign that value to the variable on the left.

Notes   1. The programmer must have provided a value for each variable on the right-hand side prior to execution of this statement.
    2. The mode of *arex* is converted to the mode of the *avarname* if they differ.
    3. The value of only one variable, *avarname* or *lvarname*, is altered by an assignment.

Let us study the five assignment statements in this example. Assume that the modes and values of variables before execution of statement 10 are as follows.

KOUNT	14	integer	ON	.TRUE.	logical
LIST(3)	6	integer	VALUE	15.3	real
LIST(5)	4	integer	I	3	integer

In statement 10 the expression 2.7*2 is evaluated as 5.4 and should be assigned to KOUNT. But since KOUNT is of integer mode, truncation occurs and KOUNT is assigned the value 5. (See note 2 above.) For the next statement, 6+1 or 7 is assigned to LIST(3). Thus LIST(3) has been changed from 6 to 7 . In statement 20, the logical expression is evaluated as .FALSE. (since the value of KOUNT is now 5 and LIST(3) is 7), and .FALSE. is assigned to ON. For the following statement, the value to be assigned is ((4**3)/2)-7 or 25 . But the mode of VALUE is real, and so it is assigned the value 25.0 . In statement 30, LIST(5) is assigned the value 7*7 or 49 .

After execution of the five assignment statements, the values of these six simple variables and array elements are:

KOUNT	5		ON	.FALSE.
LIST(3)	7		VALUE	25.0
LIST(5)	49		I	3

0.5 INPUT/OUTPUT STATEMENTS

In this section we discuss input and output (I/O) statements. Data values input with a READ statement are assigned to the variables listed in the READ. With WRITE and PRINT statements you can display the current values of variables on a device such as a printer. Some FORTRAN dialects (e.g., WATFIV) allow free-format I/O; with this form the programmer need not specify in exactly which positions data is placed on a record. All FORTRAN dialects recognize formatted I/O, in which the programmer indicates the exact form of each data record.

0.5.1 Lists of Variables for Input and Output

We begin this section with a description of variable lists for input and output.

> *iolist* denotes
>   1. *varlist*
>   2. *iolist, iolist*
>   3. (*iolist, ivar = initial, final* [*, increment*])
>
> where *varlist* is a list of simple variables, array elements, and array names
>   *ivar* is a nonsubscripted integer variable
>   *initial, final*, and *increment* are integer constants or simple integer varia-
>   bles, each having a value greater than zero. *Default*: if omitted, incre-
>   ment is 1

A simple variable or an array element in an *iolist* indicates that a single value is to be used for output or replaced by input. If an unsubscripted array name is part of an *iolist*, it represents *all* elements of the array in (column-major) storage order. The third form of *iolist* uses a contruct, called the *implied* DO, that resembles the DO statement used for repetition. (The full DO statement will be studied in Section 0.6.4.) The implied DO is a useful notational shortcut for constructing lists of variables, especially array elements. All items of the *iolist* are generated for each value of the implied DO variable, *ivar*, from the *initial* value, in increments of *increment*, through the *final* value. Hence the implied DO of (Y(2*I-1), X(I), I = 3, 8, 2) is expanded by the FORTRAN compiler to: Y(5), X(3), Y(9), X(5), Y(13), X(7). The next value of the implied DO variable, I, is 9, which exceeds the requested final value. The compiler builds the *iolist* (Y(2*I-1), X(I)) for I having values 3, 5, and 7, to create an *iolist* of 6 variables.

Example

List	Represents
(a) SUM, TOP(I), J	SUM, TOP(I), J
(b) (X(I), I = 3,5)	X(3), X(4), X(5)
(c) ((Y(K,J), K = 1,5), J = 1,M)	Y(1,1), Y(2,1), Y(3,1),...,Y(5,1), Y(1,2), Y(2,2),...,Y(5,M)

0.5.2 Free-format Input

The free-format input of WATFIV and other dialects is convenient for beginning programmers, since the programmer does not need to specify the columns in which the input appears on a data card. Data values appear in any positions of a data card, with items separated by blanks and/or commas. The free-format input statement is the READ statement, which is described below.

[label] READ, iolist

or

[label] READ (indev, * [, END=exit]) iolist

where   label is an optional statement number
   iolist is as previously defined in this section
   indev is an integer constant or variable designating the input unit number
   * denotes free-format
   exit is the statement number of an executable statement

Examples   (a)   READ, I, TOP, (LIST(J), J=1,5,2)
   (b)   READ (5, *, END=99) I, TOP, (LIST(J), J=1,5,2)
   card:

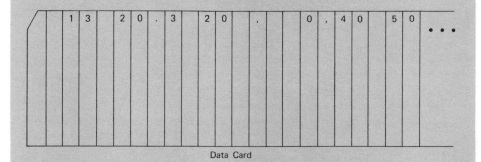

Data Card

Effect   (Either example) Input 5 values from the next card and assign them in order to the iolist variables:

```
   I    TOP  LIST(1) LIST(3) LIST(5)
  13   20.3    20       0      40
```

Notes   1. Every execution of a READ statement inputs a new card.
   2. Free-format data values may appear anywhere on a card, separated by commas and/or blanks.
   3. Each data value must agree in mode with the variable to which it is assigned.
   4. A READ statement will input only as many values as iolist designates; extra numbers are ignored. If more numbers are required,

then more cards are input until all elements of *iolist* are defined, or until the last card is exhausted.

5. The value of *indev* is dialect-dependent. For IBM 360-370 with WATFIV, *indev* = 5 for cards.

6. Once all data cards have been read, another execution of any READ statement on the same device will result in an I/O error and execution termination, if no END= option has been given. If an END= exit has been specified, execution resumes at the statement *exit*.

0.5.3 Free-format Output

Free-format output is produced by the PRINT statement. Like the free-format READ statement, this statement is helpful to beginning programmers, since the programmer does not need to specify in exactly which positions the output data values are to be printed. The PRINT statement is also quite useful during debugging where it may be important to display values at certain stages of the computation; a PRINT statement can then be easily inserted to display these values. The form of the PRINT statement is as follows.

[*label*] PRINT, *outlist*

where   *label* is an optional statement number
outlist is a list having the same form as an *iolist*, but possibly containing constants and expressions, in addition to simple variables, array elements, and array names

Example   PRINT, I, (X(J), J=1,2), SUM, '= TOTAL'
where I = 3   X(1) = 30.   X(2) = 87.2   SUM = 117.2
Effect   The following line is printed.
3   0.300000 E 02   0.872000 E 02   0.1172000 E 03 = TOTAL

Notes   1. Each execution of a PRINT begins on the next line of the line printer.
2. More than one line is printed if more space is needed to output all of the values in *outlist*.
3. Integers are output right-justified with leading zeros suppressed.
4. Reals are usually printed in scientific (E) notation.
5. All values are output in the order of *outlist*.

0.5.4 The FORMAT Statement and Formatted I/O

Free-format input and output, as implemented by the WATFIV READ and PRINT statements, is convenient for beginning programmers. As programming problems become more sophisticated, however, it becomes more important to arrange data precisely on a printed page, or to have the ability to select the positions in which input data will appear. It is also convenient to be able to ignore certain columns of input or to produce spacing other than single spacing for output. For these and similar situations, the precise control of formatted input and output is needed.

In formatted input and output, as the term suggests, the data values are in a precise arrangement called a *format*. A record is a sequence of fields, and a FORMAT statement simply identifies the fields of a record. A FORMAT statement is a template; it defines the position, size and type of the data on the record. Each field contains a single data value. The FORMAT statement has the following form.

> *label*   FORMAT (*format list*)

where   *label* is a mandatory statement number
  format list is a series of one or more format codes separated by commas. Each format code is one of the codes below[1].

In the following list, n, w and d must be unsigned integer constants; n may be omitted, implying a value of 1.

nIw: n integers of width w.
nF$w.d$: n decimal (real) numbers of width w, with d digits after the decimal point.
nE$w.d$: n scientific representation real numbers of width w, with d digits after the decimal point.
nAw: n alphanumeric values of w characters each.
wH*string-of-w-characters*: literal field consisting of the w characters immediately following the H.
'*any-string*': literal field (not acceptable in all dialects).
nX: ignored (input) or blank (output) field of n spaces.
Tw: skip to column w (not acceptable in all dialects).
/: end of current record (line or card).
n(*format list*): repeat group of n repetitions of the series of codes in the parenthesized list.

Example 100   FORMAT (5X, I2, F6.2, 2(3X, A4))

Effect   Defines seven fields, starting at the beginning of the record, as follows.

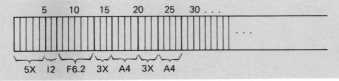

---

[1] Consult a FORTRAN *manual for additional codes.*

Notes   1. A FORMAT statement need not describe an entire record.
2. A FORMAT statement may be referenced by more than one I/O statement.
3. Literal constant fields (H codes and quoted strings) are normally used only for output.
4. A FORMAT statement may be placed anywhere in a program; it is a nonexecutable statement.
5. When all field codes in the FORMAT statement have been used but there remain variables in the associated READ or WRITE list, a new record is begun at the repeat group associated with the last right parenthesis (ignoring the right parenthesis closing the entire FORMAT statement). If there is no repeat group, the entire FORMAT is reused.

0.5.5 Formatted READ

The formatted READ statement has the following form.

[*label*]   READ (*indev*, *fmt* [, END=*exit*]) *iolist*

where   *label* is an optional statement number
indev is an integer designation of the input device
fmt is the label of the associated FORMAT statement
exit is the number of an executable statement (Not all dialects permit use of the END= option.)
iolist is a list as defined in Section 0.5.1

Example
```
READ (5, 101, END=50) I, TOP, (LIST(J), J=1, 5, 2)
101 FORMAT(I2, 4X, F5.1, 3(2X,I2))
```

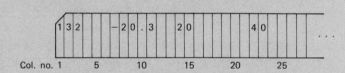

Col. no. 1   5   10   15   20   25

Effect   Input five values from the next card in accordance with FORMAT statement 101. If the end of the data is encountered, branch to statement 50. In this example the *iolist* variables are assigned the following values.

I	13
TOP	-20.3
LIST(1)	20
LIST(3)	0
LIST(5)	40

Notes 1. Every execution of a READ statement begins its input with a new record.
2. Values are assigned to the *iolist* variables in accordance with the referenced FORMAT statement.
3. Each data value input must agree with the mode of the FORMAT field and with the mode of the variable to which it is assigned, except that any variable may receive input under an A format code.
4. Blanks are interpreted as zeros in numeric fields.
5. The value of *indev* is dialect-dependent. For IBM 360-370, *indev* = 5 for cards; for DEC-10, *indev* = 2 for cards, and *indev* = 5 for terminal input.

Let us consider two examples of READ under format control to illustrate how the FORMAT statement acts under card input.

Example 1: *Integer input*

```
INTEGER LIST(50), N
READ (5,100) N, (LIST(I),I=1,N)
100 FORMAT (16(I3, 2X))
```

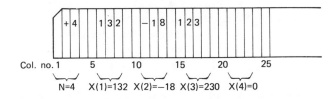

In this example, the first value on the data card (4) provides a value for N; the remaining values are assigned to the first N elements of LIST. Notice that a sign counts as part of the field size. Since blanks are interpreted as zeros, integers must be right justified to prevent any trailing blanks from changing the value punched. With the data shown the entire format (16 integer fields) was not used, yet no error resulted. We need not use all fields of a FORMAT statement. We often write formats to define the maximum number of data items that might appear on a record, such as 10I8 or 8I10 for cards.

Example 2: *Mixed-type input*

```
REAL Y(10)
INTEGER LOC, KOUNT
READ (5,101) LOC, KOUNT, (Y(I), I=1, 4)
101 FORMAT (2I5 / 3(F4.1,1X))
```

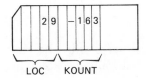
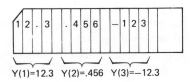
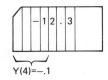

In this case, three cards are read, since the format described only five fields and we requested six numbers. The first card was used to provide values for LOC and KOUNT. The / terminated use of that record (card) and caused three F4.1 fields to be taken from the second card. After this second card was exhausted, control returned to the start of the last repeat group, using a new data card. The last F4.1 field was taken from the third data card. Note that a decimal point appearing anywhere in the field is retained in that position in the input value, but a value without a decimal point has one placed *d* digits from the right end of the input value. The sign and the punched decimal point, if either is present, occupy one position in the field.

We urge you to input using the END= option. This allows you to use the end-of-data condition to signal completion of one phase of processing. If the end-of-data was unexpected, you can then output a message along with the values of key variables and halt under programmer control.

0.5.6 Formatted WRITE

In this section we define formatted output with the WRITE statement.

[*label*] WRITE (*outdev*, *fmt*) [*iolist*]

where *label* is an optional statement number
outdev is an integer constant or variable designating the output device
fmt is the statement number of the associated FORMAT statement
iolist is an optional I/O list

Example Assume RMAX and SUM are real variables having values -13.2 and 183.765, respectively.

```
    WRITE (6,100) RMAX, SUM
100 FORMAT (' RMAX = ', F7.2, 5X, 'TOTAL IS $', F6.2)
```

Effect The following output is produced.

```
    RMAX =  -13.20    TOTAL IS $183.77
```

Notes 1. If *outdev* refers to a line printer, the first character of the output line controls the movement of the paper before the line is printed. This character is called a *carriage control character* and is not printed. Carriage control symbols and their meanings are: '+': print on the same line, ' ': single space, '0': double space and '1': new page.
2. The value of *outdev* is dialect-dependent. For IBM 360-370, *outdev* = 6 for printer; for DEC-10, *outdev* = 3 for printer, and *outdev* = 5 for terminal output.
3. The mode of each variable output must agree with the mode of the FORMAT field under which it is transmitted, except that

data from any variable may be transmitted under an A FORMAT code.

4. Real numbers are rounded if the associated fields request fewer digits after the decimal point than are present in the value.

5. Each data item must fit into its associated field.

6. The negative sign (and decimal point in an F or E field) counts as part of the field width w.

7. The format may not produce a record longer than the maximum record size for the specified device. Typical sizes for printers are 121 or 133. Terminals may be 72 or 80 characters wide, and punched cards are generally 80 character records. A format may, of course, define more than one output record.

8. The skip field, nX, places n blank characters in the output wherever encountered.

9. Character values (Aw, nH, or literals) are placed left-justified in the output record; integer and real values are placed right-justified with leading zeros suppressed.

One additional example below shows typical use of the FORMAT statement for output. The FORMAT demonstrates the use of the end of record (/) code and repeated use of a group within a FORMAT. Assume we wish the output to look like the following, starting with a new page,

```
            * * SUMMARY REPORT * *

   # BOUGHT:  53     # SOLD: 138      PROFIT: $1390.50

         PART #           STOCK     TOTAL =    141
         ------           -----
            1               13
            2               28
            3                0
            4               50
            5               18
            6               32
```

where BOUGHT, SOLD and TOTAL are simple integer variables, STOCK is an integer array of size N and PROFIT is a simple real variable.

```
    WRITE (6,100) BOUGHT, SOLD, PROFIT, TOTAL, (I, STOCK(I), I=1,N)
100 FORMAT ('1',15X, '* * SUMMARY REPORT * *', //
   1   5X,'# BOUGHT:', I4, 5X,'# SOLD:', I4, 7X,'PROFIT: $', F7.2//
   2   T12, 'PART &#', 10X, 'STOCK', 5X 'TOTAL = ', I5/
   3   T12, '------', 10X, '-----'/
   4   (T12, I4, 2X,   10X, I4) )
```

FORMAT 100 defines 12 records that result in 10 output lines. The last group of FORMAT 100 defines only two usable fields (each I4), and hence it is reused six times to output our 12 values. Each time, the T12 field causes single-spaced carriage control, since the first print position (which is not printed) will contain a blank.

This concludes the discussion of input and output through cards, terminal, and printer in FORTRAN. In Chapter 4 you will learn about input and output to other devices such as tapes and disks and about other forms of data arrangement on these devices.

0.6   LOCAL CONTROL OF EXECUTION

The programmer has control over the order in which statements are executed in a program. Normally statements are executed sequentially, one after another. A programmer can alter this order by causing execution termination (STOP), unconditional transfer (GO TO), conditional transfer (IF), and repetition (DO). In this section we discuss these statements which provide for control of order of execution.

0.6.1   Execution Termination

Program execution can be halted at any time by executing a STOP statement:

> [*label*]   STOP

where   *label* is a statement number

Example   15   STOP

Effect   Execution of this statement, in the main program or in any subprogram, immediately terminates execution.

Note   As many STOP statements as desired may be placed in a program.

0.6.2   Unconditional Branching

The branching commands of FORTRAN enable a programmer to alter the normal sequential execution of statements. Here we define two statements that perform unconditional branches; execution of these statements will always result in a branch. The simplest form of unconditional branch is the FORTRAN GO TO statement.

> [*label1*]   GO TO *label2*

where   *label1* and *label2* are statement numbers

Example   GO TO 5

Effect   Execution control is transferred to the statement labeled 5.

Notes   1. *label2* must be the statement number of an executable statement in the same main program or subprogram as this GO TO statement.
2. The GO TO should be used with discretion, since a knot of code tangled with GO TO statements is quite unreadable. Some remarks on program structure and the proper uses of GO TO are presented in Chapter 1.

A more flexible form of unconditional branch is provided by the *computed GO TO* statement. During execution the value of an integer variable determines which label from a list of labels will be the destination of a branch. The computed GO TO has the following form.

[*label0*]   GO TO (*label1*,*label2*,...,*labeln*), *ivar*

where   *label0* is an optional statement number
label1, *label2*, etc., are statement numbers of executable statements in the same main program or subprogram as this GO TO statement
ivar is a simple (unsubscripted) integer variable

Example   GO TO (10, 2, 15, 15), K

Effect   If K=1, branch to statement 10; if K=2, branch to statement 2; if K=3 or K=4, branch to statement 15.

Note   If a computed GO TO contains a list of n labels, then the value of *ivar* must be between 1 and n.

0.6.3 Conditional Branching

The conditional branch statements enable the programmer to impose conditions under which a branch is to be taken. There are two forms of FORTRAN IF statements for conditional branching: the arithmetic IF and the logical IF. The arithmetic IF statement is used to define an arithmetic condition on which the branch is based. The arithmetic IF statement has the form:

[*label*]   IF (*arex*) *neg, zero, pos*

where   *label* is a statement number
arex is an arithmetic expression
neg, zero, and *pos* are statement numbers

Example   IF (X/2 - A) 3, 5, 4

Effect   Compute (X/2-A) and branch to statement 3 if the value is negative, to statement 5 if zero, and to statement 4 otherwise.

Although the expression in an arithmetic ɪꜰ may be as complex as desired, it is generally quite simple. An expression of any type is permitted; however, care must be taken when using real expressions. Because of error in the approximation of a real value, such a value may not be exactly zero, even if the correct evaluation of *arex* is zero. Thus the *pos* or *neg* branch might be taken when the *zero* one was expected.

The other conditional control statement is the logical ɪꜰ statement. It allows for the testing of more complex conditions than does the arithmetic ɪꜰ; it handles only two-way branches, while the arithmetic ɪꜰ can handle three-way branches. (The uses of three-way branches in programming are rare, however.) The logical ɪꜰ need not always branch, but it could cause a card to be read, a line printed, an assignment performed, or execution halted. The strongest advantage of the logical ɪꜰ is that it is far more readable than the arithmetic ɪꜰ.

[*label*]   IF (*logex*) *stmt*

where   *label* is a statement number
logex is a logical expression
stmt is any executable statement except an arithmetic ɪꜰ or ᴅᴏ

Example   IF (A .GT. 10.0) GO TO 32

Effect   If A is greater than 10.0, branch to statement 32; otherwise proceed to the next statement.

Notes   1. If *logex* is .TRUE. then *stmt* is executed.
2. If *stmt* is executed but is not a ɢᴏ ᴛᴏ, sᴛᴏᴘ or ʀᴇᴛᴜʀɴ, then the statement immediately following the ɪꜰ is also executed. If *stmt* is not executed (i.e., if *logex* is false), then the statement immediately following the ɪꜰ is executed next.

As another example of the logical ɪꜰ, let us replace each element of the *n*-element array X by its absolute value, and then print the entire array after the values have been changed.

```
      I = 1
   2  IF (X(I) .LT. 0.) X(I) = -X(I)
         PRINT, X(I)
         I = I+1
      IF (I .LE. N) GO TO 2
```

Note that regardless of whether the logical expression in statement 2 is true or false, the PRINT statement is executed for each value of I from 1 through N.

0.6.4   Automatic Looping

A principal source of power in computing is the ability to repeat a simple activity many times. Since repetition or "iteration" is such a common task, there is a statement, the DO statement, specifically designed for loop control. The form of the DO loop is described below.

[label]   DO *foot dovar* = *initial, final* [, *increment*]

where   *label* is an optional statement number
   foot is the statement number of some executable statement following the DO statement
   dovar is a simple integer variable called the *index* of the DO loop
   initial, final, and *increment* are each either simple integer variables or integer constants, each having a value greater than zero

Example   DO 32 I = 1, 10, 2

Effect   Execute the statements from here through statement 32 five times, with successive I values of 1, 3, 5, 7, 9.

Notes   1. A DO loop always executes at least once.
   2. The values of *dovar, initial, final*, and *increment* should not be altered by the programmer within the DO loop.
   3. One may branch out of a DO loop. One may also branch from a statement within the loop to another statement within the loop; however, from a statement outside a DO loop, one may branch only to the DO statement itself, not to any statements within the DO loop.
   4. The statement labeled *foot* may not be a STOP, GO TO, RETURN (see Section 0.7.4), a logical IF with any of these, a DO, or an arithmetic IF.
   5. DO loops may be nested one within another, as long as all statements of each inner loop are contained within the outer loop. (Two or more DO loops may share the same *foot*, however.)
   6. *Default*: If *increment* is omitted, the value 1 is used.

Perhaps the clearest way to define a DO loop is to show the actual effect on the source code. Figure 0-7 illustrates an example DO loop and its equivalent in non-DO structure.

```
      D3 32 I = 1,10,2                 I = 1                  <==INITIALIZE
      TOP = TOP + I               5    TOP = TOP + I
          :                                :
          :                                :
      X(I) = X(I) + 1                  X(I) = X(I) + 1
   32 PRINT, X(I)                      PRINT, X(I)
                                       I = I+2                <==INCREMENT
                                       IF (I.LE.10) GO TO 5  <==TEST
```

FIGURE 0-7   The Effect of the DO Statement

We will now study the CONTINUE statement. This instruction provides a statement with which to associate a statement number; it causes no action by itself. It is frequently used as the foot of a DO loop.

[*label*]   CONTINUE

where   *label* is an optional statement number

Example   20 CONTINUE

Effect   None; this statement acts as a placeholder for label 20.

Note   This statement is often used as the foot of a DO loop. When so used, the compiler will generate the code to increment and test the loop index immediately after the CONTINUE. In this case executing the CONTINUE has the effect of moving to the next iteration of the loop.

Let us consider a more complex DO loop example. Assume we have vectors X and Y of sizes N and M, respectively. We wish to output every positive element of vector X that appears in vector Y, and the list of locations where the X values appear in Y.

```
      DO 10 I = 1, N
         IF (X(I) .LE. 0.) GO TO 10
         DO 20 J = 1, M
   20       IF (X(I) .EQ. Y(J)) PRINT, 'MATCH', X(I), 'AT J=', J
   10 CONTINUE
```

We see the CONTINUE used at statement 10 as the foot of the outer loop. This was necessary since, if an X element were less than or equal to zero, we would want to ignore it and look at the next one. We thus need to skip the second loop entirely. Notice that the inner loop uses a different index (J), because the outer index (I) cannot be altered within its own loop. The inner loop could equivalently be coded as:

```
    DO 20 J = 1,M
       IF (X(I) .EQ. Y(J)) PRINT, 'MATCH', X(I), 'AT J=', J
 20 CONTINUE
```

The use of a CONTINUE to terminate a DO loop is preferable because it clearly marks the end of the loop, and so we will use it in our examples.

Our final example of DO loops demonstrates the use of the value of the index after exiting the DO loop. Assume we wish to read data cards, stopping when the data cards are exhausted or when 100 cards have been read. We will place values from the cards into a vector X and then use NCARDS, the actual number of cards read, to output the number of elements of X that exceeded the value of X(NCARDS). The entire program to do this task is shown in Figure 0-8.

```
C. . . . . . . . PROGRAM TO OUTPUT THE NUMBER OF VALUES ...
C. . . . . . . . EXCEEDING THE LAST ONE INPUT...
      INTEGER X(100), NCARDS, IN, OUT, FINAL, NCM1, COUNT
      DATA COUNT/0/, IN/5/, OUT/6/, NCARDS/100/
C. . . . . . . . INPUT THE TEST DATA...
      DO 10 I=1,NCARDS
         READ (IN,100,END=15) X(I)
 10 CONTINUE
      GO TO 20
C. . . . . . . . IF PREMATURE LOOP TERMINATION, FEWER THAN 100 VALUES;
C. . . . . . . . USE LAST ONE AS TEST VALUE...
 15 NCARDS = I-1
      IF (NCARDS .GT. 1) GO TO 20
         WRITE (OUT,102) NCARDS
         STOP
C. . . . . . . . LOCATE FINAL INPUT VALUE AND COMPARISON LIMIT ...
 20 FINAL = X(NCARDS)
      NCM1 = NCARDS-1
      DO 30 I = 1,NCM1
         IF (X(I) .GT. FINAL) COUNT = COUNT+1
 30 CONTINUE
C. . . . . . . . OUTPUT FINAL RESULTS ...
      WRITE (OUT,101) NCARDS, COUNT, FINAL
      STOP
 100 FORMAT (I5)
 101 FORMAT (5X, 'OF THE ', I3, ' NUMBERS INPUT,'
    1 I3, ' VALUES EXCEEDED THE FINAL VALUE OF ', I6)
 102 FORMAT (' ***ERROR: ONLY ', I3, 'NUMBERS INPUT...ABORT***')
      END
```

FIGURE 0-8 Use of the DO Index after Exit from the Loop

Note that we have indented the statements in the body of each DO loop for greater readability. As we stated earlier, FORMAT statements may appear anywhere; in this example, we chose to place all of them just prior to the END statement. The END= option in the READ statement creates a branch to statement 15 if the data deck is exhausted; we must decrement the index, NCARDS, by 1 to indicate the actual number of array elements defined by the input loop. It is unwise to use the value of a DO index if execution falls through the foot of the loop, that is, if the loop terminates normally after having completed the required number of iterations. In that case, the value of the index is compiler-dependent. Finally, the IF statement following statement 15 ensures that the second DO loop is not executed if not enough numbers were input. Without this statement the program would fail in the second DO loop because of the final value of zero.

0.7 SUBPROGRAMS

0.7.1 Introduction

Subprograms are an important tool of the advanced FORTRAN programmer. The proper use of subprograms makes a program easier to develop, to debug, to document and to maintain. We will discuss the relationship between subprograms and program modularity in Chapter 1. In this section we describe the mechanics of writing FORTRAN subprograms.

A subprogram is an independent section of code. Because subprograms are very much like the main programs that we have already described, subprograms and main programs are collectively called *program units*, or *program modules*. We say that a subprogram is *called* from another program unit. At the time of the call, control of execution passes from the calling program unit to the called subprogram. The subprogram then computes using any of the tools of FORTRAN: assignment statements, control transfers (IF, GO TO, DO) and I/O statements. Subprograms may also call other subprograms. A subprogram may declare and initialize its own storage locations by statements such as REAL, INTEGER, LOGICAL, DIMENSION, IMPLICIT and DATA statements. At some time, the called subprogram *returns* to its calling program unit, which means that execution control reverts to a point immediately after the spot from which the call occurred. (In Chapter 2 we will see that control can also return to locations other than the point of call.)

All program units are independently compiled; this means that there is no relationship between statement numbers or variable names used in two program units. It is thus possible to use the name K or the statement number 10 in several program units without confusion.

The exchange of information among program units is not by names, since there is no relationship between names in different program units. There are three ways by which information is passed between calling and called program units. First, the *function subprograms* return one single arithmetic or logical value. This provides only one-way communication from the function subprogram to its calling program unit. Two-way communication is possible through the *argument list*, a series of values and variables that the calling program explicitly gives to a subprogram at the time of the call. The subprogram may use the values for computation and may assign results to the variables. At the time of the return, the calling program unit then has access to the results that the subprogram has placed in the variables. A third means of sharing data between two program units is called COMMON. By this technique, certain variables are stored in locations that are accessable to any program unit. In this section we will examine only the first two means of communication: function values and argument lists; COMMON will be studied in Section 2.6.

0.7.2 Argument Lists

As described above, an argument list is a series of values and variables passed between program units. The argument list consists of one or more items separated by commas; the entire list is enclosed in a pair of parentheses. The items in the argument list may be any combination of constants, simple variables, expressions, array names, and array elements. The argument list in the calling program unit is called the *actual argument* list, since these are the actual values and variables passed as a result of the call.

The subprogram must have a similar list called the *dummy argument* list. This list consists of only simple variables and array names. Since names cannot be shared between program units, the relationship between these two lists is by position: the first actual argument is associated with the first dummy argument, etc. (Where feasible, it certainly improves program readability and maintainability to use the same names in the two argument lists. Be aware, however, that the association is by position within each list, not by name.) You may think of the dummy variables as merely representatives for the variables and values provided in the call. Each change to a dummy argument (by an assignment or READ statement, for example) has the effect of changing the associated actual argument.

Because the dummy argument is merely a representative for an actual argument, the two need to be similar data items. We call this *agreement of arguments*. Dummy and actual arguments must agree in the following aspects.

Mode.   Each actual argument must be of the same mode as its corresponding dummy argument.

Kind.   A single data value (constant, simple variable or expression) must be associated with a simple variable in the dummy argument list. An array element in the actual argument list is normally paired in the dummy list with a simple variable; an array element may, however, be associated with an array name in the dummy argument list. This latter form associates the passed element and all elements after it with elements (1), (2), etc. of the dummy array.

Dimension.   Because of storage mapping functions used to locate array elements, an actual array name should associate with a dummy array name having the same dimension. An exception to this restriction is for one-dimensional arrays, where the dimension of the dummy array may be smaller than the actual array. The actual dimensions of an array can also be passed as arguments.

Quantity.   There must be the same number of items in the actual argument list as there are in the dummy list.

There are two different types of subprograms: function subprograms and subroutines. These two varieties differ both in the manner in which they are called and in the way in which they return results.

Function subprograms normally return a single arithmetic or logical value. A function subprogram is invoked by the use of its name, followed by an argument list, as a term in an arithmetic or logical expression. The result of that function is then returned as the value of the term and is combined with any other terms in the expression. The invocation of a function has the following form:

> *name* (*arglist*)

where   this is a term in an arithmetic or logical expression
name is the name of the function subprogram
arglist is a list of simple variables, array elements, array names, constants, or expressions

Example   `REAL P, BIG`
`P = 5.0`
`GROSS = BIG (P, -1.75)`

Effect   Variable GROSS is assigned the value computed by function BIG acting on arguments P and -1.75 .

0.7.3   Built-in Functions

There are a series of function subprograms that are used in many computing tasks. These include functions to compute square root, trigonometric sine and cosine, logarithm, absolute value, and so forth. The code for these functions is supplied as an integral part of many FORTRAN compilers, and so the functions are called *built-in* functions. We have included a table of the common built-in functions as Appendix 1. In using that table, you should note the types of arguments that each function requires and supply arguments of the correct types when invoking the function. We will not comment further on the mathematical functions, since their uses should be reasonably clear. Several other functions are, however, worth explaining here.

First, the FLOAT and IFIX functions are convenient for creating expressions of types other than their arguments. FLOAT returns a real value equivalent to its integer argument; IFIX returns an integer value equivalent to its real argument with any fractional part truncated. These can be quite useful in matching argument types for subprogram calls. Suppose you wish to compute the square root of an integer, K. The table of Appendix 1 indicates that SQRT computes square roots, but its argument must be of real type. Therefore SQRT(K) would be in error. One solution to this problem is to select a real variable, say AK, and assign to it the value of K, as in AK = K. However, this introduces an unnecessary variable, and makes the program slightly more complicated to read. Another solution is to use the FLOAT function to obtain a real result equivalent to K. Then SQRT(FLOAT(K)) may be used to determine the square root of this value. This shortens the program, and does not confuse the reader with variables that will be used only once.

The MAX and MIN functions accept a variable number of arguments and return the largest or smallest, respectively, among those arguments. Suppose you wish to perform a loop at least once, no more than 20 times, and $(K+1)/2$ times if that value is between 1 and 20. This can be accomplished by the following statements.

```
NTIMES = MAX0( 1, MIN0( (K+1)/2, 20) )
DO 55 KOUNT = 1, NTIMES
```

The four MAX functions vary by the types of arguments and the types of their results. AMAX0 and AMAX1 return real results, while MAX0 and MAX1 return integers; AMAX0 and MAX0 accept only integer arguments, while AMAX1 and MAX1 compute using real arguments only. The MIN functions are similarly defined. For the MAX and MIN functions, all arguments must be listed explicitly; the arguments must be simple variables, constants, expressions or array elements—array names are not acceptable. For this reason, even if TABLE is an integer array of 20 elements, MAX0 (TABLE) can *not* be used to determine the largest value of that array.

0.7.4 User-Defined Function Subprograms

User-defined subprograms are composed of the same statements as are main programs: declarations, assignment statements, READ, WRITE, FORMAT, IF,

GO TO, DO, STOP. Like a main program, each subprogram must terminate with an END statement to mark the physical end of the program unit. There is one additional statement, the RETURN statement, used to cause control transfer back to the point of call. This statement has the form shown below.

[*label*] RETURN

where   *label* is an optional statement number

Example   20   RETURN

Effect   Causes execution to resume at the point from which this subprogram was called. At the time of return, the values of all dummy arguments are associated with their actual arguments from the call.

Function subprogram definitions are identified by the FUNCTION statement that indicates the type of the function result, the name of the function, and the names of the dummy arguments. It has the following form.

[*mode*] FUNCTION *name* (*arglist*)

where   *mode* explicitly declares the mode of the function result. *Default*: If no mode is given, then the mode of the function is the default mode of the *name* by the I through N convention
name is the name of the function and is used to return the result. It is formed by the same rules as a variable name
arglist is a list of simple variables or array names making up the dummy argument list of this function

Example   REAL FUNCTION BIG (X,Y)

Effect   Declares BIG to be a function of type real, indicates that this is the start of the definition of that subprogram, and declares that there are two dummy arguments: X and Y.

We can now study examples of function subprograms.

```
EXAMPLE
        REAL FUNCTION BIG (X,Y)
        REAL X,Y
        BIG = X
        IF (X .LT. Y) BIG = Y
        RETURN
        END
```

Effect   Given two real values called X and Y, respectively, function BIG returns as its value the larger of the two values.

Notes   1. A value must be assigned to the function *name* before a RETURN is executed since this is the means by which a value is assigned as the result of the function.
   2. The function name may be used like any unsubscripted variable within the function definition.
   3. A function cannot invoke itself, either directly (A cannot call A) or indirectly (if A calls B, then neither B nor any subprogram B calls can call A).
   4. A function should not alter the value of any dummy argument.

The name of a function subprogram is used in two ways in this example. During execution of the subprogram, it is a conventional variable and may be used in computation. At the time a RETURN statement is executed, the current value of the function name is the result returned by the function. Returning a value through the function name is normally the only means by which a function communicates with the program unit that called it.

If the above function were coded, it could be used as in the following example.

```
REAL A,B,C,D
READ (-,-) A,B,C
D = BIG (A,B)
D = BIG (D,C)
WRITE (-,-) D
```

In the first call, the current values of A and B replace the values of the dummy arguments X and Y, respectively. The value of BIG becomes that of X (=A). However, if Y (=B) is larger, then the value of BIG is replaced by that of Y. The RETURN sends the current value of BIG back to the right hand side of the first assignment statement. In the second call, the previous result, D, is passed back to BIG as a value for X, and the value of C is passed to Y. The computation procedes as before, with BIG returning the larger of these values. An acceptable alternative to this example is to use the expression BIG(A,B) as one of the arguments to BIG. Thus

```
D = BIG( BIG(A,B), C )
```

would produce the same result as the two assignment statements above.

Before going on to subroutines, let us consider another function example. In the following example we show several invocations of a subprogram AVG; this subprogram computes the average of the first N elements of a real vector of size 100.

```
REAL X(100), Y(100)              REAL FUNCTION AVG (X,N)
REAL AVG, RES                    REAL X(100)
   :                             INTEGER N
1 RES = AVG(X,10)                AVG = 0.
   :                             IF (N.LT.1 .OR. N.GT.100) RETURN
2 IF (AVG(Y,J) .LE. 0) GO TO 5   DO 1 I = 1, N
   :                                AVG = AVG + X(I)
3 X(I) = X(I) - AVG(Y, 100-I)  1 CONTINUE
   :                             AVG = AVG/N
   :                             RETURN
STOP                             END
END
```

Function AVG is invoked and executed three times in this program (if statements 1, 2 and 3 are each executed once). In the first invocation the average of the first 10 elements of vector X is computed. In the second call vector Y and variable J are transmitted to AVG as arguments, and the result represents the average of elements Y(1) through Y(J). In the third call an expression is used as the calling argument: if I has value 32, then the result of the function is the average of elements Y(1) through Y(68).

Function subprograms are useful where one result needs to be returned. However, for more complicated communication, a different type of subprogram, the *subroutine*, is needed. This will be described in the next section.

0.7.5   Subroutine Subprograms

Subroutine subprograms are invoked by means of a separate statement, the CALL statement. This statement is shown below.

[*label*] CALL *name* [(*arglist*)]

where *label* is an optional statement number
     name is the name of the subroutine
     arglist is a list of simple variables, constants, expressions, array elements and array names

Example
```
REAL ALARGE, P
DATA P/5.0/
CALL MAX (P, 4.7, ALARGE)
```

Effect Subroutine MAX is entered with arguments P, 4.7, ALARGE, and the values of these data items are transmitted to the subprogram.

User-written subroutines are headed by a SUBROUTINE statement.

SUBROUTINE *name* [(*arglist*)]

where *name* is a name that identifies the routine. It is formed by the same rules as a variable name

arglist is a list of one or more simple variables or array names separated by commas

Example SUBROUTINE ORDER (X,Y)

Effect Indicates the beginning of a subroutine named ORDER, having two dummy arguments, X and Y.

The body of a subroutine subprogram is similar to that for a function subprogram; the same declaration, assignment, control transfer, and input/output statements are used. The RETURN statement presented with function subprograms is also used in subroutines to cause control transfer back to the point from which the subroutine was called. However, unlike in functions, the name of a subroutine may *not* be used as a variable; it is used only to identify the subroutine. Also, unlike functions, subroutines are permitted to modify the values of the dummy arguments; this is the means by which subroutines return values to the calling program unit. We will now show examples of subroutines.

Example
```
SUBROUTINE ORDER (X,Y)
REAL X, Y, LARGER
IF (X .GT. Y) RETURN
LARGER = Y
Y = X
X = LARGER
RETURN
END
```

Effect Given two real values, called X and Y, respectively, subroutine ORDER places the larger of its two inputs in X, and the smaller in Y.

Notes 1. The values of variables in the argument list may be changed in the subprogram.
2. A RETURN statement may appear anywhere in the executable portion of the subprogram.
3. The name of the subroutine is not a variable; it merely identifies the subprogram. It has no mode and hence is not declared.
4. No other subprogram or variable in the subroutine or invoking program unit may have this same name.
5. A subroutine cannot call itself, either directly (A cannot call A) or indirectly (if A calls B, neither B nor any subprogram B calls can call A).

The mechanism for returning values is different between subroutines and function subprograms. Whereas a single value was returned through the name of the function, subroutines return values through their arguments. At the time a RETURN is executed, the values of all dummy arguments are effectively copied back into their corresponding actual arguments. This can cause surprising results or errors if the dummy argument corresponding to a constant has been modified. In Section 2.2 we discuss the different mechanisms by which arguments are passed; for now, we will advise you simply that if you modify the value of a dummy argument, that dummy argument must correspond to an actual argument that is a simple variable, an array element or an array name.

Because it returns values through the argument list, a subroutine may return more than one value. Each simple variable in the argument list may be assigned a value by the subroutine, and that value is transmitted back to the calling program unit at return time. For arrays in the dummy argument list, one value may be transmitted back in each element of the array. Thus the number of results returned by a subroutine subprogram is bounded only by the number of dummy arguments and the dimensions of the arrays used as dummy arguments.

On the other hand, a subroutine does not need an argument list at all. Consider a subroutine whose purpose is to print a fixed title at the top of a report; it is called each time a new page is to begin. There is no information that this subroutine would need, nor is there any result that it would want to send back to its calling program unit. Thus, it would not need any arguments. The SUBROUTINE and CALL statements for this subroutine would be written without either the argument list or the enclosing pair of parentheses.

A larger subroutine example is shown below. Subroutine INPUT reads N values, placing them in the passed array, and setting ERROR to TRUE if insufficient data exists.

```
      REAL X(30), Y(30), Z(40)          SUBROUTINE INPUT (X, N, ERROR)
      LOGICAL EOF                       REAL X(N)
      INTEGER M                         LOGICAL ERROR
      M = 30                            ERROR = .FALSE.
      CALL INPUT (X, 10, EOF)           IF (N.LE.0) RETURN
      IF (EOF) GO TO 99                 READ (5,4,END=1) (X(I),I=1,N)
         :                              RETURN
      CALL INPUT (Y, M, EOF)          1 ERROR = .TRUE.
         :                              RETURN
      CALL INPUT (Z, M+10, EOF)       4 FORMAT (16I5)
         :                              END
   99 WRITE (6,199)
  199 FORMAT (' OUT OF DATA')
      STOP
         :
```

The flow of execution for the first call of this subprogram is as follows. 1. At the time of the call, the values of vector X, constant 10 and variable

EOF are transmitted to subroutine INPUT. These are associated with arguments X, N and ERROR, respectively, in the subroutine.

2. Execution proceeds in subroutine INPUT until either N values have been read or all cards have been used.

3. When a RETURN statement is executed, the current values of vector X and variables N and ERROR are transmitted back to the actual arguments, in this case X, 10, and EOF.

4. Execution resumes with the statement immediately after the CALL statement in the calling program unit.

Notice in this example that the dimension of the array has been passed as an argument, and that dummy argument, X, has been declared as an array in a REAL statement. Arrays passed as arguments are not allocated space in a subprogram. The REAL statement is needed to identify X as an array, and the dimensions are used in calculating the storage mapping function for array element references. An array may have a variable subscript in a declaration statement only if *both* the array name *and* the dimensions are dummy arguments. Furthermore, the dimensions must be integers. This form is called the use of *adjustable dimensions*.

As the first call in this example illustrates, it is acceptable for the adjustable dimension of an array to be smaller than the actual array size. It is not, however, possible to use an adjustable dimension larger than the size of the array. With multidimensional arrays, since the passed dimensions are used for calculation of the storage mapping function, they should agree exactly with the true dimensions of the array being passed.

This completes our description of the preliminary elements of FORTRAN. We will conclude this chapter with an example using many of these forms. As you study the code of the example, you may want to refer back to the definition of a particular statement type to verify what it does, or why something has been coded as it has.

0.8   AN EXAMPLE

In this section we present an example to show the use of the statements discussed in this chapter. The INFO Company is a firm specializing in mail-order sales. They maintain a list of names and addresses of potential customers; this list is sorted by patron id. Any new names that can be added to the master are valuable to this company, so the company has agreements to purchase names for their mailing list. In the past, however, people have delivered lists and been paid, with the company learning later that many names were in fact duplicates of ones they already had. We are to develop a merge and charge program that updates the master list and credits the supplier with $.25 for each new name added.

To simplify our program, we will assume that all input is on cards, that the master file consists of at most 1000 unique five-digit patron id's, that each update list is ordered and has fewer than 100 entries, and that each update list ends with a 99999 card. The general design of our solution is shown in Figure 0-9. After reading the master file, and until an end-of-file (EOF) condition occurs from the input deck, we perform the following repeatedly.

1. Read next update file.
2. Perform merge, discarding duplicates.
3. Output bill for this list.

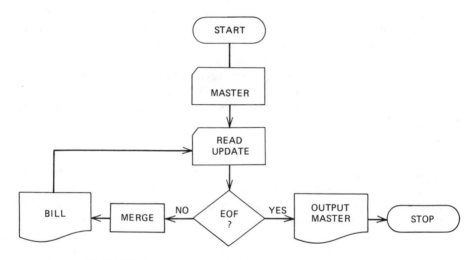

FIGURE 0-9   General Solution Flowchart Design

Following is an example showing how the merge portion of this program should work.

```
MASTER      UPDATE      MERGED FILE
  1           2            1
  3           3            2    <== NEW ENTRY
  8           5            3
 10           8            5  .  <== NEW ENTRY
                           8
                          10
```

Although it is possible to perform a merge so that the resultant merged file is the same array originally containing the master list, this would require two passes through the master file. Instead, we will store two masters in a two-column array, with one column representing the current master and the other column representing the result of our merge operation.

We must be able to perform alternating merges if more than one update file is input; initially we merge to the first column, then to the second, then to the first again, etc. Instead of writing the same merge code twice, we design a MERGER subroutine to do either merge. We will similarly use a subroutine INPUT to do the reading of input files. Figure 0-10 shows the main program logic.

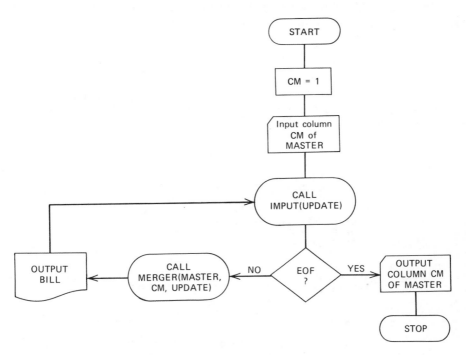

FIGURE 0-10 Main Program Logic Flowchart

Now we can finalize the design of our two subprograms and code the solution to the problem. Subroutine INPUT's argument list must contain an integer vector argument to represent the UPDATE file it is to read and transmit back to the main program. The main program must know the number of patron id's that INPUT has read, and so we transmit this back in a variable UPSIZ. Finally, if we wish to output the input list id number with the bill, then subroutine INPUT must return this value; we will call this UPNUM. Thus a main program call to subroutine INPUT will have this form.
Camera-ready insert number 2b

Further analysis of subroutine MERGER reveals that the subroutine must know the sizes of the master file and of the update list; we will call these OMSIZ and UPSIZ. Also, the merge subprogram must know which column of MASTER contains the current master list; this will be called OMCOL. We see that upon completion of the merge, the main program must know how many new items were added and the length of the new master file. Instead of adding other arguments for these return values, we will place these values in UPSIZ and OMSIZ, since the previous values of these variables are no longer needed.

In Figure 0-11 below, we show the main program subprograms to perform the merge charge algorithm.

```
C========================================================================
C= MERGE-CHARGE PROGRAM =                                              =
C========================                                              =
C=                                                                     =
C= THIS PROGRAM UPDATES A MASTER CUSTOMER ID FILE WITH AN ARBITRARY    =
C= NUMBER OF INPUT FILES. MERGING IS DONE WITH DUPLICATES OMITTED.     =
C= EACH NEW ADDITION TO THE MASTER FILE RESULTS IN A PAYMENT OF .25    =
C= TO THE PATRONS' CREDIT. THE AMOUNT OWED FOR EACH UPDATE IS PRINTED. =
C= UPON COMPLETION OF ALL UPDATES, THE NEW MASTER IS PRINTED.          =
C=                                                                     =
C= MAJOR VARIABLES:                                                    =
C=     UPDATE - UPDATE FILE FROM CARD                                  =
C=     MASTER - EACH COLUMN IS USED ALTERNATELY FOR MASTER             =
C=     OMCOL  - WHICH COLUMN OF MASTER CONTAINS OLD MASTER             =
C=     UPSIZ  - NUMBER OF ID'S IN LATEST UPDATE FILE                   =
C=     UPNUM  - FILE NUMBER OF THIS UPDATE                             =
C=     OMSIZ  - NUMBER OF ENTRIES IN LATEST MASTER                     =
C=     COST   - AMOUNT LATEST UPDATE WILL COST US                      =
C=                                                                     =
C= SUBPROGRAMS CALLED:                                                 =
C=     INPUT  - ALL UPDATE FILES ARE READ IN THIS SUBPROGRAM           =
C=     MERGER - MERGES LATEST UPDATE WITH MASTER FILE                  =
C=                                                                     =
C= PROGRAMMER: ---                DATE: ---                            =
C========================================================================
C
      INTEGER UPDATE(100), MASTER(1000,2), UPSIZ, UPNUM, OMSIZ, OMCOL
      INTEGER RDR, PRT
      REAL COST
      DATA OMCOL/1/, RDR/5/, PRT/6/
C------------INPUT AND ECHO CURRENT MASTER FILE
      READ (RDR,100,END=99) OMSIZ, (MASTER(I,OMCOL), I=1,OMSIZ)
  100 FORMAT (I5 / (16I5) )
      WRITE (PRT,110) (MASTER(I,OMCOL), I=1,OMSIZ)
  110 FORMAT ('1', 20X, 'CURRENT MASTER FILE:' // 8(5X, I5) )
C------------MORE MERGING TO DO?
   10 CALL INPUT (UPDATE, UPSIZ, UPNUM)
      IF (UPSIZ .EQ. 0) GO TO 20
C------------ECHO UPDATE FILE, THEN MERGE AND RECORD PAYMENT OWED
      WRITE (PRT,120) UPNUM, (UPDATE(I), I=1,UPSIZ)
  120    FORMAT ('0', 20X, 'UPDATE FILE NUMBER', I6, ':' // 8(5X, I5) )
      CALL MERGER (UPDATE, UPSIZ, MASTER, OMSIZ, OMCOL)
      COST = .25*UPSIZ
      WRITE (PRT,130) UPNUM, COST, UPSIZ
  130    FORMAT ('0', 2X, 'FILE NUMBER', I6, ' TO BE PAID $', F6.2,
     X        ' FOR', I5, ' NEW ADDRESSES')
      GO TO 10
C------------ALL DONE: OUTPUT CURRENT MASTER FILE AND HALT
   20 WRITE (PRT,110) (MASTER(I,OMCOL), I=1,OMSIZ)
      WRITE (PRT,140)
  140 FORMAT ('0', '*** JOB COMPLETED ***')
      STOP
C------------MASTER INPUT FILE ERROR: NOTHING CAN BE DONE
   99 WRITE (PRT,150)
```

```
  150 FORMAT (' *** MASTER FILE INPUT ERROR: HALTING IN MAIN ***')
      STOP
      END



      SUBROUTINE INPUT (FILE, N, FNUM)
C=============================================================================
C= IF NO PRIOR END-OF-FILE FOUND, THEN INPUT NEXT UPDATE FILE              =
C=                                                                         =
C= MAJOR VARIABLES:                                                        =
C=    FILE   - ARGUMENT SPACE FOR NEW UPDATE TO BE RETURNED                =
C=    N      - ARGUMENT TO BE ASSIGNED SIZE OF NEW UPDATE                  =
C=    FNUM   - ARGUMENT TO BE ASSIGNED NEW FILE NUMBER                     =
C=    EOF    - SET TO .TRUE. ONLY IF END-OF-FILE FOUND                     =
C=    MARKER - VALUE WHICH INDICATES END OF UPDATE: CURRENTLY 99999        =
C=============================================================================
      INTEGER FILE(100), N, FNUM
      INTEGER NEWVAL, MARKER, RDR, PRT
      LOGICAL EOF
      DATA MARKER/99999/, EOF/.FALSE./, RDR/5/, PRT/6/
C--------------IF PRIOR END-OF-FILE, THEN QUI
      I = 1
      IF (.NOT. EOF) GO TO 10
         N = 0
         RETURN
C--------------READ FILE NUMBER, THEN EACH FILE VALUE UNTIL MARKER FOUND
   10 READ (RDR,100,END=30) FNUM
  100 FORMAT (I5)
      DO 20 I = 1, 100
         READ (RDR,100,END=30) FILE(I)
         IF (FILE(I) .EQ. MARKER) GO TO 40
   20 CONTINUE
C--------------ENSURE THAT MARKER OR END-OF-FILE FOUND
      I = 101
      READ (RDR,100,END=30) NEWVAL
      IF (NEWVAL .EQ. MARKER) GO TO 40
C--------------TOO MANY (OVER 100) UPDATE ENTRIES
      WRITE (PRT,110) FNUM
  110 FORMAT (' *** TOO MANY UPDATES IN FILE', I6, ' ***')
      STOP
C--------------END-OF-FILE ENCOUNTERED: REMEMBER FOR NEXT CALL
   30 EOF = .TRUE.
   40 N = I-1
      RETURN
      END



      SUBROUTINE MERGER (UPDATE, UPSIZ, MASTER, OMSIZ, OMCOL)
C=============================================================================
C= MERGE LIST UPDATE WITH COLUMN OMCOL OF ARRAY MASTER; MERGE INTO         =
C= OTHER COLUMN OF MASTER                                                  =
C=                                                                         =
C= MAJOR VARIABLES:                                                        =
C=    UPDATE - LIST TO BE MERGED INTO MASTER                               =
C=    UPSIZ  - SIZE OF UPDATE FILE; ON EXIT, NUMBER UNIQUE                 =
C=    MASTER - COLUMN OMCOL IS MASTER; OTHER COLUMN RECEIVES NEW MASTER=
C=    OMSIZ  - NUMBER OF ENTRIES IN CURRENT MASTER                         =
C=    OMCOL  - COLUMN OF 'MASTER' CONTAINING CURRENT MASTER                =
C=    NMCOL  - COLUMN OF MASTER TO RECEIVE MERGED FILE                     =
C=    UPPTR  - MERGE POINTER FOR UPDATE LIST                               =
C=    OMPTR  - MERGE POINTER FOR OLD MASTER                                =
C=    NMPTR  - MERGE POINTER FOR NEW MASTER                                =
C=    MSIZ   - DIMENSION OF MASTER FILE (CURRENTLY 1000)                   =
C=============================================================================
```

43

```
      INTEGER UPDATE(100), UPSIZ, MASTER(1000,2), OMSIZ, OMCOL, NMCOL
      INTEGER UPPTR, OMPTR, NMPTR, PRT
      DATA PRT/6/
C-------------ASSIGN NMCOL TO POINT AT NEW MASTER COLUMN
      NMCOL = 1
      IF (OMCOL .EQ. 1) NMCOL=2
C-------------START AT TOP OF EACH LIST
      UPPTR = 1
      OMPTR = 1
      NMPTR = 1
C-------------DETERMINE FROM WHICH LIST TO GET NEXT ELEMENT
   10 IF (UPPTR.GT.UPSIZ .AND. OMPTR.GT.OMSIZ) GO TO 50
      IF (UPPTR .GT. UPSIZ) GO TO 40
      IF (OMPTR .GT. OMSIZ) GO TO 20
      IF (UPDATE(UPPTR) - MASTER(OMPTR,OMCOL)) 20, 30, 40
C-------------COPY AN ELEMENT FROM UPDATE; CHECK FOR OVERFLOW FIRST
   20 IF (NMPTR .GT. 1000) GO TO 99
      MASTER(NMPTR,NMCOL) = UPDATE(UPPTR)
      NMPTR = NMPTR+1
      UPPTR = UPPTR+1
      GO TO 10
C-------------MOVE PAST ELEMENT IN UPDATE (BRANCH HERE TO SKIP DUP)
   30 UPPTR = UPPTR+1
      GO TO 10
C-------------COPY ELEMENT FROM OLD MASTER; CHECK FIRST FOR OVERFLOW
   40 IF (OMPTR .GT. OMSIZ) GO TO 50
      IF (NMPTR .GT. 1000) GO TO 99
      MASTER(NMPTR,NMCOL) = MASTER(OMPTR,OMCOL)
      NMPTR = NMPTR+1
      OMPTR = OMPTR+1
      GO TO 10
C-------------MERGE COMPLETE: ASSIGN VALUES TO OMCOL, JPSIZ AND OMSIZ
   50 UPSIZ = NMPTR-OMSIZ-1
      OMSIZ = NMPTR-1
      OMCOL = NMCOL
      RETURN
C-------------OVERFLOW OCCURRED: QUIT HERE
   99 WRITE (PRT,100)
  100 FORMAT (' *** MASTER FILE SIZE EXCEEDED: HALTING IN MERGER ***')
      STOP
      END
```

FIGURE 0-11   Merge Charge Program

Exercises

0.01 Given two integers, determine the largest integer that divides both with zero remainder. (This value is called the greatest common divisor, or g.c.d.)

0.02 A *perfect* number is an integer that equals the sum of its divisors. For instance, 6 is a perfect number because the sum of its divisors, 1, 2 and 3, equals 6. Write a program to read an arbitrary number of integers and output those integers that are perfect.

0.03 Write an inventory control program for a drugstore. Each unique item has a nine-digit ID, a cost price, and a markup. Your program will handle sales and deliveries of items input as follows. Positive quantities are deliveries and the store must pay for them; negative quantities are sales and the customers must pay cost plus markup if the item is available. When the input is exhausted, produce a complete stock and profit report

0.04 Write a program to output bank statements such as you receive each month. Each check or deposit is listed by value and date accepted, and a daily running balance is displayed.

0.05 Referring to subroutine MAX in Section 0.7.5, write a similar routine to handle vectors. You are to write subroutine MAXV having arguments (X,N,Y,M,AMAX). This subroutine is to assign to AMAX the largest value found among X(1) through X(N) and Y(1) through Y(M), where N,M $\leq$ 50.

0.06 Given array PRICE of N elements, write the code segment to output N+1 lines as follows.

```
         CLOSING  STOCK  PRICES
STOCK  #1         CLOSED AT      $53.20
STOCK  #2         CLOSED AT      $21.40
   ETC.              ETC.          ETC.
```

0.07 Write subroutine FLIP that reverses the elements of a vector. For example, FLIP applied to vector X produces the result shown below.
    Initial values of X: 3, 4, 12, 9, 8
    Result after FLIP(X): 8, 9, 12, 4, 3
Do this using only one vector.

0.08 As a handicapper you watch all Formula I races each year. For each driver in each race you prepare one card with the driver's number, the driver's average speed for the race and the position in which the driver finished. At the end of the year you sort the cards by driver number. Write a program to determine the top five drivers according to average speeds over all races in which they completed. Drivers who have never won a race or who have driven in fewer than five races are not to be considered for this count of the top five drivers.

0.09 Your company, SLOP (SLOw but sure Programming) has contracted to do a job for ARRAYS INC. (Always Ready to Rip-off Another Yekel Sale). This company, as is obvious from its name, produces Yekels of all different sorts. Your job, as chief programmer at SLOP, is to write the program to compute a production report for ARRAYS INC. Each time Yekels are produced, the overseer punches a card containing values for TYPE, QUANT, HOURS and COST, representing Yekel type, quantity produced, hours involved and production cost.

There can be more than one card for each Yekel type produced, since a YEKEL may require work by people at different work stations or at different times of the day. At the end of each week the janitor turns in all work cards. There is no limit on the number of work cards, and they are not sorted in any way.

Draw a flowchart and write the program to do the following. For each Yekel type produced on a given day, compute the total hours, total cost, and total units produced. Although at most 100 different Yekel types can be produced on any given day, ARRAYS INC. can make thousands of variations of Yekels, and they are each identified by a nine-digit number. Your output should show only those Yekel types produced that day. Your weekly report will show five parts of output, one for each day of the week. There is a card giving the Julian date (e.g., 77032 is 2/1/77) in front of each day's set of work cards; for distinguishability this value is negative. Your input logically consists of the first date card followed by the first day's work cards, the second date card followed by the second day's work cards, up to the fifth day's date card and the fifth day's work cards.

SAMPLE OUTPUT HEADER AND CONTENTS:

```
*ARRAY INC.   PRODUCTION REPORT:   JULIAN DATE 77023
*YEKEL PART #      TOTAL UNITS      TOTAL HOURS      TOTAL COST
      328              150             2.3             800.58
      ETC              ETC             ETC              ETC
*ARRAY INC. PRODUCTION REPORT:   JULIAN DATE   77024
          REPORT HERE, ETC.
```

0.10 Write the referee program for the 3 by 3, X and O game. A referee must ask each player, in turn, to make a move; the move (placement of a X or O) must be to an empty square; referee declares the winner when 3 X's or O's in a row are found. Test the referee by either reading player moves from the terminal (interactive) or writing subroutines X and O which decide where to place the next marker. (Represent X and O by the integers 1 and 0, respectively.)

0.11 A symmetric matrix is a two-dimensional array in which $A(I,J)=A(J,I)$ for all values of I and J. For example, the matrix

$$
\begin{array}{ccc}
1 & 4 & 5 \\
4 & 2 & 6 \\
5 & 6 & 3
\end{array}
$$

is symmetric and is uniquely representable by its lower triangular matrix:

$$
\begin{array}{ccc}
1 & & \\
4 & 2 & \\
5 & 6 & 3
\end{array}
$$

Write a subroutine SYM to test matrices of arbitrary dimension less than 25 for symmetry, output the lower triangular matrix if so, and return a logical value .TRUE. or .FALSE., depending on whether the matrix is or is not symmetric.

CHAPTER 1

Programming Style

Programming is a form of expository writing. Any program that will have a life greater than one execution needs to be carefully planned and constructed, just as does a position paper, an article, an advertisement, or any other piece of writing with which one seeks to communicate. In this chapter we discuss programming style.

In this and following chapters we will highlight sensible techniques that we have seen good programmers use. Of course, rather than your memorizing all of these techniques and trying to apply them mechanically, you should review them, try to understand their motivation, and work to develop a style of your own that meets the same objectives. These are techniques that we use; they are not inflexible rules.

1.1 AN EXAMPLE

We begin this chapter with an example that exhibits many bad programming practices. This is a contrived example, but it is so only because of space limitations. We have actually seen each of the stylistic faults shown here in one or more programs. Some of these were student programs, others were running production programs, and others were portions of larger systems being developed.

The program, shown in Figure 1-1, is a simple bookseller's inventory control program. It works with a file of present inventory (book numbers and quantities), and it processes purchase requests against that inventory. The program does run (remarkably!). You should now try to analyze what the program does and how.

In the rest of this chapter, we will describe some of the faults in this program; we will also survey topics such as program structure and debugging. As you read about these topics, you may want to compare the comments given there with the content of this program. We do not, however, intend to patch this program in order to make it good. Hopefully you will learn a very important lesson from looking at this example. Sometimes it is better to throw away a bad program than to try to repair it.

```
C
C       PROGRAM BINGO - VERSION III, LEVEL 8   JULY 17
C
        INTEGER A(100,2),BQ,CCL,AA(100,2)
        DATA A/200*0/,IPA/0/
C       FIRST GET VALUES OF NL AND ND
        KE=0
        READ(5,107) NL,ND
C       BEGIN MAIN DO LOOP
        DO 8 K=1,2
        IF (K.EQ.1) GO TO 84
107     FORMAT(I9,I9)
        IF(K.NE.1) GO TO 11
84      MN=NL
        GO TO 18
11      MN=ND
C       BEGIN INNER DO LOOP
18      DO 3 IX=1, MN
        READ (5,204)  LN,   CCL
        IF (K-1) 16,43,70
204     FORMAT(I8,I9)
C       CASE A: NEW CARD
43      A(IPA+1,1)=LN
        A(IPA+1,2) = CCL
        IPA=IPA+1
        GO TO 67
C       AN ERROR HAS OCCURRED
16      GO TO 701
C       HERE WE TAKE CARE OF OLD CARDS
70      DO 505 BQ=1,NL
        BBQ = 100-NL+BQ
        IF (A(BBQ,1).EQ.LN) GO TO 644
        GO TO 505
644     A(BBQ,K)=-CCL+A(BBQ,K)
505     CONTINUE
67      GO TO  3
3       KK=K
        JJ=    100
        IF (KK.NE.2) GO TO 19
        WRITE (6,1919)A
1919    FORMAT(2X,7I10)
        STOP
C       THIS MUST BE FIRST TIME; DON'T STOP YET
19      DO 6 I=1,100
        JJJ=I+1
        IF((JJJ-1)/100.NE.KK) GO TO 153
        GO TO 6
174     JJ=JJ-1
        GO TO 702
153     DO 999 J=JJ J,JJ
        IF (.NOT.A(J,1).LT.A(I,1)) GO TO 302
        AA(I,2)=A(J,2)
        A(J,2)=A(I,2)
        A(I,2)=AA(I,2)
C       CHECK IF A(I,1) IS LESS THAN A(J,1)
302     IF (A(I,1).LT.A(J,1)) GO TO 17
        AA(J,1)=A(I,1)
        A(I,1)=A(J,1)
        A(J,1)=AA(J,1)
17      IF (I.LT. J) GO TO 999
C       AN ERROR HAS OCCURRED
        GO TO 703
999     CONTINUE
6       CONTINUE
        GO TO 8
703     KE=KE+1
702     KE=KE+1
701     KE=KE+1
        WRITE(6,704) KE
704     FORMAT(' ERROR; KE=',I5)
8       CONTINUE
        STOP
        END
```

FIGURE 1-1   Book Inventory Example Program

1.2 DOCUMENTATION

When you hear the term "documentation," you probably think of comments within a program. This is a good response, but only a partial one. Documentation needs to exist both inside and outside a program. The outside or "external documentation" is necessary to distribute to users who may never see the actual source program. External documentation is also convenient to explain things at greater length than is reasonable to do in comments. Comments (a part of "internal documentation") are, of course, essential to help a person (even yourself) follow the source code you have written.

1.2.1 External Documentation

External documentation serves two different groups of people, program users and program maintainers. External documentation for program users contains information to enable a person to use the given program. Such documentation, called a *user's guide*, provides such information as:

1. Program name.
2. Briefly what the program does.
3. Form and meaning of inputs to the program.
4. Meaning of output from the program and any means to control the amount or types of output produced.
5. Unusual conditions in the program and limitations of the method used.
6. A sample run of the program showing full input submitted and output acquired.
7. Means to contact the author or principal maintainer in case of erroneous results.
8. Acknowledgements and references.

In any given program, some of these topics will need less coverage, and some will need more. With experience, you will be able to judge this for yourself.

Now let us compare these suggestions with what has been provided on the bad sample. One paragraph of explanation preceded this sample. If you needed to use the sample program, you would not know how to prepare input to it, nor would you be able to interpret output. You can readily appreciate the value of a user's guide.

The deficiency of external documentation in this program is even more noticeable for the maintainer. If you were given the task of extending this program or of correcting some incorrect results, you would be lost. This program is, unfortunately, typical of too many production programs: it runs correctly on the "standard" input, meaning that it worked for the author's test case and for the first set of actual data on which it was run. There are many sets of data on which it will not operate properly. Eventually one of these bugs will appear. If you were called upon to repair this program, you would have no idea where to begin looking for a bug.

External documentation for the maintainer is often called a *program logic manual*, because the logical structure of the program is explained in it. A program logic manual (PLM) normally contains:

1. Program purpose.
2. Names and purposes of principal modules.
3. Calling sequences of modules—list of modules called by each module.
4. Names and purposes of major variables.
5. Program flow—order of the principal activities that occur during program execution.
6. Description of features to aid debugging and how to invoke them.
7. Extensions that the original author planned for and how to interface these extensions to the rest of the program.

Again, this information will vary from one program to the next. You should place yourself in the position of a potential user or maintainer of your program and try to anticipate questions or problems that that person will have.

We have spoken of the user's guide and the PLM as if they are to be written after the program. Although the final polishing is an *ex post facto* task, the bodies of these manuals are laid out as an important part of the initial program development. After all, if these documents would help someone to understand or to use the code, couldn't they help you to do the same thing as you develop or debug the program?

Consider identifying modules, parameters, and purposes. This is surely an important part of the design task. We generally iron out the problems of which module does what with what before worrying about how each module works. We prefer to keep our attention on the high points of a large amount of work before narrowing our scope to the details of any one of these high points. (This program construction technique is called stepwise refinement. We will be using it later to remake the above program in Section 1.9.)

1.2.2 Internal Documentation

The author of a novel must do two things. First, the scene must be set, the plot unveiled and the characters introduced. After the reader understands the background, then it is time to proceed to the exposition of the plot. In nonfiction a similar sequence occurs. This book, for example, starts with one chapter to insure that all readers speak the same language at a certain minimum degree of proficiency; after that introduction, new material is presented.

The writing of a computer program should follow the same pattern. First you must introduce your program. What is it, how (generally) does it work, what are the inputs and outputs, and what are the key variables? After this introduction, you may proceed to develop the code, confident that anyone reading can follow what you intend to do and roughly how you intend to do it.

To this end, we will divide internal documentation into two parts: a "header" or "block" of comments at the top of the program, and "step comments" within the program.

We generally put the following information into the header comments.

1. Program name and descriptive title.
2. Programmer name.
3. Date, (and version number if program has had substantial change).
4. Concise statement of what is to be done, brief synopsis of the algorithm used, outline of order of events that occur.
5. Inputs expected.
6. Names and meanings of the important variables.
7. Subprograms called.
8. Non-standard or system-dependent features that have been used (these should be avoided wherever possible).
9. Peculiar conditions or exceptions to the program's execution.

Compare these suggestions to the header documentation given in the sample program. We will now show the level of documentation we normally would supply if we were writing such a program.

```
PROGRAM BINGO -- BOOK INVENTORY GENERATOR

PROGRAM TO MAINTAIN LIST OF BOOK NUMBERS AND
       QUANTITIES OF THOSE BOOKS.

THIS PROGRAM HAS FOUR PHASES:
1. READ CARDS CONTAINING BOOK NUMBERS AND QUANTITY ON HAND
2. SORT INVENTORY DATA IN ASCENDING ORDER BY BOOK NUMBER
3. READ CARDS CONTAINING BOOK NUMBERS AND QUANTITY SOLD
4. PRINT SUMMARY REPORT OF BOOK NUMBERS AND QUANTITY ON HAND

INPUTS:
1. HEADER CARD TELLING HOW MANY CARDS WILL BE READ IN PHASE 1
       AND HOW MANY IN PHASE 3  (ONE BOOK NUMBER PER CARD)
2. BOOK NUMBER/QUANTITY-ON-HAND CARDS FOR PHASE 1
3. BOOK NUMBER/QUANTITY-SOLD CARDS FOR PHASE 3

PRINCIPAL VARIABLES
NBOOKS - HOW MANY BOOK/QUANTITY CARDS FOR PHASE 1
NSALES - HOW MANY BOOK/SALES CARDS FOR PHASE 3
BOOKNO - ARRAY OF BOOK NUMBERS
QTY    - QUANTITY ON HAND -- QTY(I) IS QUANTITY OF BOOKNO(I)
CBOOK  - CURRENT BOOK NUMBER BEING PROCESSED
NENTRY - NUMBER OF ENTRIES IN BOOKNO/QTY ARRAYS

PROGRAMMER: ---              DATE: ---
```

This documentation certainly conveys much more information than did the single header comment in the original program. (Also note that this documentation gives clues of structural changes that we will make later.)

Now examine the rest of the documentation within our example program. Two comments tell you that a DO loop follows (which you would certainly have noticed without the comments), two comments warn of an error having occurred, without identifying the source or type of the error, and others worry about "new cards," "old cards," or "first time." In short, the comments within the program provide no information to the reader at all.

We have found that the following techniques help produce effective documentation.

1. Use comments that describe the intent of a segment of code, without echoing the code itself. A comment such as "ADD 1 TO COUNT" preceding COUNT=COUNT+1 is far less useful than "INCREMENT COUNT OF DATA CARDS READ."
2. Do not comment every statement. The purpose of comments is to explain actions in a program. It is rare for actions to be accomplished in one statement each, and so it should also be rare for one comment to describe one statement. Comments should help a person to follow the execution of a program.
3. Use comments to break a program into meaningful sections. These sections have one purpose and are usually about 5 to 10 statements long.
4. Use more comments to break a program into larger phases. These phases represent one major activity and will probably be under a page in length.
5. It is often helpful to indent the text of a comment somewhat from the rest of the code. Thus, for statements beginning in column 7, comments might begin about column 15. This separation makes it possible for someone to read either comments alone, or code alone, or both.

You might want to refer to the program at the end of Chapter 0 to compare the documentation there with the suggestions given here. We will not show the comments now that we would use inside the sample program for this chapter. As we modify the approach to that program, however, we will include comments adhering to these standards. The entire program is shown in Section 1.9.

1.2.3   Additional Techniques

So far we have described internal documentation solely in terms of comments. But the precise meaning of the verb "document" is to convey information. Thus, anything done within a program to convey information is a part of the documentation. The following techniques all help your program to communicate by itself.

1. Choose meaningful names. X=Y/I conveys far less information than AVG=SUM/N .
2. Be aware of the I-N convention for integers. FORTRAN programmers have lived with this for long enough that they often assume that variables beginning with I, J, K, L, M, or N are integers. Help the reader of your program by following this convention wherever feasible.
   a. The names I, J, K, and N should always be integers. (By convention also, I, J, and K should be used only as loop indices, counters, or subscripts.)
   b. However, do not destroy otherwise meaningful names to make them conform to the I-N convention. Names for reals such as MILES or MEDIAN should *not* be changed to XMILES or EMDIAN just to match this guideline. The purpose of this suggestion is to improve communication, not to obscure it. It is hard to improve names such as MILES or MEDIAN.
3. Do things in an obvious manner. If a piece of code needs to compute

$$\frac{-b \pm \sqrt{b^2 - 4ac}}{2a}$$

then

```
DSCRM = SQRT(B**2 - 4*A*C)
ROOT(1) = (-B+DSCRM) / (2*A)
ROOT(2) = (-B-DSCRM) / (2*A)
```

is certainly much easier to follow than

```
   J=1
   DSCRM=(B*B-4*A*C)**0.5
10 ROOT(2-(J+1)/2) = (-B + J*DSCRM) / (2*A)
   J=-J
   IF (J .LT. 0) GO TO 10
```

4. Break long statements into readily understood sections; avoid excessive subdivision, however. This suggestion has two motivations. First, the human mind can keep about five different partial pieces of information active at one time. Thus, a complicated expression of more than five nontrivial parts is not easy to follow. Second, the longer an expression is, the more potential places there are for misplaced parentheses, unintended operators, and incorrect variables. It is reasonable to divide a long statement into pieces that anyone can follow easily, and that you can debug easily. The expression above involving computation of the discriminate of a quadratic equation is an example of extracting a series of related terms from a long expression.

5. Similarly, use redundant parentheses and spaces to help convey your intent. A term such as

```
IF (A+(B*C).GT.8 .OR. (I.LT.5 .AND. J.GT.2)) GO TO 10
```

is easier to understand than

```
IF (A+B*C.GT.8.OR.I.LT.5.AND.J.GT.2) GO TO 10
```

6. Indentation is a powerful technique that can make a program easier to follow. Good PL/I and ALGOL programmers have for years used this technique, but only recently have FORTRAN programmers broken themselves of the habit of starting each statement in column 7. DO loops and IF groups are prime candidates for indented treatment. Consider the following sample.

```
      DO 200 HOURNO = 1, 24
         WRITE(IOUT,100) HOURNO
100      FORMAT(' PROGRESS REPORT FOR HOUR',I4)
         DO 150 I = 1, N
            SUM=SUM+X(I)
            IF (X(I).LE.10) GO TO 120
               X(I)=X(I)-10.
               GO TO 150
120         WRITE(IOUT,125) I, X(I)
125         FORMAT(' SAMPLE ', I2,' HAS VALUE ', F10.4)
            X(I)=0.
150      CONTINUE
         WRITE(IOUT,175) SUM
175      FORMAT(' TOTAL SUM FOR THIS HOUR IS', F12.4)
         SUM=0.
200   CONTINUE
      STOP
      END
```

Even without understanding what this example does, you can easily see its structure. We have found that these guidelines are useful for indentation.

a. The body of a loop is indented three spaces more than either its head or its foot. This applies both to conventional DO loops and to "manufactured" loops. (These are loops that, for some reason, you must code explicitly with IF and GO TO statements.)

b. Another type of code body that should be indented three spaces is the "false" portion of an IF when that portion is more than one statement long. For example:

```
      IF (X(I) .LE. X(I+1)) GO TO 40
         TEMP = X(I)
         X(I) = X(I+1)
         X(I+1) = TEMP
40    CONTINUE
```

c. One or both action clauses of an IF-THEN-ELSE construct may be indented. (An IF-THEN-ELSE construct is described in Section 1.3.2. It is simply a form of an IF statement that has two different actions, depending on whether the condition tested is true or false.) Here is an example of indentation for an IF-THEN-ELSE.

```
      IF (HOURS .GT. 40.) GO TO 450
          PAY = RATE*HOURS
          TAX = 0.23*PAY
      GO TO 500
  450   PAY = RATE*HOURS + 0.5*RATE*(HOURS-40.)
          TAX = .23*PAY + .08*RATE*(HOURS-40.)
          NOVRT = NOVRT+1
  500 NEMP = NEMP+1
      ETC.
```

d. Readability of DO loops and of most manufactured loops is enhanced by terminating the loop with a CONTINUE statement.

We encourage you to use indentation to make your programs more readable. It is surprising, but true, that programs on which you take the time to indent carefully, are easier to debug.

7. Use some consistent, logical pattern for statement numbers. In the middle of a program, if you see the statement GO TO 675, and the last statement number you saw was 403, you would expect to begin looking for 675 lower in the program. Good programmers use statement numbers (as well as comments, of course) to inform the reader that a new section of code is about to begin. Each major section has assigned to it a range of numbers (e.g. 1000 to 1999, 2000 to 2999, etc.) and all statement numbers within the section are taken from that range. Then, as sections are divided into subsections, each subsection gets a portion of the section's range (1000 to 1199, 1200 to 1399, etc.). With such a pattern it becomes easy to locate statement numbers and to follow related blocks of statements.

8. Avoid easily confused variable names and statement numbers. Names such as MEAN and MEEN, or II and I1, and statement numbers such as 1883 and 1383, or 9099 and 9909 are too easily mistaken. These labels can cause difficulties as you write code; they can cause disastrous results from innocent keypunch errors; and they can make code hard to read.

In summary, you should consider the people who will read your code, for it is almost certain that someone, maybe even you, will read your code. Maintenance of programs is a nontrivial task. Whether you need to refer back to your program one year after writing it, or someone else needs to try to interpret your logic, or you need to try to interpret the logic in someone else's program, you will be thankful if the code is readable.

1.3 PROGRAM STRUCTURE

You are probably at the point now of having written some fairly complicated (longer than about thirty statements) programs. On short programs, structure is generally a moot point since, for these programs, there often is not enough complexity to allow for differences in structure. Just as with documentation, program structure is a matter that will vary from programmer to programmer and from project to project. We want you to read this section and to appreciate the motivation behind each technique we describe.

1.3.1 The GO TO Controversy

In 1968, a noted computer scientist, Edsger Dijkstra (pronounced DIKE-stra), wrote an essay stating, in essence, that use of the GO TO statement was a hinderance to program readability. The truth of this statement is apparent to all who have read substantial numbers of FORTRAN programs. The purpose of his statement was to encourage future language designers to provide a rich enough vocabulary of control structures to make use of the GO TO statement unnecessary. However, that pronouncement has received enough attention that it is appropriate to consider the motivation behind Dijkstra's remarks.

Dijkstra intended that a language contain facilities for controlling loops, for performing alternate actions depending on one or more conditions, and for selecting one of a group of statements to handle a particular subcase.

The problem is that we are faced with the language FORTRAN, which is over twenty years old. It has been updated several times, but features such as Dijkstra proposes would require substantial revision to the FORTRAN language. One goal in each revision to FORTRAN has been to preserve upward compatibility as far as possible; a program that did compile properly under the old standard should also do so under the new. (Of course, new features and extended meanings may mean that not all programs that compile under the new standard also do so under the old.) In essence we cannot expect to see drastic change in FORTRAN; we must learn to make intelligent use of what exists.

People often seek easy, mechanical solutions to their problems. A simplistic solution is to assume the converse of Dijkstra's statement: if a program with GO TO's is bad, then a program without GO TO's must be good. Wrong! Through deep nesting of subprograms calls and DO's, through sparse documentation, through illogically-ordered statements, and through other similar impediments, you can write unintelligible but GO TO-free code. Thus a program without GO TO's is not necessarily a good program.

Good code can be written in FORTRAN, even though FORTRAN has a limited set of control structures. Even without fancy tools, the craftsman can produce a notable object.

FORTRAN has the advantage of being a standardized language; this means that programs written in standard FORTRAN can be run on a wide variety of machines. Furthermore, FORTRAN is simple enough that compilers for it are reasonably small, and thus it is available on a number of minicomputers. FORTRAN is widely used; you are apt to find programs already written that may suit your needs. There are a number of well-tested compilers available; some of these have special features, such as debugging aids or object code optimization. Finally, and most important to this discussion, the desirable control features can be simulated in standard FORTRAN, often without substantial loss in efficiency or in readability. Thus, FORTRAN is a perfectly acceptable medium for advanced programming.

Some people have designed extended or "structured FORTRAN" processors. Generally, these take the form of a preprocessor that accepts some extended version of FORTRAN and produces as output an equivalent standard FORTRAN program; this output is then the input to a FORTRAN compiler, and the compiler produces machine object code.

These processors are nonstandard. Furthermore, there are many of them, but there is no agreement on what extensions should be provided. Thus there are many different dialects of "structured FORTRAN." Use of one of these processors will restrict you to running programs at your installation or at others that have a compatible processor. This clearly defeats one of the strongest advantages of FORTRAN: transportability of code.

On the other hand, these processors may allow you to code algorithm steps in a more "natural" syntax. They do not, however, make programs necessarily better, just as the mechanical elimination of GO TO's does not make a program necessarily better. If you have such a preprocessor available and if you like the features it provides, you may want to use it. The use of one of these preprocessors does add to the compile time of a program. We take the position, however, that a little machine time is far less valuable than a lot of programmer time. If these tools can help you to program more quickly or with fewer errors, the extra machine cost is well spent.

1.3.2   Control Structures

In this section, we will present some of the structures used in good algorithms. Good programmers have used such constructs for years. Examine them and keep them in mind as you plan computer solutions to problems. You will find, we are sure, that solutions to many problems are naturally represented using these forms.

1. IF-THEN. If a condition holds, then perform a certain group of actions. This form may arise in situations such as sorting (if two elements are out of order, then exchange them); inventory systems (if a sufficient quantity of part x exists, then process an order to ship   y   quantity of part   x); or simulations

(if more events remain to be done, then take the earliest event and effect it). This form is readily implemented by a logical IF statement as shown below.

```
      IF (NAME(I).LE.NAME(I+1)) GO TO 50
         TNAME = NAME(I)
         NAME(I) = NAME(I+1)
         NAME(I+1) = TNAME
   50 I = I+1
```

2. IF-THEN-ELSE. If a condition holds, then perform a certain group of actions; if the condition does not hold, then perform a different group of actions. Often these two groups of actions will merge again at a common statement. This form may arise when processing checking account deposits and withdrawals or finding the roots of a quadratic equation. This form is represented in FORTRAN either by two IF statements, or by a single IF and a pair of GO TO's. When implemented by two IF's, one tests the required condition, and the other tests the complement (the logical .NOT.) of the condition. When using an IF and two GO TO's, the code resembles

```
      IF (CONDITION) GO TO SN1
         CODE TO PERFORM IF CONDITION FALSE
         •••
      GO TO SN2
   SN1   CODE TO PERFORM IF CONDITION TRUE
         •••
   SN2 NEXT STATEMENT
```

3. ITERATE. This form requires repetition of a series of actions, depending on a condition. The condition can be for a certain number of repetitions, while a certain relationship holds, until a certain event occurs, or some combination of these. This form may arise when approximating the square root of a number until a desired level of accuracy has been achieved or until a particular number of repetitions have occurred, or when searching a table for a particular value until the value is found or until the whole table has been searched. This construct would ordinarily be implemented by a DO statement and, in fact, in languages such as PL/I, ALGOL, COBOL, and PASCAL, it is implemented by a single repeat statement. However, even in FORTRAN 77, the DO is so restrictive that complicated repetition forms are frequently implemented by IF and GO TO statements. Examples of situations for IF/GO TO loops include needing two independent stopping conditions, progressing at some nonconstant increment, needing to test for completion prior to executing the loop instead of after. There are two classic types of iterations statements: the test *before* performing the actions within the loop, and the test *after* performing the loop body. Other names for these iterative groups are DO-WHILE and REPEAT-UNTIL.

4. CASE. This form entails selection of one of a number of action groups, depending on the value of a variable. All action groups merge at a common

point after the last action group. An example that may call for this type of construct is a library circulation file program, where the cases would be new book acquired, book checked out, book returned, book withdrawn from circulation, location of book desired, borrower's name desired, etc. Some languages implement this form directly, but in most, the programmer must simulate it using a computed GO TO. For small numbers of cases, IF-THEN-ELSE constructs are probably more readable than the computed GO TO form. Good documentation is essential when using this form. When coded using a computed GO TO, a case statement has this form.

```
          GO TO (SN1, SN2, ..., SNM), ACTION
C
C                     FIRST TYPE OF EVENT
    SN1 CODE TO PERFORM FOR EVENT 1
          ...
          GO TO SNX
C                     SECOND TYPE OF EVENT
    SN2 CODE TO PERFORM FOR EVENT 2
          ...
          GO TO SNX
          ...
C                     LAST TYPE OF EVENT
    SNM CODE TO PERFORM FOR LAST EVENT
          ...
          GO TO SNX
C
C                     COMMON MERGE POINT
    SNX REST OF PROGRAM
```

5. SUBPROCEDURE. This form uses a separate block of code to accomplish a specific task. This construct is useful in situations such as (a) when nearly the same action must be performed in several places, perhaps on different sets of data, (b) when a self-contained set of actions can be separated from the rest of a group of code to improve understandability, or (c) when one segment of a process can be separately coded and debugged. This form is generally implemented in FORTRAN through use of a function subprogram or a subroutine.

These five forms are the major ones used by good programmers. We urge you to study them and to start thinking of solutions to programming problems in terms of them. It seems presumptuous to assert that all problems are amenable to solution using these forms; however, natural solutions to most problems seem to fall within these frameworks.

In Section 1.2 you saw the importance of comments to prepare the program reader for what is to come. Similarly, the use of these control structures helps to alert the reader to the form of your program. Before a person begins looking at a sequence of code, it is helpful to know that it is part of a loop structure.

Note, also, that the order of execution of these structures is "top down." All branches (GO TO's) transfer to points later (forward) in the program, with the exception of the iterative structure. Well-structured programs exhibit this forward-moving control flow.

1.4 DEFENSIVE PROGRAMMING

Without exception, major programs have bugs. These bugs can come from such sources as misunderstanding the problem, writing bad code, or writing or punching wrong statements. The programmer usually has control over these problem sources.

Another potential source of error is out of the programmer's control: errors in input data. In a commercial environment once the initial program debugging has been completed, the programmer turns the program over to others to use, and cannot prevent input errors such as mispunched data, misplaced or omitted data, and missing trailer cards.

You should protect your program against input errors. This protection involves several steps.

1. Minimize restrictions on the input. Use a trailer card to signal the end of the input deck, instead of using a header card to indicate the count of cards to follow. It is too easy to miscount. If your compiler permits it, use of the END= option on the READ is preferable to a trailer card.
2. Validate the input. In many applications, there is an acceptable range for input values. The number of hours an employee worked in a week must fall between 0 and 7*24 hours, or the weights of humans should range between 1 and 200 kilograms, for example. Your program should thus check each input value for reasonableness.
3. Echo check input. You should print each value read, immediately after reading; this output should be clearly labeled. This technique will provide you or the user of your program with a listing of exactly what values were received (in case some value was mispunched). Also, for debugging purposes, you then have a listing of all data received by your program, so that you can perform a full trace by hand.
4. Crash softly. If your program expects input data but receives none, your program should print a message and terminate. Similarly, if you expect a nonzero value but receive a zero (perhaps from no value having been punched in the required columns), you should not proceed with execution and produce erroneous results. In general, whenever your program finds an unacceptable situation of any kind, it should print a message and terminate.

1.5   DEBUGGING TECHNIQUES

Programmers seem to be extraordinarily optimistic. Beginners assume that a program is correct if there are no syntax errors. As programmers mature, they acknowledge the existence of semantic bugs. However, in spite of strong evidence to the contrary, they assume that each program will run perfectly the first time. Even after accepting that their programs will always initially contain errors, beginning programmers still feel that when they mature, this situation will reverse. This, too, is a fallacy. It takes quite a while for programmers to adopt the philosophy that bugs will occur and to plan to locate these bugs as easily as possible.

1.5.1   Tools for Debugging

Debugging is an investigative, experimental science. It is therefore important to know the techniques of debugging and to learn to apply them successfully. Here are some tools that we have found useful.

1. Learn about the debugging aids available to you.

Many compilers have extensions to the FORTRAN language to provide additional information in the event of an error. WATFIV, for example, provides the DUMPLIST statement, and the DEC FORTRAN-10 has the FOR-DDT package. Even production compilers such as the IBM FORTRAN G compiler allow the use of DEBUG packets. We will not go into detail about any one of these facilities, since their precise form varies so widely. The services often provided include

a. Post-mortem dump. In the event of abnormal termination (and sometimes for normal terminations), the values of all or of a selected group of variables are displayed as they were at the time of termination.

b. Flow trace. The programmer sets bounds or key points. Each time execution proceeds within the bounds, a "map" is produced identifying all statements executed within that area. This often is of the form of a statement number or a control transfer trace: "You executed statements numbered 1,2,3, 4,5,6, 4,5,6, 4,5,6, 7,8" or "Execution began at 1. Change of flow at 6 to 4. Change of flow at 6 to 4. Termination at 8." This latter form assumes sequential execution (1 then 2 then 3 ...) except as noted (change of flow at 6 to 4).

c. Check for defined variables. Variables that have not yet been assigned a value (by DATA initialization, input, assignment, or some other technique) are said to be "undefined." Each variable is associated with a word in storage, and each word contains some value. If you have not explicitly put something there, the word contains whatever was there previously—a part of another program or some random piece of data. The meaning of "undefined" variables is really that their value is "unpredictable" or "meaningless." Some compilers monitor variable references to guarantee that each time a variable is referenced, its value has previously been defined.

d. Check for legality. Subscripts must be less than or equal to the dimension of an array. Calling arguments must be of the same type and number as the dummy arguments. The results of arithmetic computations must not exceed the sizes of the variables in which they are to be stored. In some compilers, such activities are monitored, and the program abnormally terminates in the event of an error.

2. Let your compiler help you.

Use the debugging aids provided by your compiler and operating system. Some novice programmers suffer from a strange form of machismo in which they feel it is shameful to use the debugging features available from their compiler. Often their reasoning is that subscript checking increases the running time of a program (which it does), but during the initial debugging runs, this is a false economy. A small bit of machine time is certainly worth less than a large amount of programmer time, and perhaps an even larger amount of time from those waiting to use the program.

Another reason cited for not using debugging aids is "I'll learn more by debugging without assistance." If the problem has been carefully designed, then the programmer is already quite aware of the program's structure and flow. A programmer learns more from a new project than from remaining with an old one. Thus, to maximize the amount of material learned, the programmer needs to maximize the number of new projects, which comes from minimizing debugging time. This should not be interpreted as a recommendation for shoddy or incomplete debugging but, rather, as a justification for making full use of all available debugging tools.

3. Plan to make errors.

a. Locate potential trouble spots as you plan your program. We have recommended checking for reasonableness of input data, since this is one of the major trouble spots of a program. We recommend now that you similarly test for reasonableness at internal trouble spots. For example, if you are about to divide A by B, you might test if B has a nonzero value. If your compiler does not check subscripts, you might verify that 3*(IGRADE+1)/4 + IPLUS would be within legal bounds before using it as a subscript.

b. Identify key flow points within your program. Each time you enter a new phase in your computation, it is useful to know that your program has concluded one task and begun another. Include output statements at these crucial points as you first write your program. Then, if your program fails, you have some idea where this failure occurred.

c. Write debugging code as you write the program. In the long run, it takes less effort to include debugging code while your mind is fully attuned to the program flow. For example, you should automatically put output statements at the beginning and end of each subprogram.

d. Avoid shuffling debugging code in and out of a program. Once you have found the appropriate spots for debugging code and have placed helpful statements there, leave the debugging code in your program. It seems to be a law among program bugs that once you think you have isolated and corrected the last bug and you have removed all the code to assist you in debugging, then another bug appears.

Instead of removing the debugging code, you may simply deactivate this code. For example, consider a subprogram to calculate the amount of depreciation of an item by the double declining balance method of accounting. Such a function might resemble this.

```
      REAL FUNCTION DDECLN(COST,NYEARS,YEARNO)
C        CALCULATE DOUBLE DECLINING BALANCE DEPRECIATION
C        INPUTS:
C        COST    NEW COST OF ITEM BEING DEPRECIATED
C        NYEARS SPAN OF YEARS OVER WHICH DEPRECIATION IS
C                BEING CALCULATED
C        YEARNO YEAR FOR WHICH DEPRECIATION AMOUNT IS DESIRED
C               (E.G. YEARNO=1 MEANS FIRST YEAR)
C        OUTPUTS:
C        DDECLN AMOUNT OF DEPRECIATION TO CLAIM FOR GIVEN YEAR
C
      INTEGER NYEARS, YEARNO
      REAL COST
      LOGICAL DEBUG/.TRUE./
      INTEGER IDBOUT/6/
C             DEBUGGING OUTPUT FOR PROGRAM TRACE
      IF (DEBUG) WRITE (IDBOUT,100) COST,NYEARS,YEARNO
100   FORMAT (' **DEBUG** DDECLN ENTERED WITH COST=',F10.2,
     X ' NYEARS,YEARNO=',2I5)

      ...REST OF COMPUTATION...

C             DEBUGGING OUTPUT FOR PROGRAM EXIT TRACE
      IF (DEBUG) WRITE (IDBOUT,101) DDECLN
101   FORMAT (' **DEBUG** DDECLN EXITED WITH VALUE',F10.2)
      RETURN
      END
```

When the programmer first executes the subprogram DDECLN, there may be some errors. These should not be difficult to spot since, on each call to the subprogram, all entry and exit values are displayed. Therefore, if the subprogram is producing consistently erroneous results, some general part of the subprogram code is suspect. However, if only one set of data causes incorrect results, you have all the input values as received, and you can trace the processing of those values through the subprogram.

The important point is that debugging code should *not* be removed after the program module is working. Instead, change one card to

```
      LOGICAL DEBUG/.FALSE./
```

This will inhibit output from the debugging statements. However, if in the future, the integrity of module DDECLN is ever questioned, a single card change reinitializing DEBUG to value .TRUE. will reactivate the debugging code in that module. At a much later date, it may be difficult to remember the key debugging points in a program, while locating them during algorithm development is relatively easy. Furthermore, it is wasteful of your time to have prepared meaningful output labels, only to throw them away and to have to rewrite the same statements for subsequent debugging. It is false economy to discard all the information built up during debugging.

It is possible to generalize this technique. One possibility is to make DEBUG a parameter or a global variable (through the use of COMMON, as explained in Section 2.6). One logical variable will then activate debugging code in the entire program. A related technique is to have special inputs turn the debugging switch(es) on and off. Then, instead of needing to recompile a source program after changing the initialization statement for variable DEBUG, you can indicate that the variable is to be turned on or off by special values in the input data. In this way, if something is awry with the processing of one portion of the input data, you can activate debugging for that one portion of the input data only, thereby limiting your output to the crucial parts.

Another variant on this scheme is to assign a "level of confidence" to each piece of debugging output. Thus, a straightforward routine performing simple computations might have a high level of confidence, whereas a crucial routine that does many intricate computations might have a low level of confidence. DEBUG would be a numeric variable. During execution, if the value of DEBUG was not higher than the level of confidence of a particular routine or output statement, no output would be produced. If, however, DEBUG had a higher value than the level of a particular section of code, debugging output would be produced for that code section. Local debug statements might look like this.

```
IF (DEBUG.GT.4)   WRITE (-,-) MAXVAL, COST
```

You start with a high value of DEBUG; this produces output from all your debugging points. As program debugging progresses and you build more confidence in the program modules, you decrease the value of DEBUG. A value of zero would mean no debugging output at all.

One argument frequently raised is the overhead (use of computer resources such as time, memory space, or paper) from leaving debugging code in a program. This argument is often raised by experienced programmers who have programmed on older machines that were slower and smaller than many of the machines today. Relative to a nontrivial program, the time to test one logical variable or the space required for the code of   IF (--) WRITE(-,-) --- is inconsequential. You should, of course, be judicious in your use of debugging statements, placing them where they will not be repeatedly executed, if possible. (Inside a DO loop that will execute 1000 times is, for example, a bad place to locate a debugging statement, unless you need to monitor each iteration of the loop. You might, however, use a "sampling" technique that displays values on the 10th, 20th, 30th, ... iterations.) The choice between efficient execution and easily debugged execution leans more toward efficiency for the true production program that will be used many times or on massive volumes of data; even then, however, the ease of debugging makes a strong argument in favor of leaving debugging code in the program. We will explore the issue of efficiency more carefully in Section 1.6.

e. It is easier to debug a correct algorithm than an incorrect one. The time spent honing, refining, and checking a program design (called an *algorithm*) before it is coded is time well spent. Do not be too anxious to produce code, for you will generally be less willing to revise or even scrap code than to rework a program design.

f. It is useful to explain your algorithm (in detail) to someone else. In the process of talking it out, you may find points that you have neglected, or the person may ask about a segment that just doesn't "look right." Often the person needs only to be a listener; you will find flaws yourself as you try to explain your algorithm. Many commercial programming teams use what are called "code walk-throughs." In these, all members of a programming team explain their design to their teammates. Management is usually not present at these meetings, and so the team members do not feel as if they are being judged. The teammates offer suggestions, but frequently just the act of having to explain a program's logic causes its author to locate potential problems. Of course, this technique can also be used by students debugging projects; all it takes is another student who is willing to listen.

1.5.2 So How Does One Debug?

You may have been amazed as you wrote your first programs and took them to a more experienced programmer for help. That person could quickly locate and correct your errors. That person could work quickly because of knowing the language well, understanding the potential trouble spots in your (relatively simple) beginning programs, and having seen the symptoms of many varied errors before. As you have acquired maturity in programming, the speed with which you debug should also have increased. It is not possible to detail all the steps used to debug a particular project or to explain all the debugging techniques used. Some of the best debugging seems to involve pulling together unrelated facts and forming plausible hypotheses. However, we will present some of the more concrete debugging techniques used by mature programmers.

You must first understand the diagnostic messages produced by the compiler. Unfortunately, some compilers produce one vague message ("SYNTAX

ERROR") for all ill-formed statements. In this event you must verify the syntax of a statement with the language reference manual, watching for matching parentheses, missing commas, superfluous operators, etc.

Other more enlightened compilers produce more meaningful messages, based on the best guess of what a statement probably was meant to be. Sometimes, however, these compilers can be fooled. A classic case is that in FORTRAN, there are only two cases in which a term in an arithmetic expression may consist of a name immediately followed by a left parenthesis: an array reference or a function reference. Using the process of elimination, if the compiler has not seen a declaration or dimension for an array of the given name, it deduces that a name followed by a left parenthesis is a call to a function. Forgetting to declare an array or misspelling an array name can produce some misleading messages about references to nonexistent functions. Only experience will help in this case; therefore, you should know your error messages. Each time you find a new error message or a new set of circumstances that causes one error message, you should note the circumstances and the matching message.

Still more enlightened compilers may make corrections where possible. For example, items in a FORMAT list must be separated by commas. In some cases, such as after the closing apostrophe of a character string, it is obvious where the comma must be placed. In the case of the error

```
12    FORMAT (' ANS =' 10X, A5)
```

the compiler could not only tell you that you must have a comma between ' ANS =' and 10X, but the compiler could insert one, show you what correction has been made, and proceed to compile the "corrected" program. The person who designed the compiler analyzed the cases where an apostrophe could precede a digit and determined that in the majority, say 80% of the cases, what was intended was a comma between them. This is fine for the majority of cases, but what if your error falls into the minority group? In this case, the "correction" may lead you even farther from the correct code than what you started with. Thus, if your compiler produces a message saying "missing comma," for example, or if it corrects a statement for you by inserting a comma, recheck your syntax. You, not the compiler, wrote the original statement, and you, not the compiler, know what you intended.

After you have mastered the error messages produced by your compiler and have a program that compiles successfully, you are ready to proceed into execution. At this point, you should get one clean source listing of your program, including all of your documentation describing names and purposes of major variables, turn on all your debugging code, make a listing of the input data being supplied, and execute your program.

For actual debugging, nothing has been found to beat hand simulation, although a few techniques have been found to reduce the drudgery of this process. In a hand simulation you take a pencil and your program and "play computer"; you record the values of variables and follow the flow of the program. As you progress you compare each value produced to the value that that variable should have at the corresponding step of the algorithm.

One aid to you in this hand simulation can be the flow trace, produced either by the compiler or by your own debugging output. If you are making the flow trace yourself, then you will need numerous "here I am" output messages in the program. These can be simple messages printed each time you move from one step in the algorithm to another; they would say, for example, "SORTING COMPLETE; BEGIN TO COMPUTE MEDIAN." (The few extra keystrokes needed to make the message more meaningful than, for example, "SPOT 1" certainly pay off in speed of debugging.) Entry and exit to each nontrivial subprogram are two points for flow trace output, since these are frequently associated with crucial steps in the algorithm.

Often just a map of where the algorithm is going and in what order is sufficient to help you locate your error. Sometimes, however, your program may be going to the right places in the proper order, but producing the wrong answers. If so, you need a more careful simulation; you must then follow the computation of values as execution progresses.

You must take all variables and perform computations just as you direct in your program. If the error is small, you must perform all computations to full accuracy. (Be aware, also, of roundoff and truncation errors as explained in Chapter 6.) If the error is large, it is generally sufficient to approximate the value of each step of the computation, remembering if the approximation is likely too high or too low, and by what order of magnitude.

Of use during this phase of debugging is the value trace. This computer output is similar to the flow trace, except instead of saying "Here I am," you say "I just computed the value of X as ---." The same points that were key flow points are also often key value points. Again, output from these trace statements should be clearly labeled to indicate (1) where they are in the program, (2) what are the names of the variables being reported, and (3) what are their values.

Be reasonable during this phase. It is often not necessary to see all values in an array. If the array is to be sorted, the values of the first ten elements may be sufficient to demonstrate that the sort is working. If items are continually being added to an array, the values of the last (most recent) half dozen entries added may suffice. Produce enough output so that you can monitor execution, but not so much that you become inundated with useless information.

Another debugging technique that can be quite useful is to work backward through a program. Suppose that you are at statement 200, and the value of X is incorrect. You then look above this point in the program, watching where X most recently received its value. This, of course, is not as simple as progressing up one statement at a time, because a GO TO or an IF might have altered the flow of execution. If X is assigned the value Y+Z at some point, then either Y or Z might have contributed to the erroneous value; you then continue tracing back Y and Z. You are effectively constructing a tree where each manner in which X can receive a value is represented by a unique branch. Note that one of the X branches could split into a Y and a Z branch if X depends on Y and Z. Each of these two new branches is then also followed backward. One by one you prune these branches because (1) your simulation and program output confirm that this computation and all its input are correct, or (2) your simulation and program output confirm that this branch was never executed. You put in more debugging code in the remaining branches to narrow the search for the faulty computation by determining exactly which branch was executed and what were the initial and final values of all variables along the branches. Eventually this technique will lead to the points of error. A few compilers are capable of performing the process of backing up the path your program executed for you.

Probably the hardest act in debugging is to admit that there may be more than one error. You should examine all output and make sure that you have found as many errors as can be identified from the output produced. Many programmers practice "iterative debugging," in which they get output, find one bug, fix it, resubmit, get more output, find one more bug, fix it, get more output, find one more bug, etc. It is a more efficient use of your time to continue a hand simulation until you have traced a substantial part of the program, regardless of whether you have found 1 or 100 errors. Once you are in the right frame of mind for simulation, it is easier to continue than to break and have to begin the simulation again with the next run. It is tempting to fix the "one last bug," but mature programmers realize that the "last bug" is often mythical.

1.6 EFFICIENCY

Efficient programs are those that use the minimum amount of resources. It is important to recognize that there are many different resources: computer time and memory are two important ones, but so also are auxiliary storage (tape and disk, as described in Chapter 4) and paper. Two frequently overlooked and very valuable resources are programmer time and user time. When we use the term "efficiency," we must be careful to identify which resources are economized and what offsetting increases occur in the uses of other resources. The relative values of these resources will vary between different computer installations and different individuals. It is important to apply a reasonable value to each resource, however.

1.6.1   Machine Time/Space Efficiency

Efficient use of machine time means using the smallest amount of time to produce the desired output. Clearly, you should avoid unnecessary computations. The classic cases of obviously inefficient code are listed below.

One serious piece of inefficient code involves recomputing the same value over and over again. You should move constant computation outside of a program loop. As an example, consider

```
    DO 10 I = 1,N
        B(I) = A(I)/(C**2 - 4*D)
10  CONTINUE
```

It is obvious that (C**2 - 4*D) will not change within this loop. However, most compilers cause the term (C**2 - 4*D) to be recomputed with each pass through the loop. A simple alternative is to move the invariant calculation outside the loop.

```
    DENOM = (C**2 - 4*D)
    DO 10 I = 1, N
        B(I) = A(I) / DENOM
10  CONTINUE
```

Cases similar to these are frequent.

Another obvious source of inefficiency is the use of real numbers, integers, and conversions between them. On many machines, real number calculations are significantly more time consuming than integer calculations; in fact, on small machines, each arithmetic operation on two real numbers results in a subprogram call. Conversions from one type to another are also costly. You should thus use integer computations wherever the choice between real or integer is arbitrary. Similarly, you should avoid unneeded conversions. Where possible, mixed-mode expressions should contain only one term of the foreign type, and it should be placed so that the fewest conversions possible occur.

A third obvious source for time reduction is in the use of subscripts. Recall from Chapter 0 that the storage mapping function for subscripted variable references involves one added term for each extra dimension, and that the more dimensions, the more multiplications per term. For this reason, reference to single-dimension arrays is preferable to double-dimension arrays, etc. Notice however, that if the subscript becomes an expression as complicated as (3*I*J + 7*I - J), it may be more complicated than reference to the two subscripts (I,J). Of course, simple variables are most easily referenced, and so they are preferable to arrays, where feasible.

It is not fair, however, to ignore the role of the compiler in this process. The above hints are well-known techniques of efficiency. Just as programmers have followed these guidelines for a long time, so also have compiler writers. Many production environment compilers today detect these inefficient forms shown above and generate efficient code for them. This is so because many of these code forms have been a by-product of the generation of object code from FORTRAN statements. Take, for example, repeated computations within a loop. Many occurrences of this problem are due to the compiler generating code to compute the storage mapping function for an array reference, or to set up addresses for a subprogram call. These pieces of code are something over which the programmer cannot achieve direct control, and so it must be the compiler that optimizes this type of situation. Thus, many compilers will extract invariant computations from a loop, regardless of whether you or the compiler caused the computation to be within the loop.

Our recommendation is that you not write obviously inefficient code. However, to brood over code in order to remove the last wasted microsecond is, in our opinion, not the mark of a mature programmer. In the long run, differences in execution time between a well-coded implementation and the best implementation of the same algorithm are likely to be inconsequential. Even more important, as a person uses more and more tricky code to eke out "efficient" executions, readability often declines; we consider this to be a serious misordering of priorities. In short, we recommend a healthy concern for efficient construction, but not an obsession.

1.6.2 Algorithm Efficiency

We have taken a rather dim view of the low-order variety of efficiency that worries over the best way to code a particular algorithm step. What is of far more importance, however, is the inherent complexity of the algorithm being implemented. Let us consider two examples, involving searching and sorting.

There are many methods of looking for a particular value in a list of values. The easiest of these is the brute force sequential search technique. In this, you compare the value for which you are looking against each element in the list of values, starting with the top element and moving sequentially through the list. It is clear that on the average, you will have to look halfway through the list to locate the desired element. If the list has N elements, this means an average of $N/2$ comparisons.

Now consider the running time of this algorithm. On a list of N elements, there will be an average of $N/2$ comparisons plus $N/2$ loop index increments and tests plus some constant number of other statements executed. Thus the running time of this algorithm is $c*(N/2)+d$ where c and d are constants that depend on the time for a particular machine to perform an increment or a comparison. Clearly this algorithm runs at a speed proportional to N, the number of data items processed; we say that it is an algorithm of *time complexity* N.

This is not, however, the most efficient search technique. When looking up numbers in a phone book, people do not do a straight sequential scan.

The more common human lookup technique involves successive guesses, moving forward if the guess is too low and backward if the guess is too high. As one gets closer to the desired spot in the book or table, the sizes of the jumps between guesses become successively smaller. We can approximate this pattern of lookup by a technique known as the "binary search." In this technique, our initial probe is halfway into the table. If the desired value is smaller than or larger than the middle table element, then we confine our search to the first or last half of that table, respectively. We next probe to the middle of that half (which is the one quarter or three quarter mark of the original table) and then confine our search to the top or bottom of these quarters, depending on whether the desired value is lower or higher than the examined value. The process of successively halving the table continues until either the desired entry is found, or the size of the table is reduced to zero.

We present the binary search formally as a subprogram in Figure 1-2.

The execution time of this approach is considerably better than that of the simple sequential search. Each time we divide the list, we discard half of it. In one step, the list is reduced to half of the previous one; in two steps, to one fourth; in three steps, to one eighth; etc., until in k steps, it is reduced to $1/(2**k)$ of the original. If the size of the original list is N, and if $(2**k)>N$, then the list has been exhausted, and we are done. Thus, the maximum number of steps the search can take is the smallest k such that $(2**k)>N$. This value of k is $\log_2(N)+1$. So in the worst case we must make no more than $\log_2(N)$ comparisons before the list is exhausted. The time complexity of this process can be no worse than $\log_2(N)$. For large values of N, this technique achieves a great advantage over the sequential scan. However, this technique applies only to sorted tables, which is a severe limitation.

We have run a test of the number of comparisons needed to locate values in a sorted table of 100 elements, each of which was a value between 1 and 1000. We selected 10 elements at random and found them, using both the sequential and the binary search techniques. The number of comparisons for each of these techniques are shown in Table 1-1 following the program.

The table confirms the time complexity statistics derived earlier, since $100/2$ is 50 and $\log_2(100)$ is between 6 and 7. The advantage of the binary search is even more pronounced as the size of the table increases; $1000/2$ is 500, but $\log_2(1000)$ is less than 10. The disparity between $N/2$ and $\log_2(N)$ increases as N grows larger.

Let us now examine another common computing activity: sorting. By sorting, we mean putting a series of values in order so that each value is less than[1] its successor. Assume that we have N elements, A(1) through A(N).

---

[1] *We will use the term "less than" for simplicity only. It should be clear, however, that the same techniques apply if there are duplicate entries (in which case "less than or equal to" would be a more appropriate phrase) or if the sort should run in descending order (in which case "greater than" would be more appropriate).*

```
      SUBROUTINE BISRCH (ARG, TABLE, TABSIZ, LOCN)
C
C          BINARY SEARCH SUBROUTINE
C
C          TABLE LOOKUP OF "ARG" IN "TABLE," BY BINARY SEARCH
C              PROCESS OF SUCCESSIVELY HALVING THE TABLE UNTIL
C              THE DESIRED ARGUMENT IS FOUND, OR THE TABLE IS
C              EXHAUSTED.
C
C          INPUT ARGUMENTS:
C          ARG      VALUE TO BE LOOKED FOR
C          TABLE    LIST IN WHICH TO LOOK FOR VALUE
C          TABSIZ   SIZE OF TABLE
C
C          OUTPUT ARGUMENT:
C          LOCN     LOCATION AT WHICH "ARG" WAS FOUND, OR
C                        0 IF ARGUMENT WAS NOT FOUND
C
C          INTERNAL VARIABLES:
C          LOW      LOWEST SUBSCRIPT IN CURRENTLY ACTIVE TABLE PORTION
C          HI       HIGHEST SUBSCRIPT IN CURRENTLY ACTIVE TABLE PORTION
C          MID      MIDPOINT OF CURRENTLY ACTIVE TABLE
C          SIZE     SIZE OF CURRENTLY ACTIVE TABLE
C
C          PROGRAMMER: ---           DATE: ---
C
      INTEGER ARG, LOCN, TABSIZ, TABLE(TABSIZ)
      INTEGER LOW, HI, MID, SIZE
      INTEGER IDBOUT
      LOGICAL DEBUG
      DATA DEBUG/.FALSE./,IDBOUT/6/
      IF (DEBUG) WRITE (IDBOUT,11)
   11 FORMAT (' ENTRY TO BISRCH')
C
C              INITIAL SCAN IS FOR ENTIRE TABLE, FROM 1 TO TABSIZ
      LOW = 1
      HI = TABSIZ+1
      SIZE = TABSIZ
C              LOCN SET TO NOT FOUND INITIALLY; WILL BE RESET IF FOUND
      LOCN = 0
C
C              *** MAIN LOOP ***
C
C              CHECK IF TABLE EXHAUSTED
   25 IF (SIZE .LE. 0) GO TO 150
C              THIS PASS WILL SPLIT TABLE IN HALF; COMPUTE MIDPOINT
      SIZE = SIZE/2
      MID = (LOW+HI)/2
      IF (DEBUG) WRITE (IDBOUT,35) LOW, HI, ARG, MID, TABLE(MID)
   35 FORMAT (' BISRCH LOOP: LOW, HI BOUNDS=',2I10, '; COMPARING',I10,
     X    ' TO TABLE(',I6,') =',I10)
      IF (ARG .LT. TABLE(MID)) HI = MID
      IF (ARG .GT. TABLE(MID)) LOW = MID
      IF (ARG .NE. TABLE(MID)) GO TO 25
C
C              DESIRED ENTRY FOUND
      LOCN = MID
C
C              COMMON RETURN POINT: FOUND OR NOT FOUND
  150 IF (DEBUG) WRITE (IDBOUT,151) ARG, LOCN
  151 FORMAT (' BISRCH EXIT: ARG=',I10,',  LOCN=',I10)
      RETURN
      END
```

FIGURE 1-2 Binary Search Subprogram

| TRIAL | LOOKING FOR | COMPARISONS | |
		SEQUENTIAL	BINARY
1	418	51	1
2	946	95	6
3	477	56	7
4	3	1	7
5	725	74	6
6	326	38	3
7	432	53	7
8	656	70	6
9	51	5	6
10	401	49	6
AVERAGES		49.20	5.50

Table 1-1   Comparison of Binary and Sequential Search

The classic "bubble sort" involves comparing successive pairs of numbers and exchanging them when they are out of order—when the larger precedes the smaller. This process continues through the array again and again until a pass has been made through the array without changes. The algorithm can be presented like this.

1. M = N-1
2. If M < 2, stop.
3. Switch = "off"
4. Perform for I = 1 to M:
   If A(I) and A(I+1) are out of order (A(I)>A(I+1)),
   then exchange them and set switch to "on."
5. M = M-1
6. If switch is off, then stop; otherwise return to step 2.

We wish to determine the time complexity of this algorithm. The loop in step 4 involves the most activity so we will first estimate the number of times it repeats. Since M is reduced by 1 at step 5, the number of times the statements in step 4 are executed decreases by 1. The first time N-1 comparisons are made, the second time N-2, until the last time 1 comparison is made. The average number of comparisons made in step 4 is N/2.

We would like to know how many times in step 6 the switch will be on. The switch is on just in case two adjacent elements were exchanged in step 4. Notice that in the event of an exchange, we immediately move to the next element. Thus, a small element can make only one step upward per pass. However, the largest element is pulled to the bottom in a single pass. In the next pass, the second-largest element is pulled to its spot. Thus (N–1) passes are sufficient to move all elements to their places. Although the number of passes to sort this data depends on the initial arrangement of the data, on the average N/2 passes are required to sort N numbers.

Since step 4 involves an average of N/2 comparisons per pass, and since there are an average of N/2 passes, the number of comparisons for the complete sort is proportional to N∗∗2. Therefore, we say that this is an algorithm of order N∗∗2.

This implies that if we increase the size of an array to sort by a factor of 10, we can expect the running time of the sort to increase by a factor of 100, or 10∗∗2. This certainly makes one think twice before using this algorithm to sort a thousand numbers, since that would require on the average one million comparisons.

None of the efficiency hints given previously, nor any tricky or careful code will improve that situation dramatically, because this is inherently an N∗∗2 algorithm. The N∗∗2 complexity is a characteristic of the *algorithm* itself, and not of the *coding* of that algorithm. If we wish to solve this problem more efficiently, we must consider a faster algorithm, not a different coding.

A better algorithm is the Quicksort, due to C.A.R. Hoare. The sort does not involve exchanging adjacent pairs of elements, since that is the source of much of the inefficiency of the bubble sort. Instead, this sort locates a "dividing" point, such that all elements on one side of the element at the dividing point are less than the dividing point, and all elements on the other side are greater than it. (Note that the elements on either side may not be in proper ascending order; however, all elements on the left will be less than, and all elements on the right will be greater than, the dividing element.) This then produces two lists, one on either side of the dividing point. These two lists may be sorted independently, since the elements in the one list will all be larger than those in the other. Furthermore, each of these lists will be smaller than the original list.

We will make one of the end elements be our dividing element; assume that we make the left element our dividing element. Then we will start at the right end of the list examining all elements and passing over those which are greater than the dividing element. We are trying to locate the dividing point and, since these elements are larger than the dividing element, they will stay to the right of it. However, when we find an element on the right that is smaller than the dividing element, then it must be moved to the other side. We do this by interchanging the dividing element and this smaller element. We now proceed with this same process working from the left; that is, we pass over elements on the left as long as they are smaller than the dividing element. When a larger element is found, we exchange it with the dividing element. Notice that each time we exchange, it is to move a small element to the left of the dividing element or to move a large element to the right.

We continue this process until all elements have been split into two lists: those smaller than the dividing element and those larger than it.

The technique will be shown first by an example. In it, we will use two pointers, L and R, to indicate the element currently being compared to the dividing element.

1.	45	32	62	22	18	75	57
	L				x	←	R

2.	18	32	62	22	45	75	57
	L	→	x		R		

3.	18	32	45	22	62	75	57
			L	x	←	R	

4.	18	32	22	45	62	75	57
			L	→	R		

5.	18	32	22	45	62	75	57
				Div			

In the first step of this process, the element identified by the right pointer (57) is compared to the element pointed to by the left pointer (45). As long as the left element is less than the right element, we move the right pointer toward the left. However, when a right element is greater than the left, we exchange them (18 and 45, exchanged at line 2). We then start moving the left pointer until the right element (45) is less than the left element (62), and exchange them (shown in line 3). We repeat the process of moving the right pointer as far as possible, exchanging, moving the left pointer as far as possible, and exchanging, until the two pointers meet. The element at which the pointers meet is our dividing element.

We then repeat this entire sequence on each of the two lists on the two sides of the dividing point. If either of these lists has zero or one elements, it is already sorted. The stopping condition is for all lists to have been sorted. The algorithm is formally stated in Figure 1-3.

Complete analysis of the running time of this algorithm is beyond the scope of this book. Knuth has determined that the number of comparisons made in this algorithm is proportional to $N*\log_2(N)$, where N is the size of the array being sorted. So that you can see some of the justification for this time estimate, we describe the number of comparisons performed in the best case. First we start with one list of size N. This list divides into two lists, and the size of each will be about N/2, in the best case. (Since the initial right end element becomes the dividing point, the exact size of each new list

To sort an array A of size N into ascending order.
1. LISTS—TO—SORT = (1,N)

2. DO STEPS 3–7 WHILE LISTS—TO—SORT is not empty.

3.   Remove last pair from LISTS—TO—SORT stack.
     Let LEND be the first element of that pair, and
     let REND be the second element of that pair.
     LPT=LEND; RPT=REND

4.   DO STEPS 5–6 WHILE LPT < RPT

5.   ** First move left pointer as far as possible **
         DO WHILE (A(LPT) ≤ A(RPT))
               LPT = LPT+1
               IF (LPT ≥ RPT) GO TO STEP 7
         END
         ** Have found an out of order element; **
         ** Move the left element to the right side **
         Exchange A(LPT) and A(RPT)

6.   ** Now move right pointer as far as possible **
         DO WHILE (A(LPT) ≤ A(RPT))
               RPT = RPT–1
               IF (LPT ≥ RPT) GO TO STEP 7
         END
         ** RPT element belongs on other side; exchange **
         Exchange A(LPT) and A(RPT)

7. ** RPT is dividing point **
   ** Split list into two, and sort each independently **
   ** Avoid sorting empty lists. **
   IF (RPT–1 > LEND) put (LEND,RPT–1) on LISTS—TO—SORT
   IF (RPT+1 < REND) put (RPT+1,REND) on LISTS—TO—SORT
   END

FIGURE 1-3 Quicksort Algorithm

depends on how well balanced the list was with respect to that dividing point.)
Each of these two lists divides into two lists, thus making 4 lists of size N/4,
which become 8 lists of size N/8, etc. In the best case, this process terminates
with (2**k) lists of size N/(2**k), for the largest k for which (2**k) ≤ N. This
value of k is just $\log_2(N)$. The process of dividing all present lists in two can

be performed $\log_2(N)$ times. Notice that to split a list requires examination of all elements of the list, and that the number of elements in all lists is nearly N (minus any dividing points). Therefore, each of these $\log_2(N)$ passes involves about N comparisons. Therefore, the number of comparisons made by this algorithm can be as small as $N*\log_2(N)$.

For all values of N, $\log_2(N)$ is smaller than N, and as N grows, $\log_2(N)$ does so at a much smaller rate. For example, $\log_2(10)$ is over 3, but $\log_2(1000)$ is slightly less than 10. We therefore have reduced the 1,000,000 comparisons for a bubble sort of 1000 elements to 10,000 comparisons using the Quicksort. This is, obviously, a substantial savings. The advantage of choosing a good algorithm and implementing it in a straightforward and readable manner is substantial.

1.7   MODIFIABILITY

Nearly all major production programs will require modification. In some cases, the modification is as simple as changing the form of employee numbers from 12345 to 12-345, or changing the format for output reports. In other cases, the modification is more extensive, such as adding new capabilities to the program, performing additional calculations, or revising the action performed when a particular input is received. The structure of a program can greatly affect how easy these modifications are to implement. Here are some guidelines to improve program modifiability.

a. Document extensively. The person modifying a program needs to know not only where a particular function is performed, but also what is the full environment of that function.

For example, if you must exit from a DO loop and intend to use the value of the index, J, later, then the person modifying your program should be warned not to modify the value of J. The most sensible way to do this is to place the code depending on J close to the end of the loop. If that is impossible, you should put a comment at the end of the loop warning that the value of J must not be changed.

We have already stated that each subprogram and each major section of code should be preceded by a list of important variables. This list is especially important for achieving program modifiability.

b. Don't use tricky code. We have warned that from an efficiency standpoint the use of tricky or "cute" code is a practice of questionable value. For reasons of modification, this practice is definitely detrimental.

c. Write modular code. This means that your program should be carefully divided into single action modules, and the inputs and outputs of each module should be clearly described. Then, a person needing to modify this code can rapidly find those sections to change or can model extensions after similar pieces of existing code.

d. Write table-driven code. Suppose you are writing a text editor, that is, a program to input lines of text and to output this same information in a "printed page" format. Your program might fill (run together text from different input lines, printing as many words as will fit on each output line) or not; right-justify (insert additional blank spaces to make all output lines the same length, like the lines of this book) or not; single or double space; skip n lines, and so forth. To control this, you decide to allow users to add editing commands to cause or to stop right-justification, to skip n lines, to determine the length of an input or output line, etc. You decide that these commands will be inserted on lines beginning with a period and followed by a two letter acronym for the action. This list might be:

```
.JU       RIGHT-JUSTIFY
.NJ       DO NOT RIGHT-JUSTIFY
.SS       SINGLE SPACE OUTPUT
.DS       DOUBLE SPACE OUTPUT
.SP N     LEAVE   N  BLANK LINES
.OL N     CREATE OUTPUT LINES OF LENGTH N
.IL N     USE THE FIRST N CHARACTERS FROM EACH INPUT LINE
```

There are some common actions to be performed, and there are actions to be performed for some, but not all, editing commands. For those commands that affect the output, you want to print the current output line and then have the command be effective on subsequent output lines. The common actions are summarized in the table below.

COMMAND	PRINT CURRENT OUTPUT LINE?	SEEK NUMBER AFTER COMMAND?	DEFAULT NUMBER
.JU	YES	NO	–
.NJ	YES	NO	–
.SS	YES	NO	–
.DS	YES	NO	–
.SP	YES	YES	1
.OL	YES	YES	80
.IL	NO	YES	72

This code can be naturally represented by a series of arrays, one containing the command, two containing 1 and 0 (or .TRUE. and .FALSE.) for the two yes or no columns, and a last one for the default values. (In Chapter 3 we will discuss representing alphabetic data in FORTRAN.) Let us call these arrays COMAND, PRLINE, NUMBER, and DEFLT, respectively. Then we can outline the handling of an input command in the code sketch of Figure 1-4.

```
C                 LOOK UP INPUT TEXT EDITOR COMMAND
      ...
      ...
C                 ASSUME IT WAS FOUND AT COMAND(K)
C
C                 CHECK IF MUST BEGIN A NEW LINE
      IF (PRLIN(K) .EQ. 1) CALL PRINT(LINE,LINLEN)
C                 CHECK IF A NUMBER TO BE GOTTEN
      IF (NUMBER(K) .EQ. 0) GO TO 2
          CALL GETNUM (INPUT,N,FOUND)
          IF (.NOT.FOUND) N = DEFLT(K)
C
C                 NOW COMMON PROCESSING DONE;
C                 HANDLE EACH COMMAND SEPARATELY
    2 GO TO (10,15,20,25,30,40,50),K
C                 JU NJ SS DS SP OL IL
C
C                 .JU - SET SWITCH TO BEGIN RIGHT JUSTIFICATION
   10 ADJSW = .TRUE.
      GO TO 100
C
C                 .NJ - SET SWITCH TO STOP JUSTIFICATION
   15 ADJSW = .FALSE.
      GO TO 100
C
C                 .SP N - LEAVE  N  BLANK LINES
   30 DO 35 I = 1,N
          CALL PRINT (BLANKS,1)
   35 CONTINUE
      GO TO 100
C
      ...
      ...
C                 PROCESSING DONE; GET NEW CARD
  100 CALL GETCRD
      RETURN
      END
```

FIGURE 1-4   Example of Table-Driven Code

Notice that the processing of each option is quite short, since we have already performed any common actions. Notice also that to add a new option, you merely add a new line to the table (extend the arrays) and write the code unique to that editing command. Filling in all of the arrays guards against our forgetting to perform some routine task with the new option. We call this programming style "table-driven code," since the table entries drive the actions of the algorithm.

The primary advantage of table-driven code is that it is easy to modify. In addition, because of the uncomplicated implementation of an often complex set of decisions, such code tends to be quite easy to read. Again, because the structure is relatively simple, it is not prone to errors and thus is easy to debug. In the next section we will present another technique for enhancing the readability of table-driven code.

1.8   SHARED STORAGE LOCATIONS: THE EQUIVALENCE STATEMENT

The EQUIVALENCE statement permits two or more variables to share one storage location. Since, of course, one location can contain only one value at a time, this statement really provides synonyms or alternate names under which one location may be accessed. The EQUIVALENCE statement has the following form.

EQUIVALENCE (*names1*) [, (*names2*), etc.]

where   each *names* list must be a series of simple variables and array elements with constant subscripts

Example
```
EQUIVALENCE (KOUNT, ICOUNT)
KOUNT = 10
ICOUNT = ICOUNT + 1
WRITE (-,-) KOUNT
```

Effect   Declares that KOUNT and ICOUNT are to refer to the same location in memory. The value printed by the WRITE statement will be 11; since KOUNT and ICOUNT are equivalenced, the third statement has the same effect as

```
KOUNT = KOUNT + 1
```

Note   EQUIVALENCE is a nonexecutable statement and must appear after all specification statements but before the first executable statement of a program unit.

Two cautions need to accompany the EQUIVALENCE statement. First, recall that integer and real are only means of interpreting patterns of bits, and that on most machines the bit pattern of an integer number is quite different from the pattern of the same real value. For example, the following code segment appears similar to the example above.

```
REAL COUNT
INTEGER KOUNT
EQUIVALENCE (COUNT, KOUNT)
KOUNT = 10
COUNT = COUNT + 1.0
WRITE (-,-) KOUNT
```

The answer produced will vary between different compilers, but it will almost certainly *not* be 11! On the IBM 360, for example, the result is 1,091,567,616. (In Chapter 6 we will discuss the internal representations of variables, so that you will be better able to understand this peculiar-looking answer.) Because integer and real representations are seldom the same, you must be wary of equivalencing variables of different types.

The second caution concerning the use of EQUIVALENCE is to remember that an array is a series of *contiguous* storage locations. Thus an equivalence between elements of two arrays also implies an equivalence between other elements of those arrays. To understand what this means, consider the arrays A and B, of sizes 10 and 6, respectively. Assume that the statements

```
REAL A(10), B(6)
EQUIVALENCE (A(3),B(1))
```

appear in a program. We know that A(4) immediately follows A(3) in memory, and that B(2) follows B(1). Furthermore, B(1) and A(3) are to refer to the same memory location; call that location X. The memory location immediately following X belongs to A(4), since A(4) directly follows A(3). The location after X also belongs to B(2), since B(2) directly follows B(1). Thus both A(4) and B(2) refer to the single location directly after X. Therefore, the equivalence of A(3) and B(1) causes an implied equivalence of A(4) to B(2), of A(5) to B(3), and so on. We can represent this equivalence with a picture.

A(1)	A(2)	A(3)	A(4)	---	A(7)	A(8)	A(9)	A(10)
		B(1)	B(2)	---	B(5)	B(6)		

It is possible to equivalence more than two arrays, but one must not attempt to "stretch" or to "buckle" any array by distorting the implied alignment of equivalenced elements. For example, the following is *not* acceptable.

```
REAL A(10),B(6),C(4)
EQUIVALENCE (A(3),B(1)), (C(1),A(1)), (C(4),B(1))
```

This is illogical because it requires B(1) to be in two places at once: both at A(3) and at A(4). The equivalence involving C improperly places B.

In an EQUIVALENCE statement, you may refer to an element of a multidimensional array by a single (constant) subscript. This subscript identifies the element number relative to the first element, under FORTRAN's column-major array storage. Assume you have a 20 by 25 array A, and you wish the first 100 elements of that array to be equivalenced to array B of size 100, and you wish the last 400 elements of A to be equivalenced to array C of size 400. The following statement is an appropriate way to do this, since it avoids your having to compute which element of A is the 101st.

```
EQUIVALENCE (A(1),B(1)), (A(101),C(1))
```

This statement seems of very limited use—it seems unnecessary to refer to the same quantity by two names. However, there are several very good uses of the EQUIVALENCE statement.

The first example is the simplest to follow. Two programmers might be working on a large program, planning to combine their separate pieces of code. They find, however, that one has used the name QY while the other has used the variable QTY, meaning the same thing. This discrepancy can be easily patched with an equivalence. (However, this does not solve the readability problem of having two apparently different names refer to the same value. We call this a "patch" for an unfortunate situation, as opposed to a "solution." Of course, two people working on the same project are seldom this badly out of communication.)

Second, equivalences can save memory space by permitting two independent uses of the same space. In determining to what family of animals an unidentified species belongs, one technique scientists use is this. First, they take measurements of the members of the species. These measurements may include length, weight, wingspan, number of legs, presence of feelers, etc. Then they discard the few highest and lowest values of each measurement as aberrant and compute the mean of the remaining values. This yields a profile of a "typical" or "average" member of the species. Finally, they compare this profile with the profiles of identified species and decide which known species the unknown one resembles most.

In a program to perform the mechanics of this task, there are two large data areas needed: first, one to store the measurements of all the samples of the new species, and second, one to store the profiles of all known species. However, these are independent uses; once the determination of the average characteristics is completed, the area to contain the measurements is no longer needed. Thus, this space can be shared with the space for profiles. This mutually exclusive sharing of space can be accomplished with an EQUIVALENCE, an example of which is shown below.

```
INTEGER SAMPLS(100,10), PROFIL(100,50)
EQUIVALENCE (SAMPLS, PROFIL)
```

A third use of an equivalence is to provide descriptive names for portions of an array. For example, in writing a program to average student scores and to compute grades, you would need to know the cutoff values—the lowest score for an A, for a B, for a C, and for a D. For ease of looking up a student's score, you might want this to be an array CUTOFF of size 4. However, if at some point in the program you need to count the number of students receiving passing marks, then a statement like

```
IF (SCORE .GE. PASS) --
```

is more meaningful than

```
         IF (SCORE .GE. CUTOFF(4)) --
```

The following EQUIVALENCE statement will solve this problem.

```
         EQUIVALENCE (PASS, CUTOFF(4))
```

Another use of equivalences is related. If there are a substantial number of simple variables that need to be reset to zero several times during the execution of a program, you can equivalence each of the variables to a different element of an array, and zero the whole array with a DO loop. The following example outlines how this might be done.

```
     REAL COUNT,SUM,AVG,STDEV,ZEROS(4)
     EQUIVALENCE (ZEROS(1),COUNT), (ZEROS(2),SUM), (ZEROS(3),AVG),
   X    (ZEROS(4),STDEV)
```

Another use of equivalences uses multiple names to refer to portions of an array. In the discussion of table-driven code above, we worked with four different arrays. Sometimes it is convenient to work with one array of four columns and yet be able to refer to the columns by individual names. Since arrays are stored in column order in FORTRAN, we can equivalence a vector to a column of an array. In the table-driven example, we might have:

```
     INTEGER CONTAB(7,4), COMND(7),PRLINE(7),NUMBER(7),DEFLT(7)
     EQUIVALENCE (CONTAB(1,1),COMND), (CONTAB(1,2),PRLINE),
   X    (CONTAB(1,3),NUMBER), (CONTAB(1,4),DEFLT)
```

In this way, we can use CONTAB as we would use any two-dimensional array, to initialize data or to change the values of an entire row, for example. We can also refer to the elements of CONTAB by the more readable names COMND or DEFLT.

The EQUIVALENCE statement is a very powerful one, perhaps too powerful for some programmers. Some consider it "cute" to change the value of a variable without ever referring to it by name; some enjoy coding using dialect-dependent tricks with EQUIVALENCE. We cannot prevent these uses, but such games are not the mark of a mature programmer.

1.9   A REVISED EXAMPLE

Now it is time to revise the example program with which this chapter began. It will be developed using the technique of stepwise refinement. To use this technique, you first state the program actions in a few very general steps. Then take each step and refine it, making the one step into several smaller ones. Continue refining each step into several smaller steps, until the entire algorithm is expressed in clear, simple steps.

In order to recall the gist of this program, you should review the header documentation in Section 1.2. We repeat here the four basic steps of the program outline:

1. Read cards containing book numbers and quantities on hand.
2. Sort the inventory data from those cards in ascending order by book number.
3. Read cards containing book numbers and quantity sold.
4. Print a summary report of book numbers and quantity on hand.

This constitutes the first level of our stepwise refinement. Now to refine the steps, the first becomes as follows.

1.1. Determine how many book-on-hand cards are to be read.
1.2. If no cards are to be read, halt.
1.3. Read and process the cards.

Steps 1.1 and 1.2 are sufficiently detailed to make it possible to code them directly. Step 1.3, however, needs further refinement.

Perform 1.3.1 through 1.3.3 for each book-on-hand card.
1.3.1. If no space for a new book number exists, print an error message and stop.
1.3.2. Read BOOKNO(NENTRY) and QTY(NENTRY)
1.3.3. Check if this book number is a duplicate. If yes, print an error message and ignore it. Else increment NENTRY.

Since the book number cards are not in any particular order, we cannot use the binary search for step 1.3.3. We will instead use the common sequential search as the book tables are being built. For the second step, we will use the Quicksort algorithm to sort the data. Thus, we will not refine step 2, since its refinement would be precisely the algorithm shown in Section 1.6.

Step 3 involves several refinements. We will present all refinements at once, since much of this development matches that of step 1. You might write your refinement steps in this order, if you can clearly see the logical development of step 3. The important feature of stepwise refinement is that it help you to code a program. You should not feel hindered by some mechanical restriction of the stepwise refinement process; instead let it help you in your thinking.

3.1. Determine how many book-sales cards are to be read.

3.2. If no cards are to be read, halt.

3.3. Process book-sales cards.

      DO for each book-sales card to be read:

          Read CBOOK and CQTY, the data for one sale

          Look up CBOOK in BOOKNO array.

              If NENTRY = 0, done; not found.

              DO for J = 1 to NENTRY.

                    IF BOOKNO(J) = CBOOK, done; found.

                    If BOOKNO(J) > CBOOK, done; not found.

              If loop terminates normally, done; not found.

          If not found, print error message and get next card.

          If found, then process sale.

              If quantity sold less than or equal to quantity on hand, reduce on-hand; else set on-hand to zero and print message.

Step 4 merely involves printing the contents of the BOOKNO and QTY arrays.

Now we can start looking for redundant code in an attempt to simplify the algorithm. There are two searches used, one in step 1 and the other in step 3. They are similar in purpose, but not identical. We can exploit this similarity with a common subprogram to perform the table lookup. We will make (NENTRY-1) or NENTRY a parameter, as well as BOOKNO(NENTRY) or CBOOK. We can also add a parameter to show if the array is sorted or not, since only the search in step 3 makes use of the order of the data. The subprogram for this is shown in Figure 1-5.

```
      SUBROUTINE LOOKY (TABLE, TABSIZ, ENTRY, SORTED, FOUND, WHERE, DBG)
C * * * * * * * * * * * * * * * * * * * * * * * * * * * * * * * * * *
C  TABLE LOOKUP SUBROUTINE
C
C  ENTRY VALUES:
C     "TABLE" IS AN ARRAY OF SIZE "TABSIZ" IN WHICH WE ARE TO SEARCH
C     FOR "ENTRY."  IF THE TABLE IS IN ASCENDING ORDER, THEN VARIABLE
C     "SORTED" IS TRUE; ELSE IT IS FALSE.  "DBG" CONTROLS DEBUGGING
C     OUTPUT: NONZERO MEANS TRACE ON EXIT.
C
C  EXIT CONDITIONS:
C     IF THE ENTRY WAS FOUND, THEN "FOUND" IS TRUE, AND "WHERE" IS THE
C        INDEX WITHIN THE TABLE WHERE THE ENTRY APPEARED.
C     IF THE ENTRY WAS NOT FOUND, THEN "FOUND" IS FALSE, AND THE VALUE
C        OF "WHERE" IS NOT CHANGED.
C
C  PROGRAM OPERATES BY A SIMPLE SEQUENTIAL LOOKUP.
C  IF THE TABLE IS IN SORTED ORDER, THEN THE SEARCH CONTINUES ONLY UNTIL
C     AN ELEMENT LARGER THAN THE DESIRED ENTRY IS FOUND;
C     ELSE THE ENTIRE TABLE MUST BE SCANNED.
C
C  PROGRAMMER: ---              DATE: ---
C * * * * * * * * * * * * * * * * * * * * * * * * * * * * * * * * * *
```

```
      INTEGER TABSIZ, TABLE(TABSIZ), ENTRY, WHERE, DBG, DBOUT
      LOGICAL SORTED, FOUND
      DATA DBOUT/6/
C               ASSUME ENTRY WILL NOT BE FOUND
      FOUND = .FALSE.
C
C               IF TABLE HAS NO ELEMENTS, THEN NO SEARCH NEEDED
      IF (TABSIZ .LE. 0) RETURN
C
C               LOOP TO EXAMINE EACH ELEMENT
      DO 10 I = 1,TABSIZ
         IF (TABLE(I) .EQ. ENTRY) GO TO 50
         IF (TABLE(I) .LT. ENTRY) GO TO 10
         IF (SORTED) GO TO 99
   10 CONTINUE
C
C               IF LOOP TERMINATES NORMALLY, ENTRY DOES NOT EXIST
      GO TO 99
C
C               COME HERE IF ENTRY IS LOCATED
   50 FOUND = .TRUE.
      WHERE = I
C .
C               COMMON RETURN POINT; FOUND SET PROPERLY
   99 IF (DBG .EQ. 0) RETURN
      IF (FOUND) WRITE (DBOUT,101) ENTRY, WHERE
      IF (.NOT. FOUND) WRITE (DBOUT,102) ENTRY, TABSIZ
      RETURN
  101 FORMAT (' EXIT FROM SUBR. LOOKY: ITEM', I8, ' FOUND AT POS.', I8)
  102 FORMAT (' EXIT FROM SUBR. LOOKY: ITEM', I8, ' NOT FOUND IN TABLE',
     X        ' TABLE SIZE IS', I6)
      END
```

FIGURE 1-5 Table Lookup Subprogram

The sorting process, although it appears only once, can be made into a subprogram to modularize this program. The coding of this subprogram follows the outline in Section 1.6.2, and so we omit the precise listing of that code.

There are also several points from which an error message is issued. This also makes a good sequence of code to isolate, because such messages are peripheral to the actual program and can obstruct the reading of it. Also, this module can be trivially coded for initial program debugging (merely printing an error message number), and later it can be "prettied up" with intelligible error message statements. The subprogram will receive as arguments an error number, and an indication of whether the error is fatal (processing cannot continue), or simply a warning (processing can continue). A third argument is the book number associated with the error, or 0 for those errors that are unrelated to a book number. The subprogram appears on the next page.

Having developed all subprograms needed for this program, we will now show the code for the main program. In this program, we have followed one of our own suggestions by using a trailer card to mark the end of each of the two parts of the input deck. A book number of -1 will now mark the end of each part. Notice that in the calls to ERRMSG, we have used mnemonic

```
      SUBROUTINE ERRMSG (ERRNO, FATAL, BOOKNO)
C           GENERAL ERROR MESSAGE HANDLER
      INTEGER ERRNO, BOOKNO, OUT
      LOGICAL FATAL
      DATA OUT/6/
C           PRODUCE ERROR MESSAGE
      WRITE (OUT,1) ERRNO
    1 FORMAT (' ERROR NUMBER ', I3, ' OCCURRED.')
      IF (BOOKNO .NE. 0) WRITE (OUT,2) BOOKNO
    2 FORMAT (' INVOLVING BOOK NUMBER', I10)
C           CHECK SEVERITY OF ERROR
      IF (.NOT. FATAL) RETURN
      WRITE (OUT, 3)
    3 FORMAT (' EXECUTION TERMINATING')
      STOP
      END
```

variable names such as OVFLOW, DUPL, NEWBK, etc. Using these names, we do not need to remember the numeric codes assigned to different error messages. We have similarly used a mnemonic technique to indicate fatal or nonfatal errors. The full program is shown in Figure 1-6.

```
C * * * * * * * * * * * * * * * * * * * * * * * * * * * * * * * *
C
C  BOOK INVENTORY MAINTAINER PROGRAM
C
C  THIS PROGRAM ACCEPTS A SET OF BOOK NUMBERS AND QUANTITIES ON HAND
C     OF THOSE BOOKS, AND PROCESSES SALES AGAINST THAT INITIAL INVENTORY
C     THE PROGRAM PRINTS A FINAL REPORT OF BOOKS ON HAND.
C  IF AN ATTEMPT IS MADE TO SELL MORE BOOKS THAN ARE AVAILABLE,
C     THIS PROGRAM PRINTS A MESSAGE AND SETS THE INVENTORY OF THAT
C     BOOK TO 0.
C
C  INPUTS:
C  A SERIES OF BOOK NUMBER/QUANTITY INITIALLY ON HAND CARDS.
C  THESE ARE TERMINATED BY A CARD WITH BOOK NUMBER -1 .
C  A SERIES OF BOOK NUMBER/QUANTITY SOLD CARD.
C  THESE ARE TERMINATED BY A CARD WITH BOOK NUMBER -1 .
C
C  THERE ARE FOUR PHASES TO THE PROGRAM:
C  1. READ INITIAL INVENTORY CARDS
C  2. SORT THE INITIAL BOOK NUMBER AND QUANTITY ARRAYS
C  3. READ THE SALES CARDS
C  4. PRINT ENDING QUANTITIES ON HAND BY BOOK NUMBER
C
C  SUBPROGRAMS CALLED:
C    LOOKY: TO PERFORM A TABLE LOOKUP
C    QSORT: TO SORT AN ARRAY HAVING TWO COLUMNS
C    ERRMSG: TO PRINT ERROR MESSAGES
C
C  PRINCIPAL VARIABLES:
C    BOOKNO - NUMBERS OF BOOKS IN INVENTORY SYSTEM
C    QTY    - QUANTITIES OF THOSE BOOKS.
C             QTY(I) IS QUANTITY OF BOOKNO(I)
C    BOOKS  - MATRIX CONSISTING OF COLUMNS BOOKNO AND QTY
C    NENTRY - CURRENT NUMBER OF BOOKS IN SYSTEM
C    CBOOK  - CURRENT BOOK, USED IN THIRD STEP
C    CQTY   - CURRENT QUANTITY, USED IN THIRD STEP
C    MAXBKS - MAXIMUM NUMBER OF BOOKS HANDLED BY SYSTEM (200)
C    DBG    - DEBUGGING CONTROL: =0 NO DEBUGGING,   =1 SUBROUTINE CALLS,
C             =2 CALLS PLUS INPUT ECHO,   =3 CALLS, ECHO, TABLE DUMP
C             AFTER SORTING
C
C  PROGRAMMER: ---          DATE: ---
C * * * * * * * * * * * * * * * * * * * * * * * * * * * * * * * *
C
```

```
          INTEGER BOOKS(200,2),BOOKNO(200),QTY(200),CBOOK,CQTY,MAXBKS,
     X     IN,OUT,WHERE,NENTRY
          EQUIVALENCE (BOOKS(1,1),BOOKNO), (BOOKS(1,2),QTY)
C               ERROR MESSAGE NAMES/CODE NUMBERS
          INTEGER OVFLOW,DUPL,NEWBK,OVSOLD,EOF1,EOF2, DBG, DBOUT
          DATA OVFLOW/1/,DUPL/2/,NEWBK/3/,OVSOLD/4/,EOF1/5/,EOF2/6/
C               MNEMONIC NAMES FOR EXPRESSIONS SHOWING FATAL/NON-FATAL
C               ERRORS, SORTED/NOT SORTED
          LOGICAL FOUND, FATAL,SORTED
          DATA FATAL/.TRUE./,SORTED/.TRUE./
          DATA IN/5/,OUT/6/,MAXBKS/200/,DBG/0/,DBOUT/6/
C
C
C         **** PHASE 1: READ INITIAL INVENTORY VALUES ****
          NENTRY = 1
C               CHECK FOR EXCEEDING SIZE OF BOOK ARRAYS
  100 IF (NENTRY .GT. MAXBKS) CALL ERRMSG (OVFLOW,FATAL,0)
C               READ A BOOK NUMBER/QUANTITY PAIR
          READ (IN,110,END=190) BOOKNO(NENTRY), QTY(NENTRY)
  110 FORMAT (2I10)
          IF (DBG .GT. 1) WRITE (DBOUT,111) NENTRY, BOOKNO(NENTRY),
     X                              QTY(NENTRY)
  111 FORMAT (' ENTRY NO.', I8, ' BOOK NO.', I10, ' QUANTITY', I10)
C               CHECK FOR END OF DATA
          IF (BOOKNO(NENTRY) .EQ. -1) GO TO 200
C
C               CHECK FOR DUPLICATE BOOK NUMBER
  120 CALL LOOKY (BOOKNO, NENTRY-1, BOOKNO(NENTRY), .NOT. SORTED,
     X          FOUND, WHERE, DBG)
          IF (.NOT. FOUND) NENTRY = NENTRY + 1
          IF (     FOUND) CALL ERRMSG (DUPL, .NOT.FATAL, BOOKNO(NENTRY))
          GO TO 100
C
C               COME HERE ON END OF FILE WHILE READING INITIAL INVENTORY
  190 CALL ERRMSG (EOF1,FATAL,0)
C
C         **** PHASE 2: SORTING THE DATA ****
C               END OF DATA; DROP "-1" BOOK NUMBER
          NENTRY = NENTRY-1
  200 CALL QSORT (BOOKS, MAXBKS, NENTRY)
          IF (DBG .GT. 2) WRITE (DBOUT,201) (BOOKS(I), I=1,NENTRY)
  201 FORMAT(' SORTED BOOK TABLE:'/ 10(1X,I10))
C
C         **** PHASE 3: PROCESS SALE REQUESTS ****
C
  300 READ (IN,110,END=390) CBOOK,CQTY
          IF (DBG .GT. 1) WRITE (DBOUT,301) CBOOK, CQTY
  301 FORMAT (' TRANSACTION TRACE: BOOK NO., QUANTITY:', 2I10)
C               CHECK IF AT END OF DATA
          IF (CBOOK .EQ. -1) GO TO 400
C
C               FIND BOOKNUMBER SO CAN PROCESS SALE
          CALL LOOKY (BOOKNO, NENTRY, CBOOK, SORTED, FOUND, WHERE, DBG)
          IF (FOUND) GO TO 350
C
C               BOOK SHOULD HAVE BEEN ENTERED DURING FIRST PHASE;
C               ERROR IF NOT. IGNORE SALE REQUEST
          CALL ERRMSG (NEWBK,.NOT.FATAL,CBOOK)
          GO TO 300
C
C               BOOK FOUND; SEE IF SUFFICIENT STOCK TO HANDLE SALE
  350 IF (QTY(WHERE) .GE. CQTY) GO TO 360
C               OVERSOLD ON BOOK; PRINT MESSAGE AND SHOW HOW MANY
C               WERE NOT DELIVERED
          CALL ERRMSG (OVSOLD,.NOT.FATAL,CBOOK)
          NQTY = CQTY - QTY(WHERE)
          WRITE (OUT, 351) NQTY
  351     FORMAT(' QUANTITY NOT SHIPPED IS ', I10)
          QTY(WHERE) = 0
          GO TO 300
C
```

```
C            LEGAL SALE
  360 QTY(WHERE) = QTY(WHERE) - CQTY
      GO TO 30)
C               UNEXPECTED END OF PHASE 3 INPUT;
C               TREAT AS IF HAD SEEN "-1" TO TERMINATE THAT DATA
  390 CALL ERRMSG (EOF2,.NOT.FATAL,0)
C
C    **** PHASE 4: OUTPUT REPORT ****
C
  400 IF (NENTRY .LE. 0) GO TO 500
      WRITE (OUT,4)1) (BOOKNO(I),QTY(I), I=1,NENTRY)
  401 FORMAT ('1ENDING INVENTORY REPORT'///
      X    5X, 'BOOK NUMBER = QUANTITY ON HAND'/
      X    5(3X, I10, '=', I10, ';') )
C
  500 STOP
      END
```

FIGURE 1-6 Revised Book Inventory Program

REFERENCES

The letter by Dijkstra, "Go To Statement Considered Harmful", appeared in Communications of the ACM, volume 11, number 3, pages 147 to 148. The Quicksort algorithm was first presented by Hoare in "Quicksort", Computer Journal, volume 5, number 1, pages 10 to 15. Knuth's analysis of the running time of that algorithm appears in The Art of Computer Programming, Volume 3: Sorting and Searching, published by Addison-Wesley Publishing Company in 1973.

CHAPTER 2

Advanced Features of Subprograms

Effective use of subprograms is one of the first steps in a programmer's transition from a novice to a professional. As noted in Chapters 0 and 1, subprograms are a tool for making programs more efficient, more readable, easier to maintain, and easier to write and debug. This chapter expands upon the basics that you have already learned and introduces you to the more advanced features of FORTRAN subprograms.

2.1 ELEMENTARY CHARACTERISTICS OF FORTRAN SUBPROGRAMS

The FORTRAN language allows two types of procedural subprograms: functions and subroutines. A function is a procedure that returns a single result based upon the value of its arguments. A subroutine is more general and may return zero or more results.

FORTRAN subprograms take the form of a header card followed by a set of declarations, the body of the procedure, and then an END statement. The header statement declares the subprogram's name, its type (function or subroutine), and a set of dummy arguments. The declaration section provides information such as the type and dimension of each of the arguments and each of the procedure's local variables.

Statement numbers employed within any program module (main program or subprogram) are treated as local to that module. Thus, statement numbers may be reused in each separate subprogram. Statements within a given program module can reference statement numbers only within that same module.

Variables and arrays that are not dummy arguments are treated, by default, as local to the program module in which they are defined. This means that, unless otherwise specified, a variable K used in one program module has a different storage area associated with it than a variable K used in some other program module. (In Section 2.6, we discuss how variables and arrays may be declared to be global instead of local.) For now, all variables and arrays used in our examples will be either dummy arguments or local to the module in which they are declared.

2.1.1 Review of Function Subprograms

A *function* subprogram is defined by a sequence of statements starting with one of the form

[*type*] FUNCTION *name* (*dummy argument list*)

and ending with the next END statement. The *type* of a function may be INTEGER, REAL, or LOGICAL, or it may be omitted. If omitted, the function type is determined by the first letter of its *name* (I-N integer, else real). The dummy argument list consists of a set of variable and array names that are associated with the corresponding actual variables and arrays.

A function is invoked whenever an arithmetic or logical expression is executed that contains the function name followed by an appropriate list of actual arguments. The execution of a function causes the function's name to be assigned a result value. This is accomplished by the use of the function name as a variable. The last value assigned to this name is then the function's result. A return to the calling routine is effected whenever a RETURN statement is executed within the function.

Function subprograms should be used only when a single result is to be returned. Although the rules of FORTRAN do not explicitly prohibit the returning of additional results by changing values of arguments, this practice is not condoned. To see why, consider the following trivial function F. Here function F returns the value I+1, given the original argument value I.

```
INTEGER FUNCTION F(I)
INTEGER I
I = I+1
F = I
RETURN
END
```

In doing this, it produces the side effect of modifying the value of its argument. Observe the result when F is called by the statement

```
K = F(J) + F(J) + J
```

where J has value 3. The first call to F returns the value 4 and also changes J to 4. The second call returns 5 and changes J to 5. As a consequence, K is assigned the value 14 (4+5+5) and, as a side effect, J is assigned the value 5.

This is clearly confusing but, what is worse, the above scenario may, in fact, not occur. Some compilers are designed to recognize and eliminate inefficiencies. A compiler of this sort might reasonably assume that

```
K = F(J) + F(J) + J
```

is equivalent to

```
K = 2*F(J) + J
```

But then K is assigned the value 12 (2*4+4), not 14, and J is changed to 4, not 5.

Although the following is a guideline, not a rule, of FORTRAN, it is a rule of good FORTRAN programming. We strongly encourage you to obey it.

> A function subprogram should never modify the value
> of any of its arguments.

Similarly, it is a good programming practice to avoid performing input/ output operations within a function. This restriction is a consequence of the fact that we cannot always predict the frequency of calls to a function. Our previous example shows this, as would also a call of the form

```
IF ((J.EQ.0) .OR. (F(J).EQ.K)) GO TO 7
```

In this example, if J=0, then it would not be necessary to call function F to determine whether control should proceed to statement number 7. Some dialects of FORTRAN will always call F, while others will not. If F reads a card or prints a line then differing results may be obtained by different dialects. This point is summarized by the following guideline.

> A function subprogram should not perform any input
> or output (except, of course, the execution of output
> statements used for debugging.)

2.1.2 Review of Subroutine Subprograms

A *subroutine* subprogram is defined by a sequence of statements starting with one of the form

SUBROUTINE *name* [(*dummy argument list*)]

and ending with the next END statement. Subroutine *name* is invoked whenever a statement of the form

CALL *name* [(*actual argument list*)]

with an appropriate number of arguments, is executed. Results may be returned to the calling program by changing the values of one or more of the subprogram's arguments. A return to the calling routine is effected whenever a RETURN statement is executed within the subroutine.

2.2 ARGUMENT PASSING

2.2.1 Basic Rules of Actual/Dummy Argument Association

Whenever a function or subroutine reference is executed, an association occurs between each actual argument and its corresponding dummy argument. The first actual argument is associated with the first dummy argument, the second with the second, etc. The number of actual arguments must be the same as the number of dummy arguments.

An actual argument may be a variable, an array element, an arithmetic or logical expression, or an array. (Other possibilities are discussed in later sections.) A dummy argument may be a variable or an array. Whenever a dummy argument is a variable, the corresponding actual argument may be either a variable, an array element, or an expression. A dummy argument that is an array must be matched with either an array or an array element. The type (REAL, INTEGER, or LOGICAL) of each actual argument must be the same as that of the corresponding dummy argument. It is good practice for the number and size of the dimensions of a dummy array to agree with those of its associated actual argument. However, the rules of FORTRAN require only that the size (total number of components) of the dummy array not exceed that of the actual argument. In the case where the actual argument is an array element, the size of the argument array is considered to be the size of the array in which this element exists, less the number of elements preceding the argument element. (Refer to Section 0.2 for a description of how FORTRAN arrays are stored.)

2.2.2 Common Implementation Techniques for Argument Association

According to the American National Standards (ANS) definition of FORTRAN, an actual argument that is not an expression is associated with its dummy argument *by name*; where an actual argument is an expression, the association is *by value*. The meaning of "by name" and "by value" were intentionally left undefined in order to allow computer manufacturers to choose methods of implementation best suited to their computers' architectures. The designers of FORTRAN, foreseeing the inconsistency of results obtained by differing implementations, placed the following restrictions on argument modifying.

> If two or more dummy arguments are associated with the same variable, array element or array, then none of these dummy arguments may be assigned a value.

> A dummy argument associated with an expression may not be assigned a value.

We will now describe common methods of implementing argument association by name and by value, and show the differing results that can be obtained if either of the above restrictions is not followed.

2.2.3 Association by Name

Argument association by name is commonly implemented by one of two methods: *by value/result* or *by location* (this latter method is also referred to as *by address* and *by reference*). When association is by location, every reference to the dummy argument becomes a reference to the storage associated with the actual argument. Thus, every assignment of a value to the dummy argument is, in fact, an assignment to the actual argument. In contrast, if an association is by value/result, then the value of the actual argument is initially copied into a storage area allocated to the dummy argument. An assignment of a value to the dummy argument results in the value being stored in the storage allocated to the dummy, not the actual argument. When a RETURN statement is executed, the current value of the dummy argument is copied back into the actual argument's storage area.

Argument association by location is used within all FORTRAN dialects with which we are familiar whenever the dummy argument is an array. The reason for this should be clear from consideration of subroutine PRLIST.

```
      SUBROUTINE PRLIST (LIST,N)
C** * * * * * * * * * * * * * * * * * * * * * * * * * **
C* PRINT THE CONTENTS OF THE FIRST N ELEMENTS OF THE   *
C* ONE-DIMENSIONAL ARRAY, LIST, 5 PER LINE             *
C** * * * * * * * * * * * * * * * * * * * * * * * * * **
      INTEGER LIST(500), N, I, PRT
      DATA PRT/6/
      WRITE (PRT,200) (LIST (I), I = 1, N)
200   FORMAT ('1', (20X,5I5) )
      RETURN
      END
```

If association by value/result were used, then the 500 elements of the actual argument would need to be copied into the storage allocated to LIST as a result of a call to PRLIST. These 500 values would then be copied back as a result of execution of the RETURN. Clearly, this is wasteful of computer time and storage.

The differing results obtained by the use of location versus value/result are demonstrated by the program of Figure 2-1.

```
C* * * * * * * * * * * * * * * * * * * * * * * * * * * * * * * *
C* THIS PROGRAM DEMONSTRATES THE DIFFERENCES BETWEEN THE TWO COMMON   *
C*  ARGUMENT ASSOCIATION TECHNIQUES OF "BY LOCATION" AND "BY VALUE/    *
C*  RESULT".  THESE DIFFERENCES ARISE AS A RESULT OF THE MAIN PROGRAM  *
C*  CALLING SUB WITH M INDICATED IN BOTH ARGUMENT POSITIONS.           *
C* * * * * * * * * * * * * * * * * * * * * * * * * * * * * * * *
      INTEGER M, PRT
      DATA PRT/6/
C
```

```
C                    ASSIGN THE VALUE 1 TO M AND THEN CALL SUB WITH M
C                    ASSOCIATED WITH BOTH OF SUB'S DUMMY ARGUMENTS.
      M = 1
      CALL SUB (M, M)
C
C                    SEE WHAT VALUE M WAS ASSIGNED. THIS VALUE MAY DIFFER EVEN
C                    ON TWO SYSTEMS BOTH OF WHICH USE VALUE/RESULT
      WRITE (PRT,200) M
200   FORMAT (10X, 'M=', I1)
      STOP
      END

      SUBROUTINE SUB (J, K)
      INTEGER J, K, PRT
      DATA PRT/6/
C
C                    CHANGE VALUE OF FIRST DUMMY ARGUMENT. IF ASSOCIATION IS
C                    BY LOCATION, THEN THIS ALSO CHANGES VALUE OF SECOND DUMMY
      J = J+1
C
C                    SEE WHAT EFFECT THIS HAD ON K
      WRITE (PRT,200) J, K
200   FORMAT (11X, 'J=', I1, 3X, 'K=', I1)
      RETURN
      END
```

FIGURE 2-1 Demonstrate "by location" versus "by value/result".

If association by location is used, execution of the assignment statement J=J+1 causes the actual argument M to attain the value 2; consequently, the dummy argument K also takes on the value 2. Execution of the WRITE within SUB results in the output.

$$J=2 \quad K=2$$

Consider now what happens if association is by value/result. In this case there are storage areas assigned to J and K and, upon execution of the CALL statement, J and K are both assigned the value 1. Execution of the statement J=J+1 causes J to be assigned the value 2, but no corresponding change occurs to K's value. Consequently, execution of the WRITE statement within SUB results in the output

$$J=2 \quad K=1$$

In addition to the inconsistency of results produced by the two methods discussed above, there can be different results produced by two dialects, both of which use association by value/result. Referring again to our example, what value should M possess after control is returned from the subprogram? If the value of J is copied into M and then the value of K is copied, the most recent value of M will be the value of K, namely 1. However, if K is copied before J, then M will possess the value 2.

2.2.4 Association by Value

Association by value is more consistently handled by FORTRAN dialects than is association by name. The by value technique, which is used for expression arguments, requires that storage be allocated within the calling (not the called) program module for the value of the argument. The expression is evaluated just once before entry into the called module, and its value is stored into the specially allocated storage area.

The problem with association by value occurs when the actual argument is a constant. Some FORTRAN dialects short-circuit the evaluation process for this one case and associate the dummy argument directly with the storage area reserved for that constant. This can cause disastrous side effects. For example, consider the program of Figure 2-2. If this program were executed using one of the aforementioned dialects, the storage that is intended to possess the constant value 1 would be assigned the value 2 as a result of executing the subprogram ADD1. Imagine your reaction to the fact that the result of executing the statement

$$J = 1$$

is to assign the value 2 to J!

```
C* * * * * * * * * * * * * * * * * * * * * * * * * * * * * * * * * * * *
C* THIS PROGRAM IS DESIGNED TO DEMONSTRATE HOW THE VALUE OF A CONSTANT *
C*  CAN ACTUALLY BE MODIFIED IF IT IS PASSED TO A DUMMY ARGUMENT WHICH *
C*  IS ASSIGNED A VALUE. NOTE: IF YOU HAVE AN IBM 360-370 AVAILABLE,   *
C*  RUN THIS PROGRAM UNDER ONE OF THE PRODUCTION COMPILERS (E.G.,      *
C*  FORTRAN G, NOT WATFIV). THE SURPRISING RESULT IS THAT THE PROGRAM  *
C*  PRODUCES THE OUTPUT   J=2                                          *
C* * * * * * * * * * * * * * * * * * * * * * * * * * * * * * * * * * * *
      INTEGER J, PRT
C             PRINTS TO UNIT NUMBER 6 ARE APPROPRIATE FOR IBM 360-370
      DATA PRT/6/
C
C             CALL ADD1 WITH CONSTANT ARGUMENT VALUE 1
      CALL ADD1 (1)
C
C             SEE IF CONSTANT IS CHANGED
      J = 1
      WRITE (PRT,200) J
200   FORMAT (10X, 'J=', I1)
      STOP
      END

      SUBROUTINE ADD1 (I)
      INTEGER I
      I = I+1
      RETURN
      END
```

FIGURE 2-2 Modifying a constant which is passed to a subprogram.

2.3 ADVANCED SUBPROGRAM FEATURES

This section introduces four advanced concepts associated with subprograms: alternate exits from subroutines, multiple entries, subprograms as arguments, and adjustable dimensions. Here we present examples of each of these features individually. Section 2.4 presents an example that incorporates all of them into a single program.

2.3.1 Alternate Exits from Subroutines

Many FORTRAN dialects provide a capability for subroutines to return to a statement other than the one that directly follows the subroutine call. In order to do so, the subroutine statement must include one asterisk (*) in the dummy argument list for each alternate exit. These asterisks should be coded before any other dummy arguments. Although such an ordering is not required by any FORTRAN dialect, doing so helps to ensure portability among the different dialects that do provide for alternate exits.

Execution of a statement of the form

RETURN n

where n is an integer constant or variable, causes a return to the nth alternate exit. If there are k alternate exits, designated by k asterisks, then the argument list in a call to the subroutine must start with k label arguments. Each label argument is of the form &s_n (or *s_n, in some dialects) where s_n is the statement number of some executable statement in the calling program.

Figure 2-3 presents a program containing a subroutine with two alternate exits. The first alternate exit is taken if the table LIST is sorted in ascending order; the second, if LIST is in descending order; and a normal return is taken if LIST is unsorted. (*Note.* A list which is in both ascending and descending order, that is, one whose elements are all equal, is considered to be in ascending order.)

```
C* * * * * * * * * * * * * * * * * * * * * * * * * * * * * * * * * *
C* THIS PROGRAM READS IN A LIST, INSPECTS IT AND PRODUCES A MESSAGE   *
C*  INDICATING WHETHER OR NOT THE LIST WAS SORTED, AND IF SO,         *
C*  WHETHER IT IS IN ASCENDING OR DESCENDING ORDER                    *
C*                                                                    *
C* SUBROUTINES CALLED: SORTED                                         *
C*                                                                    *
C* MAJOR VARIABLES:                                                   *
C*    LIST - THE INTEGER LIST TO BE INSPECTED. SIZE IS 50.            *
C*    N    - THE NUMBER OF VALUES IN LIST                             *
C* PROGRAMMER'S NAME: ---                      DATE WRITTEN: ---      *
C* * * * * * * * * * * * * * * * * * * * * * * * * * * * * * * * * *
      INTEGER LIST(50), N, I, RDR, PRT
      DATA RDR/5/, PRT/6/
C
```

```
C          READ LIST TO BE INSPECTED AND CALL SORTED. RETURN IS
C          NORMAL IF THE LIST IS UNSORTED. RETURN IS TO LABEL 10 IF
C          THE LIST IS IN ASCENDING ORDER; TO LABEL 20 IF IN
C          DESCENDING ORDER
       READ (RDR,2) N
2      FORMAT (I2)
       IF ((N .LE. 0) .OR. (N .GT. 50)) STOP
       READ (RDR,3) (LIST(I), I = 1, N)
3      FORMAT (5I10)
       CALL SORTED (&10, &20, LIST, N)
       WRITE (PRT,4)
4      FORMAT (' LIST IS UNSORTED')
       STOP
10     WRITE (PRT,11)
11     FORMAT (' LIST IS IN ASCENDING ORDER')
       STOP
20     WRITE (PRT,21)
21     FORMAT (' LIST IS IN DESCENDING ORDER')
       STOP
       END

       SUBROUTINE SORTED (*, *, LIST, N)
C* * * * * * * * * * * * * * * * * * * * * * * * * * * * * * * * * * *
C* SUBROUTINE SORTED (*, *, LIST, N) :                               *
C*    PURPOSE: INSPECTS THE ELEMENTS OF LIST TO SEE IF IT IS SORTED  *
C*             IF LIST IS NOT SORTED, A NORMAL RETURN OCCURS         *
C*             IF LIST IS IN ASCENDING ORDER, ALT RETURN1 IS TAKEN   *
C*             IF ALL ELEMENTS ARE EQUAL, ALT RETURN1 IS TAKEN       *
C*             IF LIST IS IN DESCENDING ORDER, ALT RETURN2 IS TAKEN  *
C*                                                                   *
C* ARGUMENTS:  LIST - INTEGER LIST TO BE INSPECTED. SIZE IS 50       *
C*             N    - NUMBER OF ELEMENTS IN LIST                     *
C*                                                                   *
C* SIDE EFFECTS: NONE                                                *
C* * * * * * * * * * * * * * * * * * * * * * * * * * * * * * * * * * *
       INTEGER LIST(50), N, I
       LOGICAL ASCEND, DESCND
C
C          A LIST OF 1 ELEMENT IS SORTED
       IF (N .LE. 1) RETURN1
C
C          ASSUME LIST IS IN BOTH ASCENDING AND DESCENDING ORDER
C          CHANGE VALUE OF APPROPRIATE LOGICAL VARIABLE IF EVER WE
C          FIND A PAIR OUT OF ORDER
       ASCEND = .TRUE.
       DESCND = .TRUE.
C
C          INSPECT EACH PAIR LOOKING FOR ELEMENTS OUT OF ORDER
       DO 10 I = 2, N
          IF (LIST(I-1) .GT. LIST(I)) ASCEND = .FALSE.
          IF (LIST(I-1) .LT. LIST(I)) DESCND = .FALSE.
10     CONTINUE
C
C          RETURN BASED ON RESULT OF SCANNING LIST PAIRS
       IF (ASCEND) RETURN1
       IF (DESCND) RETURN2
       RETURN
       END
```

FIGURE 2-3 Alternate exits.

2.3.2 Multiple Entries

The situation often arises where we have two or more closely related tasks for which we require subprograms. For example, the sine, cosine and many other trigonometric functions may be approximated by essentially the same algorithm; only some initial coefficient values need be different.

Normal entry to a subprogram results in execution starting at the first executable statement of the subprogram. Many dialects of FORTRAN provide an ENTRY statement so that execution may be started at alternate points. The form of an ENTRY statement is

ENTRY *name* [(*dummy argument list*)]

If this statement appears within a subroutine, then a CALL statement referencing *name* causes execution of the subroutine to start at the first executable statement following this entry. If it appears within a function, then a function reference to *name* causes execution to start at the first executable statement following this entry. Although not strictly required, the dummy argument lists of all entry statements should be the same as that of the subroutine or function statement in which they appear. Moreover, an entry name within a function should be declared the same type as the name on the function statement. Failure to follow either of these guidelines can result in a program that runs correctly in one dialect but not in another.

Figure 2-4 presents a short example of a function having two entries. Entry through the name LOOK1 results in the table LIST being sorted and then ARG being looked up in LIST. Entry through LOOK2 assumes LIST is sorted and merely results in ARG being looked up. In either case, the function returns the value K if this is the least value such that ARG=LIST(K), and zero otherwise. Note that we assign a return value only to the name LOOK1. This is possible, since all entry names to a function refer to the same storage area. Hence the name LOOK1 is synonymous with LOOK2 within this function.

```
      INTEGER FUNCTION LOOK1 (LIST, N, ARG)
C* * * * * * * * * * * * * * * * * * * * * * * * * * * * * * * * * * * * *
C* TABLE LOOKUP FUNCTION. THIS FUNCTION PERFORMS A TABLE LOOKUP OF THE *
C*  VALUE 'ARG' IN THE TABLE 'LIST'. IF 'LIST' IS SORTED THEN ENTRY    *
C*  SHOULD BE THROUGH THE NAME 'LOOK2'. IF NOT SORTED THEN ENTRY IS    *
C*  THROUGH THE NAME 'LOOK1'. IN THIS LATTER CASE 'LIST' IS SORTED BY  *
C*  A CALL TO THE SUBPROGRAM 'SORT'. IF 'ARG' IS FOUND AT 'LIST(K)'    *
C*  THEN THE VALUE K IS RETURNED.  IF 'ARG' CANNOT BE FOUND THEN ZERO  *
C*  IS RETURNED.                                                       *
C*                                                                     *
C* ARGUMENTS:                                                          *
C*   LIST - THE LOOKUP TABLE. MAY BE SORTED OR UNSORTED.               *
C*          TYPE IS INTEGER. SIZE IS 50.                               *
C*   N    - NUMBER OF ITEMS CURRENTLY IN TABLE 'LIST'                  *
C*   ARG  - INTEGER VALUE TO BE LOOKED UP                              *
C*                                                                     *
C* ENTRY POINTS:                                                       *
C*   LOOK1 - USED IF 'LIST' IS NOT SORTED.                             *
C*   LOOK2 - USED IF 'LIST' IS SORTED IN ASCENDING ORDER.              *
C*                                                                     *
C* SUBPROGRAMS CALLED:                                                 *
C*   SORT(LIST, N) - SORTS THE N ELEMENTS OF 'LIST' IN ASCENDING ORDER*
C*                 **NOTE** SORT IS NOT SHOWN HERE.                    *
C* * * * * * * * * * * * * * * * * * * * * * * * * * * * * * * * * * * * *
      INTEGER LIST(50), N, ARG, LOOK2
C
```

```
C               LIST IS UNSORTED. PERFORM SORT
        CALL SORT (LIST, N)
C
C               ENTER HERE FOR SORTED LIST
        ENTRY LOOK2 (LIST, N, ARG)
C
C               SEE IF 'ARG' IS IN 'LIST'
        DO 10 LOOK1 = 1, N
           IF (LIST(LOOK1) .GE. ARG) GO TO 20
10      CONTINUE
C
C               BRANCH TO NOTE NOT IN 'LIST'
        GO TO 30
C
C               IF 'ARG' IS IN, THEN IT MUST BE AT POSITION LOOK1
20      IF (LIST(LOOK1) .EQ. ARG) RETURN
C
C               'ARG' IS NOT IN, RETURN VALUE OF ZERO
30      LOOK1 = 0
        RETURN
        END
```

FIGURE 2-4 Example of multiple entry points.

2.3.3 Subprograms as Arguments

In FORTRAN it is possible for the names of functions and subroutines to appear as arguments to other subprograms. When this is done it is usually necessary, and always desirable, to include an EXTERNAL statement. Its general form is

EXTERNAL *list of names*

All subprogram names appearing as arguments should be listed in an EXTERNAL statement. Any subprogram name appearing only in the context of an argument list must be so declared. If this is not done, the FORTRAN compiler assumes the name to be that of a simple variable.

Consider the problem of approximating the area under a curve f in the domain from point a to point b. A simple technique for doing this is called the *trapezoidal rule*. In its simplest form this involves approximating the area as

$$(b-a) * (f(a)+f(b))/2$$

This is, in fact, the area of the trapezoid having edges $(a,0)$, $(a,f(a))$, $(b,f(b))$, $(b,0)$ (See Figure 2-5(a).) A better approximation is obtained by dividing the interval $[a,b]$ into n subintervals of equal length.

$$[a,a+(b-a)/n], [a+(b-a)/n,a+2*(b-a)/n], ..., [b-(b-a)/n,b]$$

The area in any one of these subintervals $[c,d]$ is then approximated by

$$(d-c) * (f(c)+f(d))/2$$

The sum of these n approximations is then an approximation to the area from a to b. (See Figure 2-5(b).)

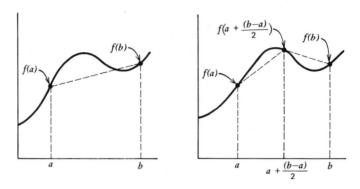

FIGURE 2-5 The trapezoidal rule.

Figure 2-6 presents a subprogram AREA having four arguments: A, B, N, and F. A and B are real values representing the beginning and end, respectively, of the interval in which the approximation is to occur, N is the number of subintervals to be taken, and F is a dummy argument that is used as a function subprogram name. The actual argument associated with F must be the name of the real-valued function that defines the curve forming the area to be approximated.

```
C* * * * * * * * * * * * * * * * * * * * * * * * * * * * * * * * * * * *
C* PROGRAM TO COMPUTE THE AREA UNDER THE CURVE X**2-X BETWEEN 1 AND 4  *
C* THE AREA IS APPROXIMATED USING THE TRAPEZOIDAL RULE.               *
C*  12 SUBINTERVALS ARE USED IN CALCULATING THIS APPROXIMATION        *
C*                                                                    *
C* SUBPROGRAMS CALLED:                                                *
C*    AREA(A,B,N,F) - USES TRAPEZOIDAL RULE TO APPROXIMATE THE AREA   *
C*                    UNDER F IN THE INTERVAL A TO B. N SPECIFIES THE  *
C*                    NUMBER OF SUBINTERVALS TAKEN                     *
C*                                                                    *
C* UNUSUAL FEATURES:                                                  *
C*    THE FUNCTION SUBPROGRAM FCN IS PASSED AS AN ARGUMENT TO THE     *
C*    SUBPROGRAM AREA. AS CURRENTLY WRITTEN, FCN COMPUTES X**2-X      *
C* PROGRAMMER'S NAME: ---                 DATE WRITTEN: ---           *
C* * * * * * * * * * * * * * * * * * * * * * * * * * * * * * * * * * * *
        INTEGER PRT
        REAL APPROX, AREA
        DATA PRT/6/
C
C              AN EXTERNAL STATEMENT MUST BE USED SO THAT COMPILER IS
C               INFORMED THAT FCN IS A SUBPROGRAM, NOT A VARIABLE
        EXTERNAL FCN
C
C              APPROXIMATE THE AREA UNDER FCN IN THE INTERVAL 1 TO 4
        APPROX = AREA(1., 4., 12, FCN)
        WRITE (PRT,200) APPROX
200     FORMAT('0', 5X, 'THE AREA UNDER X**2-X BETWEEN 1 AND 4 IS', F10.2)
        STOP
        END
```

```
      REAL FUNCTION FCN (X)
C* * * * * * * * * * * * * * * * * * * * * * * * * * * * * * * * * * * *
C* COMPUTE X**2 - X. IF YOU WISH TO TRY THIS PROGRAM ON A MORE COMPLEX *
C* FUNCTION, THEN CHANGE THIS SUBPROGRAM TO COMPUTE WHATEVER FUNCTION *
C* YOU DESIRE. ALSO BE SURE TO CHANGE THE MAIN PROGRAM TO REFLECT THE *
C* NEW INTERVAL IN WHICH YOUR APPROXIMATION IS TO BE TAKEN.          *
C* * * * * * * * * * * * * * * * * * * * * * * * * * * * * * * * * * * *
      REAL X
      FCN = X**2 - X
      RETURN
      END

      REAL FUNCTION AREA (A, B, N, F)
C* * * * * * * * * * * * * * * * * * * * * * * * * * * * * * * * * * * *
C* APPROXIMATE AREA UNDER F USING TRAPEZOIDAL RULE                   *
C*                                                                   *
C* ARGUMENTS:                                                        *
C*    A - LOWER BOUND OF INTERVAL (REAL VALUE)                       *
C*    B - UPPER BOUND OF INTERVAL (REAL VALUE)                       *
C*    N - NUMBER OF SUBINTERVALS TO BE TAKEN (INTEGER VALUE)         *
C*    F - REAL-VALUED FUNCTION WHOSE CURVE FORMS AREA                *
C* * * * * * * * * * * * * * * * * * * * * * * * * * * * * * * * * * * *
      INTEGER N, I
      REAL A, B, F, INTRVL, C, D
C
C           DIVIDE AREA UP INTO SUBINTERVALS OF LENGTH (B-A)/N
C           CALCULATE AREA OF TRAPEZOID IN EACH OF THESE SUBINTERVALS
C           SUM ALL SUCH AREAS TOGETHER TO FORM APPROXIMATION
      AREA = 0.
      INTRVL = (B-A) / N
      DO 10 I = 1, N
         C = A + INTRVL*(I-1)
         D = A + INTRVL*I
         AREA = AREA + INTRVL*(F(C) + F(D))/2.
10    CONTINUE
      RETURN
      END
```

FIGURE 2-6 Integration by trapezoidal rule.

2.3.4 Adjustable Dimensions

Although the sort and search routines that we have written have been general in that the list to be sorted or searched is provided as an argument, they are limited since the subprograms provide specific list dimensions. For example, the routine of Figure 2-4 is designed to search tables of size 50 only.

Dummy array arguments may have adjustable, instead of fixed, dimensions. In order to accomplish this, the desired dimension of the array must also appear as an argument. The DIMENSION statement (or type declaration) then takes the following form

```
      DIMENSION LIST1(N), LIST2(N,M)
```

where LIST1, LIST2, N and M are dummy arguments. This declares LIST1 to be of size N and LIST2 to be of size N by M. Since arrays are always associated by location, no space is actually reserved for LIST1 or LIST2. The DIMENSION statement is used only to declare LIST1 and LIST2 arrays, to limit their legal subscript values, and to compute the storage mapping function. When this technique is used, the actual arguments must be dimensioned to contain at least N and N*M components, respectively.

2.4 TABLE LOOKUP BY HASH CODING

In Chapter 1 we presented two methods for organizing and searching a table of n values. The first method was a linear search and required on the order of n comparisons to perform a search request. The second method, a binary search, used a sorted list and required only on the order of $\log_2(n)$ comparisons. The disadvantage in the binary search is its dependence on a sorted table. Since general sorting algorithms require, on the average, the execution of at least $n*\log_2(n)$ steps, their use introduces a fairly severe overhead, especially if the table tends to grow during use or if the number of searches is small.

A third commonly used method of table organization and searching is called *hash coding*. The order of time required to insert or find an element using this technique is dependent on how full the list currently is and not on its size. The following presents several examples of the average number of probes based on the percentage of used entries in a hash table.

Percentage of Table Full	Average Number of Probes
10	1.06
50	1.50
75	2.50
90	5.50

Hash coding works as follows. We choose a function h that maps items (e.g., book call numbers) onto table positions. For instance,

$$h(k) = k - (k/100)*100 + 1$$

maps any k into a number between 1 and 100. Specifically, if the last two digits of k represent the number q, then $h(k)=q+1$. Now, if the last two digits of the values of k to be used are evenly distributed between 00 and 99, then the values of $h(k)$ will be evenly distributed between 1 and 100.

A perfect hash coding function is one in which there is a unique table position for each potential data or search item. That item is then stored or found at its hash coded position. For example, hash function h, above, is perfect if the values of k are allowed to range only between 0 and 99. If, however, we can have 9-digit values (e.g., social security numbers), then a perfect hash would need to reference a table of size one billion. Clearly, the general case is one where the range of values is larger than the number of computer words we wish to allocate to the table required to store such data. Under these circumstances, we will not be able to allocate one table slot per potential data value. This problem leads to a *collision*, which means we wish to insert a value k and find that position $h(k)$ is already filled. Whenever a collision occurs, we must find a different position for data item k. The frequency at which collisions occur and the amount of probing required to find secondary slots is what determines the order of complexity of hash coding.

Collisions may be resolved by a large number of different techniques. Here we concentrate on the simplest technique, *linear probing*. If we wish to insert an item k, then we inspect the slot at $h(k)$. If this is unavailable, we try the next slot at $h(k)+1$ [or 1 if $h(k)=n$]. This process continues with $h(k)+2$, $h(k)+3$, ..., until an available slot is found, k is found to already be in the table, or the table is found to be full.

The following is a high-level description of the processes of initializing, building, and searching a hash table. Our search table is comprised of n elements; k is the item to be inserted or searched for; h is the hash function; and all values of the k's are greater than 0.

Initialization: /Set all table entries to empty/
    $table(i) \leftarrow -1$, $i=1,n$ /All slots empty/

Lookup: /See if key value k is in the table/
    $p \leftarrow h(k)$ /Start probe at hashed slot/
    $s \leftarrow p$ /Remember starting point/

    scan1: /Check p-th slot. If not there, try next one/
        if $table(p)=k$ then return('success at slot k') /Found it?/
        if $table(p)=-1$ then return('fail')   /Empty slot found?/
        $p \leftarrow p+1$ /Increment to next slot/
        if $p>n$ then $p \leftarrow 1$ /Treat table as circular/
        if $p=s$ then return('fail')   /Back to starting point?/
        go to scan1   /Try this next slot/

Insert: /Insert key value k/
    $p \leftarrow h(k)$ /Start probe at hashed slot/
    $s \leftarrow p$ /Remember starting point/

    scan2: /Check p-th slot. If not there, try next one/
        if $table(p)=k$ then return('duplicate')   /Found it?/
        if $table(p)=-1$ then   /Empty slot found?/
            begin   /Put into empty slot/
                $table(p)=k$
                return('success')
           end
        $p \leftarrow p+1$ /Increment to next slot/
        if $p>n$ then $p \leftarrow 1$ /Treat table as circular/
        if $p=s$ then return('overflow')   /Is table full?/
        go to scan2   /Try this next slot/

Figure 2-7 contains a set of subprograms that might be used to implement our hash table management algorithms. Subroutine INIT performs table initialization. Subroutine HASH has two entry points, LOOKUP and INSERT; one is to perform table lookup and the other is to perform data insertion. The argument TABLE is the hash table, K is the data item to be searched for or inserted, and H is the hash function. If entry to HASH is via INSERT then the following occurs.

1. If K is at TABLE(P) then a normal return is taken with POS assigned the value P.

2. If K is not found and TABLE(P) is the first empty slot encountered, then TABLE(P) is assigned the value K and alternate return 1 is taken.

3. If K is not found and the table is full, then alternate return 2 is taken.

If entry to HASH is through LOOKUP, then the actions taken are exactly as for INSERT except in case 2. Here we exit by alternate return 1, but we do not insert K into the table.

```
C* * * * * * * * * * * * * * * * * * * * * * * * * * * * * * * * * * * * *
C* USE OF HASH FUNCTIONS IN TABLE CREATION AND SEARCH                    *
C*  THIS PROGRAM DEMONSTRATES MULTIPLE ENTRY POINTS, ALTERNATE EXITS     *
C*  AND ADJUSTABLE DIMENSIONS                                            *
C*                                                                       *
C* INPUT:                                                                *
C*    A CARD SPECIFYING THE NUMBER OF INSERTS (I3 FORMAT)                *
C*    ONE CARD PER INSERT GIVING THE INSERTED VALUE (I6 FORMAT)          *
C*    ONE CARD PER NUMBER TO BE LOOKED UP (I6 FORMAT)                    *
C*                                                                       *
C* SUBPROGRAMS CALLED:                                                   *
C*    INIT, INSERT, LOOKUP                                               *
C*                                                                       *
C* MAJOR VARIABLES:                                                      *
C*    TABLE - TABLE INTO WHICH VALUES ARE TO BE PLACED USING HASH CODE   *
C*            TYPE IS INTEGER, SIZE IS 100                               *
C*    ITEMS - NUMBER OF INTEGERS TO BE STORED IN TABLE (TYPE INTEGER)    *
C*                                                                       *
C* RESTRICTIONS:                                                         *
C*    ONLY POSITIVE NUMBERS MAY BE PLACED IN TABLE. NEGATIVE VALUES      *
C*     SIGNIFY FREE SPACE.                                               *
C*                                                                       *
C*   PROGRAMMER'S NAME: ---                       DATE WRITTEN: ---      *
C* * * * * * * * * * * * * * * * * * * * * * * * * * * * * * * * * * * * *
      INTEGER TABLE(100), K, POS, ITEMS, RDR, PRT
      DATA RDR/5/, PRT/6/
      EXTERNAL H
C
C            INITIALIZE ALL TABLE ELEMENTS TO -1 (EMPTY)
      CALL INIT (TABLE, 100)
C
```

```
C               READ IN NUMBER OF ITEMS FOLLOWED BY VALUES TO BE STORED
C               PRINT OUT WARNING MESSAGE WHENEVER A DUPLICATE IS FOUND
C               TERMINATE WITH ERROR MESSAGE IF TABLE OVERFLOWS
      READ (RDR,2) ITEMS
2     FORMAT (I3)
      DO 10 I = 1, ITEMS
         READ (RDR,6) K
6        FORMAT (I6)
C
C               SUCCESSFUL INSERT BRANCHES TO 10, OVERFLOW TO 888
C               NORMAL RETURN IF A DUPLICATE WAS FOUND
         CALL INSERT (&10, &888, TABLE, 100, K, POS, H)
         WRITE (PRT,7) K, POS
7        FORMAT (' DUPLICATE ITEM', I7, ' FOUND AT POSITION', I4)
10    CONTINUE
C
C               WRITE OUT CURRENT CONTENTS OF TABLE
      WRITE (PRT,15) TABLE
15    FORMAT ('0',T30, 'HASH TABLE AFTER ALL INSERTIONS' // ( 10I8) )
C
C               READ IN LOOKUP ARGUMENTS UNTIL END-OF-FILE. FOR EACH SUCH
C               ARGUMENT K, SEE IF IT IS IN TABLE. IF YES, INDICATE WHERE
C               IT IS. IF NO, PRINT A MESSAGE INDICATING THIS FACT
20    READ (RDR,6,END=999) K
C
C               IF K IS NOT IN TABLE BRANCH TO 25, ELSE CONTINUE
      CALL LOOKUP (&25, &25, TABLE, 100, K, POS, H)
         WRITE (PRT,22) K, POS
22       FORMAT (' ITEM', I7, ' FOUND AT POSITION', I4)
      GO TO 20
25       WRITE (PRT,26) K
26       FORMAT (' ITEM', I7, ' NOT FOUND')
      GO TO 20
C
C               COME HERE IF TABLE HAS OVERFLOWED
888   WRITE (PRT,889)
889   FORMAT (' *** TABLE OVERFLOW ***')
999   STOP
      END

      SUBROUTINE INIT (TABLE, N)
C* * * * * * * * * * * * * * * * * * * * * * * * * * * * * * * * * * * *
C* INITIALIZES ALL N ELEMENTS OF THE INTEGER LIST 'TABLE' TO -1       *
C*  THIS VALUE OF -1 IS INTERPRETED AS MEANING THE POSITION IS UNUSED *
C* * * * * * * * * * * * * * * * * * * * * * * * * * * * * * * * * * * *
      INTEGER N, TABLE(N), I, EMPTY/-1/
      DO 10 I = 1, N
         TABLE(I) = EMPTY
10    CONTINUE
      RETURN
      END

      INTEGER FUNCTION H (K)
C* * * * * * * * * * * * * * * * * * * * * * * * * * * * * * * * * * * *
C* HASH FUNCTION: GIVEN INTEGER VALUE K, THIS RETURNS ONE MORE THAN THE*
C*  2-DIGIT NUMBER FORMED BY THE RIGHTMOST 2 DIGITS OF K               *
C* * * * * * * * * * * * * * * * * * * * * * * * * * * * * * * * * * * *
      INTEGER K
      H = K - (K/100)*100 + 1
      RETURN
      END
```

```
        SUBROUTINE HASH (*, *, TABLE, N, K, POS, H)
C* * * * * * * * * * * * * * * * * * * * * * * * * * * * * * * * * * * *
C* INSERT OF LOOK UP VALUE 'K' IN 'TABLE' USING HASH FUNCTION 'H'       *
C*   IF 'TABLE' IS NOT FULL AND 'K' IS NOT IN IT, EXECUTE RETURN1,      *
C*     AFTER HAVING INSERTED 'K' IF CALL WAS FOR THAT PURPOSE           *
C*   IF 'TABLE' IS FULL AND 'K' IS NOT IN IT, THEN EXECUTE RETURN2      *
C*   IF 'K' IS ALREADY IN 'TABLE', THEN EXECUTE A NORMAL RETURN         *
C*                                                                      *
C* ARGUMENTS:                                                           *
C*   TABLE - HASH TABLE; TYPE INTEGER; SIZE N                           *
C*   N     - SIZE OF TABLE; TYPE INTEGER                                *
C*   K     - KEY TO BE INSERTED OR LOOKED UP; TYPE INTEGER              *
C*   POS   - POSITION K IS INSERTED OR FOUND AT; TYPE INTEGER           *
C*   H     - HASH FUNCTION SUBPROGRAM; TYPE INTEGER                     *
C*                                                                      *
C* ENTRY POINTS:                                                        *
C*   INSERT - USED TO INSERT K INTO TABLE                               *
C*   LOOKUP - USED TO SEE IF K IS ALREADY IN TABLE                      *
C* * * * * * * * * * * * * * * * * * * * * * * * * * * * * * * * * * * *
        INTEGER N, TABLE(N), K, POS, H, S, EMPTY/-1/
        LOGICAL PUTIN
C
C              ENTER HERE TO INSERT K INTO TABLE; PUTIN IS SET TO .TRUE.
C                 TO INDICATE OUR DESIRE TO INSERT THIS VALUE
        ENTRY INSERT (*, *, TABLE, N, K, POS, H)
        PUTIN = .TRUE.
        GO TO 10
C
C              ENTER HERE TO LOOK K UP IN TABLE. PUTIN IS SET TO .FALSE.
C                 TO INDICATE OUR DESIRE TO NOT STORE THE VALUE OF K
        ENTRY LOOKUP (*, *, TABLE, N, K, POS, H)
        PUTIN = .FALSE.
C
C              COMMON CODE SECTION. BOTH ENTRIES MERGE TO HERE
C
C              CALCULATE HASH POSITION FOR K AND REMEMBER THIS POSITION
C                 FOR USE DURING LINEAR PROBING PHASE
10      POS = H(K)
        S = POS
C
C              USE LINEAR PROBE TO FIND SLOT FOR K OR TO DETECT THAT IT
C                 IS ALREADY IN THE TABLE.. EXIT TO LABEL 30 IF A SPACE IS
C                 FOUND. EXECUTE RETURN IF K IS FOUND. EXECUTE RETURN2
C                 IF TABLE IS FULL AND K IS NOT ALREADY IN.
20      IF (TABLE(POS) .EQ. K) RETURN
        IF (TABLE(POS) .EQ. EMPTY) GO TO 30
C
C              MOVE TO NEXT POSITION TREATING TABLE AS CIRCULAR
        POS = POS + 1
        IF (POS .GT. N) POS=1
C
C              IF WE'RE BACK TO THE START POINT, QUIT
        IF (POS .EQ. S) RETURN2
        GO TO 20
C
C              FOUND A PLACE FOR K, INSERT IF REQUIRED
30      IF (PUTIN) TABLE(POS)=K
        RETURN1
        END
```

FIGURE 2-7 Hash table organization.

108

2.5 DATA STATEMENTS IN SUBPROGRAMS

In Chapter 0 we discussed the use of DATA and type specification statements for initializing the values of variables, arrays and array elements prior to execution. Note that, when using data initialization within subprograms, one may not data initialize the value of a dummy argument. This is clearly a sensible rule, since a dummy argument acquires a value only as a result of an actual argument association. An initial value would therefore have no use. More important, if association is by location, then no storage would be assigned and therefore no initial values could be kept.

2.6 COMMON—FORTRAN'S WAY TO MAKE DATA GLOBAL

2.6.1 Local Versus Global

Except for dummy arguments, the data items (variables and arrays) used within a FORTRAN program module (subprogram or main program) are by default treated as local to that module. This means that a variable called A in any one module is distinct from the variable A (or, for that matter any other variable) referenced within another module. This locality has two main advantages. First, it allows two or more programmers to work independently on different modules of some large program. Each programmer may chose variable names without having to worry about avoiding duplication of the names being used by one of the others.

A second advantage of this locality is the way in which it reduces unintended side effects by FORTRAN subprograms. If the only data items used within a subroutine SUB are either local or dummy argument names, then a call to SUB can change values of only the actual arguments passed to it from a calling routine. This makes debugging far easier than in the situation where a subprogram might modify the values of variables in the calling routine other than those explicity stated in the argument list. Futhermore, readability of a program is enhanced whenever it is possible to determine a subprogram's potential side effects, without actually reading the code that comprises such a module.

There do, however, arise programming situations in which FORTRAN's default local status for data items is inconvenient. If some set of variables and arrays is used by a large number of program modules or if some modules require a large number of arguments, then coding of argument lists can become very cumbersome and, consequently, error prone. In order to alleviate this problem, FORTRAN allows variables to be declared global, that is, shared by more than one module. The tool for doing this is the COMMON statement, which we now define and discuss.

2.6.2 COMMON—Its Standard Usage

Before a FORTRAN program is executed, computer storage is allocated for each of its modules. This storage is divided into two distinct parts. The first is comprised of all machine code; the second provides storage for local variables and constants.

In addition, a single block of storage is reserved for use by all modules. This block is called *common*. A module expresses its intent to share data from common by including a COMMON statement among its declarations. The general form of such a statement is

$$\text{COMMON } name_1, name_2, ..., name_n$$

This declares that, so far as this module is concerned, the beginning of common storage is reserved for $name_1$, the next portion for $name_2$, etc.

A COMMON statement that is too long to be specified on a single card image may be continued by the normal rules of FORTRAN or may be continued by starting a new COMMON statement. Thus,

```
          COMMON A, B, C
```

has the same meaning as

```
          COMMON A, B,
     *          C
```

which is the same as

```
          COMMON A
          COMMON B, C
```

and so on.

As a first example of the use of COMMON, consider the following set of statements.

```
          INTEGER DOLLAR, CENT, LIST(2,3)
          REAL CASH
          COMMON LIST, CASH, DOLLAR, CENT
```

If these exist in some program module A then, during its execution, the common storage area is considered to be organized as follows.

LIST(1,1)	Word 1
LIST(2,1)	Word 2
LIST(1,2)	Word 3
LIST(2,2)	Word 4
LIST(1,3)	Word 5
LIST(2,3)	Word 6
CASH	Word 7
DOLLAR	Word 8
CENT	Word 9

If some other module B contains the same set of statements then each reference it makes to LIST, CASH, DOLLAR or CENT is a reference to the same storage accessed by these names within module A. The effect is to make these data areas not local to a single module but common to any that include an appropriate COMMON statement.

Figure 2-8 contains a simple example of the use of COMMON. This program reads in data that is organized as follows.

Card Number	Value		Comments
1	n		An integer value in columns 1-2
2	j_1		An integer value in columns 1-4
3	j_2		As above
.	.	.	
.	.	.	
$n+1$	j_n		As above
$n+2$	m		An integer value in columns 1-2
$n+3$	k_1		An integer value in columns 1-4
$n+4$	k_2		As above
.	.	.	
.	.	.	
$n+m+2$	k_i		As above

It then merges the sets of integers $(j_1,...,j_n)$ and $(k_1,...,k_i)$ and prints the merged version. (*Note.* This program assumes that the j and k values are each sorted in ascending order.)

```
C* * * * * * * * * * * * * * * * * * * * * * * * * * * * * * * * * * * *
C* MERGE TWO SORTED LISTS. DUPLICATES DO NOT APPEAR IN THE MERGED      *
C* LIST. SORTED LISTS APPEAR AS CARD INPUT                            *
C*                                                                    *
C* INPUT:                                                             *
C*    A CARD CONTAINING NUMBER OF ENTRIES IN FIRST LIST (FORMAT I2)   *
C*    ONE CARD PER ENTRY IN FIRST LIST (FORMAT I4)                    *
C*    A CARD CONTAINING NUMBER OF ENTRIES IN SECOND LIST (FORMAT I2)  *
C*    ONE CARD PER ENTRY IN SECOND LIST (FORMAT I4)                   *
C*                                                                    *
C* SUBPROGRAMS CALLED:                                                *
C*    READ, MERGE, PRINT                                              *
C*                                                                    *
C* MAJOR VARIABLES:                                                   *
C*    LIST1 - FIRST INTEGER LIST; SIZE 50                             *
C*    LIST2 - SECOND INTEGER LIST; SIZE 50                            *
C*    LIST3 - MERGE OF LIST1 AND LIST2; SIZE 100                      *
C*    S1    - NUMBER OF ENTRIES STORED IN LIST1                       *
C*    S2    - NUMBER OF ENTRIES STORED IN LIST2                       *
C*    S3    - NUMBER OF ENTRIES STORED IN LIST3                       *
C*                                                                    *
C* PROGRAMMER'S NAME: ---                     DATE WRITTEN: ---       *
C* * * * * * * * * * * * * * * * * * * * * * * * * * * * * * * * * * * *
      INTEGER S1, S2, S3, LIST1(50), LIST2(50), LIST3(100)
C
C            COMMON AREA IS USED TO SHARE VALUES IN LISTS WITH MERGE,
C            AND PRINT. READ DOES NOT SHARE THIS COMMON AREA
      COMMON S1, S2, S3, LIST1, LIST2, LIST3
C
```

```
C                    READ TWO LISTS, MERGE AND PRINT. IF ANY ERRORS ARE FOUND
C                    BY READ DURING INPUT, TERMINATE ALL PROCESSING
      CALL READ (&999, S1, LIST1)
      CALL READ (&999, S2, LIST2)
      CALL MERGE
      CALL PRINT
999   STOP
      END

      SUBROUTINE READ (*, SIZE, LIST)
C* * * * * * * * * * * * * * * * * * * * * * * * * * * * * * * * * * *
C* READ SIZE THEN VALUES FOR ELEMENTS OF LIST. IF SIZE IS CODED WRONG *
C* (LESS THAN 1 OR GREATER THAN 50) THEN A RETURN#1 IS EXECUTED.      *
C* THIS ACTION ALSO OCCURS IF AN END-OF-FILE IS DETECTED             *
C* * * * * * * * * * * * * * * * * * * * * * * * * * * * * * * * * * *
      INTEGER SIZE, LIST(50), RDR, PRT, I
      DATA RDR/5/, PRT/6/
      READ (RDR,100,END=888) SIZE
100   FORMAT (I2)
      IF ((SIZE .LT. 1) .OR. (SIZE .GT. 50)) GO TO 888
      READ (RDR,101,END=888) (LIST(I), I = 1, SIZE)
101   FORMAT (I4)
      RETURN
C
C                    ENTER HERE ON ANY ERROR CONDITION
888   WRITE (PRT,889)
889   FORMAT (' *** ERROR IN DATA ***')
      RETURN1
      END

      SUBROUTINE MERGE
C* * * * * * * * * * * * * * * * * * * * * * * * * * * * * * * * * * *
C* MERGE COMMON LISTS, LIST1 AND LIST2, INTO LIST3                    *
C*                                                                   *
C* MAJOR VARIABLES:                                                  *
C*    LIST1 - MERGE LIST FROM COMMON; TYPE INTEGER; SIZE MAX OF 50    *
C*    LIST2 - MERGE LIST FROM COMMON; TYPE INTEGER; SIZE MAX OF 50    *
C*    LIST3 - LISTS MERGED TO THIS COMMON AREA; SIZE MAX OF 100       *
C*    S1    - ACTUAL NUMBER OF ENTRIES IN LIST1 (COMMON VARIABLE)     *
C*    S2    - ACTUAL NUMBER OF ENTRIES IN LIST2 (COMMON VARIABLE)     *
C*    S3    - NUMBER OF ENTRIES IN MERGED LIST3 (COMMON VARIABLE)     *
C*            DURING MERGE PROCESS THIS IS PTR TO CURRENT END OF LIST3 *
C*    P1    - MERGE PTR FOR LIST1, POINTS TO ELEMENT BEING USED NOW   *
C*    P2    - MERGE PTR FOR LIST2, POINTS TO ELEMENT BEING USED NOW   *
C* * * * * * * * * * * * * * * * * * * * * * * * * * * * * * * * * * *
      INTEGER P1, P2, S1, S2, S3, LIST1(50), LIST2(50), LIST3(100)
      COMMON S1, S2, S3, LIST1, LIST2, LIST3
C
C                    START AT TOP OF EACH LIST
      P1 = 1
      P2 = 1
      S3 = 0
C
C                    DETERMINE FROM WHAT LIST TO COPY A VALUE INTO LIST3
10    IF (P1 .GT. S1) GO TO 30
      IF (P2 .GT. S2) GO TO 20
      IF (LIST1(P1) - LIST2(P2)) 20, 40, 35
C
C              COME HERE IF WE ARE TO COPY AN ELEMENT FROM LIST1
20    S3 = S3 + 1
      LIST3(S3) = LIST1(P1)
      P1 = P1 + 1
      GO TO 10
C
C              ARE BOTH LISTS EXHAUSTED? IF SO, QUIT
30    IF (P2 .GT. S2) RETURN
C
```

112

```
C               COME HERE IF WE ARE TO COPY AN ELEMENT FROM LIST2
35        S3 = S3 + 1
          LIST3(S3) = LIST2(P2)
C
C               MOVE PAST ELEMENT IN LIST2 (BRANCH HERE TO SKIP DUPLICATE)
40        P2 = P2 + 1
          GO TO 10
      END

      SUBROUTINE PRINT
C* * * * * * * * * * * * * * * * * * * * * * * * * * * * * * * * * * * *
C* PRINT COMMON LIST - LIST3. SIZE OF THIS LIST IS S3               *
C* * * * * * * * * * * * * * * * * * * * * * * * * * * * * * * * * * * *
      INTEGER S1, S2, S3, LIST1(50), LIST2(50), LIST3(100), PRT, I, K
      COMMON S1, S2, S3, LIST1, LIST2, LIST3
      DATA PRT/6/
      WRITE (PRT,200) (LIST3(I), I = 1, S3)
200   FORMAT ('0 MERGED LIST' // (I7) )
      RETURN
      END
```

FIGURE 2-8 Use of common in a merge program.

Storage allocated to the program of Figure 2-8 would be organized as follows.

Code for main routine	MAIN
Code for subprogram READ Storage for local variable I,RDR,PRT Storage for constants 1 and 50 If association by value/result is used, then storage for SIZE	READ
Code for subprogram MERGE Storage for local variables P1,P2 Storage for constants 1 and 0	MERGE
Code for subprogram PRINT Storage for local variables I,PRT Storage for constant 1	PRINT
S1 Word 1 S2 Word 2 S3 Word 3 LIST1 Words 4 to 53 LIST2 Words 54 to 103 LIST3 Words 104 to 203	COMMON

2.6.3 Inconsistent Definitions of COMMON

In most programming languages, variables and arrays are made global by allowing modules to access the same storage areas by the same names. In FORTRAN, however, access is shared by allowing all modules to share common using whatever names they wish. Reconsidering modules A and B from the previous section, assume a third module C contains statements

```
INTEGER UNIT1, UNIT2, ARRAY(2,3)
REAL MONEY
COMMON ARRAY, MONEY, UNIT1, UNIT2
```

Then it considers common to be organized as

ARRAY(1,1)	Word 1
ARRAY(2,1)	Word 2
ARRAY(1,2)	Word 3
ARRAY(2,2)	Word 4
ARRAY(1,3)	Word 5
ARRAY(2,3)	Word 6
MONEY	Word 7
UNIT1	Word 8
UNIT2	Word 9

not as

LIST(1,1)	Word 1
LIST(2,1)	Word 2
LIST(1,2)	Word 3
LIST(2,2)	Word 4
LIST(1,3)	Word 5
LIST(2,3)	Word 6
CASH	Word 7
DOLLAR	Word 8
CENT	Word 9

which is the format for modules A and B. Now, any references C makes to ARRAY would be to the same storage area accessed by A and B when they refer to LIST. References to MONEY, UNIT1, and UNIT2 correspond to references to CASH, DOLLAR, and CENT, respectively.

Even more extreme, a module D might contain statements

```
INTEGER L, Q
REAL A(2), S(3)
COMMON L, A, Q, S
```

which result in common being treated as

L	Word 1
A(1)	Word 2
A(2)	Word 3
Q	Word 4
S(1)	Word 5
S(2)	Word 6
S(3)	Word 7

A reference in module D to the variable L would result in its accessing the same word of storage as would be gotten in A or B by referring to LIST(1,1) or in module C by ARRAY(1,1); A(1) is allocated the same storage as LIST(2,1) and ARRAY(2,1), etc. References to DOLLAR and CENT in A and B, UNIT1 and UNIT2 in C, have no counterparts in module D, since it accesses only the first seven words of common.

Clearly, inconsistent specifications of common cause a program to be hard to comprehend. Furthermore, such practices often lead to errors. To avoid potential pitfalls and to make your programs more readable, we recommend that you obey the following guideline.

> All modules which contain a COMMON statement should specify precisely the same organization of the common area.

The best way to achieve this is to make up one copy of your common declarations, including the appropriate REAL, INTEGER, and LOGICAL specifications, and then reproduce this copy for each module that needs to share common.

2.6.4 Named COMMON

The type of common that we discussed in the previous two subsections is called *blank common* or *unnamed common*. One may also define other, independent common blocks, called *named commons*. A set of variables and arrays is assigned to the named common area called *name* by a statement of the form

COMMON /name/ list of variables and arrays

Before a program is executed, one block of storage is allocated for each distinct named common area that was specified within any of the program's modules.

Named common is often used in programs that have two or more sets of subprograms, where the members of one set communicate with each other but not with the members of any of the other sets. Each set then has its own named common area. By using this technique, instead of merging all named commons into a single block, there is less chance of some routine modifying a common data item unintentionally. Misspellings are therefore more likely to have only a local effect.

2.6.5 The Interaction of COMMON and EQUIVALENCE

A variable or array appearing within a common area may be equivalenced with local variables or arrays. When this is done, no space is actually allocated for the local name, since it serves as an alternate way to reference storage within a common block. Equivalences of this sort may be used for all the reasons set forth in Chapter 1 (e.g., treating a multi-dimensional array as one-dimensional in order to improve efficiency). There is, however, one restriction on such equivalencing: no portion of the equivalenced local area may be assigned to a storage area preceding the first word of common.

Consider the following sequence of statements.

```
INTEGER A(20), B(16), C, D, E(6)
COMMON B, C, D
EQUIVALENCE (C,E(1)), (C,A(20))
```

The common area comprised of B, C, and D is 18 words long. Starting with element B(1), the first equivalence pair specifies that C may be referred to by the array element E(1). Since D immediately follows C in the common area, D and E(2) refer to the same word of storage. Although it is poor practice, this equivalence is legal and has the side effect of declaring the common area to be 22 instead of 18 words long. In essence this extends common to the right.

The second equivalence pair (C,A(20)) is illegal. Since B(16) would immediately precede C in common, then B(1) is equivalenced to A(4). This would then require A(1), A(2), and A(3) to precede B(1), thereby extending common to the left. Since a common block is preceded in storage by either another common block or by the area associated with some program module, the assigning of values to either of these items could cause unintended side effects, even the destruction of code.

It is legal to equivalence common areas with local ones, but it is not legal to equivalence a common area with a dummy argument or another common area. The first of these restrictions is logical, since dummy arguments must be identified with their corresponding actual arguments, not with some fixed common variable or array. The sensibility of the second restriction may be seen from the following example.

```
INTEGER A, B, C, D, E
COMMON/COM1/ A, B
COMMON/COM2/ C, D
EQUIVALENCE (A,B), (A,C), (D,E), (B,E)
```

The first equivalence pair (A,B) is illogical since it requires the second word of common block COM1 to share storage with the first word. This is asking B to be in two places at once. The second pair is similarly illogical since common areas COM1 and COM2 are assigned distinct, nonoverlapping areas of storage. Although the third and fourth pairs are not illegal by themselves, their combined effect is illegal, since it requires B and D to share the same word of storage.

We now summarize the restrictions just discussed on the use of equivalence with elements belonging to common blocks.

1. Equivalence may not extend the size of a common block to the left, that is, to storage preceding the first word of the common area.

2. A variable or array in a common block may not be equivalenced with any other element in a common block.

3. A variable or array in a common block may not be equivalenced with a dummy argument.

2.6.6 Data Initialization of Elements in Common Blocks

The rules of FORTRAN do not allow any variable or array element that appears in unnamed common to be data initialized. However, it is possible to do so with members of a named common block. In order to do this we must create a nonexecutable program module called a BLOCK DATA subprogram.

A BLOCK DATA subprogram starts with the statement

```
BLOCK DATA
```

ends with an END statement, and contains no statement types other than named COMMON, mode specifications, DIMENSION, and DATA. An example of a BLOCK DATA subprogram is

```
BLOCK DATA
INTEGER A, B, C(3), D(2,2)
REAL E(4,2), Q, R
COMMON/PASS1/ A, B, E
COMMON/PASS2/ C, D, Q, R
DATA A/15/, E/8*0.0/, D/1,2,3,4/
END
```

This specifies that named common PASS1 contains three items, A, B, and E. Of these, A and E are data initialized and B is not. PASS2 is comprised of four items, C, D, Q, and R. Only D is data initialized, while the values associated with C, Q, and R are unpredictable when execution starts.

2.7 STATEMENT FUNCTIONS

In addition to providing the facilities to create function subprograms, the FORTRAN language allows a programmer to define simple functions that are internal to the program module in which they are defined and referenced. These functions are called *statement functions*. Each statement function is defined by a single assignment statement that must appear after all specification statements and prior to the first executable statement of the program module in which it is to be used. The general form of such a statement is

$$name(a_1, a_2, ..., a_n) = expression$$

where *name* is any variable name, the a's are dummy arguments, and *expression* is any arithmetic or logical expression that does not include references to array elements or to statement functions that are not previously defined within the same module. The mode of the function is that of *name*.

A statement function is invoked just like any other function. Whenever we include a call to a statement function, the compiler acts as if we had coded the associated function expression with each of the dummy arguments replaced by actual ones. Thus, if we define the function, SAMPLE, as

```
SAMPLE(Y,Z) = Y*(Z+Y)**2-L
```

then the statement

```
RESULT = A+SAMPLE(A,B)
```

is compiled as if we had written

```
RESULT = A + (A*(B+A)**2-L)
```

Note that the variable L is used without regard to the actual arguments since it does not appear among the dummy arguments.

Statement functions do not result in any decrease in storage requirements as is generally achieved through the use of function subprograms. Their main use is to improve program readability and reduce tedious writing of commonly needed arithmetic or logical expressions. This often leads to a reduction of errors since programmers tend to get sloppy when they feel that their work is overly repetitive. This also can aid in making a program easier to modify, if this common calculation should ever need to be changed.

As an example of the use of a statement function, consider the efficient storing of a matrix A, for which all values above the major diagonal are zero.

(That is, if J>I then A(I,J)=0.) Such a matrix is called a *lower triangular matrix* and arises in many applications. If A is a 50 by 50 lower triangular matrix, than allocating storage using

```
DIMENSION A(50,50)
```

is wasteful since 1225 of the 2500 words are guaranteed to be assigned the value zero. A more efficient approach is to allocate storage as

```
DIMENSION A(1275)
```

The I,J component of A $(I \geq J)$ is then located at $A((I*(I-1))/2+J)$. With this scheme in mind we might define the statement function

```
INDEX(I,J) = (I*(I-1))/2 + J
```

We can then access the I,J component by coding A(INDEX(I,J)), provided, of course, $I \geq J$ and that our dialect allows subscript expressions to involve function calls.

2.8 A FINAL EXAMPLE— RANDOM NUMBER GENERATORS

2.8.1 The Notion of Pseudo-Random Sequences

Whenever we are faced with the job of debugging a complicated program, one of the hardest tasks is to generate meaningful data. For example, consider the problem of generating a set of social security numbers required as input to a program to be tested. We surely would not input all possible numbers since there are one billion of these. Instead, we need to pick a manageable number of test values (e.g., 1000 of them). We wish to have these values be randomly distributed across the set of all possible numbers. Clearly, choosing social security numbers 0 through 999 would not generally be satisfactory.

A method by which we might accomplish our task would be to have a 10-sided die with sides numbered from 0 to 9. Each throw of the die gives us a random digit. Nine throws provide us with a randomly chosen social security number, and 9000 throws provide us with the 1000 test values desired. The question at hand is how can we write a program that has the property of producing random numbers, since all computer programs execute in a deterministic (not random) manner. To see how this may be done, we must first consider what properties we desire from a random sequence.

True randomness means that each event (choice of a number) is independent of any previous event. Thus, the sequence of 1000 social security numbers, each of which is the number 555026281, might be the result of the random generation of 1000 nine digit numbers. When we use the term random, one criterion we desire is that the sequence of numbers be uniformly distributed in the desired range (0 to 999999999). We would probably expect that out of our 1000 numbers, approximately 500 would be in the range 0 to 499999999. Furthermore, we would not expect to see any obvious sequences of recurring number patterns. For example, the sequence 0,5,10,15,... would not be acceptable, although its numbers are evenly distributed. Sequences satisfying the above criteria are often called *pseudo-random*, since they have the appearance of randomness without the anomalies that can occur in truly random sequences.

2.8.2 A Multiplicative Random Number Generator

Much research has gone into the study of techniques for generating random sequences. Among the methods that have been studied and found to be quite reasonable are those classified as *multiplicative*.

A sequence generated by a multiplicative random number generator is defined by a starting number, $r(0)$, called the *seed*, and a formula

$$r(k+1) = (a * r(k)) \text{ modulo } (m)$$

that calculates the next number in the sequence. Thus, the first number of such a sequence is

$$r(1)=(a*r(0))\text{modulo}(m)$$

the second is

$$r(2)=(a*r(1))\text{modulo}(m)$$

and so on. The properties of sequences generated by such a method are highly dependent on the choices of values for $r(0)$, a, and m. Good choices of these values for one machine may be extremely bad choices for another. Often, the value of m is chosen as one greater than the largest integer that can be represented on our machine. Such a choice has two advantages. First, it permits numbers to range as high as possible. Second, the modulo function for such a value of m can be trivially computed on most machines.

2.8.3 Monte Carlo Integration

We now present a program that uses random numbers to approximate the area under a curve. (See Figure 2-6 for another solution to this problem.) The technique used here is generally called *Monte Carlo*. It approximates the area under a curve F, in the interval [A,B], as follows. Draw a box having corners (A,0), (B,H), (B,H), and (B,0). The area of this box is BOX=H*(B-A). The area under F in the interval [A,B] is approximated by BOX*FPART, provided FPART is an approximation to the percentage of this box that is under the curve formed by F. (See Figure 2-9.) Our Monte Carlo technique, presented in Figure 2-10, estimates the value of FPART by generating a large number of (1000) random points within the box and calculating what percentage of these lie below the curve of F.

The random number generator, RAND, used here, is a multiplicative one that is appropriate for use of an IBM 360-370 machine. It produces real numbers in the interval [0,RMAX] , where RMAX is its only argument. To do this, it first produces a random integer, g, in the range from 1 to $2^{31}-1$ (the largest integer represented on an IBM 360-370). Each such number, g, is then normalized into the interval from 0 to RMAX. This normalization is performed by calculating the value $((g-1)/(2^{31}-2))*RMAX$.

When studying this example, you need to recall that RAND is designed specifically for an IBM 360-370. It may not be appropriate for your machine. You should also be aware of the fact that, while Monte Carlo techniques can produce very good results, they are usually much slower to converge than methods such as the trapezoidal rule.

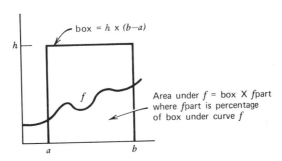

box = h x $(b-a)$

Area under f = box X $f$part
where $f$part is percentage
of box under curve f

FIGURE 2-9 Basis of Monte Carlo integration.

```
C* * * * * * * * * * * * * * * * * * * * * * * * * * * * * * * * * * * *
C* APPROXIMATE AREA UNDER X**2-X IN THE INTERVAL FROM 1 TO 4.          *
C*  TECHNIQUE USED IS MONTE CARLO INTEGRATION.                         *
C*                                                                     *
C* SUBPROGRAMS CALLED: AREA                                            *
C*                                                                     *
C*  PROGRAMMER'S NAME: ---                      DATE WRITTEN: ---      *
C* * * * * * * * * * * * * * * * * * * * * * * * * * * * * * * * * * * *
      INTEGER PRT
      REAL APPROX, AREA
      DATA PRT/6/
C
C              THE FUNCTION TO BE COMPUTED IS DEFINED BY SUBPROGRAM FCN
C                  THIS SUBPROGRAM NAME IS PASSED TO AREA AS AN ARGUMENT
      EXTERNAL FCN
C
C              APPROXIMATE AREA AND PRINT OUT RESULT
C              VALUE 12 PASSED AS FIRST ARGUMENT INDICATES THE LARGEST
C              VALUE ASSUMED BY FCN IN THE INTERVAL FROM 1 TO 4
C              THIS IS NEEDED BY THE MONTE CARLO INTEGRATION ALGORITHM
      APPROX = AREA(12., 1000, 1., 4., FCN)
      WRITE (PRT,200) APPROX
200   FORMAT ('0', 5X, 'THE AREA UNDER X**2-X FROM 1 TO 4 IS', F10.2)
      STOP
      END
```

```
      REAL FUNCTION FCN (X)
C* * * * * * * * * * * * * * * * * * * * * * * * * * * * * * * * * *
C* RETURN VALUE X**2-X                                              *
C* * * * * * * * * * * * * * * * * * * * * * * * * * * * * * * * * *
      REAL X
      FCN = X**2 - X
      RETURN
      END


      REAL FUNCTION AREA (HIGH, N, A, B, F)
C* * * * * * * * * * * * * * * * * * * * * * * * * * * * * * * * * *
C* USES MONTE CARLO INTEGRATION TO APPROXIMATE AREA UNDER FUNCTION 'F' *
C*   IN THE INTERVAL FROM A TO B                                    *
C*                                                                  *
C* ARGUMENTS:                                                       *
C*    HIGH  - A NUMBER AT LEAST AS LARGE AS LARGEST VALUE OF F IN    *
C*              INTERVAL FROM A TO B (TYPE REAL)                    *
C*    N     - NUMBER OF RANDON POINTS IN PLANE TO BE USED IN ESTIMATING*
C*              AREA UNDER F (TYPE INTEGER)                         *
C*    A     - BEGINNING OF INTERVAL (TYPE REAL)                     *
C*    B     - END OF INTERVAL (TYPE REAL)                           *
C*    F     - REAL FUNCTION UNDER WHICH AREA IS TO BE APPROXIMATED   *
C*                                                                  *
C* MAJOR VARIABLES:                                                 *
C*    HITS  - NUMBER OF RANDOM POINTS WHICH WERE UNDER CURVE (INTEGER) *
C*    INTVAL- DISTANCE BETWEEN B AND A (TYPE REAL)                  *
C*                                                                  *
C* SUBPROGRAMS CALLED:                                             *
C*    RAND, FLOAT                                                   *
C* * * * * * * * * * * * * * * * * * * * * * * * * * * * * * * * * *
      INTEGER N, I, HITS
      REAL HIGH, A, B, INTVAL, X, Y
C
C              COMPUTE N RANDOM POINTS AND CALCULATE THE NUMBER OF "HITS"
C              (POINTS UNDER THE CURVE FORMED BY F)
      INTVAL = B - A
      HITS = 0
      DO 10 I = 1, N
        Y = RAND(HIGH)
        X = RAND(INTVAL) + A
        IF (F(X) .GE. Y) HITS = HITS+1
10    CONTINUE
C
C              AREA IS THEN PERCENTAGE IF "HITS" TIMES TOTAL AREA IN
C              BOX FORMED BY POINTS (A,0),(A,HIGH),(B,HIGH),(B,0)
      AREA = HIGH * INTVAL * (FLOAT(HITS)/N)
      RETURN
      END


      REAL FUNCTION RAND (RMAX)
C* * * * * * * * * * * * * * * * * * * * * * * * * * * * * * * * * *
C* COMPUTE RANDOM REAL VALUE IN THE INTERVAL FROM 0 TO RMAX          *
C*  AS WRITTEN THIS PROGRAM IS APPROPRIATE FOR USE ON ANY 32-BIT TWOS *
C*  COMPLEMENT MACHINE. IN PARTICULAR IT MAY BE USED ON AN IBM 360-370 *
C* * * * * * * * * * * * * * * * * * * * * * * * * * * * * * * * * *
      REAL RMAX
      INTEGER IRAND, MULT, LARGE
      DATA IRAND/137462873/, MULT/65539/, LARGE/2147483647/
C
C              COMPUTE A NEW RANDOM NUMBER IN THE RANGE 1 TO 2**31-1
      IRAND = IRAND * MULT
      IF (IRAND .LT. 0) IRAND = (IRAND + LARGE) + 1
C
C              COMPUTE DESIRED REAL-VALUED NUMBER
      RAND = RMAX*(IRAND-1) / (LARGE-1)
      RETURN
      END
```

FIGURE 2-10 Monte Carlo integration

Exercises

2.01 Discuss the problems posed by altering the first argument to the following function M.

```
        J = 2
        I = 0
        IF ((I.EQ.0) .OR. (M(I,J).EQ.J)) WRITE (6,20) I
   20   FORMAT (I12)
        STOP
        END

        INTEGER FUNCTION M(I,J)
        IF (J.GT.I) I=J
        M = I
        RETURN
        END
```

2.02 Consider the following program.

```
        COMMON I,J
        L = 2
        J = 3
        CALL SUB (I,L)
        WRITE (6,20) I,J,L
   20   FORMAT (3I12)
        STOP
        END

        SUBROUTINE SUB (K,L)
        COMMON I,J
        I = L
        K = J + 1
        L = I
        RETURN
        END
```

What values are printed for I, J and L if
(a) I and L are passed to SUB *by value/result*?
(b) I and L are passed to SUB *by location*?

2.03 Using alternate exits, write a CALL statement and a subroutine to do the following. The call passes numeric arguments 3.*X**2, 4.*Z, 2.*(X-Z) and ANS. The subroutine has corresponding dummy arguments A, B, C and D. It calculates the value D = B**2 - 4*A*C. If the value of D is positive, a normal return is executed. If D is zero, the subroutine returns to statement 20 in the calling routine. If D is negative, control is returned to statement 99.

2.04 Write a real-valued function that has two entry points, SUM and ABSSUM, and two arguments, A and N. If entry is made using the name SUM, then the sum of the first N elements of the real list A is returned. If entry is through ABSSUM, then the absolute value of this sum is returned. The subprogram you write may have only one loop which sums the elements of A. Test your subprogram with an appropriate main program.

2.05 Write a real-valued function with two entry points, called FMAX and FMIN, and four arguments, F, A, B and N. F is a real-valued function. A and B are real values representing the start and end of some interval. N is an integer value. Entry through FMAX results in the return of an approximation to the maximum value obtained by F in the interval A to B. FMIN is used to calculate the minimum. These approximations are calculated by inspecting the values of F at A, A+(B-A)/N, ..., B-(B-A)/N, B. Test this with an appropriate main program and several real-valued function arguments.

2.06 The program of Figure 2-6 implements the trapezoidal rule in order to approximate the area under some curve F, between the values of A and B. The *midpoint rule* is similar to the trapezoidal rule. It divides the interval (A,B) into N subintervals. However, in this method the area in a subinterval (C,D) is approximated by (D-C) $*$ F((C+D)/2). Write a program that compares these methods for the functions X**3-X**2 and X*SQRT(X) in the interval 2 to 10. In each case, divide this interval into 24 subintervals.

2.07 If the machine on which you are running your program is other than an IBM 360 or 370, find out if the random number generator of Figure 2-10 is appropriate for your use. If not, acquire or write one that will work for you. *Note*. Many computer centers provide such a function as part of their FORTRAN library.

2.08 Write and test a subroutine RNDSEQ that has two integer arguments, LIST and N, where LIST is a list of size N. RNDSEQ is to use a random number generator to create a sequence of N random integer numbers, $r(1)$, $r(2)$, ..., $r(N)$. Each number must be in the range from 1 to N and there may be no duplicates. This sequence is to be returned by assigning $r(1)$ to LIST(1), $r(2)$ to LIST(2), etc. *Warning*. This may require more than N calls to your random number generator, since it is possible that duplicates will occur.

2.09 The hash table method of Section 2.4 resolves collisions by the technique called linear probing. This is not considered to be the best method. An alternative, *random probing*, generates a sequence of $n-1$ unique random numbers, $r(1)$, $r(2)$, ..., $r(n-1)$, each in the range 1 to $n-1$. If a collision occurs at position $h(k)$, then we try $h(k)+r(1)$, $h(k)+r(2)$, ..., $h(k)+r(n-1)$. As with linear probing, the table is treated as circular. Write a program that compares the number of probes required by linear probing and random probing. Create several sets of data to carry out this comparison. *Suggestion*. Your random number generator is an ideal tool for creating such test data.

2.10 Assume some program module contains the statements

```
INTEGER LIST(3), MATRIX(2,3)
REAL COEFF, EIGEN(2)
COMMON LIST, COEFF, MATRIX, EIGEN
```

Which variables and array elements are assigned to each of the 12 words of the common area?

2.11 Consider the statement sets below. Indicate which are legal and which are illegal. For illegal ones, explain why. For the legal ones comment on any nonobvious side effects.

a)
```
INTEGER J(5), K, L(13,2)
REAL M(30)
COMMON J, K, L
EQUIVALENCE (L(1,1),M(1))
```

b)
```
INTEGER J(5), K, L(13,2), M(30)
COMMON J, K, L
EQUIVALENCE (K,M(7))
```

c)
```
INTEGER J(5), K, L(13,2), M(30)
COMMON J, K, L
EQUIVALENCE (J(1),M(1)), (L(1,1),M(8))
```

d)
```
INTEGER LIST(3), MATRIX(2,3), SIX(6)
REAL COEFF, EIGEN(2), FIVE(5)
COMMON LIST, COEFF, MATRIX, EIGEN
EQUIVALENCE (SIX(1),MATRIX(2,2))
```

e)
```
INTEGER LIST(3), MATRIX(2,3), SIX(6)
REAL COEFF, EIGEN(2), FIVE(5)
COMMON LIST, COEFF, MATRIX, EIGEN
EQUIVALENCE (SIX(2),FIVE(3))
EQUIVALENCE (FIVE(1),LIST(1))
EQUIVALENCE (SIX(1),MATRIX(1,1))
```

2.12 What are the contents of the 2 by 2 array A printed by

```
      INTEGER A(2,2), I, J, ARG, Z, FN, FILL
      COMMON Z
      FILL (ARG) = FN(3-ARG)
      Z = 0
      DO 2 I = 1,2
         DO 1 J = 1,2
            A(I,J) = FILL(I+J)
   1     CONTINUE
   2  CONTINUE
      WRITE (6,20) A
  20  FORMAT (1X,2I7)
      STOP
      END
```

```
INTEGER FUNCTION FN(P)
INTEGER P, Z
COMMON Z
FN = P
IF (Z .LE. P) RETURN
FN = Z
Z = Z+1
RETURN
END
```

2.13 It is possible to represent a map of driving distances between cities by an integer array. Consider, for example, the following map.

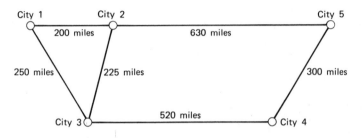

This can be represented by the 5 by 5 array

0	200	250	-1	-1
200	0	225	-1	630
250	225	0	520	-1
-1	-1	520	0	300
-1	630	-1	300	0

Here, -1 indicates an unknown distance. For this assignment, you are to read in an integer value N (N $\leq$ 5) followed by an N by N integer matrix PATHS. Your program is then to check to see if PATHS is a proper representation of a map. (That is, check that PATHS(I,J) = PATH(J,I), for all I, J $\leq$ N.) If it is not proper, terminate. Otherwise, you are to replace all -1 positions with the shortest distance between these two cities. Care must be taken since there may not be any such path. If this is true, leave the value -1. After doing this, print out the array PATHS.

2.14 Write an inventory control program. Based on predefined input commands, it must be able to update an inventory file for new purchases and sales, print inventory reports and print purchase orders. Input to your program starts with a set of zero or more inventory cards, each of the form

Columns	Type of Data
1-9	Part number
11-14	Quantity on stock
16-19	Total number of sales to date
21-27	Wholesale price
31-37	Retail price

The end of all inventory cards is signalled by a card that contains a negative number in the part number field. These inventory cards are followed by a set of command cards, each of the form

Columns	Type of Data
1	Transaction code
6-14	Part number
16-19	Quantity
21-27	Wholesale price
31-37	Retail price

where the transaction code field is interpreted as follows.

Code = 1 - A purchase has been made. The file is to be updated. If this part number has not appeared previously, add it to list, maintaining sorted order by part number. If it has appeared before; ignore retail and wholesale prices as they should remain constant, i.e., just use the quantity field to update our stock on hand value. Print out summary statistics on this activity.

Code = 2 - A sale is to be made. Columns 21 and beyond are ignored. (These columns should be blank.) Check to see if the sale can be satisfied. If not, assume we will sell all remaining stock of this item (if there is any). In either case decrement stock quantity on hand appropriately, and increment total sales.

Code = 3 - Print a list of all items that need to be ordered because of low levels of them on hand. Our criterion is to reorder any part whose stock is less than or equal to three items. A sample reorder notice is given in FORMAT 1.

Code = 4 - Print the complete inventory report. A sample inventory form is shown in FORMAT 2.

Code = 5 - Stop processing. *Note.* In an actual inventory system we might choose to output the current inventory file for future use.

FORMAT 1
PURCHASE ORDER

PART NUMBER	QUANTITY ON HAND	TOTAL SALES	WHOLESALE PRICE	RETAIL PRICE	UNIT PRICE
57256	3	10	28.75	38.88	10.13
64031	0	623	14.25	26.99	22.74

FORMAT 2
INVENTORY REPORT

PART NUMBER	QUANTITY ON HAND	TOTAL SALES	WHOLESALE PRICE	RETAIL PRICE	UNIT PRICE
57256	3	10	28.75	38.99	10.13
57921	542	67	4.75	6.95	2.25
64031	0	623	14.25	26.99	12.74
96021	4	0	425.00	625.00	200.00

CHAPTER 3   Nonarithmetic Programming

3.1   CHARACTERS AS DATA

The FORTRAN language was designed primarily to solve scientific problems. For this reason exponentiation is a built-in operation and square root and trigonometric sine subprograms are supplied by most manufacturers. Nevertheless, the manipulation of characters is an important class of the applications of computers. FORTRAN does not have as powerful a set of direct character manipulating facilities as it does arithmetic facilities. There are thus a series of techniques that programmers have developed for character applications. In this chapter we will show you the techniques and explain their basis so that you can apply them and develop your own.

To clarify the terms we will be using, we call any single symbol a *character*. This symbol may be a letter (A through Z), a digit (0 through 9), or any of a number of extra symbols such as the characters (),.= and "blank space." (We will represent the blank by b in instances where it is necessary to make this symbol visible.) These latter symbols are often called *special characters*. The input and output devices with which you are familiar probably transmit all 26 letters, all 10 digits, and some number of special characters. Some sophisticated devices will allow lowercase letters, numeric subscripts, Greek letters, and other special characters used in certain applications. A series of zero or more characters is called a *character string* or simply a *string*. The *length* of a string is the number of characters of which it is composed.

3.2   CHARACTER ENCODINGS

You should understand that all information stored in computer memory is a pattern of bits; the interpretation and use of these patterns give them meaning. There are several coding schemes by which a character is represented as a pattern of bits. For example, the string of four characters, '1020', is encoded in one word on IBM 360-370 machines as

11110001	11110000	11110020	11110000	binary
'1'	'0'	'2'	'0'	character

Notice that there is no obvious correspondence between the representation of a character string and the representation of an equivalent integer or real.

(The decimal integer 1020 would be represented in binary as 00000000 00000000 00000011 11111100 on this same machine.)

There are three character encoding schemes in general use: BCD (Binary Coded Decimal) represents each of 64 different characters as a 6 bit value, ASCII (American Standard Coding for Information Interchange) encodes each of 128 different characters as a 7 bit value, and EBCDIC (Extended Binary Coded Decimal Interchange Code) uses 8 bits to represent each of 256 different characters. One of these schemes will probably be used in the FORTRAN dialect with which you are working. However, it is generally unimportant for the FORTRAN programmer to know which scheme is used, and it is quite possible to write code that will execute properly under all of these schemes.

Taking two words containing characters, and comparing them as if they contained arithmetic values (integers, for example) induces an ordering on the characters. In all three encodings, the integer representation of the character A is less than that of the character B which is less than that of the character Z . The encoding of the character 0, interpreted as an integer, is less than that of the character 1, which is less than that of the character 9. The arrangement of characters from lowest to highest, when viewed as integers, is called the *collating sequence*. We can use the fact that the collating sequence preserves alphabetic order when we wish to sort character data. The order of the special characters, as well as the relative order of the three groups (special characters, letters, digits), is not consistent between the coding schemes. Thus, you can write programs that are independent of the coding scheme used if you test only whether one string is equal to or not equal to another. Testing for "less than" on special characters produces dialect-dependent code.

In many FORTRAN dialects, there is no "character" data type. Instead, character encodings may be placed in integer, real or logical variables. The codings of several characters will fit in one variable; the number of characters depends on the coding scheme (BCD, ASCII or EBCDIC) used and on the size of the computer word. For example, on the IBM 360-370 computers, EBCDIC (8 bits per character) is used, and the word size is 32 bits; thus 4 characters can be encoded per word. The DEC-10 uses a 36 bit word with ASCII encodings (7 bits per character), yielding 5 characters per word, with the rightmost or "low order" bit unused. Univac 1100 machines use BCD encodings (6 bits per character) in 36 bit words, permitting 6 characters to be represented in a word.

3.3 CHARACTER INPUT AND OUTPUT

The A type format code is used to convert symbols on an external medium to/from internal character encodings, in much the same way that the I type code is used to convert to/from internal integer representation. The A type code has form Aw where w is the width of the field being processed. Assume that an Aw type format code is being used to transfer data to or from a variable which is capable of holding n encoded characters. If the operation is input and $w \leq n$, the character encodings occupy the leftmost w positions of the variable, and the rightmost $(n-w)$ positions are filled with the encoding of blanks. If $w \geq n$ only the rightmost n characters of the input field are encoded in the variable. If the operation is output and $w<n$, the leftmost w characters are transferred. If $w>n$, all n characters are transferred, and the leftmost $(w-n)$ positions of the output field are filled with blanks.

An example should clarify these rules. Suppose the machine being used allows five characters per integer word. Execution of the following READ/FORMAT pair

```
        READ (IN,100) INCH1, INCH2, INCH3
    100 FORMAT (A3, A5, A8)

        DATA CARD: CATZEBRADOGHOUSE
```

causes the following values to be assigned to these variables. (The results will be shown in character form, not as their numeric encodings. The character b will be used to denote a blank space.)

    INCH1: CATbb   INCH2: ZEBRA   INCH3: HOUSE

Output of the contents of these variables using FORMAT 101 yields the following output.

```
        WRITE (IOUT,101) INCH1, INCH2, INCH3
    101 FORMAT (1X,'OUTPUT = **', A4, A5, A8, '**')

    OUTPUT = **CAT ZEBRA   HOUSE**
```

In practice, unless you have specific need to remember these rules, we suggest that you remember the following more logical suggestions.

1. If your computer can represent n characters per word, use FORMAT codes Aw where $w \leq n$. If you want additional blanks on output, get them with X format codes.
2. Be consistent; if you input under an Aw format code, then output as Aw also. This eliminates concern over the number of significant characters and their positions in a variable.
3. In applications where this is feasible, many programmers choose one packing density, say A4, and use that on all variables that hold character data.

3.4   CHARACTER CONSTANTS

Character constants may generally be represented in two ways. First, a character constant may be as a string of characters preceded by the letter "H", with the H preceded by the length of the string (excluding the H). The other manner is to enclose the string in single quotes (apostrophes), representing an apostrophe in the string by two apostrophes (only one of these two is preserved in the character constant itself). Of these two methods, only the first is standard; however, because it is cumbersome and error-prone to count characters, most compilers also allow the latter. Below are some examples of character constants and the strings they represent.

```
CONSTANTS:    '*'    4HPL/I    10H'TAIN'T SO    '''TIS TOO'
REPRESENT:     *     PL/I       'TAIN'T SO       'TIS TOO
```

In the 1966 FORTRAN standards, such constants are legal only in three contexts: in DATA initialization statements, as items in FORMAT statements, or as arguments of subprograms. However, some compilers will tolerate character constants in more places and, in FORTRAN 77, this restriction is relaxed. (See Section 3.8 for more information on character manipulation under FORTRAN 77.)

3.5   CHARACTER OPERATIONS

Once data has been placed in a variable, the variable can be manipulated using arithmetic or logical operations. For example, if STR1 and STR2 are two integer variables containing character data, then the statements

STR1=STR2   and   IF (STR1 .EQ. STR2)

are meaningful and legal. Because the encoding of a string of numeric digits is unrelated to the representation of those digits as a real or an integer value,

STR1=10.*STR2   or   IF (STR1 .EQ. 10)

is not meaningful and will not produce the desired results. Also, since the same pattern of bits is interpreted differently as a real or as an integer, the following comparison will fail.

```
INTEGER ISTR/4HSAME/
REAL RSTR/4HSAME/
IF (ISTR .EQ. RSTR)
```

Although the bit patterns in ISTR and RSTR are the same, the comparison fails because their interpretations as integer or real values differ.

Sensible programmers adopt the policy of keeping all character data in variables of the same type. Logical type is limiting, since it is not legal to compare two such variables for equality, less than, etc. On most machines integer operations (assignment, comparison) can be done at least as fast as real and normally faster. Thus we recommend this technique.

> Characters should be stored only in variables of one type; this type will generally be integer.

3.6   EXAMPLE: FORMAT-FREE INTEGER INPUT

A common computing activity is to read input values and process them. In some applications it is reasonable to have these values in certain fixed positions on the card. However, it is often easier for the user if you allow these numbers to be punched in any locations on the card. This is especially true when you are dealing with inexperienced computer users who do not appreciate the serious consequences of being one column off in the punching or of not right-justifying values in specified fields.

When an integer value is being converted under I format input, these three actions occur.

1. Locate and analyze the sequence of characters within the designated field.
2. Calculate the binary value equivalent to the integer represented by those characters.
3. Store the binary value in a specified variable.

We wish to achieve this effect, except we will relax the first restriction. Instead of using characters from prespecified columns on the card, we will begin at any user-specified location on the card and use the first contiguous string of numeric characters found.

Note that an I or F type format code is inappropriate here, because we do not require the input to be in fixed card positions. Thus, we will be doing most of the work done by the format processor—converting a number represented on the 80 columns of an input card into the equivalent binary internal form. Actually, our task is the same as is performed under free-format I/O.

The steps to be performed are:

1. Locate the first character of the number to be converted (i.e., the first non-blank punch on the card).
2. Locate the end of the string of characters representing the number to be converted (i.e., find the first non-digit after the first nonblank or the end of the card, whichever comes first).
3. Compute the integer represented by this sequence of characters.

The first step is a straightforward process. It is essentially a sequential table lookup, where the table elements are the columns of the input card. We will be looking for anything that could be the first character of a number: a sign or a digit. We wish to ignore blanks until we find this proper first character. The lookup fails if there is a character that is neither a sign nor a digit, or if the end of the card is reached before finding a nonblank. If the lookup fails, we will stop the conversion process and produce a value of zero for the output integer.

The second step is also simple. All we need to do is to examine each character after the first. Situations that can occur are (1) non-digit found, (2) end of card reached, and (3) too many digits found. The first case is a normal termination, and the location of this non-digit separator should be noted in case we wish to search for a subsequent value on the same card. The second case is another form of normal termination. This one must be noted so that no later searches will be made for data on this card. The third case, however, is an error. There is a fixed limit on the maximum size of an integer; this limit will vary between different computers, being based on the word size of the machine. We will use the arbitrary figure of nine decimal digits, because most large-scale computers can represent all nine-digit integers in one word.

The third step can be done easily. There are really two phases to this step. First, we must find a way to pair each numeric character with the equivalent binary integer. Second, we must combine these separate integers into one result. The first phase merely amounts to a table lookup. To the character '0', we want to match the integer 0; to the character '1', the integer 1; etc. Notice that since the character '1' and the integer 1 have different internal representations, we must bring about this correspondence ourselves. (There is a relationship between the representations, but it is machine dependent.)

This correspondence can be achieved through a two-dimensional array, one column of which contains the character forms of the digits '0' through '9', and the other column of which contains the integer to which each character corresponds.

character	represents
'0'	0
'1'	1
...	...
'9'	9

Observe that each value in the second column of this table equals the row number minus 1. Thus the second column is unnecessary, since its elements can be readily computed by subtracting 1 from the subscript value. We will use this technique in our program.

Let us now consider the second phase of the last step—that of combining the integers corresponding to the digits of some number. Let the number be the character string C1C2...Cn and let i1,i2,...,in be the integers corresponding to characters C1,C2,...,Cn. The value of this string is

$$i_n + 10*i_{n-1} + 100*i_{n-2} + ... + 10^{n-2}*i_2 + 10^{n-1}*i_1$$

We can thus work from right to left, multiplying by successively higher powers of 10. Another more convenient technique is to rearrange the formula above,

$$10^{n-1}*i_1 + 10^{n-2}*i_2 + ... + 10^2*i_{n-2} + 10^1*i_{n-1} + i_n$$

and regroup multiplications

$$((...(((i_1)*10 + i_2)*10 + i_3) ...*10 + i_{n-1})*10 + i_n)$$

This leads to the obvious loop-oriented algorithm.

1. TERM=0;
2. DO INDEX=1 to N:
   TERM=TERM*10 + I(INDEX)

This algorithm has several advantages over the approach noted first.

1. The digits are scanned left to right, making the program a bit easier to comprehend.
2. It is not necessary to run a prepass across the data to find the right end of the digit string.
3. Only n multiplications are needed. Under the previous approach, the calculation of each 10**k factor could involve up to k multiplications, or an exponentiation, depending on the technique chosen. This 10**k factor would then have to be multiplied by the I(k) value. Thus at least 2*n multiplications or exponentiations would previously have been needed. Both of these operations are costly of machine time, and so it is worthwhile to try to eliminate them.

These are nontrivial concerns. As we noted in Chapter 1, from an efficiency standpoint it is wiser to select a good algorithm and to implement it in a straightforward manner, rather than to select a bad algorithm and then try to compensate with tricky and unreadable code. A subroutine implementing this algorithm is shown in Figure 3-1.

This program needs little discussion since the code reflects the design decisions made before the program was developed. Note, however, that the only reference to the input length being 80 is in the first data initialization statement; all subsequent uses of this value access variable ENDCOL. Thus, if it should be convenient later to consider only the first 72 columns of a card, this change could be effected easily. It would not be necessary to search through the program locating all statements containing the value 80, or to

```
      SUBROUTINE EDCHIN (CARD, COL, INT, ERFLAG)
C * * EDCHIN * * EDIT CHARACTERS TO INTEGERS * * * * * * * * * * * * * * S
C
C     INPUT:
C         CARD: AN ARRAY OF 80 CHARACTERS, REPRESENTING THE
C             COLUMNS OF A CARD, ONE CHARACTER PER ELEMENT
C         COL:  THE POSITION WITHIN "CARD" WHERE THE SEARCH
C             FOR A NUMERIC STRING IS TO BEGIN
C
C     OUTPUT:
C         COL:  THE POSITION WITHIN "CARD" WHERE THE SEARCH
C             FOR MORE NUMERIC CHARACTERS STOPPED.
C             A. COL=81 IF NO NON-DIGIT IS FOUND TO STOP THE
C                SEARCH AFTER COLUMN 80 HAD BEEN EXAMINED.
C             B. COL=THE POSITION OF THE CHARACTER AFTER THE LAST
C                OF A SERIES OF NUMERIC CHARACTERS, IF ANY FOUND.
C         INT:  THE BINARY VALUE EQUIVALENT TO
C             THE NUMERIC STRING FOUND.
C             A. INT=0 IF NO INTEGER LOCATED BEFORE
C                THE FIRST ILLEGAL CHARACTER
C             B. INT=THE VALUE REFLECTED BY THE FIRST 9 DIGITS IF
C                A STRING LONGER THAN 9 DIGITS WAS FOUND.
C             C. INT=THE INTEGER IF A LEGAL ONE WAS FOUND.
C         ERFLAG:  A FLAG TO REPORT ERROR CONDITIONS ENCOUNTERED
C             A. ERFLAG=-1 IF NO DIGITS FOUND
C             B. ERFLAG= 0 IF NORMAL INTEGER FOUND AND CONVERTED
C             C. ERFLAG=+1 IF MORE THAN 9 DECIMAL DIGITS FOUND
C
C     METHOD:
C         COLUMN BY COLUMN THE ARRAY IS EXAMINED, LOOKING FOR
C         A. ONE OR MORE BLANKS, WHICH ARE IGNORED
C         B. AN OPTIONAL SIGN (+ OR -) WHICH DETERMINES THE SIGN
C            OF THE RESULT INTEGER.
C         C. A DIGIT WHICH BEGINS THE SEARCH FOR A CONTIGUOUS
C            STRING OF NUMERIC CHARACTERS.
C         D. AN ILLEGAL CHARACTER (ANYTHING OTHER THAN ONE OF THE ABOVE)
C            WHICH TERMINATES EXECUTION OF THE SUBPROGRAM.
C         ONCE THE FIRST DIGIT IS FOUND, THEN ONLY MORE DIGITS
C            ARE ALLOWED; NO BLANKS AND NO SIGNS ARE LEGAL
C         A MAXIMUM OF 9 DIGITS IS USED.
C
C     PROGRAMMER: ---              DATE: ---
C
C * * * * * * * * * * * * * * * * * * * * * * * * * * * * * * * * * * F
C
      INTEGER CARD(80),COL,INT,ENDCOL,ERFLAG
      INTEGER PLUS,MINUS,BLANK,SIGN,END,DFIND
      DATA PLUS/'+'/,MINUS/'-'/,BLANK/' '/,ENDCOL/80/
      SIGN=+1
      ERFLAG=-1
      INT=0
C          CHECK FOR LEGALILTY OF INITIAL VALUE OF COL
      IF (COL .GT. ENDCOL) GO TO 99
C
C          BEGIN SEARCH FOR FIRST DIGIT
   10 DO 20 I=COL,ENDCOL
         IF (CARD(I) .EQ. MINUS) GO TO 30
         IF (CARD(I) .EQ. PLUS) GO TO 35
         IF (CARD(I) .NE. BLANK) GO TO 40
C             IF NOT BLANK OR SIGN, THEN WE HAVE EITHER A DIGIT OR
C             AN ILLEGAL CHARACTER.  DECIDE LATER
   20 CONTINUE
C             IF FALL OUT, ALL COLUMNS WERE BLANK.
C             ERROR RETURN
      COL = ENDCOL+1
      RETURN
C
C          HERE HAVE FOUND MINUS SIGN
   30 SIGN = -1
C          HERE HAVE FOUND PLUS OR MINUS SIGN.
C          IF PLUS, "SIGN" WAS SET PROPERLY ON ENTRY
C          GO TO NEXT COLUMN IN EITHER CASE
   35 I = I+1
C          TAKE CARE SIGN ISN'T IN LAST COLUMN
```

```
         IF (I .GT. ENDCOL) RETURN
C
C             BEGIN SEARCH FOR STRING OF DIGITS ONLY (AT MOST 9)
   40 END = MINO (ENDCOL, I+8)
      DO 50 J=I,END
C             CALL FOR LOOKUP OF A DIGIT.
C             ROUTINE RETURNS INTEGER 0 TO 9 IF DIGIT FOUND,
C             RETURNS -1 IF NON-DIGIT FOUND.
         M = DFIND (CARD(J))
C             IF HAVE FOUND NON-DIGIT, STOP NOW;
C             ELSE ACCUMULATE VALUE AND PROCEED.
         IF (M .LT. 0) GO TO 60
         INT = 10*INT + M
         ERFLAG=0
   50 CONTINUE
C
C             IF FALL OUT, END OF CARD OR 9 CONSECUTIVE DIGITS FOUND.
C             MOVE TO FIRST NON-DIGIT OR END OF CARD.
      IF (END .LT. ENDCOL) GO TO 55
C             CASE 1: END OF CARD; IMMEDIATE HALT
         J = ENDCOL+1
         GO TO 60
C
C      IF (END .LT. ENDCOL)
C             CASE 2: 9 DIGITS CONVERTED; FIND NEXT NON-DIGIT
   55 END = END+1
      J = END
C             IF TENTH CHARACTER NON-DIGIT, STRING ACCEPTABLE
      IF (DFIND(CARD(J) .EQ. -1) GO TO 60
      ERFLAG=+1
      DO 58 J = END,ENDCOL
         IF (DFIND(CARD(J)) .LT. 0) GO TO 60
   58 CONTINUE
C             IF FALL OUT, HAVE REACHED END OF CARD
      J = ENDCOL+1
C
C             RETURN INTEGER VALUE COMPUTED
   60 INT = INT*SIGN
      COL = J
      RETURN
C
C             ILLEGAL "COL" VALUE; RETURN VALUE 0 WITH
C             COL = LAST-CARD-COLUMN + 1
   99 INT = 0
      COL = ENDCOL+1
      ERFLAG = -1
      RETURN
      END


      INTEGER FUNCTION DFIND (CHAR)
C
C      THIS ROUTINE RECEIVES A SINGLE CHARACTER INPUT,
C         DETERMINES IF THAT CHARACTER IS A DIGIT,
C         AND RETURNS THE INTEGER EQUIVALENT TO THAT DIGIT CHARACTER
C      A NON-DIGIT CAUSES RETURN OF -1
C      OPERATION IS BY TABLE LOOKUP IN THE TABLE "DIGIT"
C      NOTE THAT CHARACTER '0' IS THE 1ST TABLE ENTRY, '1' IS THE 2ND,
C         AND SIMILARLY FOR OTHER DIGIT CHARACTERS.
C         THUS, IF A CHARACTER MATCHES A TABLE ENTRY,
C         ITS INTEGER VALUE IS 1 MORE THAN ITS TABLE LOCATION.
C
      INTEGER CHAR, DIGIT(10)
      DATA DIGIT/'0','1','2','3','4','5','6','7','8','9'/
C             FIRST TAKE DEFAULT VALUE
      DFIND = -1
C
C             LOOK UP CHARACTER;
C             IF FOUND, NOTE ITS POSITION
      DO 10 I = 1, 10
         IF (CHAR .EQ. DIGIT(I)) DFIND = I-1
   10 CONTINUE
      RETURN
      END
```

FIGURE 3-1 Character to Integer Conversion Routine

136

suffer the problems of debugging when one reference to the ending column was missed. The ending column could also be made a parameter. Similarly, notice that the digit lookup has been confined to a separate subprogram, DFIND. This is partly for readability and partly because this DFIND module might have use elsewhere. These suggestions can be summarized as follows.

1. Write programs that are as general as is reasonable (without, of course, grotesquely affecting the structure or the efficiency).
2. Plan programs for convenient modification. Anticipate what will be likely changes and structure code so that you or someone else can readily see how to make these changes. Make separate segments out of those portions that could be useful elsewhere.

3.7 OTHER CHARACTER MANIPULATING TECHNIQUES

We conclude this segment on representing one character per word with a discussion of techniques to perform more complex character operations. We will examine especially a technique for performing concatenation (joining together of two character strings) and for locating substrings.

We have been using a single-dimension array to represent a string of characters. If we wish an array of strings of characters, we use a two-dimensional array. Suppose we wish an array of at most 200 names, and each name is at most 25 characters long. Then

```
INTEGER NAME (25,200)
```

can be used to store these characters. Notice that it is immaterial to most applications whether the array is 25 by 200 or 200 by 25. However, since FORTRAN arrays are stored by columns, and since most references to this array will be for all the characters of one name, it makes more sense to store the characters in the order they will normally be accessed. Thus the dimension shown above is preferable.

Now in order to read the Nth name, for a predetermined value of N, we execute

```
READ (-,-) (NAME(I,N),I=1,25)
```

Similarly, to test if the Kth and the (K+1)th names are the same, we perform

```
          DO 50 J = 1,25
              IF (NAME(J,K) .NE. NAME(J,K+1)) GO TO 400
       50 CONTINUE
    C                    THE NAMES ARE THE SAME IF
    C                    LOOP TERMINATED NORMALLY
```

The process of concatenation is not quite so simple. To concatenate two strings, we need an array large enough to hold both of them, and then we need to move them to adjacent positions in that array. This move needs to be done element by element. Suppose that strings STRA and STRB are to be concatenated, and that the lengths of STRA and STRB are contained in variables LENA and LENB, respectively. If the result of this concatenation is to be stored in array STRC and the length is to be placed in LENC, the following segment of code can be used.

```
         IF (LENA)  99,     20,      11
C                   ERROR, NO STRA, NORMAL
   11    DO 15 I = 1, LENA
         STRC(I) = STRA(I)
   15    CONTINUE
   20 IF (LENB)  99,     40,      21
C                   ERROR, NO STRB, NORMAL
   21    DO 25 I = 1, LENB
         STRC(I+LENA) = STRB(I)
   25    CONTINUE
   40 LENC = LENA + LENB
         ...
C              ERROR: LENA<0 OR LENB<0
   99 ...
```

The length value stored with each string is important in this implementation. It is just an integer variable, the same as the elements of the character string. In order to aid in debugging and to localize references to memory during execution, we can keep the length of a string in the first element of the array, and store the actual characters in the second and following elements. Thus a 5 character string 'HELLO' might be represented in a 6 element integer array A as

5	'H'	'E'	'L'	'L'	'O'

Note that for readability it may be desirable to use different names for the length and for the characters themselves, such as LENA and STRA in the above example. This can be accomplished conveniently through an EQUIVALENCE, as in this example:

```
INTEGER A(101), LENA, STRA(100)
EQUIVALENCE (A(1),LENA), (A(2),STRA(1))
```

This organization facilitates debugging, since all information about string "A" is contained in one set of locations and can be conveniently dumped in one statement.

Another convenient tool in character manipulation is the substring operation. A substring of a string is any contiguous portion of the string, including the string itself. One common character manipulation task is to look for a substring matching a particular pattern, such as finding a substring consisting solely of blanks, or locating the longest substring of a string that contains no occurrences of the character '?'. Algorithms to solve these problems should be obvious and will not be examined further here.

Other uses of the substring operation include assignment (assigning to one variable a particular substring of another variable) and replacement (replacing a substring of one variable with another substring). A technique to achieve replacements will be demonstrated in the last example of this chapter. Here we will consider how to assign to one variable a substring of another.

Substrings are usually identified as "the substring of string X beginning with the Ith character, for a length of J characters," with appropriate values for I and J. Let us assume the representation of strings as arrays, with a length variable and a sequence of elements containing one character each. We want to assign to the string DEST the substring of string SOURCE beginning at position POS for a length contained in variable SUBLEN. Assume the lengths of DEST and SOURCE are contained in variables DSTLEN and SRCLEN, respectively. The following code will accomplish our desired task.

```
      IF((POS+SUBLEN-1) .GT. SRCLEN) GO TO 999
C         ERROR: STRING SHORTER THAN DESIRED SUBSTRING
C
      DO 10 I=1,SUBLEN
         DEST(I) = SOURCE(POS+I-1)
   10 CONTINUE
      DSTLEN = SUBLEN
```

Programs using the technique of storing one character in each integer variable have one primary advantage: they will run correctly on any machine that accepts at least the full 1966 ANS FORTRAN standard. You can then use any readily accessible computer to debug programs destined to run on a small, limited-access machine. You can also write code to be exchanged among users of several different computers. This advantage can be achieved under few other languages. However, it leads to cumbersome programming, as we will see in the next section.

3.8 CHARACTER DATA TYPE— WATFIV AND FORTRAN 77

The technique just outlined requires much code to achieve rather simple operations. Merely to move a string requires a loop and many subscript references. Simple and readable comparisons (e.g. IF(X .EQ. 'HOUSE')) are not legal, nor are natural assignments (Y='ALPHA'). These circumstances are understandable from a historic perspective, since character manipulation facilities were not in the original design of the FORTRAN language. Compilers accepting only the character features presented so far are likely to be available for some time, and adhering to those features does produce code that is widely transportable.

However, programmers have sought compilers containing more natural character manipulation facilities. A widely used compiler that has extended character manipulation facilities is the student-oriented WATFIV compiler from The University of Waterloo. In fact the facilities in that compiler are so sensible that they have been drafted almost without change into FORTRAN 77.

One of the added features is a CHARACTER data type. This addition puts character strings on an equal level with integer or real numeric values. There is thus a CHARACTER statement, similar to an INTEGER or REAL statement, by which you declare certain variables to be of CHARACTER type. It is also possible to declare on this statement a length for each variable. The length is specified as a constant value, preceded by a *. The length may either follow the word CHARACTER (in which case it indicates the length of each variable on that statement) or it may follow the name of a variable (in which case it tells the length of that variable alone, overriding any length specified after the word CHARACTER.) If no length is given on a CHARACTER statement, CHARACTER*1 is assumed. The following examples show how character variables are declared.

```
CHARACTER*5 STRG1, STRG2
CHARACTER NAME*20, ADDR*30, CITY*23, STATE*2, ZIP*5
CHARACTER    LETR, ALPH*26, DIGIT
```

The first example declares two character variables, each containing 5 characters. The second declares five variables, to contain 20, 30, 23, 2, and 5 characters, respectively. The last declares LETR and DIGIT to each contain one character, and ALPH to contain 26.

It is also possible to declare arrays of character variables, with meaning analogous to numeric arrays. For example, the following declares NAME to be an array of 100 elements, each of which is a string of 20 characters.

```
CHARACTER*20  NAME (100)
```

3.8.1 Character Constants

Given a character data mode, it is natural to inquire what are the constants in that data type, and what are the operations. Character constants are as described previously: a string of characters enclosed within apostrophes; in such a string, the character "apostrophe" is represented as two successive apostrophes. However, character constants may appear in more contexts than previously indicated. A character constant may be used as before in a FORMAT statement, in a data initialization statement, or as a subprogram argument. In addition, a character constant can be used as the right side of an assignment statement or as a term in a logical IF comparison. Thus statements like IF(STR1 .LT. 'A') and STR2 = 'ABC' are now legal.

As before, the value of a character string is not the same as an integer constant, a real constant or a variable name. Thus statements such as IF ('500' .EQ. 500) or A='A+1' may be syntactically acceptable to some compilers, but they are not what they appear to be at first glance.

A CHARACTER*n variable will have a string of exactly n characters as its value. (The value is, of course, unpredictable if the variable has never been given a value.)

If the value being assigned to a CHARACTER*n variable is longer than n characters, only the leftmost n characters are used; if the value is shorter than n characters, the rightmost positions of the variable are filled with blanks. The same rule applies regardless of whether the value is a variable or a constant. Let STR4A and STR4B be CHARACTER*4 variables; then both of the following statements assign the same value to STR4A, and likewise to STR4B.

```
STR4A = 'ABCDEF'          STR4B = 'XYZ'
STR4A = 'ABCD'            STR4B = 'XYZ '
```

In comparisons, the shorter operand is considered as if it were padded on the right with blanks to the length of the longer operand.

A variable that is CHARACTER*n is an inseparable block of n characters. Assignment replaces all n characters of the value; comparison tests all n characters (plus any blanks to pad a short operand.) It is possible, however, to use an EQUIVALENCE to permit examination or modification of one character out of a CHARACTER*n variable.

Consider a CHARACTER*20 variable CITY that has been used as a block of 20 characters for alphabetic sorting. Now, however, we wish to output only the city name, ignoring any blanks on the right to fill the value to 20 characters. The following code locates the rightmost nonblank, thereby determining the precise length of the city's name.

```
      CHARACTER*20 CITY
      CHARACTER*1 C1(20)
      EQUIVALENCE (CITY, C1(1))
      DO 10 I = 1, 20
         IF (C1(21-I) .NE. ' ') GO TO 20
   10 CONTINUE
    C                    +++ ERROR - STRING ALL BLANK
         :
         :
    C                    ... FOUND LAST NON-BLANK
   20 LNBLNK = 21-I
```

In this code we use an equivalence to force the following two variables to begin at the same point in memory.

(1) CITY, which occupies the next 20 consecutive character positions in memory.
(2) C1, an array of 20 contiguous elements, each occupying one character position.

It is clear that these variables both reference the same memory locations, so the value of one is the value of the other. However, each CHARACTER*1 array element is a single character from the value of the CITY string. Thus we have the best of two worlds; we can manipulate 20 characters at once under the name CITY, and we can operate on any single character from that string as the elements of array C1.

3.9   EXAMPLES

We conclude this chapter with examples of two utility programs. The first can be used to produce a printed document describing each of the modules of a program. The second can be used to reformat the source text of a program to reflect the control flow of the program more clearly; it will perform tasks such as indenting the bodies of DO loops and changing one variable name to another. Both of these programs make extensive use of character manipulations.

In the first example, we will construct a Program Logic Manual (or PLM). We have explained the purpose and contents of such a document in Chapter 1. For review, that should contain one section for each module of the program; this section will outline the module's function, its algorithm, names and uses of arguments and major variables, entry and exit conditions, names of modules called by this module, and names of modules that call this module.

Clearly this information cannot be readily determined by a program. This information is, however, precisely the information we normally show in the comment blocks at the top of each module. It is valuable as a part of the source listing to help in debugging and to aid in understanding a program. Furthermore, the form of this documentation can readily be made recognizable. We will design a program that accepts the source code of another program and extracts comments to form a PLM.

First we must settle on the form in which the block comments will be entered so that we can select only those comments which comprise the module description. This form is, of course, arbitrary, so we will use something like this.

```
C * * NAME (ARG1, ARG2, ...., ARGN) * * * * * * * * * * * * * * * * * *
C   SUBROUTINE   "NAME"                                                *
C   ENTRY CONDITIONS ...                                               *
C   EXIT CONDITIONS ... ETC.                                           *
C * * * * * * * * * * * * * * * * * * * * * * * * * * * * * * * * * *  F
```

In the first line, *name* will be the name of the module, and the *arg*'s will be symbolic arguments. In case this module is the main program, the first line will be filled with alternating asterisks and blanks. The *t* in column 71 will be either M (start of a main program), S (start of a subprogram), or or E (entry point of a subprogram). The comment block will be terminated by C * * in columns 1 to 6 and F (finish) column 71.

1. Read a card. If none remains, halt.
2. Are columns 1-6 'C * * ' ? No, go to step 1.
3. Is column 72 = 'F'? Yes, go to step 1.
4. Replace NAME by the contents of columns 7 through 12.
5. Is column 72 = 'M'? Yes, then NAME = 'M/PROG'.
6. Is column 72 = 'M' or 'S', or are there fewer than 5 lines left on the current page? Yes, then skip to a new page.
7. Print columns 1-72 of the card, replacing column 1 and column 72 by blanks.
8. Read a card; if none left, halt.
9. Are columns 1-6='C * * '? Yes, go to step 1. No, are there any lines left on current page? No, skip to new page.
10. Column 1=' ', column 72=' '.
11. Go to step 7.

Notice within this module outline that the IF-THEN, IF-THEN-ELSE construct has been heavily used. We will place the output section in a separate subprogram. This is for two reasons. First, we can write this module trivially (one WRITE statement and a RETURN) at first just to test the rest of the program; then, when things are running well, we can worry more about the aesthetics of formatting the output. Second, this routine is a separable body of related code. By removing it from the main program, we reduce the length of the main program and simultaneously increase its understandability. As we noted in Chapter 1, routines should ideally be short enough that the code of a major section fits on a single page of a source listing. One way to reduce the apparent length of a module is to make judicious use of subprograms.

The program to implement this algorithm is shown in Figure 3-2.

A portion of the output of this program is shown in Figure 3-3. The program has been run on itself to produce a PLM for the PLM producing program.

```
C * * * * * * * * * * * * * * * * * * * * * * * * * * * * * * * * * * * M
C
C     PROGRAM LOGIC MANUAL  (PLM)   PRODUCING PROGRAM
C
C     THIS PROGRAM TAKES A BLOCK OF PROGRAM SOURCE CODE, AND EXTRACTS
C        THE BLOCK COMMENTS OF EACH ROUTINE TO PRODUCE A PLM.
C
C     LOGIC FLOW:
C        CARDS ARE READ LOOKING FOR THE SEQUENCE 'C * * ' IN COLUMNS 1-6.
C        IF FOUND, THEN THIS MARKS THE START OF A BLOCK OF COMMENTS.
C        THEN COLUMN 72 IS INSPECTED TO DETERMINE IF THIS IS A
C           MAIN PROGRAM (COL. 72 = 'M')
C           SUB PROGRAM (COL. 72 = 'S')
C           ENTRY POINT (COL. 72 = 'E')
C        IF A MAIN PROGRAM, THEN THE NAME OF THE MODULE BECOMES 'M/PROG'.
C        IF A SUBPROGRAM OR ENTRY POINT, THEN THE NAME BECOMES THE
C           ALPHABETIC STRING LISTED IN COLUMNS 7-12.  THIS NAME IS
C           PRINTED AT THE TOP OF EACH PAGE OF THE PLM.
C        LISTING OF STATEMENTS OF THE PLM CONTINUES UNTIL THE NEXT CARD
C           CONTAINING 'C * * ' IN COLUMNS 1-6 AND 'F' IN COLUMN 72.
C        THEN THE SEARCH RESUMES FOR THE FIRST CARD OF THE COMMENT BLOCK
C           OF A NEW PROGRAM MODULE.
C
C     MAJOR VARIABLES:
C        NAME:   NAME OF MODULE (MAIN PROGRAM, SUBPROGRAM OR ENTRY POINT)
C        LINE:   CARD MOST RECENTLY READ.  THROUGH EQUIVALENCES, THIS
C                NAME ALSO REFERS TO:
C           COL:    A CHARACTER*1 ARRAY OF 72 ELEMENTS
C           C1TO6:  A CHARACTER*6 VARIABLE REFERING TO COLUMNS 1-6.
C           C7TO12: A CHARACTER*6 VARIABLE REFERING TO COLUMNS 7-12.
C        PAGENO: NUMBER TO BE PRINTED AT THE TOP OF THE CURRENT PAGE
C        LINCNT: COUNT OF LINES REMAINING ON CURRENT PAGE
C
C     SUBPROGRAMS CALLED:
C        OUTPUT: TO FORMAT AND PRINT THE NEXT LINE OF OUTPUT
C        HEADER: TO BEGIN NEXT PAGE AND RESET LINE COUNT
C
C     STATEMENT FUNCTIONS:
C        LETTER(C): -LOGICAL- TESTS IF CHARACTER "C" IS A LETTER
C        DIGIT(C):  -LOGICAL- TESTS IF CHARACTER "C" IS A DIGIT
C        **NOTE** BOTH OF THESE FUNCTIONS ARE DEPENDENT ON THE EBCDIC
C                 AND ASCII CODING SCHEME WHERE NO CHARACTERS OTHER
C                 THAN LETTERS (DIGITS) APPEAR BETWEEN 'A' AND 'Z'
C                 ('0' AND '9', RESPECTIVELY).
C
C     PROGRAMMER: ---               DATE: ---
C
C * * * * * * * * * * * * * * * * * * * * * * * * * * * * * * * * * * * F
      INTEGER PAGENO, IRDR
      LOGICAL LETTER, DIGIT
      CHARACTER LINE*72, COL*1(72), NAM1*1(6), C*1
      CHARACTER*6 C1TO6, C7TO12, NAME
      EQUIVALENCE (LINE,COL(1),C1TO6), (COL(7),C7TO12), (NAME,NAM1(1))
      DATA IRDR/5/
C
C                STATEMENT FUNCTION DEFINITIONS:
      LETTER(C) = (C.GE.'A' .AND. C.LE.'Z')
      DIGIT(C) = (C.GE.'0' .AND. C.LE.'9')
C
      LINCNT = 0
      PAGENO = 1
```

144

```
C
C       *** MAIN PROGRAM LOOP ***
C
C                  READ A CARD, AND SEE IF IT BEGINS NEW COMMENT BLOCK
  100 READ(IRDR,101,END=999) LINE
  101 FORMAT(A72)
      IF (C1TO6 .NE. 'C * * ') GO TO 100
C
C                  HAVE FOUND START OF NEW COMMENT BLOCK
C                  BEGIN SEARCH FOR NEW PROGRAM MODULE NAME
      NAME = ' '
      DO 200 I = 7,12
         IF (.NOT.LETTER(COL(I)) .AND. .NOT.DIGIT(COL(I))) GO TO 250
         NAM1(I-6) = COL(I)
  200 CONTINUE
C                  NOW HAVE COLLECTED AT MOST 6 CHARACTERS FOR NAME
  250 IF (COL(72) .EQ. 'M') NAME = 'M/PROG'
C
C                  BEGIN NEW OUTPUT PAGE IF (A) NEW MAIN PROGRAM OR
C                  (B) NEW SUBPROGRAM OR (C) NEW ENTRY AND FEWER THAN 5
C                  LINES REMAIN ON CURRENT PAGE.
      IF (COL(72).EQ.'M' .OR. COL(72).EQ.'S' .OR. LINCNT .LT.5)
     1    CALL HEADER (NAME, PAGENO, LINCNT)
C
C                  FORMAT AND PRINT SINGLE LINE OF PLM
  275 CALL OUTPUT (COL, LINCNT, PAGENO, NAME)
C                  GET NEW LINE AND CONTINUE PRINTING
C                  UNTIL REACH FINISH OF COMMENT BLOCK
      READ (IRDR,101,END=999) LINE
      IF (C1TO6.EQ.'C * * ' .AND. COL(72).EQ.'F') GO TO 100
      GO TO 275
C
  999 STOP
      END
      SUBROUTINE OUTPUT (COL, LINCNT, PAGENO, NAME)
C
C * * OUTPUT * * FORMAT AND PRINT OUTPUT LINES  * * * * * * * * * * * S
C
C   SUBPROGRAM TO FORMAT AND PRINT ONE LINE OF A PLM
C
C   INPUT ARGUMENTS:
C     COL:    THE LINE TO BE PRINTED - CHARACTER*1 ARRAY OF 72 ELEMENTS
C     LINCNT: COUNT OF LINES REMAINING ON CURRENT OUTPUT PAGE
C     PAGENO: NUMBER OF CURRENT OUTPUT PAGE
C     NAME:   NAME OF CURRENT PROGRAM MODULE
C
C   OUTPUT ARGUMENTS:
C     LINCNT: REVISED TO REFLECT LINES REMAINING AFTER PRINTING
C             DESIRED LINE
C     PAGENO: INCREMENTED IF A NEW PAGE HAD TO BE STARTED
C
C   ACTIONS: CHARACTER "C" BLANKED OUT FROM POSITION 1 OF LINE,
C            COLUMN 72 ALSO CHANGED TO BLANK.
C
C * * * * * * * * * * * * * * * * * * * * * * * * * * * * * * * * * * F
      INTEGER LINCNT, PAGENO, IPRT
      CHARACTER COL*1(72), NAME*6
      DATA IPRT/6/
C
C                  IS THERE ROOM ON CURRENT PAGE?
      IF (LINCNT .LT. 1) CALL HEADER(NAME, PAGENO, LINCNT)
C
```

```
      COL(1) = ' '
      COL(72) = ' '
      WRITE (IPRT,100) COL
100   FORMAT(1X,72A1)
      LINCNT = LINCNT-1
      RETURN
      END

      SUBROUTINE HEADER (NAME,PAGENO,LINCNT)
C * * HEADER * * OUTPUT PAGE HEADINGS * * * * * * * * * * * * * * * S
C
C  FORMAT AND PRINT PAGE HEADINGS
C
C  INPUT ARGUMENTS
C    NAME:   NAME OF CURRENT PROGRAM MODULE
C    PAGENO: NUMBER TO AFFIX TO PAGE HEADING FOR NEW PAGE
C
C  OUTPUT ARGUMENTS:
C    PAGENO: VALUE FOR NEXT OUTPUT PAGE NUMBER (INPUT VALUE OF
C            PAGENO + 1).
C    LINCNT: COUNT OF LINES WHICH MAY BE PRINTED ON NEW PAGE
C
C * * * * * * * * * * * * * * * * * * * * * * * * * * * * * * * * * F
C
      INTEGER PAGENO, LINCNT, IPRT, MAXLN
      CHARACTER NAME*6
      DATA IPRT/6/, MAXLN/56/
      WRITE(IPRT,100) NAME, PAGENO
100   FORMAT ('1', 2X, 'PROGRAM LOGIC MANUAL',  10X,
     1  'ROUTINE: ',  A6,     T61, 'PAGE: ', I4 / )
      PAGENO = PAGENO+1
      LINCNT = MAXLN
      RETURN
      END
```

FIGURE 3-2   PLM Producing Program

```
PROGRAM LOGIC MANUAL              ROUTINE: M/PROG            PAGE:    1

* * * * * * * * * * * * * * * * * * * * * * * * * * * * * * * * * * *

   PROGRAM LOGIC MANUAL   (PLM)  PRODUCING PROGRAM
   PROGRAMMER: ---                DATE: ---

   THIS PROGRAM TAKES A BLOCK OF PROGRAM SOURCE CODE, AND EXTRACTS
      THE BLOCK COMMENTS OF EACH ROUTINE TO PRODUCE A PLM.

   LOGIC FLOW:
      CARDS ARE READ LOOKING FOR THE SEQUENCE 'C * * ' IN COLUMNS 1-6.
      IF FOUND, THEN THIS MARKS THE START OF A BLOCK OF COMMENTS.
      THEN COLUMN 72 IS INSPECTED TO DETERMINE IF THIS IS A
         MAIN PROGRAM (COL. 72 = 'M')
         SUB PROGRAM (COL. 72 = 'S')
         ENTRY POINT (COL. 72 = 'E')
      IF A MAIN PROGRAM, THEN THE NAME OF THE MODULE BECOMES 'M/PROG'.
      IF A SUBPROGRAM OR ENTRY POINT, THEN THE NAME BECOMES THE
         ALPHABETIC STRING LISTED IN COLUMNS 7-12.  THIS NAME IS
         PRINTED AT THE TOP OF EACH PAGE OF THE PLM.
      LISTING OF STATEMENTS OF THE PLM CONTINUES UNTIL THE NEXT CARD
         CONTAINING 'C * * ' IN COLUMNS 1-6 AND 'F' IN COLUMN 72.
      THEN THE SEARCH RESUMES FOR THE FIRST CARD OF THE COMMENT BLOCK
         OF A NEW PROGRAM MODULE.
```

MAJOR VARIABLES:
   NAME: NAME OF MODULE (MAIN PROGRAM, SUBPROGRAM OR ENTRY POINT)
   LINE: CARD MOST RECENTLY READ. THROUGH EQUIVALENCES, THIS
           NAME ALSO REFERS TO:
     COL: A CHARACTER*1 ARRAY OF 72 ELEMENTS
     C1TO6:   A CHARACTER*6 VARIABLE REFERING TO COLUMNS 1-6.
     C7TO12: A CHARACTER*6 VARIABLE REFERING TO COLUMNS 7-12.
   PAGENO: NUMBER TO BE PRINTED AT THE TOP OF THE CURRENT PAGE
   LINCNT: COUNT OF LINES REMAINING ON CURRENT PAGE

SUBPROGRAMS CALLED:
   OUTPUT: TO FORMAT AND PRINT THE NEXT LINE OF OUTPUT
   HEADER: TO BEGIN NEXT PAGE AND RESET LINE COUNT

STATEMENT FUNCTIONS:
   LETTER(C): -LOGICAL- TESTS IF CHARACTER "C" IS A LETTER
   DIGIT(C): -LOGICAL- TESTS IF CHARACTER "C" IS A DIGIT
   NOTE BOTH OF THESE FUNCTIONS ARE DEPENDENT ON THE EBCDIC
            AND ASCII CODING SCHEME WHERE NO CHARACTERS OTHER
            THAN LETTERS (DIGITS) APPEAR BETWEEN 'A' AND 'Z'
            ('0' AND '9', RESPECTIVELY).

PROGRAM LOGIC MANUAL   ROUTINE: OUTPUT   PAGE: 2

* * OUTPUT * * FORMAT AND PRINT OUTPUT LINES * * * * * * * * * * *

 SUBPROGRAM TO FORMAT AND PRINT ONE LINE OF A PLM

 INPUT ARGUMENTS:
    COL: THE LINE TO BE PRINTED - CHARACTER*1 ARRAY OF 72 ELEMENTS
    LINCNT: COUNT OF LINES REMAINING ON CURRENT OUTPUT PAGE
    PAGENO: NUMBER OF CURRENT OUTPUT PAGE
    NAME: NAME OF CURRENT PROGRAM MODULE

 OUTPUT ARGUMENTS:
    LINCNT: REVISED TO REFLECT LINES REMAINING AFTER PRINTING
            DESIRED LINE
    PAGENO: INCREMENTED IF A NEW PAGE HAD TO BE STARTED

 ACTIONS: CHARACTER "C" BLANKED OUT FROM POSITION 1 OF LINE,
          COLUMN 72 ALSO CHANGED TO BLANK.

PROGRAM LOGIC MANUAL   ROUTINE: HEADER   PAGE: 3

* * HEADER * * OUTPUT PAGE HEADINGS * * * * * * * * * * * * * * * * *

 FORMAT AND PRINT PAGE HEADINGS

 INPUT ARGUMENTS
    NAME: NAME OF CURRENT PROGRAM MODULE
    PAGENO: NUMBER TO AFFIX TO PAGE HEADING FOR NEW PAGE

 OUTPUT ARGUMENTS:
    PAGENO: VALUE FOR NEXT OUTPUT PAGE NUMBER (INPUT VALUE OF
            PAGENO + 1).
    LINCNT: COUNT OF LINES WHICH MAY BE PRINTED ON NEW PAGE

FIGURE 3-3 Sample Output from PLM Producing Program

147

For the last sample program in this chapter, we will show a program reformatter. Consider some of the points suggested in Chapter 1; code is easier to read if it begins in consistent columns, loops are clearer to follow if the loop body is indented, and code is easier to understand if names of variables are meaningful. However, not everybody adheres to these practices. What we will present is a program to take poorly formatted FORTRAN programs and perform the cosmetic changes listed above.

The development of the algorithm will be presented in essentially the same sequence as the author designed it. We stress that this is certainly not the only possible development. You are being shown many different program development and documentation styles in this book; you must work to develop one that is natural and effective for you.

The problem: given a FORTRAN program, produce a program identical except for appearance. The changes to be effected are

1. Begin all statements initially in column 7.
2. On the appearance of the word DO, indent each succeeding card 3 spaces more than present indentation.
3. On the appearance of the word CONTINUE, decrease the identation by 3.
4. Never indent beyond column 25 (six levels deep); never begin text prior to column 7 (no indentation).
5. Do not move FORMAT statements.
6. Given any string of characters, be able to replace all occurrences of that string by any other string (e.g., be able to change one variable name consistently to another).
7. Assume that no blanks exist in the control words FORMAT, DO, or CONTINUE. (These may, of course, be preceded or followed by blanks.)

After setting down this reasonably rigorous problem definition, we identify the major steps to perform.

1. Read card and find start of statement.
2. Look for keyword DO, CONTINUE, or FORMAT.
3. Look for replacement pattern.
4. Move text, watching for continuation lines.
5. Repeat to process all statements.

This rough sketch of actions is the first level in a top down development of this program. Because the logic of this process is straightforward, we will not show a full flowchart or algorithm development of it. In the development of this program three activities reappear—move text, look for a particular series of characters, and look for the first nonblank. These three repeated activities make good candidates for subprograms. Therefore, we will refine and debug the routines CHMOVE, CHFIND, and NOBLNK. Given these three basic support routines it was easy to code the main routine. The code of this whole program is shown in Figure 3-4.

```
      SUBROUTINE CHMOVE (TO,TOPOS,TOLEN, FROM,FRPOS,FRLEN, MOVLEN)
C * * CHMOVE * * * * * * * * * * * * * * * * * * * * * * * * * * * * *  S
C
C     GENERAL PURPOSE CHARACTER MOVE SUBROUTINE
C
C     MOVES DATA FROM "FROM" ARRAY TO "TO" ARRAY.
C     THESE ARRAYS HAVE MAXIMUM SIZES "FRLEN" AND "TOLEN," RESPECTIVELY
C     THE POSITIONS FROM WHICH AND TO WHICH MOVEMENT IS TO OCCUR
C        ARE CONTAINED IN "FRPOS" AND "TOPOS," RESPECTIVELY.
C     THE LENGTH OF MOVEMENT IS IN VARIABLE "MOVLEN"
C
C     ERRORS DETECTED:
C     IF MOVEMENT EXCEEDS THE SIZE OF EITHER THE "FROM" OR
C        "TO" ARRAY, ONLY MOVEMENT WITHIN THE ARRAY IS PERFORMED.
C     "MOVLEN" CONTAINS THE AMOUNT OF DATA MOVED. IN ANY CASE.
C
C     MOVEMENT IS ONE CHARACTER AT A TIME, LEFT TO RIGHT.
C     ARRAYS "TO" AND "FROM" MAY OVERLAP, IF DESIRED.
C
C     PROGRAMMER: ---           DATE: ---
C
C * * * * * * * * * * * * * * * * * * * * * * * * * * * * * * * * * *  F
      INTEGER TOLEN, FRLEN, TOPOS, FRPOS, MOVLEN
      CHARACTER*1 TO(TOLEN), FROM(FRLEN)
C
C. . . . . .DETERMINE MAXIMUM AMOUNT WHICH CAN BE MOVED
C. . . . . .TOLEN-TOPOS+1 = MAXIMUM AMOUNT OF DATA LEFT IN "TO" ARRAY
C. . . . . .SIMILARLY FOR "FROM" ARRAY
      MOVLEN = MIN0 (MOVLEN, TOLEN-TOPOS+1, FRLEN-FRLEN+1)
      IF (MOVLEN .LE. 0) RETURN
C
C. . . . . .LEGAL MOVE GUARANTEED; MOVE CHARACTERS 1 AT A TIME
      DO 10 I = 1, MOVLEN
         TO(TOPOS+I-1) = FROM(FRPOS+I-1)
   10 CONTINUE
      RETURN
      END



      SUBROUTINE CHFIND (TARGET, PATTRN, PATL, COL, SKIP, FOUND)
C * * CHFIND* * * * * * * * * * * * * * * * * * * * * * * * * * * * *  S
C
C     CHARACTER STRING FIND ROUTINE
C
C     LOOK FOR STRING "PATTRN" OF LENGTH "PATL" IN STRING "TARGET."
C     THE SEARCH IS TO BEGIN AT THE "COL" POSITION OF "TARGET."
C
C     IF THERE ARE NOT "PATL" POSITIONS LEFT IN TARGET,
C        I.E. IF COL+PATL-1 .GT. CARDL (=80), THEN
C        FOUND IS SET TO .FALSE. AND RETURN OCCURS IMMEDIATELY.
C
C     IF THE NEXT "PATL" POSITIONS OF "TARGET" MATCH "PATTRN,"
C        THEN "FOUND" IS SET TO .TRUE., COL IS UNCHANGED, AND RETURN.
C     SKIP CONTROLS WHETHER THE MATCH MUST BEGIN AT POSITION "COL,"
C        OR CAN BEGIN AT A LATER COLUMN.
C     IF "SKIP" IS .TRUE., THEN FAILING TO MATCH BEGINNING AT "COL",
C        THE SEARCH CONTINUES AT COL+1, COL+2, ..., UNTIL EITHER
C        (A) A MATCH IS FOUND, IN WHICH CASE
C. . . . . .COL IS SET TO THE COLUMN WHERE THE MATCH BEGINS,
C. . . . . .FOUND IS SET TO .TRUE. AND RETURN OCCURS,
C        (B) THE TARGET IS EXHAUSTED: NO MATCH IS FOUND IN
C. . . . . .COL, COL1, C...,COL+K, AND COL + (K+1)+PATL-1 .GT. CARDL
C. . . . . .THEN "FOUND" IS SET TO .FALSE., "COL" REMAINS
C. . . . . .UNCHANGED FROM ENTRY, AND RETURN OCCURS.
C
C     PROGRAMMER: ---           DATE: ---
C
C * * * * * * * * * * * * * * * * * * * * * * * * * * * * * '* * * * *  F
      INTEGER PATL, COL, CARDL/80/
      LOGICAL SKIP, FOUND
      CHARACTER*1 TARGET(80), PATTRN(PATL)
      FOUND = .FALSE.
```

```
C. . . . . . .FIRST GUARANTEE LEGAL INPUTS
      IF (PATL .LT 1 .OR. COL .LT. 1) RETURN
C. . . . . . .ALSO GUARANTEE THAT "PATL" POSITIONS REMAIN IN "TARGET"
      IF (COL+PATL-1 .GT. CARDL) RETURN
C. . . . . . .BEGIN SEARCH AT "COL"
      ISTART = COL
      IEND = COL
C. . . . . . .IF SKIPPING ALLOWED, DETERMINE LAST POSSIBLE MATCH BEGINNING
      IF (SKIP) IEND = CARDL-PATL+1
C
C. . . . . . .LOOK FOR MATCH; IF FIRST LETTER OK, CHECK WHOLE PATTERN
      DO 100 J = ISTART, IEND
          IF (TARGET(J) .NE. PATTRN(1)) GO TO 100
          IF (PATL .EQ. 1) GO TO 200
C. . . . . . .COMPARE FOR FULL MATCH; SUCCESS IF NO MISMATCHES
              DO 50 K = 2, PATL
                  IF (TARGET(J+K-1) .NE. PATTRN(K)) GO TO 100
  50          CONTINUE
              GO TO 200
 100  CONTINUE
C. . . . . . .IF FALL OUT, NOT FOUND - RETURN
      RETURN
C
C. . . . . . .PROPER MATCH FOUND
 200  FOUND = .TRUE.
      COL = J
      RETURN
      END


      SUBROUTINE NOBLNK (LINE, COL, FOUND)
C * * NOBLNK* * * * * * * * * * * * * * * * * * * * * * * * * * * * * * S
C
C     THIS SUBROUTINE LOCATES THE NEXT NON-BLANK IN
C     ARRAY "LINE" OF SIZE 80, BEGINNING AT POSITION "COL"
C
C     THE SEARCH EXAMINES POSITIONS COL, COL+1, COL+2,... UNTIL
C         (A) A NON-BLANK IS FOUND,
C. . . . . . .IN WHICH CASE COL RETURNS WITH THE POSITION OF THIS BLANK,
C. . . . . . .AND FOUND = .TRUE.,  OR
C         (B) NO NON-BLANK IS FOUND, IN WHICH CASE
C. . . . . . .COL IS UNCHANGED FROM ENTRY, AND
C. . . . . . .FOUND = .FALSE.
C
C     PROGRAMMER: ---          DATE: ---
C
C * * * * * * * * * * * * * * * * * * * * * * * * * * * * * * * * * * * F
      INTEGER COL
      LOGICAL FOUND
      CHARACTER*1 BLANK/'*'/, LINE(80)
C. . . . . . .GUESS NO MATCH; RESET IF MATCH FOUND
      FOUND = .FALSE.
      IF (COL .GT. 80 .OR. COL .LE. 0) RETURN
C
C. . . . . . .CHECK EACH COLUMN FOR NON-BLANK
      DO 10 I=COL, 80
          IF (LINE(I) .NE. BLANK) GO TO 20
  10  CONTINUE
C. . . . . . .IF FALL OUT, NOT FOUND; REPORT FAILURE
      RETURN
C
C. . . . . . .COME HERE IF FOUND.  REPORT SUCCESS
  20  FOUND = .TRUE.
      COL = I
      RETURN
      END
C
C            ===================
C            == MAIN PROGRAM ==
C            ===================
C
```

```
C * * * * * * * * * * * * * * * * * * * * * * * * * * * * * * * * *   M
C
C       CARD REFORMATTER
C
C       THIS PROGRAM FORMATS PROGRAMS
C
C       IT INDENTS LOOPS AND CHANGES ANY STRING TO ANY OTHER
C       IT READS A CARD, BROKEN INTO FOUR COMPONENTS
C                             (STMTNO, CONT, INCAR, SEQFLD)
C       AND REFORMATS THIS CARD
C
C       MAJOR VARIABLES:
C       INCAR(66):  CARD JUST READ
C       OUTCAR(132):  NEXT CARD TO OUTPUT
C       INDENT:  AMOUNT OF INDENTATION FOR NEXT LINE
C       DELSTR:  STRING TO BE DELETED, OF LENGTH "DELLEN"
C       REPL:  STRING TO REPLACE DELETED ONE, OF LENGTH "REPLEN"
C
C       PROGRAMMER: ---           DATE: ---
C
C * * * * * * * * * * * * * * * * * * * * * * * * * * * * * * * * *   F
C
      EQUIVALENCE (STMTNO,COL1)
      LOGICAL ANCHOR, FOUND
      CHARACTER*1 INCAR(66),OUTCAR(132),COL1
      CHARACTER SEQFLD*8, STMTNO*5, CONT*1
      CHARACTER*1 FORMAT(6), DO(2), CONTIN(8), DELSTR(5), REPL(4)
      INTEGER DELLOC, INDENT, ENDLOC, NEXTIN, DELLEN,
     X    REPLEN, CARDLN, OUTUNT, COL, REPLOC, TOPOS
      LOGICAL ANCHOR, FOUND
      EQUIVALENCE (STMTNO, COL1)
      DATA FORMAT/'F','O','R','M','A','T'/, DO/'D','O'/
      DATA CONTIN/'C','O','N','T','I','N','U','E'/
      DATA INUNIT/5/, OUTUNT/7/, CARDLN/66/
C. . . . . . .FOR SAMPLE, REPLACE "QWXYZ" BY "XYZQ"
      DATA REPLEN/4/,REPL/'X','Y','Z','Q'/, ANCHOR/.TRUE./
      DATA DELLEN/5/,DELSTR/'Q','W','X','Y','Z'/, OUTCAR/132*' '/
      NEXTIN=1
   90 READ (INUNIT,100,END=999) STMTNO,CONT,INCAR,SEQFLD
  100 FORMAT (A5,A1,66A1,A8)
C
C. . . . . . .BEGIN SCAN OF A NEW CARD
  110 INDENT = NEXTIN
      IF (COL1 .EQ. 'C') GO TO 120
      COL = 1
C. . . . . . .GET FIRST NONBLANK ON CARD; IGNORE AN ALL BLANK CARD
      CALL NOBLNK (INCAR,COL, FOUND, CARDLN)
      IF (.NOT. FOUND) GO TO 90
C
C. . . . . . .CHECK IF THIS IS A FORMAT CARD; IF YES, NO CONVERSION
      CALL CHFIND (INCAR, FORMAT,6,COL,ANCHOR,FOUND,CARDLN)
      IF (.NOT. FOUND) GO TO 200
  120   WRITE (OUTUNT,100) STMTNO,CONT,INCAR,SEQFLD
        READ (INUNIT,100,END=999) STMTNO, CONT,INCAR, SEQFLD
        IF ((CONT.EQ.' ' .OR. CONT.EQ.'0').AND. COL1.NE.'C') GO TO 110
        GO TO 120
C
C. . . . . . .CHECK FOR CONTINUE. REDUCE INDENT, UP TO LEFT EDGE
  200 CALL CHFIND (INCAR,CONTIN,8,COL,ANCHOR,FOUND, CARDLN)
      IF (.NOT. FOUND) GO TO 250
        NEXTIN = MAX0(1, INDENT-3)
        GO TO 300
C. . . . . . .CHECK FOR DO LOOP. INCREASE INDENT, UP TO 6 LEVELS
  250 CALL CHFIND (INCAR,DO,2,COL,ANCHOR,FOUND, CARDLN)
      IF (.NOT. FOUND) GO TO 300
        NEXTIN = MIN0(INDENT+3,19)
C
C. . . . . . .BEGIN SEARCH FOR DELETE/REPLACEMENT STRINGS
  300 REPLOC = COL
      CALL CHFIND (INCAR,DELSTR,DELLEN,REPLOC,.NOT.ANCHOR,FOUND,CARDLN)
      IF (.NOT.FOUND) GO TO 400
C. . . . . . .HAVE FOUND A STRING FOR REPLACEMENT
C. . . . . . .MOVE EVERYTHING UP TO REPLACEMENT BEGINNING
```

151

```
                 TOPOS = INDENT
                 MOVELN = REPLOC-COL+1
                 CALL CHMOVE (OUTCAR,TOPOS,2*CARDLN,
        X            INCAR,COL,CARDLN, MOVELN)
                 COL = COL+MOVELN+DELLEN
C. . . . . . .MOVE REPLACEMENT PORTION
                 CALL CHMOVE (OUTCAR,TOPOS,2*CARDLN,REPL,1,REPLEN,REPLEN)
                 MOVELN = CARDLN-COL
                 TOPOS = TOPOS+REPLEN
C. . . . . . .NOW MOVE END OF STATEMENT
                 CALL CHMOVE (OUTCAR,TOPOS,2*CARDLN,
        X            INCAR,COL,CARDLN,MOVELN)
                 ENDLOC = COL+MOVELN-1
                 GO TO 500
C
C. . . . . . .SIMPLE CASE: NO REPLACEMENT
     400 CALL CHMOVE (OUTCAR,INDENT,2*CARDLN,INCAR,COL,CARDLN,CARDLN-COL+1)
                 ENDCOL = INDENT+CARDLN-COL+1
C
C. . . . . . .CARD FORMED IN "OUTCAR"; PROCEED TO OUTPUT IT
     500 WRITE (OUTUNT,100) STMTNO,CONT,(OUTCAR(I),I=1,CARDLN),SEQFLD
                 IF (ENDCOL .LE. CARDLN) GO TO 550
C. . . . . . .FOR LONG STATEMENTS, MUST MAKE CONTINUATION
                 CALL NOBLNK (OUTCAR,CARDLN+1,FOUND,2*CARDLN)
                 IF (.NOT. FOUND) GO TO 550
                 CALL CHMOVE (OUTCAR, INDENT,2*CARDLN,
        X            OUTCAR,CARDLN+1,2*CARDLN, CARDLN-INDENT)
                 ENDCOL = ENDCOL-(CARDLN-INDENT+1)
C. . . . . . .BLANK OUT SEQUENCE FIELD AND STATEMENT NUMBER OF CONTINUATION
                 SEQFLD = ' '
                 STMTNO = ' '
                 CONT = 'X'
                 GO TO 500
C
C. . . . . . .WHEN GET HERE, BLANK OUT REMNANT OF CARD
     550 J = 2*CARDLN
                 DO 560 I = 1,J
                    OUTCAR(I) = ' '
     560 CONTINUE
C
C. . . . . . .READ NEXT INPUT CARD
                 READ (INUNIT,100,END=999) STMTNO,CONT,INCAR,SEQFLD
                 IF (CONT .NE. ' '.AND. CONT .NE. '0') GO TO 300
                 GO TO 110
     999 STOP
                 END
```

FIGURE 3-4 Card Reformatting Program

Exercises

3.01 Write an INTEGER FUNCTION subprogram NXTBLK that has three arguments: STRING, STRLEN, and IPOS. STRING is an array of length STRLEN. IPOS is an integer between 1 and STRLEN. This subprogram returns the position of the next blank beginning with STRING(IPOS). It returns -1 if IPOS is negative, zero or greater than STRLEN, and it returns 0 if no element is blank.

3.02 Write an INTEGER FUNCTION subprogram NONBLK that has arguments as in the previous example. It is to return the position of the next nonblank character in STRING.

3.03 Write a subroutine NEXTWD that has three arguments: BUFFER, POSN, LEN. BUFFER is an array of size 80, and POSN is a number between 1 and 80. The subprogram is to examine BUFFER(POSN), BUFFER(POSN+1),.. looking for the first letter. Then, from that position, examine succeeding columns looking for the first blank space, mark of punctuation, or the end of the buffer. The subroutine returns with POSN containing the location of the first letter; LEN is to contain the length of the word beginning at that location.

3.04 Write a collection of six LOGICAL function subprograms CEQ, CNE, CLE, CLT, CGE and CGT that have four arguments: STR1, LEN1, STR2 and LEN2. The subprograms are to return .TRUE. if string STR1 is equal to, not equal to, etc. string STR2. The strings are to be compared one character at a time left to right (i.e., from low subscripts to high) for as many characters as the smaller of LEN1 and LEN2. The first unequal characters from the two strings determine less than or greater than. If all characters compare equal, the strings are equal if the lengths are equal. If the lengths are unequal but all characters match, the string having the smaller length is the lesser. (*Note*. These can all be written as multiple entries to a single subprogram.)

3.05 Write a program to carry out a partial simulation of a chess game. You are to consider an 8 x 8 board. Your program will randomly select three squares to receive a queen, a bishop, and a castle (all your opponent's pieces) and one square to receive your knight. Print an image of the chess board showing Q, B, C, and K for the four pieces. Then you are to examine the squares that your knight can reach in one move. Label these squares:

1 - If the knight can move here but would be taken by one of the opponents next move.
2 - If the knight can move here and cannot be taken by any opponent next move.
3 - If the knight can move here and would take an opponent in the move.

Display the image of the board with these labels on the squares. Recall that the queen can move as far as desired horizontally, vertically or diagonally. The bishop can move as far as desired diagonally. The castle can move as far as desired horizontally or vertically. The knight can move two squares horizontally and one vertically or two squares vertically and one horizontally.

3.06 One of the techniques used to determine authorship of an anonymous piece of literature is as follows. First, all words in the document are counted and a table of the frequency of appearance, by percentage, of each word is constructed. These percentages are then compared with the percentages of those who are suspected authors. Write a program that inputs a piece of text and isolates all the words in that text (ignoring marks of punctuation and using one or more blanks as the delimiters between words). Your program should output the raw frequency and percentage of occurrence for each word.

3.07 Right-justified text is text in which the right margin is even, as is the left. Write a procedure that inputs a line of text and inserts enough additional spaces between words to force the line to a particular length.

3.08 (For those having interactive capability.) An interesting demonstration game is the old children's game of "hangman." In this game a word is chosen and a number of dashes is displayed, one for each letter in the word. The contestant guesses a letter and if the letter appears in the word, the letter is displayed in each position in which it belongs. At any time the contestant is allowed to guess the entire word. The object is to identify the chosen word in the fewest guesses. Write a program to play this game. (With a challenging list of words, this game has been known to enchant adults, too.)

CHAPTER 4 Extended I/O: Tapes and Disks

A computer's main memory serves as the primary storage medium into which are placed a program, its data, the results of its calculations, and the output lines that it has formatted for printing. Each data item within this memory is directly accessible. In the FORTRAN language, such access is accomplished by referencing an item by its name. Storing and retrieving of values are accomplished at very high speeds, usually in excess of one million words per second.

However, on most machines the size of main memory is fairly limited. As a consequence, the amount of main memory allocated to a program may be insufficient for storing all the data that must be simultaneously accessible. For example, consider a program that must read, sort and then print the names and mailing addresses of 15,000 persons. If one name/address record is 80 characters long, then over one million characters of memory are needed to store the data for this program. It is a rare computer installation that would or could allocate this much main memory to a single program. We therefore need to augment main memory with a less expensive storage medium in order to solve problems of the kind just discussed.

A second deficiency of main memory is the short life span of data that we store there. After a program completes execution, the main memory that it uses is assigned to other programs. Thus, any values that we leave there are destroyed. Consider again our task of producing mailing labels. What should we do if we now wish to keep these 15,000 sorted card images for future label printing runs? We could read in the original card deck, but this would require a sort to be performed each time. Recalling that a sort of 15,000 items requires on the average about 200,000 comparisons ($15000*\log_2(15000)$), we would quickly reject this solution. We could punch the sorted card deck, but consider that 15,000 cards fill $7\frac{1}{2}$ boxes.

To alleviate the problems arising from using only cards and a computer's main memory for data storage, most computer installations provide other forms of storage devices. Two classes of such devices are usually available: those suited to processing data only in a fixed order (*sequential access*) and those that facilitate random processing (*direct access*). With the exception of unit record devices (card readers, line printers, etc.), the most commonly used sequential access device is the magnetic tape. Magnetic disk storage devices make up the most common class of direct access devices. We discuss the organization

and use of tapes in the next three sections. Disks are discussed in Sections
4.4 and 4.5.

4.1 THE PHYSICAL ORGANIZATION OF TAPES

4.1.1 Recording of Data

Computer tape reels are similar to those used on audio tape recorders. A
standard reel contains 2400 feet of magnetic tape. The width of this tape is
usually sufficient to record up to 9 bits of data. A convention is established
whereby a spot on the tape's surface that is magnetized in one direction signifies
a binary one; a zero is represented by the opposite polarity. In general, data
is recorded as 7 or 9 bits in parallel across the tape's width (called 7-track or
9-track tape, respectively). In either case, the number of bits is sufficient to
represent the encoding of a single character.

Whenever a character is written onto a tape, a bit, called the *parity bit*,
is attached to the character's encoding. Thus, BCD 6-bit character encodings
require 7-track tape and EBCDIC's 8 bits require 9-track tape. The ASCII 7 bit
encodings, while needing only eight tracks, are recorded on 9-track tape, with
one bit always set to 0.

The most common type of parity bit is called odd parity. If the number
of 1 bits in the character is even, then this bit is a 1; otherwise it is a 0.
Using this scheme, we are guaranteed that each character recorded contains
an odd number of 1 bits.

Whenever data is written, a parity bit is computed and then appended
to each character. Upon reading the data, each parity bit is checked to see if
errors have occurred. Such a technique can detect an error in a single bit,
but it fails to detect two bit errors.

A string of characters is represented on tape by recording the characters
in sequence. There is, of course, some space (unrecorded tape surface) between
the encoding of the first and second characters, the second and third characters,
etc. This space is approximately the same for all data recorded on a single
tape, but it may vary among different tapes. The density at which characters
are packed on a tape is generally 6250, 1600, 800, 556, or 200 characters per
inch. These densities are commonly denoted as 6250, 1600, 800, 556, and 200
bpi, where bpi is an abbreviation for bits per inch. Since all the bits of a
single character are stored in parallel, the figure for bits per inch is the same
as that for characters per inch.

The capacity of a tape depends on its length and its recording density.
A 2400 foot tape, recorded at 1600 bpi, can store over 45 million characters
of data. Only half as much can be stored using 800 bpi. A tradeoff between
the variety of densities occurs since the higher the density, the more chance
for recording errors on older tapes, and the more expensive the cost of the
recording device.

When we wish to record more than one block of data (string of characters) on a tape, a *gap* between blocks is used to delineate separate blocks. A gap is an erased portion of the tape. The length of a gap is usually between $\frac{1}{2}$ and $\frac{3}{4}$ inch long. The existence of these gaps reduces the realizable capacity of tapes.

Consider what happens if we fill a 2400 foot tape with 80-character card images. Using 1600 bpi, each block occupies only $\frac{1}{20}$ inch. Assume the gap associated with a block is $\frac{1}{2}$ inch long. Then, our effective density is 80 characters per $\frac{11}{20}$ inch or just 146 characters per inch. We would only be using 9% of the tape. However, if we write 3200 character blocks, each containing 40 card images, then our effective utilization is about 80%. (See Figure 4-1.)

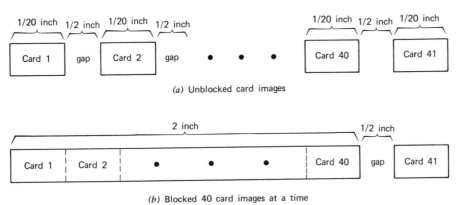

(a) Unblocked card images

(b) Blocked 40 card images at a time

FIGURE 4-1 Unblocked versus blocked records.

The concept of writing more than one data item per block is called *blocking*. Each single data item in a block is called a *logical record* and each block is called a *physical record*. Data is unblocked if each physical record consists of just one logical record. Most data written on tape is blocked since the use of large physical records results in a high percentage of the tape being effectively used. As we will see later, blocking also reduces the time required to read or write data.

Although the blocking of data has many advantages, there is a price to be paid. For any input or output activity within a program, enough main memory must be allocated to store at least one physical record. (For most applications, two or more blocks are kept in memory.) Thus, if we choose too large a block size, there may not be enough memory available for our program to execute. On the other hand, if the block size is too small, then much of the tape is full of gaps, not data.

There is unfortunately no magic formula that dictates the optimum size of a physical record. The decision must be based on factors such as the amount of data to be processed and the amount of memory allocated to our program.

It often involves concepts that are outside the scope of this book. Here, we will use physical record sizes in the range from 600 to 4000 characters. Such a range is generally acceptable for programs that are not restricted to running in a very small amount of memory and that are not required to store large volumes of data.

4.1.2 Fixed and Variable Length Records

In FORTRAN, it is possible to write data records of varying lengths to the same tape file. This variability in length is usually handled by one of three methods.

A first, and the simplest, solution is to always write logical records of some fixed length that is equal to the longest data record. The data occupies the leftmost characters of the logical record, with its remainder filled with some pad character (e.g., blank). This technique is pictured in Figure 4-2.

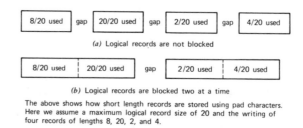

(a) Logical records are not blocked

(b) Logical records are blocked two at a time

The above shows how short length records are stored using pad characters. Here we assume a maximum logical record size of 20 and the writing of four records of lengths 8, 20, 2, and 4.

FIGURE 4-2 Short length records using pad characters.

A second solution is to follow each data record by a recognizable end-of-record character. Using this technique, we may pack more than one logical record into a single block. We may even allow a single logical record to span several blocks, since the existence of an end-of-record marker allows us to detect the end of a logical record irrespective of physical record boundaries. Figure 4-3 pictures how end markers are used on the DECsystem 10.

The above shows how records are stored using the DEC–10's end–of–record marker. Here we assume the writing of four records of lengths 8, 20, 2, and 16. We also assume that each physical record is 10 words (50 characters) long. The cent sign (¢) denotes an end–of–record. All records are rounded to a multiple of 5 characters (one word) using null characters (denoted by @).

FIGURE 4-3 Storing records using end-of-record marker.

A third solution is to write the data record preceded by some control characters that specify the actual data length. Both the IBM 360-370 OS System and the DECsystem 10 use this technique for certain types of output records. Figure 4-4 pictures the IBM variable length record method. Figure 4-5 shows how this technique is implemented by DEC.

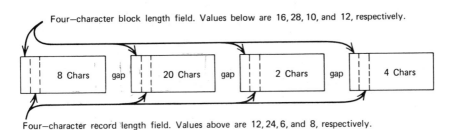

Four—character block length field. Values below are 16, 28, 10, and 12, respectively.

Four—character record length field. Values above are 12, 24, 6, and 8, respectively.

(a) Unblocked records

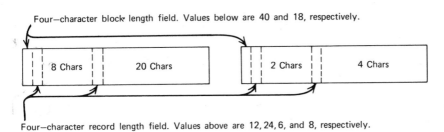

Four—character block length field. Values below are 40 and 18, respectively.

Four—character record length field. Values above are 12, 24, 6, and 8, respectively.

(b) Blocked records

The above shows how records are stored using IBM's variable length record feature. Here we assume that four records of lengths 8, 20, 2, and 4 have been written.

FIGURE 4-4 Variable length records using IBM control words.

4.1.3 The Record Update Problem

If we are using a computer tape to store employee payroll records, then the need occasionally arises to replace the data stored in one block by more up-to-date information. If the new block is of the same length as the old one, we might want to write the new block directly over the outdated block. Such a process, which is commonly called *updating in place*, cannot always be carried out successfully.

The essential problem with rewriting a block is that the positioning of the recording mechanism might not be precisely the same as when the block was first written. The result of this imprecision can be the nonerasure of an end portion of the old block or the creation of a too small gap between this

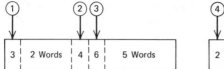
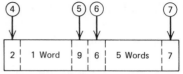

1. Start word for first record. Indicates record plus this start word occupy 3 word.
2. End word for first record. Indicates record plus start and end words occupy 4 words.
3. Start word for second record. Indicates that the first 5 words of this record are stored in this block. Count of 6 includes the start word.
4. Continue word for second record. Indicates that remaining one word of record number 2 follows. Count includes continue word.
5. End word for second record. Indicates that 9 words were used for this record, its start, continue and end words.
6. Start word for third record. Indicates record plus this start word occupy 6 words.
7. End word for third record. Indicates that record plus start and end words occupy 7 words.

The above pictures how records are stored on a DEC–10 using control information. Here we assume the writing of three records of lengths 2, 6 and 5 words. We also assume that each physical record is 10 words long.

FIGURE 4-5 Variable length records using DEC-10 control words.

new block and the one following it. (See Figure 4-6.) The net effect is that if you rewrite a block, then all subsequent ones are inaccessible.

4.1.4 Files of Data

A group of related data items stored on a computer tape is called a *file* (or *data set* by some computer manufacturers). A single tape may contain more than one file. In fact, a tape has such a large capacity that more than one file is generally recorded. Each file on a tape is terminated by a special marker block called an *end-of-file*. The last file on a tape is followed by an *end-of-volume* marker (represented on some systems by two end-of-files in succession).

Many computer systems allow files to be labeled. This means that immediately preceding (and on some systems also immediately following) each file there is a collection of records called a *label*. Information recorded in a label varies but usually includes: a user-chosen file name that must be known to anyone who wishes to read or write the file; the length of the physical records contained within the file; and the length of the logical records that comprise each physical record.

Methods by which a program may identify which file of a multifile tape it wishes to process are discussed in Section 4.3. Such techniques are not a part of FORTRAN but are specific to a given computer system.

(a) Tape before update of RECORD j

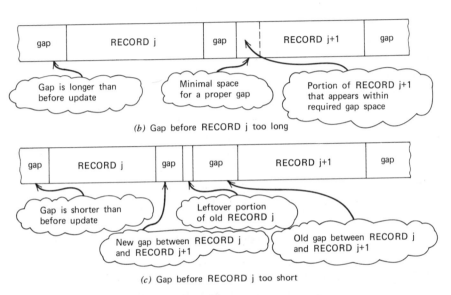

(b) Gap before RECORD j too long

(c) Gap before RECORD j too short

FIGURE 4-6 Updating tape records.

4.1.5 Physical Characteristics of Tape

The devices that read data from and write data onto magnetic tapes are called *magnetic tape units* (or tape drives or tape transports). These units have two spindles for mounting tape reels. One spindle holds the reel containing the tape to be processed; the other holds a take-up reel. Tape from the first of these reels is threaded under a read/write head and onto the take-up reel.

Whenever a read or write request is directed to a tape unit, the tape begins to move past the read/write head. Reading or writing cannot occur until the tape is moving at its full rate of speed, usually 75 to 125 inches per second. Such speed is obtainable after the tape has moved approximately half the length of a gap.

If a read operation is to be performed, the read/write head should be positioned in the middle of the gap preceding the block to be read. As movement occurs, the read/write head monitors the tape's contents awaiting the start of data. As soon as the first character beyond the gap is detected, reading begins. Reading continues until the start of the next gap is detected. The tape unit then gradually slows down, stopping about halfway through the next gap.

If a write operation is to be performed, the read/write head should be positioned about half the length of a gap after the preceding block. The read/write head erases a portion of tape during its start-up time. This completes the gap required before the new block. Once the tape is moving at full speed, the data block is written. As soon as the last character is written, the tape unit will slow tape movement to a gradual halt. During this time, the read/write head erases tape, thereby providing the start of the gap separating this new block from any that might follow it.

Two problems result from the way in which tape units operate. The first of these relates to updating blocks in place and was discussed in Section 4.1.3. The second restriction concerns block lengths. When a read is being performed, the read/write head expects some minimum length data block; otherwise it interprets what it has found as being "noise" caused by a transmission or recording error. The minimum length of an acceptable block varies among different tape units. However, a good rule of thumb is to never write blocks whose lengths are less than 20 characters.

4.1.6 Transfer Rates Achieved by Tapes

Data stored in a computer's main memory may be accessed at a very fast rate, usually over four million characters per second on today's larger machines. The rate to transfer data to and from tapes is considerably slower. Consider a tape that is recorded at 800 bpi and a tape unit which moves the tape at a rate of 75 inches per second. Ignoring start and stop time, data is transferred to or from the tape at a rate of 60,000 characters per second.

Tape transfer rates, while slower than those achieved by main memory, are considerably faster than those attained when cards are being processed. (A typical card transfer rate is 1000 cards per minute, or just 1333 characters per second.)

4.2 FORTRAN STATEMENTS
FOR TAPE PROCESSING

Each tape to be processed by a FORTRAN program is associated with a unit number. The choice of unit numbers available and the techniques whereby one associates a given tape with some unit number vary radically from installation to installation. Section 4.3 discusses this matter in more detail. For now we use variable names of the form TAPEx (x being an integer) each time we need to refer to a tape unit. An appropriate value for these variables would have to be specified before program segments presented here could be compiled.

Seven statements are provided in the FORTRAN language for processing tapes. These are the formatted READ and WRITE, the unformatted READ and WRITE, BACK-SPACE, ENDFILE, and REWIND.

4.2.1 Formatted Tape Input/Output

The formatted READ and WRITE statements used for tape processing are written in precisely the same way as those for reading cards and printing lines; only the unit numbers differ.

Execution of

```
      WRITE (TAPE1,4000) (ALPHA(I), I=1,100)
4000  FORMAT (100A1)
```

would result in the creation of a 100-character logical record to be written onto the tape mounted on a unit designated by TAPE1. If records are not blocked, this single logical record is written out as one physical record. If the computer system is performing blocking, then it merges this logical record with others it is writing to tape. This blocking activity is normally invisible to the FORTRAN programmer.

Logical records in a tape file may be read only in the order in which they were written. Thus, if we wish to read the fifth logical record, we need to first read the four preceding ones. Assuming the read/write head is positioned just before record number 1, we can achieve the desired result by

```
      READ (TAPE1,3000,END=999) (ALPHA(I), I=1,50)
3000  FORMAT (////, 50A1)
```

The first four slashes in the format cause us to read and ignore the first, second, third, and fourth records. Since the read list has not yet been satisfied, the fifth record is read. If this fifth record is 50 or more characters long, then its first 50 characters are assigned to the first 50 elements of ALPHA and any remaining characters in the record are ignored. If the record is shorter than 50 characters, an error is detected, just as it would be if we tried to read 100 characters from an 80-character card. On some systems, this is a fatal error; on others, it results in another record being read and the values from it being used to complete the read operation.

The preceding READ statement contained an END= option field. This is used just as with a card read statement to detect the end of data. In this case, if the end-of-file marker is detected before the fifth record, then execution proceeds with the statement labeled 999.

4.2.2 Unformatted Tape Input/Output

Every time a formatted WRITE statement is executed, the data values it accesses from main memory are converted in accordance with the format codes specified. Often, the formatted version of a real, integer or logical variable requires more characters than one word (the length of its internal representation). For instance, if such a variable were written with no format conversion, it would occupy four characters on an IBM 360-370 series machine and five characters on a DECsystem 10. However, if the value of such a variable is written using an I9 format code, it will be represented by nine characters. This space problem, along with the time and loss of precision associated with format conversion, may be overcome by the use of unformatted reads and writes.

In order to pack data that is written on a tape, one can use an unformatted WRITE statement. This has the general form

WRITE *(unit number) output list*

The absence of a format number identifies this as unformatted, instead of formatted.

Execution of the statement

```
WRITE (TAPE1) (LIST(I), I=1,200)
```

causes the 200 words comprising the first 200 elements of LIST to be written onto tape with no format conversion. On an IBM 360-370 series machine, the logical record produced by such a write is 800 characters long. On a DECsystem 10, this record is 1000 characters long. In contrast to this, the logical record produced by

```
      WRITE (TAPE1,3000) (LIST(I), I=1,200)
3000  FORMAT (20019)
```

is 1800 characters long.

Logical records that were written using an unformatted WRITE statement should be read using an unformatted READ statement. The general form of this statement is

READ *(unit number[,END=label]) [input list]*

The input list here is noted as being optional. We can omit it whenever we wish to skip over a record. Thus,

```
READ (TAPE1)
```

skips one logical record on the tape associated with unit TAPE1.

Although unformatted input/output is usually conservative in its use of tape, it is not always so. For example, assume we wish to write a logical record containing the values of the 500 components of an integer array A, and we are assured that all components have values between 0 and 99. The formatted write

```
            WRITE (TAPE1,4000) A
     4000   FORMAT (500I2)
```

will accomplish this task by writing a record of length 1000 characters. The unformatted write

```
            WRITE (TAPE1) A
```

will also work, but its record is 2000 characters long on an IBM 360-370 series machine and 2500 characters on a DECsystem 10. For this case, the formatted write is possibly the better choice.

Formatted writes are needed whenever we are creating a tape to be read on different types of computers. The reason for this is that unformatted output is in an internal code that is recognizable only to our computer and to similar ones. If, however, we use formatted writes, then the tape may be read by other computers using the same character code (e.g., ASCII, BCD, or EBCDIC.)

4.2.3 BACKSPACE

A BACKSPACE statement may be thought of as backing up a tape mechanism to allow reprocessing of the most recent record. Thus, if a statement of the form

BACKSPACE *unit number*

is executed then the logical record processed next will be the one preceding that which would normally be accessed. So, for example, execution of the first read in

```
            READ (TAPE1,3000) (A(I), I=1,30)
     3000   FORMAT (30I3)
            BACKSPACE TAPE1
            READ (TAPE1,3000) (B(I), I=1,30)
```

causes a new logical record to be read and the first 90 characters of this record to be treated as 30 consecutive I3 fields. The values from these fields are placed in the first 30 elements of A. The BACKSPACE command directs that the next read should process the same logical record as was just read. Thus, the first 30 elements of B are assigned the same values that were assigned to those elements of A.

The BACKSPACE statement has no effect in the case where we are positioned to read the first record of a file. Clearly, it makes no sense to back up from this point.

4.2.4 ENDFILE

After all data records are written to a tape file, an end-of-file marker must be written to signify the file termination. This is accomplished in FORTRAN by executing a statement of the form

ENDFILE *unit number*

4.2.5 REWIND

The REWIND statement has the general form

REWIND *unit number*

This command should be executed after all processing of the file has been completed. In addition, a rewind command should be given anytime you wish to reposition the read/write head to the logical beginning of the tape. (The definition of a tape's logical beginning varies among different computer systems.

```
C* * * * * * * * * * * * * * * * * * * * * * * * * * * * * * * * * * * *
C* COPY CARD DECK ONTO TAPE. READ AND PRINT TAPE CONTENTS AS A CHECK   *
C*                                                                     *
C*   PROGRAMMER'S NAME: ---                    DATE WRITTEN: ---       *
C* * * * * * * * * * * * * * * * * * * * * * * * * * * * * * * * * * * *
        INTEGER RDR/5/, PRT/6/, TAPE1/16/
        CHARACTER*80 CARD
C
C***              READ CARD AND WRITE TO TAPE
C
10      READ (RDR,15,END=20) CARD
15      FORMAT (A80)
        WRITE (TAPE1,15) CARD
        GO TO 10
20      ENDFILE TAPE1
C
C***              READ TAPE FILE AND ECHO TO PRINTER
C
        REWIND TAPE1
        WRITE (PRT,25)
25      FORMAT ('1', T40, 'CONTENTS OF TAPE FILE' /
     1            '+', T40, '_____ __ ____ ____' ////)
30      READ (TAPE1,15,END=40) CARD
        WRITE (PRT,35) CARD
65      FORMAT (T11, A80)
        GO TO 30
40      REWIND TAPE1
        STOP
        END
```

FIGURE 4-7 Card to tape copy routine.

On an IBM 360-370, this refers to the beginning of the file being processed. On a DEC-10, it is the beginning of the first file on the tape.)

A common use of tapes is for medium- to long-term storage of programs and data. Figure 4-7 demonstrates this use in a program that copies an input deck of cards onto a tape, rewinds the tape, and lists the tape file to document its contents. Omitted from this example are the details of how one logically associates a FORTRAN unit number with an actual tape unit. The next section presents some specifics of how to do this on an IBM 360-370 OS system and on a DECsystem 10.

4.3 TAPE PROCESSING: CASE STUDIES

Assume that we have written a correct program that is to process a tape file. In order to run this program we must learn and follow the conventions established by our own computer installation. Such conventions differ greatly among different computer systems and usually differ slightly among installations using the same system.

Our next two subsections present case studies of how FORTRAN program unit numbers may be associated with tape files. Our example systems are the IBM 360-370 and the DEC-10.

4.3.1 Device Assignments Using IBM OS/JCL

IBM provides two essentially different languages for controlling the operations of its 360-370 series machines. These are OS/JCL and DOS/JCL. (OS stands for Operating System, DOS stands for Disk Operating System, and JCL stands for Job Control Language.)

OS/JCL is the control language used on most large 360-370's. In this language, devices are assigned to unit numbers by means of commands called data definition statements (DD statements). Since some aspects of the specifications of DD statements are dependent on procedures established at each computer center, there are a number of issues concerning them that we cannot address (e.g., their placement within a card deck). We will, however, present much of the information that tends to be consistent across different installations and note those places where local procedures usually have an effect.

DD statements associated with the execution of FORTRAN programs are of the form

//[*stepname*.]FT*uu*F001 DD *operands*

The // must appear in columns 1 and 2 and is used to indicate that this card contains a JCL statement. The FORTRAN unit number to which we wish to assign a device is unit number *uu*.

The string of characters that must be used as a *stepname* differs from one computer installation to another and may even be omitted at some. You will need to find out whether or not you are required to specify a stepname and, if so, what it must be.

The *operands* field is a list of one or more operand values. Two commonly used ones are

```
//FT11F001 DD *
```

and

```
//FT09F001 DD SYSOUT=A
```

The first of these (∗) is used to indicate that the unit number (in this case 11) is to reference a card input deck. The cards to be read must immediately follow this DD statement. The end of the card input associated with unit 11 is either the end of all cards for this job, or the occurrence of another JCL card.

The second example shows an operand of SYSOUT=A. This declares that all writes to the unit number (in this case 9) are to be directed to a line printer.

DD statements similar to those just described are usually provided for unit 5 (∗) and unit 6 (SYSOUT=A) as part of a standard set of JCL used in processing FORTRAN programs.

The use of a unit number other than 5 for a card input file is rare. This feature can, however, be useful for running programs that were written for other computer systems. For example, the standard card file unit number in DEC FORTRAN-10 is 2 not 5. If we wish to run such a program then we might include the DD statement

```
//FT02F001 DD *
```

before our card input. This allows us to associate unit 2, instead of unit 5, with our card input. All card input statements in the program would have the form READ(2,-)- .

A more common use for the SYSOUT=A operand is to allow our programs to access two or more separate print files. This facility provides us with an extremely flexible debugging aid.

Assume that we have written a program that directs all debugging output to unit DBG. Thus all such WRITE statements are of the form

WRITE (DBG,*fmt*) *list*

Now, if we want the debugging output merged with standard output, we initialize DBG by

```
DATA DBG/6/
```

If, however, we want all debugging output to appear on a set of output pages separate from unit 6 output, we can include, for example,

```
DATA DBG/9/
```

provided our JCL specifies

```
//FT09F001 DD SYSOUT=A
```

Whenever a program is executed that produces two or more separate print files, each of these files appears as a separate part of your program's output. Thus, if our program contained the sequence

```
WRITE (6,-)  list1
WRITE (9,-)  list2
WRITE (6,-)  list3
```

where both 6 and 9 are printer units, we will not see the lines associated with *list2* between those associated with *list1* and *list3*. Instead, *list3* follows *list1* on one group of pages and *list2* is written on another group associated with all unit 9 writes.

The segregated printing referred to in the previous paragraph is effected by directing all writes for unit 6 to one file on some system storage device and all those for unit 9 to a different file. The actual printing of these files is done after our program has stopped its execution. This technique, which is called *SPOOLing*, is used by most modern computer systems.

The DD operand values for tape files are more complex than those just shown for card and printer files. We will introduce these operands by a series of examples followed by a summary of the meanings of each operand used. We are not attempting to be complete but, instead, to give sufficient information to provide you with a basic familiarity. More detailed information on DD statements may be found in the appropriate IBM manuals and from documents published by your computer center.

Example 1   Assume that we wish to associate unit 12 with a file having characteristics as follows.

1. The file is to be written on 9-track tape [UNIT=TAPE].
2. The tape is identified by the name HUGHES [VOL=SER=HUGHES].
3. The file is to be created by this run [DISP=NEW].
4. The file is labeled and is to be the first one written on this tape [LABEL=1].
5. The file is to be named MYDATA [DSN=MYDATA].
6. The file is written using formatted WRITE's. Each data record is at most 100 characters long. Logical records written to the tape are all to be of the fixed size, 100 characters. Each physical block is to contain 20 logical records [DCB=(RECFM=FB,LRECL=100,BLKSIZE=2000)].

Then the needed DD statement is

```
//FT12F001 DD UNIT=TAPE,VOL=SER=HUGHES,DISP=NEW,LABEL=1,
//             DSN=MYDATA,DCB=(RECFM=FB,LRECL=100,BLKSIZE=2000)
```

Note that, since JCL cards cannot be typed beyond column 71 (not 72, as with FORTRAN) we require two such cards. To continue a DD statement, you simply break at the comma following some operand, code // in columns 1 and 2 of the next card, leave at least column 3 blank, and then type the remaining operands, starting no later than column 16.

Example 2   The method used in example 1 always requires that logical records be 100 characters long. If the data records are usually smaller, then many of the logical records contain blank padding characters. We therefore wish to redo this example, except we now require that data records be written with no padding. This requires that variable length blocks, as pictured in Figure 4-4, be used. The only change in the DD operands is to DCB. It must now be coded as

DCB=(RECFM=VB,LRECL=104,BLKSIZE=2084)

The length of 104 allows for a 4-character length field followed by up to 100 characters of data. The length of 2084 accommodates 20*104 characters plus another 4-character length field.

Example 3   Assume that we need to associate unit 8 with a tape file described as follows.

1. The file is on a 9-track tape [UNIT=TAPE].
2. The tape is identified by the name CPP01 [VOL=SER=CPP01].
3. The file was previously created [DISP=OLD].

4. The file is labeled and is the third one recorded on this tape [LABEL=3].
5. The file is named YOURDATA [DSN=YOURDATA].
6. The logical records are each 350 characters long, are not blocked, and are to be read by a formatted READ [DCB=(RECFM=F,LRECL=350,BLKSIZE=350)].

Then the needed DD statement is either

```
//FT08F001 DD UNIT=TAPE,VOL=SER=CPP01,DISP=OLD,LABEL=3,
//            DSN=YOURDATA,DCB=(RECFM=F,LRECL=350,BLKSIZE=350)
```

or the above with no DCB operand specified. The DCB operand may be omitted since the file YOURDATA already exists, and so it has a label that contains the DCB values.

Example 4   A file is to be written to unit 13. This file is characterized as follows.

1. The file is to be written on a 9-track tape [UNIT=TAPE].
2. The tape is identified by the name ROSE [VOL=SER=ROSE].
3. The file is to be created by this job [DISP=NEW].
4. The file is unlabeled and is the second one on this tape [LABEL=(2,NL)].
5. The data records are no greater than 80 characters long. These records are written by unformatted WRITE statements and are to be packed at least 40 per block [DCB=(RECFM=VBS,LRECL=84,BLKSIZE=3364)].

The needed DD statement is

```
//FT13F001 DD UNIT=TAPE,VOL=SER=ROSE,DISP=NEW,LABEL=(2,NL),
//            DCB=(RECFM=VBS,LRECL=84,BLKSIZE=3364)
```

Note that data read or written by unformatted I/O statements must be recorded using the variable length method. Thus, we could not have specified a RECFM value of FB.

We now list each of the operand values in the preceding tape examples and give further explanations of their meanings.

UNIT=*UNIT*. The keyword UNIT signifies that we are describing the kind of device to be used. In some installations UNIT=TAPE means that we are using whatever type tape drive is standard. Such a tape drive may be expected to record 9-track data at densities of 800 or 1600 bpi. At your computer center, the standard designation for a 9-track tape may be different. For example, UNIT=2400 and UNIT=3400-4 refer to specific types of IBM tape drives.

VOL=SER=*tapename*. The keyword sequence VOL=SER specifies the name (serial number) of the tape volume that we want the operator to mount on some available tape drive. Such tape names are up to 8 characters long and are usually assigned by computer center personnel to each tape used within that installation. When a job is ready to execute, the operator receives a message requesting that the tape volume named *tapename* be mounted on some drive. Execution of your program is delayed until this tape is mounted.

DISP=*status*. The value coded with the DISP keyword indicates the status (disposition) of the file to be processed. Three status values are NEW, OLD and MOD. NEW is used when we wish to create a new file. OLD is used whenever we wish to read or rewrite an existing one. MOD is used when we wish to add records to the end of an existing file. Note, if the file does not exist then MOD is equivalent to NEW.

LABEL=*file #* or LABEL=(*file #*,NL). The LABEL keyword is used to specify which tape file is to be processed. The first form is used when the tape files are labeled; the second is used when no labels (NL) exist.

DSN=*filename*. This operand is needed if the tape file is labeled. It specifies the file's 1 to 8 character name. If this job creates the file (DISP=NEW), then *filename* is written into its label. If the file already exists (DISP=OLD), then *filename* is compared with the name that was previously written into the label. If it does not agree, then our program will not be executed. Thus, the DSN operand provides some protection against unauthorized access or unintended destruction of tape files.

DCB=(RECFM=*format*,LRECL=*rl*,BLKSIZE=*bl*). This operand describes how logical records are recorded. If RECFM=F, then all records are of fixed size *rl* and no blocking occurs. In this case, the values *rl* and *bl* must each be the size of a logical record. If RECFM=FB, then all records are of fixed size *rl*, and these are packed into blocks of size *bl*. Here *bl* must be a multiple of *rl*. If RECFM=V, then records may vary in length up to (rl-4), and each record is written as a single block. The value of *bl* must be four more than *rl*. These 4-character areas are used for control information. If RECFM=VB, then records may vary in length up to (rl-4), and these logical record segments are packed into blocks of length up to four less than *bl*. The value *rl* must be four greater than the largest possible data length. The value *bl* must be four greater than some multiple of *rl.* The designation RECFM=VBS is essentially equivalent to VB but must be specified if unformatted I/O is being used.

In addition to DD statements, a job that uses tape may require JCL cards called setup statements, one per tape. The form and positioning of these is wholly dependent on local computer center policies. Before attempting to use tape, you will need to find out if any such setup statements are required at your center and, if so, what information needs to be provided and where such statements are placed within your card deck.

4.3.2 Device Assignments Using the DECsystem 10

Using DEC FORTRAN-10, we can read or write unlabeled multifile tapes. Each block written on such a tape is of the same fixed length, usually 128 words (640 characters). The size of these blocks and their physical boundaries are unrelated to the sizes of the logical records and their boundaries. Thus, a single block may contain more than one logical record, and a single logical record may span more than one block.

Two techniques are employed to mark the boundaries of logical records. One technique is used for formatted records, the other for unformatted.

A formatted record (one written by a formatted WRITE statement) is recorded with an end-of-line character appended to it by the system. This special character marks the end of the record during any subsequent read operations. (See Figure 4-3.)

An unformatted record is written with a control word preceding it and one following it. If the record spans blocks then there is one additional control word for each block after the first. These control words contain record segment lengths and are used when the records are read or a BACKSPACE statement is executed. (See Figure 4-5.)

Whenever we code I/O statements in FORTRAN, we specify logical unit numbers. Each such unit number is, by default, assigned to some predefined class of devices. Specifically, FORTRAN unit number 2 is assigned to a card reader, unit 3 to a line printer, and unit 5 to the user's time-sharing terminal.

References to units 2, 3, or 5 are sufficient to access a card reader, printer or user terminal. However, when we wish some unit number to reference a tape, we must take explicit action. First, it is necessary to request the operator to mount the desired tape onto some tape drive. Then, we must associate our FORTRAN unit number with this tape drive. In order to accomplish these tasks we issue a MOUNT command. The form of this command, when we wish to reference a tape by unit number *uu*, is

.MOUNT MTA:*uu* /REELID:*tapename* / *access*

This command requests that the tape with reel identification *tapename* be mounted on some tape drive. In response, the operator finds the requested tape and mounts it on some available tape drive. Since reel identification names are assigned by the computer center staff, such a request is always associated with a unique tape.

The value of *access* is either RONLY or WENBL. If RONLY (Read ONLY) is coded, then the tape may be read but not written. If WENBL (Write ENaBLe) is coded, then we may issue both read and write commands. This operand helps to prevent the accidental destruction of tape files.

If more than one tape needs to be mounted, then a MOUNT command must be issued for each such tape.

When a tape is mounted, it is positioned at its beginning. This position may not be appropriate. If, for instance, we wish to process the third file, then we must skip over the first two. This is accomplished by the SKIP command. Its format is

.SKIP *uu*: *n* FILES

This causes the tape, associated with unit *uu* by a preceding MOUNT, to be spaced forward to the start of the (n+1)st file.

The SKIP command has a second format

.SKIP *uu*: EOT

This causes the associated tape to be spaced forward to the end of its last file. Such a command is of use if we wish to add new files.

After execution of a program is completed, a DISMOUNT command should be issued for each tape that was mounted. The form of this command is

.DISMOUNT *uu*:

Our discussion above gives no details as to precisely how the MOUNT, SKIP, and DISMOUNT commands are included as part of the setup of a FORTRAN program. This will vary, depending on whether you are a *batch* user (one submitting jobs by cards and receiving output by printer) or a *time-sharing* user (one submitting jobs and receiving output from a teletype or CRT device). Details on how to include these commands appear in the DEC introductions to batch and time-sharing use. You need to consult whichever manual is appropriate for you.

In either case, proper use of tapes requires that MOUNT commands be issued prior to program execution and that DISMOUNT commands be issued after execution.In addition, many installations require that a PLEASE command be directed to the operator prior to any MOUNT requests. This is done to insure availability of a tape drive. Before attempting to run any tape programs, you should find out what special procedures may be required at your installation.

4.4 DIRECT ACCESS DEVICES

While tapes are convenient devices for many applications, there are a number of tasks for which they are not well suited. Consider, for example, an airline reservation system. Such a system must have the ability to access data blocks rapidly in a random order. Since tapes are organized so that block 2 must be processed after block 1, block 3 after block 2, etc., they are not appropriate for random order processing. In fact, it takes a minimum of several minutes to read a block at the end of a tape if we are currently positioned at the beginning of the tape.

The computer storage devices that are designed to provide fast access for random order requests are called *direct access devices*. The most commonly used devices of this type are *movable head* and *fixed head* disk storage units.

A *disk storage unit* is a facility that provides read/write heads for accessing and recording data on disk packs. A *disk pack* consists of a set of circular platters, stacked one on top of the other. (See Figure 4-8.) Each such platter contains a large number of (usually over 200) concentric recording tracks on each of its two surfaces. Data is read or written either by having one read/write head per track (fixed head disk), or by each platter surface having its own read/write head that can be positioned at any selected track (movable head disk).

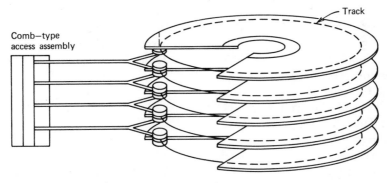

FIGURE 4-8 Disk pack with movable read/write mechanism.

Each disk pack mounted on a disk storage unit is constantly rotating at some fixed speed (usually at least 40 rotations per second) so that every data block recorded on a track passes by its read/write head once during each rotation. This constant spinning, plus the ability of movable head disks to move read/write heads to each track position, is what allows blocks on disks to be accessed at high speeds; generally, any given block may be accessed in no more than a fifth of a second, and average access time is considerably less.

Direct access to a block on a disk pack is facilitated by the fact that each block has a unique address associated with it. This address is determined by the block's position on its track, its track's position on its platter surface, and its surface's position relative to other surfaces.

In addition to direct access, disks can accommodate the need for sequential access. In fact, they are superior to tapes in the sense that one can update any block in place and can write blocks of any length, including a single character.This ability exists because of the constant rotational speeds of disks. The disadvantage of disks over tapes is an economic one. Disks, because of their sophisticated characteristics, are considerably more expensive.

4.4.1 Characteristics of Some Disks

Movable head disk units are in greater use than fixed head units. This is partly because they are less expensive but it is also a result of the fact that the disk packs on fixed head units are nonremovable. In contrast, the packs on movable head disks may be mounted and dismounted much the same as computer tapes.

Two common movable head disks are the IBM 3330 and the DEC RP03. Two common fixed head disks are the IBM 2305 and the DEC RD10. The characteristics of these four units follow.

Common User	IBM	IBM	DEC	DEC
Manufacturer	IBM	IBM	Memorex	Burroughs
Type	Movable	Fixed	Movable	Fixed
Model Number	3330-1	2305-1	RP03	RD10
Maximum Disks per Unit	8	1	8	4
Storage Capacity (in millions of characters)	100	5.75	52	2.5
Access Time (in milliseconds)				
Average	37.5	2.5	62.5	16.5
Maximum	72	5	105	33
Transfer Rate (in 1000 characters/sec)	806	3000	333	385

In studying this table you should note that the access time for fixed head devices is considerably less than that for movable head disks. This is because fixed head devices experience only *rotational delay* (the time for a selected block to rotate to its read/write head). In contrast, movable head devices experience both rotational delay and *seek delay* (the time for a read/write head to be moved to the chosen cylinder).

4.4.2 Management of Disk Space—IBM 360-370 OS

Each disk pack on an IBM disk storage unit is referred to as a volume and starts with a series of tracks on which is recorded the volume table of contents (VTOC). This table consists of one entry per file that is currently written on the pack and one entry per contiguous group of unassigned tracks. Each file entry specifies the file's name, the format of its blocks, and which tracks are assigned to it. Each free space entry points to a free track and specifies how many contiguous free tracks follow this one.

The VTOC serves a number of purposes. First, the free space entries are used each time some user wants to write a new file onto the pack. If enough room exists, tracks are removed from free space and assigned to a new file entry. When an existing file is deleted, its tracks are placed back into this pool of free space.

The VTOC file entries are also needed whenever we wish to process an existing data set. They indicate whether or not it resides on the pack and, if it is found, its location and how its blocks are formatted.

4.4.3 Management of Disk Space—DECsystem 10

The blocks on a DECsystem 10 disk pack are formatted much like a DEC-10 magnetic tape in that data is written into fixed size blocks, usually 128 words long. This fixed block size allows the allocation of file space in multiples of blocks. Such allocations are independent of track sizes.

In order to keep account of disk pack usage and free space, each pack contains a space allocation table, a master directory, and a set of user directories. The space allocation table has entries giving the status (used, unused) of every block on the pack. This table is used whenever space is needed to create a new file or space is released because of file deletion.

The master directory has one entry per user directory. This is used to find the correct directory whenever we are searching for the file of some specific user. The user directories maintain the name of each user file and the blocks that are allocated to that file.

4.4.4 Sequential Processing of Disk Files

Data can be written into and read from disk files in the same sequential manner as tape. In fact, the record formats used for disks are precisely the same as those used for tapes, and the specialized commands—BACKSPACE, ENDFILE, and REWIND— have logically the same effect as they had on tapes.

This compatability between tape and disk sequential files allows us to write programs that work for data recorded on either medium. No changes are required to the FORTRAN programs. However, for each system, certain commands (e.g., MOUNT's and DD statements) must be altered to change from one medium to another.

4.4.5 Random Processing of Disk Files

The primary advantage of disk over tape is its ability to process random ordered requests for data blocks. In order to use this capability, FORTRAN provides a mode of I/O called *random access*. Associated with this mode, there are two new statement types. In addition, READ and WRITE statements for random processing differ slightly from those used for sequential processing.

To make use of the random access mode of input/output, we must first execute a statement that describes the file to be processed. This statement is a DEFINE FILE and has the form

DEFINE FILE *uu* (*rec*, *size*, L, *avar*)

in IBM FORTRAN and the form

CALL DEFINE FILE (*uu*, *size*, *avar*, '*filename*.DAT')

in DEC FORTRAN-10. The parameters in the DEFINE FILE are coded as follows.

uu   - The FORTRAN unit number to be used for this file.
rec   - The number of logical records to be associated with this file. Each such logical record is identified by its record number, which is in the range from 1 to *rec* (not specified on DEC-10).
size - The length of each record within this file. In IBM FORTRAN, this value refers to the number of characters. In DEC FORTRAN-10, it refers to words for unformatted I/O and characters for formatted I/O.
avar - An integer variable called the *associated variable*. This variable is assigned the value 1 prior to any input/output commands being issued to unit *uu*. Subsequent to input/output being performed, its value is always one more than the record number of the last record that was processed.

The third remaining parameter is coded quite differently for our two sample systems. In IBM FORTRAN, this is specified as the letter L. (Other options exist but these will not be discussed here.) In DEC FORTRAN-10, this is the name within quotes of the random access file to be processed. Such a name is formed by writing a 6-character string followed by the string .DAT .

Execution of a DEFINE FILE results in space being acquired from disk and this space being preformatted into *rec* records each of length *size*. Since all records are of a fixed length, the system can easily calculate where any randomly requested record is located.

The READ and WRITE statements for a random access file have the following form.

1.   READ (*uu'n,format #*) *list*
2.   READ (*uu'n*) *list*
3.   WRITE (*uu'n,format #*) *list*
4.   WRITE (*uu'n*) *list*

Statements 1 and 3 are used for formatted records; statements 2 and 4 are used for unformatted. The added field n is an integer expression whose value is the record number of the record to be processed. After execution of one of these statements, the value of the associated variable (*avar*) is set to $n+1$. Thus,

```
WRITE (2'15) (S(I), I=1,20)
```

writes a 20-word record, consisting of the binary representations of $S(1)$, $S(2)$,...,$S(20)$, into the disk area associated with logical record 15 on unit 2. After this write is completed, the file's associated variable has value 16.

The automatic incrementing of a random access file's associated variable can be convenient when the file is to be processed sequentially. To convince yourself of this, consider the problem of reading in a card deck and writing it out to the random access file associated with unit 1. Assuming that DSKPOS is the associated variable, the following sequence of code suffices.

```
        DSKPOS = 1
10      READ (RDR,1000,END=99) (CARD(I), I=1,80)
1000    FORMAT (80A1)
        WRITE (1'DSKPOS,1000) (CARD(I), I=1,80)
        GO TO 10
```

Prior to executing this loop, we must have executed a DEFINE FILE. An appropriate one for IBM FORTRAN might be

```
DEFINE FILE 01 (200, 80, L, DSKPOS)
```

For DEC FORTRAN-10 we could use

```
CALL DEFINE FILE (1, 80, DSKPOS, 'FOR01.DAT')
```

In the IBM example, we assume that no more than 200 records are to be written. No such limitation is placed on the DEC-10.

When executing a program segment consisting of a loop of the form—
read a record, process it, go back to read— it would be convenient to have
the system anticipate our next read while we process the current record. Such
a feature could increase our program's efficiency by allowing it to overlap its
reading with its processing activities. In FORTRAN, it is possible to achieve such
overlap by issuing a FIND statement after each read. The FIND statement has
the general form

FIND $(uu'n)$

Its execution causes the system to initiate fetching of record n. This record
is not made available to your program until you issue a subsequent read that
again specifies record n. Thus, we can improve our program's efficiency by
writing the aforementioned loop as—read the current record, find the next
record to be processed, process the current record, go back to read.

4.5 ASSIGNMENT OF FILES
TO DIRECT ACCESS DEVICES: CASE STUDIES

4.5.1 Direct Access Device Assignment Using IBM OS/JCL

As with card readers, printers, and tapes, direct access devices are associated
with unit numbers by DD statements. In this case, the DD keywords that
are used are the UNIT, DISP, DSN and DCB which have already been discussed,
plus one new one, SPACE. The LABEL parameter, used for tapes, is not meaningful, and the VOL=SER parameter, while meaningful, is not discussed here.

The UNIT parameter should be coded
UNIT=SYSDA
This indicates that we desire to use a SYStem Direct Access device.

The DSN and DCB parameters are coded as for tape, except that the
DCB RECFM field for random access files must be written as RECFM=F.

The DISP parameter is more complicated than it was for tapes. It must
now be coded
DISP=(*status*, *disposition*)
The status is either NEW, OLD or MOD. The disposition field may be DELETE,
CATLG, or KEEP. The meanings of these disposition values are

DELETE - Remove this file from the device after this job is executed. All
space allocated is returned to the system for reallocation.
CATLG - Keep this file, recording its name and position on a system catalog.
Subsequent jobs may access this data set merely by knowing its
name.

KEEP   - Keep this file. If it was cataloged in a previous job, then it remains
so.

The SPACE parameter must be included if the file is being created, that is, when the status of DISP is NEW. This parameter specifies the file's space requirements. It is coded as

$$SPACE=(block,(init,second),RLSE)$$

The value *block* is the size of our physical blocks (the same as BLKSIZE in the DCB parameter). *init* tells for how many of these blocks we initially need space. *second* gives a secondary allocation to be used only if we exhaust our initial one. Such secondary allocations can be given up to 15 times. Thus the maximum file size is *init* + 15∗*second* blocks, each of size *block*. The code RLSE merely says that we wish to return to the system any space that is not filled by this execution.

The following show how to code DD statements for a variety of problems.

Example 1 We wish to use unit 18 to create a sequential disk file named FORT. Its logical records are 40 characters long and are blocked 80 at a time. The file is to be cataloged for future use.

```
//FT18F001 DD UNIT=SYSDA,DISP=(NEW,CATLG),DSN=FORT,
//            DCB=(RECFM=FB,LRECL=40,BLKSIZE=3200),
//            SPACE=(3200,(50,10),RLSE)
```

The space parameter shown above allocates room for 50 blocks. If these are used, our quota is raised to 60, then to 70, and so on up to a maximum of 200 blocks.

Example 2 We wish to use unit 8 to process the file created in example 1. The file is to be retained at this job's end.

```
//FT08F001 DD DISP=(OLD,KEEP),DSN=FORT
```

Example 3 We wish to use unit 12 to process the file created in example 1. At the end of the job, this file is to be deleted.

```
//FT12F001 DD DISP=(OLD,DELETE),DSN=FORT
```

4.5.2 Direct Access Device Assignment Using the DECsystem 10

Any user may acquire direct access space on DECsystem 10 disks (up to some maximum allocation dictated by the system's administrator). Unlike on the IBM 360-370 system, we do not need to preallocate space for each of our files. In fact, when we are using the CALL DEFINE FILE statement, its execution handles device assignment and file naming.

The name of a sequential disk file associated with unit *uu* is always FOR*uu*.DAT . The assigning of such a unit number to a disk occurs automatically for units 1, 20, 21, 22, 23, and 24. The disk association for other unit numbers must be declared by issuing an ASSIGN command of the form

.ASSIGN DSK: *uu*

After our program completes execution, we will have in our disk area all files created by this execution. Files that we no longer need may be deleted by the command

.DELETE *filename*.DAT

(*Note*. Those interested in further study of DEC-10 I/O should investigate the FORTRAN-10 OPEN statement. Its use provides even greater flexibility than the ASSIGN command.)

4.6 AN EXAMPLE—A KEYWORD-BASED BOOK RETRIEVAL SYSTEM

Consider the task of finding all library books related to some given area of study. One technique that is often used is to scan the library's catalogs for all titles containing some meaningful words. For example, a search for books concerned with programming languages would probably involve our checking for books whose titles include the words ALGOL, COBOL, FORTRAN, PL/I, etc. Clearly, such activity is better done by machines than by people, and so we will now consider a program that implements a keyword search procedure.

The program we wish to write has two input files. The first is a tape or disk sequential file, containing the titles of all books owned by our library. The logical records within this file are each 70 characters long and contain one book title each.

The second input file appears on cards. This card deck consists of two distinct parts. It begins with a series of one or more cards, each of which contains a keyword in columns 1 to 8. The end of all keywords is signaled by a card containing an asterisk (*) punched in column 1. Following this, there is a set of retrieval command cards. Each such card contains a one-digit code in column 1. Certain of these cards contain a keyword that is punched in columns 3 to 10. The legal command codes and their meanings are:

1   Reset retrieval system so that no books are currently selected for printing.
2   Requires a keyword argument. This command causes all titles containing this keyword to be added to the list of ones selected thus far. Thus, the sequence of commands

    1
    2 PROGRAM
    2 PROGRAMS

selects all titles that contain either the word PROGRAM or the word PROGRAMS.
3   Requires a keyword argument. This command sets the selected titles list to include only those titles previously selected that also contain this new keyword. Thus,

    1
    2 PROGRAM
    3 STYLE

selects all titles that contain both the word PROGRAM and the word STYLE.
4   Negate the selected titles list so that only those that were not chosen are now selected. Thus,

    1
    2 PROGRAM
    4

selects all titles that do not contain the word PROGRAM.
5   Print selected titles. This command prints the titles of all books that are currently selected. Thus,

    1
    2 SHARING
    2 SLICING
    3 TIME
    4
    5

prints out those titles that do not contain either of the word pairs (TIME, SHARING) or (TIME, SLICING).

The two primary data structures that are used to effect these five retrieval commands are the two-dimensional logical array TTLKEY and the logical list SELECT. During the phase of our program in which titles are first read, we scan each title to see which keywords it contains. If the Kth keyword is contained in the Ith title, then TTLKEY(I,K) is assigned the value .TRUE.; otherwise it is assigned .FALSE.

Once we enter the program phase in which retrieval commands are processed, SELECT is used to specify which titles are currently selected for printing. The value of SELECT(I) is .TRUE. just in case we have selected the Ith title. The task of the retrieval section is merely to update each component of SELECT, based on the command specified and the values found in TTLKEY. So, for example, a command

3 FORTRAN

where FORTRAN is the Kth keyword, is effected by performing

$$\text{SELECT(I)} = \text{SELECT(I)} \text{ .AND. } \text{TTLKEY(I,K)}$$

for I ranging from 1 to the number of titles. A print command (5) then results in our printing the Ith title just in case SELECT(I) has value .TRUE.

A program implementing this retrieval system follows in Figure 4-9.

```
C* * * * * * * * * * * * * * * * * * * * * * * * * * * * * * * * * *
C* KEYWORD-BASED BOOK RETRIEVAL SYSTEM                              *
C*   THIS PROGRAM INPUTS A SET OF BOOK TITLES AND KEYWORDS WHICH ARE *
C*   USED TO INDEX THE BOOKS. INPUT IS THEN RECEIVED SPECIFYING, BY  *
C*   KEYWORD, WHICH BOOKS THE USER WANTS TO ACCESS. LISTS OF RELEVANT *
C*   BOOK TITLES ARE OUTPUT UPON REQUEST.                           *
C*                                                                  *
C* INPUT FORMAT (CARD IMAGE FILE):                                  *
C*    A SET OF CARDS, EACH OF WHICH CONTAINS A KEYWORD IN COLUMN 1-8 *
C*    A TRAILER CARD CONTAINING AN * IN COLUMN 1                    *
C*    A SET OF RETRIEVAL REQUESTS EACH OF THE FORM                  *
C*        COLUMN 1    - COMMAND CODE (1,2,3,4 OR 5)                 *
C*        COLUMNS 3-10 - KEYWORD (ONLY USED IF CODE IS A 2 OR 3)    *
C* INPUT FORMAT (TAPE OR DISK SEQUENTIAL FILE):                     *
C*    A SET OF BOOK TITLES (CURRENT TITLE LENGTH IS 70)             *
C*                                                                  *
C* RETRIEVAL COMMANDS IMPLEMENTED:                                  *
C*    1 - RESET SELECT LIST                                         *
C*    2 - ADD TO SELECT LIST ALL TITLES WITH THIS KEYWORD           *
C*    3 - DELETE FROM CURRENT SELECT LIST TITLES WITHOUT THIS KEYWORD *
C*    4 - NEGATE SELECT LIST SO THAT ONLY THOSE TITLES WHICH WERE NOT *
C*        CHOSEN ARE NOW SELECTED                                   *
C*    5 - PRINT OUT THE TITLES OF ALL SELECTED BOOKS               *
C*                                                                  *
C* ALGORITHM BEING IMPLEMENTED:                                     *
C*    A) KEYWORDS ARE READ IN AND STORED IN LIST KEYTAB             *
C*    B) TITLES ARE READ IN AND STORED IN A RANDOM ACCESS FILE      *
C*    C) AS EACH TITLE IS READ, IT IS SCANNED TO SEE WHICH KEYWORDS IT *
C*       CONTAINS. IF THIS IS THE I-TH TITLE AND IT CONTAINS THE K-TH *
C*       KEYWORD, THEN TTLKEY(I,K) IS ASSIGNED THE VALUE .TRUE.     *
C*    D) THE STATUS OF THE SELECT LIST IS SET TO INDICATE THAT NO   *
C*       TITLES ARE CURRENTLY SELECTED (SELECT(I)=.FALSE., FOR ALL I) *
C*    E) RETRIEVAL COMMANDS ARE READ. ACTIONS TAKEN ARE:            *
C*       1 - SELECT(I)=.FALSE., FOR ALL I                           *
C*       2 - SELECT(I)=SELECT(I).OR.TTLKEY(I,K), FOR ALL I, WHERE K IS *
C*           INDEX OF KEYWORD SPECIFIED WITH THIS COMMAND           *
C*       3 - SELECT(I)=SELECT(I).AND.TTLKEY(I,K), FOR ALL I, K AS ABOVE*
C*       4 - SELECT(I)=.NOT.SELECT(I), FOR ALL I                    *
C*       5 - IF SELECT(I)=.TRUE. , PRINT THE I-TH TITLE             *
C*                                                                  *
```

```
C* MAJOR VARIABLES:                                                       *
C*     KEYTAB - TABLE OF KEYWORDS; CHARACTER*8; SIZE 50                    *
C*     KEYMAX - MAXIMUM SIZE OF KEYTAB; CURRENTLY 50                       *
C*     KEYNUM - ACTUAL NUMBER OF KEYWORDS                                  *
C*     TTLKEY - RETRIEVAL MATRIX; LOGICAL; SIZE 100 BY 50                  *
C*     TTLMAX - MAXIMUM NUMBER OF TITLES; CURRENTLY 100                    *
C*     TTLNUM - ACTUAL NUMBER OF TITLES                                    *
C*     TTLWTH - LENGTH IN CHARACTERS OF EACH TITLE; CURRENTLY 70           *
C*     SELECT - TITLES CURRENTLY SELECTED; LOGICAL; SIZE 50                *
C*     TRACE  - IF TRUE, TRACE ALL SUBPROGRAM CALLS AND EXITS;LOGICAL      *
C*     DEBUG  - IF TRUE, ECHO ALL INPUT AND DUMP TTLKEY; LOGICAL           *
C*                                                                        *
C* SUBPROGRAMS USED:                                                      *
C*     XTRACT - ASSIGNS VALUES TO TTLKEY IN ACCORDANCE WITH WORDS FOUND   *
C*              IN CURRENT TITLE                                          *
C*     KEYLUK - CHECK TO SEE IF SOME GIVEN WORD IS A KEYWORD              *
C*     GETKEY - READ AND STORE SET OF KEYWORDS                           *
C*     GETTTL - READ AND STORE TITLES                                    *
C*     NEXTWD - RETURN NEXT WORD IN TITLE AFTER COLUMN 'COL'             *
C*                                                                        *
C*  PROGRAMMER'S NAME: ---                     DATE WRITTEN: ---          *
C* * * * * * * * * * * * * * * * * * * * * * * * * * * * * * * * * * * * *
       INTEGER DSKPTR, KEYNDX, COMAND, I, J
       LOGICAL SELECT(50)
       CHARACTER KEYWD*8
C                  NOTE: COMMON VARIABLES ARE INITIALIZED IN BLOCK DATA
       COMMON/KEY/ TRACE, DEBUG, RDR, PRT, TRC, DBG, MASTER, DIRECT,
      *  TTLWTH, TTLNUM, TTLMAX, KEYNUM, KEYMAX, TTLKEY, TITLE, KEYTAB
       INTEGER RDR, PRT, TRC, DBG, MASTER, DIRECT, TTLWTH
       INTEGER TTLNUM, TTLMAX, KEYNUM, KEYMAX
       LOGICAL TRACE, DEBUG, TTLKEY(100,50)
       CHARACTER TITLE*70, KEYTAB*8(50)
C
C                  ALLOCATE SPACE AND ASSIGN UNIT 'DIRECT' TO A RANDOM ACCESS
C                  FILE. FORMS FOR 360-370 AND DEC-10 ARE SHOWN
       DEFINE FILE 12 (100, 70, L, DSKPTR)
C-----CALL DEFINE FILE (12, 70, DSKPTR, 'TITLES.DAT')
C
C                  PRINT OUTPUT TITLE LINE BEFORE STARTING PROCESSING
       WRITE (PRT,50)
50     FORMAT ('1', T20, 'AUTOMATED KEYWORD BOOK RETRIEVAL SYSTEM' /
      1          '+', T20, '_____ _____ ____ _____ _____' /// )
C
C                  READ AND STORE EACH OF THE KEYWORDS
       CALL GETKEY (&8000)
C
C                  IF NO KEY FOUND THEN QUIT
       IF (KEYNUM .EQ. 0) GO TO 7000
C
C                  PRINT OUT LIST OF LEGAL KEYWORDS
       WRITE (PRT,60) (KEYTAB(I), I = 1, KEYNUM)
60     FORMAT (T17, 'KEYWORDS WHICH MAY BE USED FOR RETRIEVAL ARE:'
      1          /    (1X, 8A10) )
C
C                  READ TITLES, WRITE THEM TO DISK ,CREATE RETRIEVAL MATRIX
       CALL GETTTL
C
C                  IF NO TITLES THEN QUIT NOW
       IF (TTLNUM .EQ. 0) GO TO 7500
C
C                  IN DEBUGGING STAGES DUMP OUT RETRIEVAL MATRIX
C                  IN EITHER CASE ENTER RETRIEVAL PHASE AS IF A RESET COMMAND
C                  (CODE=1) WAS JUST FOUND. THIS INITIALIZES SELECT
       IF (.NOT. DEBUG) GO TO 320
       WRITE (DBG,70)
70     FORMAT (' *** DEBUG *** RETRIEVAL MATRIX CREATED FOR THIS RUN')
       DO 100 I = 1, TTLNUM
          WRITE (DBG,80) I, (TTLKEY(I,J), J = 1, KEYNUM)
```

185

```
80      FORMAT (' TITLE', I3, ':', (T11, 50L1) )
100     CONTINUE
        GO TO 320
C* * * * * * * * * * * * * * * * * * * * * * * * * * * * * * * * * * * * *
C RETRIEVAL PHASE: ALL RETRIEVAL COMMANDS ARE PROCESSED HERE         *
C* * * * * * * * * * * * * * * * * * * * * * * * * * * * * * * * * * * * *
C
300     READ (RDR,301,END=400) COMAND, KEYWD
301     FORMAT (I1, 1X, A8)
        IF (DEBUG) WRITE (DBG,302) COMAND, KEYWD
302     FORMAT (' *** DEBUG *** RETRIEVAL CODE', I2, ' KEYWORD ', A8)
C
C               BE SURE COMMAND IS LEGAL
        IF ((COMAND .GE. 1) .AND. (COMAND .LE. 5)) GO TO 310
        WRITE (PRT,303) COMAND
303     FORMAT (' *** ERROR *** - ILLEGAL COMMAND CODE=', I1)
        GO TO 300
C
C               BRANCH OUT TO HANDLE INDIVIDUAL COMMANDS
310     GO TO (320,330,330,350,360), COMAND
C
C               CODE 1 - RESET SELECT LIST
320     DO 325 I = 1, TTLNUM
          SELECT(I) = .FALSE.
325     CONTINUE
        GO TO 300
C
C               CODE 2 AND 3 EACH REQUIRE A LEGAL KEYWORD
330     KEYNDX = KEYLUK(KEYWD)
        IF (KEYNDX .GT. 0) GO TO 332
C
C               BAD KEY - NOTE ERROR
        WRITE (PRT,331) KEYWD
331     FORMAT (' *** ERROR *** - ILLEGAL KEYWORD SPECIFIED:', A8)
        GO TO 300
332     IF (COMAND .EQ. 3) GO TO 340
C
C               CODE 2 - ADD ELEMENTS TO SELECT LIST
        DO 335 I = 1, TTLNUM
          SELECT(I) = SELECT(I) .OR. TTLKEY(I,KEYNDX)
335     CONTINUE
        GO TO 300
C
C               CODE 3 - INTERSECT SELECT LIST WITH THOSE HAVING KEYWD
340     DO 345 I = 1, TTLNUM
          SELECT(I) = SELECT(I) .AND. TTLKEY(I,KEYNDX)
345     CONTINUE
        GO TO 300
C
C               CODE 4 - COMPLEMENT SELECT LIST
350     DO 355 I = 1, TTLNUM
          SELECT(I) = .NOT. SELECT(I)
355     CONTINUE
        GO TO 300
C
C               CODE 5 - WRITE OUT SELECTED TITLES
360     WRITE (PRT,361)
361     FORMAT ('0 TITLES RETRIEVED BY LATEST COMMAND SEQUENCE ARE:' /)
        DO 365 I = 1, TTLNUM
          IF (.NOT. SELECT(I)) GO TO 365
          READ (DIRECT'I) TITLE
          WRITE (PRT,362) I, TITLE
362       FORMAT (' TITLE', I4, ' :', A70)
365     CONTINUE
        GO TO 300
C
C*****************************************************************
C**** ALL RETRIEVAL REQUESTS PERFORMED - NORMAL TERMINATION ****
400     WRITE (PRT,401)
401     FORMAT ('0*** ALL PROCESSING COMPLETED ***')
        STOP
```

```
C
C*********************************************************************
C****      ERROR TERMINATIONS ALL COME AFTER THIS POINT        ****
C
C              NO KEYWORDS
7000  WRITE (PRT,7001)
7001  FORMAT (' *** ERROR *** - NO KEYWORDS FOUND')
      STOP
C
C              NO TITLES
7500  WRITE (PRT,7501)
7501  FORMAT (' *** ERROR *** - NO TITLES FOUND')
      STOP
C
C              UNEXPECTED END-OF-FILE
8000  WRITE (PRT,8001)
8001  FORMAT (' *** ERROR *** - UNEXPECTED END OF DATA')
      STOP
      END


      SUBROUTINE GETKEY (*)
C* * * * * * * * * * * * * * * * * * * * * * * * * * * * * * * * * * *
C* READ AND STORE ALL KEYWORDS IN TABLE KEYTAB, IF THERE IS NO END OF  *
C*  KEYS CARD (*), THEN EXECUTE A RETURN1 TO CAUSE PROGRAM TERMINATION *
C* * * * * * * * * * * * * * * * * * * * * * * * * * * * * * * * * * *
C
      INTEGER I
      CHARACTER KEYWD*8, KEYCH*1(8)
      COMMON/KEY/ TRACE, DEBUG, RDR, PRT, TRC, DBG, MASTER, DIRECT,
     *  TTLWTH, TTLNUM, TTLMAX, KEYNUM, KEYMAX, TTLKEY, TITLE, KEYTAB
      INTEGER RDR, PRT, TRC, DBG, MASTER, DIRECT, TTLWTH
      INTEGER TTLNUM, TTLMAX, KEYNUM, KEYMAX
      LOGICAL TRACE, DEBUG, TTLKEY(100,50)
      CHARACTER TITLE*70, KEYTAB*8(50)
      EQUIVALENCE (KEYWD,KEYCH(1))
      IF (TRACE) WRITE (TRC,50)
50    FORMAT (' *** TRACE *** ENTERING GETKEY')
      DO 100 I = 1, KEYMAX
         READ (RDR,60,END=8000) KEYWD
60       FORMAT (A8)
         IF (KEYCH(1) .EQ. '*') GO TO 120
         IF (DEBUG) WRITE (DBG,70) I, KEYWD
70       FORMAT (' *** DEBUG *** KEYWORD NUMBER', I3, ' IS ', A8)
         KEYTAB(I) = KEYWD
100   CONTINUE
C
C              THERE ARE AT LEAST KEYMAX OF THEM
      I = KEYMAX+1
C
C              BE SURE WE FIND * . IGNORE ANY BEYOND KEYMAX-TH
110   READ (RDR,60,END=8000) KEYWD
      IF (KEYCH(1) .NE. '*') GO TO 110
120   KEYNUM =I-1
      IF (TRACE) WRITE (TRC,130)
130   FORMAT (' *** TRACE *** EXITING GETKEY - NORMAL RETURN')
      RETURN
C
C              UNEXPECTED END-OF-FILE, REPORT ERROR
8000  IF (TRACE) WRITE (TRC,8001)
8001  FORMAT (' *** TRACE *** EXITING GETKEY - END OF DATA RETURN')
      RETURN1
      END


      SUBROUTINE GETTTL
C* * * * * * * * * * * * * * * * * * * * * * * * * * * * * * * * * *
C* READ TITLES. WRITE EACH ONE TO RANDOM ACCESS FILE.            *
C*  SCAN EACH TITLE TO DETERMINE WHICH KEYWORDS IT CONTAINS       *
C*  IF I-TH TITLE CONTAINS K-TH KEYWORD THEN SET TTLKEY(I,K) TO TRUE  *
C* SUBPROGRAMS CALLED: XTRACT                                     *
C* * * * * * * * * * * * * * * * * * * * * * * * * * * * * * * * * *
```

```
      INTEGER I
      COMMON/KEY/ TRACE, DEBUG, RDR, PRT, TRC, DBG, MASTER, DIRECT,
     *  TTLWTH, TTLNUM, TTLMAX, KEYNUM, KEYMAX, TTLKEY, TITLE, KEYTAB
      INTEGER RDR, PRT, TRC, DBG, MASTER, DIRECT, TTLWTH
      INTEGER TTLNUM, TTLMAX, KEYNUM, KEYMAX
      LOGICAL TRACE, DEBUG, TTLKEY(100,50)
      CHARACTER TITLE*70, KEYTAB*8(50)
      IF (TRACE) WRITE (TRC,50)
50    FORMAT (' *** TRACE *** ENTERING GETTTL')
      DO 100 I = 1, TTLMAX
         READ (MASTER,60,END=200) TITLE
60       FORMAT (A70)
         IF (DEBUG) WRITE (DBG,70) I, TITLE
70       FORMAT (' *** DEBUG *** TITLE NUMBER', I4, ' IS:', A70)
         WRITE (DIRECT'I) TITLE
         CALL XTRACT (I)
100   CONTINUE
C
C              THERE ARE AT LEAST TTLMAX TITLES, IGNORE ANY BEYOND THIS
      I = TTLMAX+1
200   TTLNUM = I-1
      IF (TRACE) WRITE (TRC,210)
210   FORMAT (' *** TRACE *** EXITING GETTTL')
      RETURN
      END

      SUBROUTINE XTRACT (I)
C* * * * * * * * * * * * * * * * * * * * * * * * * * * * * * * * * * *
C* EXTRACT ALL WORDS FROM THE I-TH TITLE                             *
C*  NOTE EACH KEYWORD OCCURRENCE IN THIS TITLE BY MAKING APPROPRIATE *
C*   ENTRIES INTO THE RETRIEVAL MATRIX TTLKEY                        *
C* SUBPROGRAMS CALLED: NEXTWD, KEYLUK                                *
C* * * * * * * * * * * * * * * * * * * * * * * * * * * * * * * * * * *
      INTEGER COL, I, J
      CHARACTER KEYWD*8
      COMMON/KEY/ TRACE, DEBUG, RDR, PRT, TRC, DBG, MASTER, DIRECT,
     *  TTLWTH, TTLNUM, TTLMAX, KEYNUM, KEYMAX, TTLKEY, TITLE, KEYTAB
      INTEGER RDR, PRT, TRC, DBG, MASTER, DIRECT, TTLWTH
      INTEGER TTLNUM, TTLMAX, KEYNUM, KEYMAX
      LOGICAL TRACE, DEBUG, TTLKEY(100,50)
      CHARACTER TITLE*70, KEYTAB*8(50)
      IF (TRACE) WRITE (TRC,50) I
50    FORMAT (' *** TRACE *** ENTERING XTRACT, I=', I3)
C
C              INDICATE THAT NO WORDS ARE IN THIS TITLE-FIX AS NEEDED
      DO 100 J = 1, KEYNUM
         TTLKEY(I,J) = .FALSE.
100   CONTINUE
C
C              STARTING AT COLUMN 1, SCAN ENTIRE CARD
      COL = 1
C
C           FIND NEXT WORD, IF NONE BRANCH TO 300
200   CALL NEXTWD (&300, COL, KEYWD)
      KEYNDX = KEYLUK(KEYWD)
      IF (KEYNDX .EQ. 0) GO TO 200
C
C              FOUND A KEYWORD - NOTE THIS IN RETRIEVAL MATRIX
      TTLKEY(I,KEYNDX) = .TRUE.
      GO TO 200
C
C              TITLE COMPLETELY SCANNED - RETURN
300   IF (TRACE) WRITE (TRC,301)
301   FORMAT (' *** TRACE *** EXITING XTRACT')
      RETURN
      END
```

```
      SUBROUTINE NEXTWD (*, COL, WORD)
C* * * * * * * * * * * * * * * * * * * * * * * * * * * * * * * * * * *
C* STARTING AT COLUMN 'COL', FIND THE NEXT WORD IN THIS TITLE        *
C*  IF THIS NEXT WORD IS MORE THAN 8 CHARS,. TRUNCATE IT TO 8        *
C*   'COL' IS SET TO POINT AT THE CHARACTER AFTER THE NEW WORD       *
C*   NEW WORD IS STORED IN ARGUMENT 'WORD'                           *
C*  IF NO NEXT WORD EXISTS THEN EXECUTE A RETURN1                    *
C* * * * * * * * * * * * * * * * * * * * * * * * * * * * * * * * * * *
C
      INTEGER COL, I, J
      CHARACTER WORD*8, CHARS*1(8), WD*8, TTLCH*1(70)
      COMMON/KEY/ TRACE, DEBUG, RDR, PRT, TRC, DBG, MASTER, DIRECT,
     *  TTLWTH, TTLNUM, TTLMAX, KEYNUM, KEYMAX, TTLKEY, TITLE, KEYTAB
      INTEGER RDR, PRT, TRC, DBG, MASTER, DIRECT, TTLWTH
      INTEGER TTLNUM, TTLMAX, KEYNUM, KEYMAX
      LOGICAL TRACE, DEBUG, TTLKEY(100,50)
      CHARACTER TITLE*70, KEYTAB*8(50)
      EQUIVALENCE (WD,CHARS(1)), (TITLE,TTLCH(1))
      IF (TRACE) WRITE (TRC,50) COL
50    FORMAT (' *** TRACE *** ENTERING NEXTWD, COL=', I2)
C
C                IF ALREADY PAST THE END OF TITLE, QUIT
      IF (COL .GT. TTLWTH) GO TO 120
C
C                SCAN FOR NEXT NON-BLANK
      DO 100 I = COL, TTLWTH
         IF (TTLCH(I) .NE. ' ') GO TO 150
100   CONTINUE
C
C                REST OF CARD WAS BLANK
120   IF (TRACE) WRITE (TRC,121)
121   FORMAT (' *** TRACE *** EXITING NEXTWD, NO NEW WORD FOUND')
      RETURN1
C
C                FOUND A WORD, PUT IT TOGETHER
C                CLEAR RECEIVING AREA TO ALL BLANKS
150   WD = ' '
      DO 200 J = 1, 8
         IF ((I+J-1) .GT. TTLWTH) GO TO 250
         IF (TTLCH(I+J-1) .EQ. ' ') GO TO 250
         CHARS(J) = TTLCH(I+J-1)
200   CONTINUE
C
C                WORD MIGHT BE LONGER THAN 8 CHARS., IGNORE REST
      J = I+8
      DO 225 COL = J, TTLWTH
         IF (TTLCH(COL) .EQ. ' ') GO TO 300
225   CONTINUE
      COL = TTLWTH+1
      GO TO 300
C
C                WORD IS OF LENGTH LESS THAN 8, FIX COL
250   COL = I+J-1
C
C                MOVE ACCUMULATED CHARACTERS INTO 'WORD'
300   WORD = WD
      IF (TRACE) WRITE (TRC,350) WORD
350   FORMAT (' *** TRACE *** EXITING NEXTWD, WORD=', A8)
      RETURN
      END

      INTEGER FUNCTION KEYLUK (WORD)
C* * * * * * * * * * * * * * * * * * * * * * * * * * * * * * * * * * *
C* SEE IF 'WORD' IS IN KEYWORD LIST. IF NOT RETURN 0, ELSE RETURN    *
C*  THE INDEX OF THE MATCHING KEYWORD                                *
C* * * * * * * * * * * * * * * * * * * * * * * * * * * * * * * * * * *
C
```

```
          CHARACTER WORD*8
          COMMON/KEY/ TRACE, DEBUG, RDR, PRT, TRC, DBG, MASTER, DIRECT,
        *  TTLWTH, TTLNUM, TTLMAX, KEYNUM, KEYMAX, TTLKEY, TITLE, KEYTAB
          INTEGER RDR, PRT, TRC, DBG, MASTER, DIRECT, TTLWTH
          INTEGER TTLNUM, TTLMAX, KEYNUM, KEYMAX
          LOGICAL TRACE, DEBUG, TTLKEY(100,50)
          CHARACTER TITLE*70, KEYTAB*8(50)
          IF (TRACE) WRITE (TRC,50) WORD
   50     FORMAT (' *** TRACE *** ENTERING KEYLUK, WORD=', A8)
          DO 100 KEYLUK = 1, KEYNUM
              IF (KEYTAB(KEYLUK) .EQ. WORD) GO TO 200
   100    CONTINUE
          KEYLUK = 0
   200    IF (TRACE) WRITE (TRC,201) KEYLUK
   201    FORMAT (' *** TRACE *** EXITING KEYLUK, RETURN VALUE=', I2)
          RETURN
          END

          BLOCK DATA
C* * * * * * * * * * * * * * * * * * * * * * * * * * * * * * * * * * * *
C* INITIALIZE COMMON AREAS AS FOLLOWS:                                 *
C*        RDR    = 5    :IBM 360-370 READER UNIT NUMBER                *
C*        PRT    = 6    :IBM 360-370 PRINTER UNIT NUMBER               *
C*        MASTER = 11   :UNIT NUMBER FOR FILE OF TITLES                *
C*        DIRECT = 12   :UNIT NUMBER FOR RANDOM ACCESS FILE            *
C*        DBG    = 6    :DEBUGGING OUTPUT MERGED WITH STANDARD PRINT   *
C*        TRC    = 6    :TRACE OUTPUT MERGED WITH STANDARD PRINT       *
C*        TRACE  = TRUE:TRACE ALL ENTRIES AND EXITS FROM SUBPROGRAMS   *
C*        DEBUG  = TRUE:INCLUDE ALL DEBUGGING PRINTS                   *
C*        TTLMAX = 100  :NO MORE THAN 100 TITLES ALLOWED               *
C*        KEYMAX = 50   :NO MORE THAN 50 KEYWORDS                      *
C*        TTLWTH = 70   :WIDTH OF A TITLE IS 70 CHARACTERS             *
C* * * * * * * * * * * * * * * * * * * * * * * * * * * * * * * * * * * *
          COMMON/KEY/ TRACE, DEBUG, RDR, PRT, TRC, DBG, MASTER, DIRECT,
        *  TTLWTH, TTLNUM, TTLMAX, KEYNUM, KEYMAX, TTLKEY, TITLE, KEYTAB
          INTEGER RDR, PRT, TRC, DBG, MASTER, DIRECT, TTLWTH
          INTEGER TTLNUM, TTLMAX, KEYNUM, KEYMAX
          LOGICAL TRACE, DEBUG, TTLKEY(100,50)
          CHARACTER TITLE*70, KEYTAB*8(50)
          DATA RDR/5/, PRT/6/, MASTER/11/, DIRECT/12/, DBG/6/, TRC/6/
          DATA TRACE/.TRUE./, DEBUG/.TRUE./
          DATA TTLMAX/100/, KEYMAX/50/, TTLWTH/70/
          END
```

FIGURE 4-9 Keyword-based book retrieval system.

Exercises

4.01 On a 9-track tape, what is the odd parity bit associated with the following 8-bit data?
a. 10111011
b. 11111111
c. 01000000
d. 00000000

4.02 Assume the gaps on a tape are ½ inch long, data is recorded at 800 bpi, and the tape is 2400 feet long.
a. If we are told that 75% of tape is being used effectively, then how many characters are stored in a single block (assuming all blocks are of the same size)?
b. If we wish to increase our usage to 90%, how long must each block be?

4.03 Formatted records on a DEC-10 are terminated by an end-of-record marker. Why is this technique not appropriate for unformatted records?

4.04 Consider, if you are running on an IBM 360-370, the statement

```
DEFINE FILE 12 (100, 40, L, I12)
```

or, if you are running on a DEC-10, the statement

```
CALL DEFINE FILE (12, 40, I12, 'RAND.DAT')
```

a. What is the value of the integer variable I12 after execution of

```
READ (12'15,100) DATA
```

b. What is its value after execution of the sequence

```
WRITE (12'6,200) DATA
FIND (12'22)
```

4.05 Does it ever make sense to issue a REWIND to a unit number that refers to a sequential data set stored on a direct access device? Explain your answer.

4.06 Does it ever make sense to REWIND a direct access file? Explain your answer.

4.07 Assume we need to select a device to store a sequential data set. Discuss the advantages and disadvantages of using a tape or a disk.

4.08 Consider the IBM 360-370 OS/JCL DD statements.

```
//FT06F001  DD  SYSOUT=A
//FT10F001  DD  UNIT=TAPE,DSN=NEWDATA,VOL=SER=MYTAPE,LABEL=6,DISP=NEW,
//             DCB=(RECFM=VB,LRECL=84,BLKSIZE=256)
//FT12F001  DD  UNIT=TAPE,DISP=NEW,DSN=MODDATA,VOL=SER=OTHER,
//             LABEL=(3,NL),DCB=(RECFM=FB,LRECL=60,BLKSIZE=1200)
//FT14F001  DD  UNIT=SYSDA,DSN=DISKDATA,DISP=(NEW,CATLG),
//             SPACE=(200,(20,2)),
//             DCB=(RECFM=F,LRECL=200,BLKSIZE=200)
```

a. What type of device is associated with unit 6?
b. What is the significance of the 10 in FT10F001?
c. Sketch or describe the format of each record recorded on the sixth file of the tape named MYTAPE.
d. Pictorially represent the format of each record in the third file of the tape named OTHER.

e. Does MYTAPE use labels? Does OTHER?

f. What are the meaning of the three values 200, 20 and 2 in SPACE=(200,(20,2))?

g. Write a DD statement that might be used to access the newly created data set DISKDATA by unit 8 in some subsequent run.

4.09 Write a DD statement needed to create a labeled file on a tape named MINE. The tape already has four data sets. The new one is to be placed after the fourth. Its name is to be MYDATA. The records are each 100 characters long and are to be blocked in physical blocks, 10 records per block. You will reference this file by unit 9.

4.10 Assume the following sequence of DEC-10 commands are issued

```
.MOUNT    MTA:14/REELID:MINE/RONLY
.SKIP     14:2 FILES
```

a. What are the meanings of 14, MINE, and RONLY?

b. Where is the file to be located?

4.11 Assume that you are required to write a file at the end of all files currently recorded on the tape named TAPE1. Write a sequence of DEC-10 commands so that unit 8 might be used for this purpose.

4.12 Write the DEC-10 command required if unit 9 is to be used for processing a disk data set.

4.13 Write a program that processes a tape file containing 60-character records. Each such record consists of a 20-character name field followed by a 40-character address field. Your program must first read all the records, noting each unique name and the number of occurrences of this name. You must then reread the file, printing out the last record associated with each name.

4.14 In this exercise, you are being asked to write an airline reservation system. Input to your program is a set of cards each of the form

Character Positions	Information Recorded
1-20	Passenger name
21-60	Home Address
61-70	Phone number
71	Flight 1 (0 is not a legal flight number.
72	Flight 2 It is used when passenger has
73	Flight 3 fewer than 3 reservations.)

The end of all these passenger cards has a passenger name field filled with 20 asterisks. There are at most 100 passengers. You are to write each input record (except for the one containing 20 asterisks) onto a random access disk file. In addition you should create several tables. The first table, NAMES, should contain "A" in NAMES(K) if "A" is the passenger name of the Kth record. The second, RESERV, contains a K in RESERV(I,J) just in case the passenger associated with the Kth record is the Jth passenger on the Ith flight. You may assume that no flight ever contains more than 25 passengers. Thus, RESERV is declared to be a 9 by 25 integer array. Initialize RESERV to all zeros to indicate that, initially, no passengers are on any flight.

Following the reservation cards, your input is a series of commands. Each command card is of the form

Character Positions	Information Recorded
1-4	Command code
5-24	Passenger name (not used with CANC, PRINT)
25	Flight number (not used with INQ)
26-65	Home address (not used with ADD)
66-75	Phone number (only used with ADD)

Your program must interpret and print appropriate output for each such command card.

Legal commands are:

ADD - Add passenger to another flight. You must check for flight overflow and for a passenger being given reservations on more than three flights.

DELE - Remove passenger from some flight. You must check for an attempt to delete a passenger from an unassigned flight.

CANC - Cancel the reservations of all people on this flight.

PRNT - Print the list of names of all passengers on the flight.

INQ - Print the address, phone number and list of flight numbers assigned to this passenger.

CONF - Indicate whether or not this passenger holds a reservation on the specified flight.

CHAPTER 5   Data Structures

You have now seen all executable statements of the FORTRAN language. Although it does not have a large number of statement types, this language is useful in solving a wide variety of computing tasks. The power inherent in FORTRAN is not in the statements themselves but in the ways programmers use them to solve problems. Just as programmers have developed syntactic structures like the IF-THEN-ELSE and CASE described in Chapter 1, programmers have also developed ways of representing relations among data items. In this chapter we survey some structures useful for storing and manipulating data in higher-level language programs.

5.1   LISTS

Lists are the basis of most data structures. A *list* is an ordered collection of data objects. The list has a unique first object, called the *head* of the list; there is also a last object, called the *tail* of the list. Each item in the list, except the head, has a unique predecessor, and each item in the list, except the tail, has a unique successor. Physical examples of lists include a telephone directory and a filing cabinet full of folders. From these examples, you can see that the individual data objects in a list may have many components; each entry in the telephone directory, for example, consists of a name, an address, and a telephone number. Each data item is called a *record*, or a *node*, or an *element* of the list. The components of a record are called *fields*.

The following operations are commonly performed on lists.

1. Insert a node into a list.
2. Delete a node from a list.
3. Join two lists into one.
4. Split one list into two.
5. Output all nodes in a list.
6. Locate a node having a particular value in some field.
7. Sort all nodes of a list into order based on one field of the nodes.

The most common form of a list is a *sequential list*, which may be represented by an array in FORTRAN. In a sequential list each element physically follows its predecessor. Many of the programs developed in preceding chapters have performed the above operations on sequential lists. In this chapter we will consider some restricted varieties of sequential lists and several other kinds of lists.

5.2 STACKS

Imagine a store that stocks quantities of many different products. When new stock arrives, the clerks put it out on the shelves as the old stock is about to be exhausted. Since it is better not to let a shelf get completely empty, the clerks often put out new merchandise while some of the old is still available. The new stock may have a different price, but clerks put items at both prices on the shelves, relying on the customers to deplete the lower-priced stock first. If the old stock is dusty or dented, however, the customers will take the new stock first, even if it is more expensive.

At any time, the shopkeeper wants to know the value of the store's inventory, that is, the value of all goods waiting to be sold. In a store with many low-priced items (such as a grocery store), it is not feasible to maintain records on whether a can of peas put out on June 15 at $.29 or a can of peas put out on July 8 at $.31 was sold. In fresh produce, where a June 15 apple is indistinguishable from a June 18 one, this record-keeping is impossible.

To determine the value of their inventory, some stores use the LIFO method of accounting. The acronym LIFO stands for "Last In, First Out," meaning that the most recently acquired piece of merchandise is assumed to be the one sold. This method of accounting can be represented using a data structure called a stack.

A *stack* is a list in which all insertions and deletions occur at only one end. As an entry is placed on the stack, the entry previously on top of the stack becomes temporarily inaccessible. When this new entry is removed from the stack, the earlier entry, which had been inaccessible, once again becomes the top entry. The operations of adding to and deleting from a stack are called *pushing* and *popping*, respectively.

The arrangement of trays in a cafeteria operates as a stack. Clean trays are put on top of the stack, and customers remove them from the top. Some cafeterias use a spring-loaded mechanism to hold the trays, and so the push and pop operations involve physical movement of the remainder of the stack. In Figure 5-1 on the next page, we show the effects of some push and pop operations on a stack. Notice that items in a stack are removed in the reverse order from that in which they were inserted.

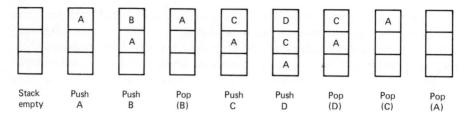

FIGURE 5-1   Stack operations.

The storekeeper wishing to model an inventory by the LIFO technique would use one stack for each item handled. As new stock is received, an entry, showing the quantity received and the price, is placed on the stack for that item. As stock is sold, the amount sold is deducted from the top element on the stack; if the quantity in that top item ever reaches zero, that entry is popped, and any remainder is deducted from the new top entry. The value of the inventory is determined by multiplying the quantity for each element by its price and summing these values for all elements.

A stack is conveniently represented in FORTRAN by an array with a pointer to indicate the position of the top. Instead of the free space appearing at the bottom of the array, as in Figure 5-1, we will represent a stack with the free space at the top. Then instead of moving the data items each time an element is added to the stack, we simply move the pointer to the stack top. Furthermore, we will represent stacks "on their sides," with the top on the right and the bottom on the left. Figure 5-2 shows a stack before and after items S has been pushed on the stack.

FIGURE 5-2   A stack implemented by an array.

If a stack is being implemented by an array of fixed size, one problem we need to consider is trying to place more entries in the stack than the array can contain. This is called stack *overflow*. The opposite of this problem is stack *underflow*, which is caused by attempting to pop an item from an empty stack. Both of these are error conditions and need to be checked for in programs that manipulate stacks.

We will now present a subroutine (STKOPS, Figure 5-3) that implements stack operations; the individual operations are entry points to that subroutine. The stack push and stack pop operations are straightforward implementations of the techniques described above. These are represented by the code associated with the entry points STKPSH and STKPOP.

The final entry point (STKINT) is used for stack initialization. Since the stack top points to the current top item in the stack, STKTOP = 0 will represent an empty stack. It is not necessary to initialize the stack itself since each push operation will always replace the contents of STACK(STKTOP+1). For debugging, however, it is helpful to dump the entire contents of the stack or the first few elements and to be able to separate stack elements from uninitialized storage locations. For this reason, the initialization code sets STKTOP and the entire stack to 0.

```
      SUBROUTINE STKOPS (*, STACK, STKSIZ, STKTOP, DATA)
      INTEGER STKSIZ, STKTOP, STACK(STKSIZ), DATA
C= = = = = = = = = = = = = = = = = = = = = = = = = = = = = = = = = = = = =
C  STACK OPERATIONS SUBROUTINE =                                         =
C= = = = = = = = = = = = = = =                                           =
C     THIS SUBROUTINE CONTAINS MODULES TO PERFORM INITIALIZATION OF      =
C          STACKS, INSERTIONS TO STACKS, AND DELETIONS FROM STACKS.      =
C                                                                        =
C     FOR EACH OF THESE ROUTINES, STACK IS AN INTEGER ARRAY BEING        =
C          USED AS A STACK; THE CURRENT TOP OF THAT STACK IS CONTAINED   =
C          IN STKTOP, AND THE SIZE (DIMENSION) OF THE STACK IS STKSIZ    =
C     PROGRAMMER: ---      DATE: ---                                     =
C= = = = = = = = = = = = = = = = = = = = = = = = = = = = = = = = = = = = =
C
C
      ENTRY STKPSH (*, STACK, STKSIZ, STKTOP, DATA)
C- - - - - - - - - - - - - - - - - - - - - - - - - - - - - - - - - - - -
C          THIS ENTRY POINT PUSHES THE VALUE IN "DATA" ONTO THE TOP    -
C          OF "STACK".                                                 -
C          IF STACK OVERFLOW OCCURS, ALTERNATE RETURN 1 IS TAKEN.      -
C          STKTOP IS UPDATED TO POINT TO THE NEW TOP OF THE STACK IF   -
C          A SUCCESSFUL PUSH OPERATION OCCURS.                         -
C- - - - - - - - - - - - - - - - - - - - - - - - - - - - - - - - - - - -
C
C . . . . . . . . CHECK FOR STACK OVERFLOW
      IF (STKTOP .GE. STKSIZ)   RETURN 1
C . . . . . . . . NO OVERFLOW, PUSH DATA ONTO STACK
      STKTOP = STKTOP+1
      STACK(STKTOP) = DATA
      RETURN
C
C
      ENTRY STKPOP (*, STACK, STKSIZ, STKTOP, DATA)
C- - - - - - - - - - - - - - - - - - - - - - - - - - - - - - - - - - - -
C          THIS ENTRY POINT POPS THE VALUE FROM THE CURRENT TOP OF     -
C          "STACK" AND PLACES THE VALUE IN "DATA".                     -
C          IF STACK UNDERFLOW OCCURS, ALTERNATE RETURN 1 IS TAKEN.     -
C          STKTOP IS UPDATED TO POINT TO THE NEW TOP OF THE STACK IF   -
C          A SUCCESSFUL POP OPERATION OCCURS.                          -
C- - - - - - - - - - - - - - - - - - - - - - - - - - - - - - - - - - - -
C
C . . . . . . . . CHECK FOR STACK UNDEFLOW
      IF (STKTOP .LE. 0)   RETURN 1
C . . . . . . . . NO UNDERFLOW, RETRIEVE DATA AND POP STACK
      DATA = STACK(STKTOP)
      STKTOP = STKTOP-1
      RETURN
```

```
C
C
      ENTRY STKINT (*, STACK, STKSIZ, STKTOP, DATA)
C- - - - - - - - - - - - - - - - - - - - - - - - - - - - - - - -
C           THIS ENTRY POINT INITIALIZES THE TOP OF STACK POINTER AND  -
C           THE ENTIRE STACK TO 0'S.                                   -
C           ALTERNATE RETURN 1 AND "DATA" ARE NOT USED IN THIS MODULE. -
C- - - - - - - - - - - - - - - - - - - - - - - - - - - - - - - -
         STKTOP = 0
         DO 10 I = 1, STKSIZ
            STACK(I) = 0
   10    CONTINUE
         RETURN
         END
```

FIGURE 5-3 Stack operation subroutine.

You should now be able to write a program that reads cards each containing a quantity purchased and its selling price, or a quantity sold, and determines the final value of the inventory by the LIFO valuation.

Stacks are an example of a *dynamic* data structure, which means that the structure logically expands and contracts during execution. Because this structure is implemented in FORTRAN using simple variables and arrays, the structure really does not change size, since variables and arrays remain of constant size. What does change is the amount of an array in use at any time. The restriction of using a fixed-sized array for a variable-sized stack is usually not too severe, since in most applications you can make a reasonable estimate of the maximum size a stack will attain.

5.3   QUEUES

The LIFO inventory valuation system is not realistic. Shopkeepers do not want to retain a large amount of old merchandise. Normally in shelving goods, they put the newer things to the back, so that stock does not age severely; this is especially important with perishable or seasonal merchandise. In these situations the FIFO inventory valuation system is more appropriate than LIFO. This system assumes that each item sold is the oldest of its type. The term FIFO stands for "First In, First Out," implying that at any time the oldest entries are those removed next. This situation is modeled by a queue.

A *queue* is a data structure in which all insertions are made at one end and all deletions are made from the other end. The end for insertions is called the *rear* of the queue, and the end for deletions is called the *front* of the queue. You are familiar with queues of people waiting in a checkout lane or queues of cars waiting for service at a filling station. New people join the queue at one end, and they leave the queue at the other end, after checking out or after being served.

Like a stack, a queue can be represented using an array. Two pointers are used to indicate the front and the rear of the queue. In Figure 5-4 we show a queue growing from left to right, with the front on the left and the rear on the right. Four operations on the queue are shown in the figure.

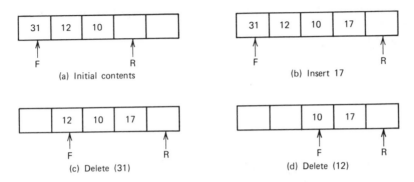

FIGURE 5-4 Queue operations.

Our sequential implementation of a stack always had one end fixed with the other end free to rise and fall. In a queue, however, both ends move, and so the active portion of the queue literally travels through the array. After one more addition to the queue in Figure 5-4(d), the queue will use the last element of the array, and so the queue will appear full. There are two empty positions on the left end of the array, however. We can use those positions by envisioning the array as a circle, with the two ends joined together. The position to the right of the rightmost position is then the leftmost. Two such insertions are shown in Figure 5-5.

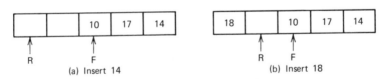

FIGURE 5-5 Circular representation of a queue.

As with stacks, the overflow and underflow conditions can exist; these need to be tested in any queue manipulation routines. Figure 5-6 presents subroutine entry points to perform initialization, insertion and deletion on queues that have the form shown in Figures 5-4 and 5-5. The front pointer always points to the oldest entry in the queue; the rear pointer always points one element to the right of the newest entry. This seemingly unnatural use of the rear pointer turns out to be convenient for distinguishing an empty list (R=F) from a full list (R=F-1). This interpretation of the rear pointer means that only $(n-1)$ items can be represented in an array of size n being used as a queue.

In addition to standard queue operation entry points, our subroutine provides an entry (QUEDMP) to help in debugging. One of the least enjoyable tasks about debugging is spending the time to produce intelligible debugging output. However, spending a few minutes writing such statements during program development can speed program debugging.

```
      SUBROUTINE QUEOPS (*, QUEUE, QUESIZ, QUEF, QUER, DATA)
      INTEGER QUESIZ, QUEF, QUER, QUEUE(QUESIZ), DATA
      INTEGER TRUER
      DATA IOUT/6/
C= = = = = = = = = = = = = = = = = = = = = = = = = = = = = = = = = = = = = = =
C  QUEUE MANIPULATION SUBROUTINE =                                        =
C= = = = = = = = = = = = = = = = = =                                      =
C  THIS SET OF MODULES MANIPULATES A SEQUENTIAL QUEUE.                    =
C  THE QUEUE IS CONTAINED IN ARRAY "QUEUE", OF DIMENSION QUESIZ.          =
C  THE QUEUE IS TREATED AS BEING CIRCULAR, AND SO POSITION "QUESIZ"       =
C  IS FOLLOWED BY POSITION "1".                                          =
C  THE FRONT AND REAR POINTERS ARE CONTAINED IN QUEF AND QUER,           =
C  RESPECTIVELY.                                                         =
C  "DATA" IS THE ITEM TO BE INSERTED OR THE ITEM DELETED.                =
C  PROGRAMMER: ---   DATE: ---                                           =
C= = = = = = = = = = = = = = = = = = = = = = = = = = = = = = = = = = = = = = =
C
C
C        ENTRY QUEINS (*, QUEUE, QUESIZ, QUEF, QUER, DATA)
C- - - - - - - - - - - - - - - - - - - - - - - - - - - - - - - - - - - -
C             THIS MODULE INSERTS "DATA" INTO THE "QUEUE".               -
C             IF A SUCCESSFUL INSERTION OCCURS, THE FRONT AND REAR       -
C             POINTERS, QUEF AND QUER, ARE UPDATED APPROPRIATELY.        -
C             IF QUEUE OVERFLOW OCCURS, ALTERNATE RETURN 1 IS TAKEN AND  -
C             NO CHANGE TO QUEF OR QUER OCCURS.                          -
C- - - - - - - - - - - - - - - - - - - - - - - - - - - - - - - - - - - -
C
C . . . . . . CHECK FOR QUEUE OVERFLOW
      IF (QUEF .EQ. QUER+1 .OR.
     X    (QUEF .EQ. 1 .AND. QUER .EQ. QUESIZ) ) RETURN 1
C . . . . . . NO OVERFLOW, PROCEED TO INSERT DATA
      QUEUE(QUER) = DATA
      QUER = QUER + 1
      IF (QUER .GT. QUESIZ) QUER = 1
      RETURN
C
C
C        ENTRY QUEDEL (*, QUEUE, QUESIZ, QUEF, QUER, DATA)
C- - - - - - - - - - - - - - - - - - - - - - - - - - - - - - - - - - - -
C             QUEUE DELETION MODULE                                      -
C             THIS MODULE DELETES AN ITEM FROM THE FRONT OF "QUEUE",     -
C             PLACING THE VALUE REMOVED IN "DATA".                       -
C             IF THE QUEUE CONTAINS NO ENTRIES, ALTERNATE RETURN 1 IS    -
C             TAKEN, AND QUEF AND QUER ARE UNCHANGED.                    -
C             IF NORMAL DELETION OCCURS, QUER AND QUEF ARE UPDATED.      -
C- - - - - - - - - - - - - - - - - - - - - - - - - - - - - - - - - - - -
C
C . . . . . . . . CHECK FOR EMPTY QUEUE
      IF (QUEF .EQ. QUER) RETURN 1
C . . . . . . . . . NO UNDERFLOW; DELETE ITEM
      DATA = QUEUE(QUEF)
      QUEF = QUEF + 1
      IF (QUEF .GT. QUESIZ) QUEF = 1
      RETURN
C
C
```

```
      ENTRY QUEINT (*, QUEUE, QUESIZ, QUEF, QUER, DATA)
C- - - - - - - - - - - - - - - - - - - - - - - - - - - - - -
C           THIS MODULE INITIALIZES A QUEUE                       -
C           THE ENTIRE QUEUE IS SET TO ZEROS, AND QUEF AND QUER ARE -
C           SET TO POINT TO THE FIRST ELEMENT.                    -
C           SINCE QUEF.EQ.QUER IS THE INDICATION OF AN EMPTY QUEUE, -
C           AN ATTEMPT TO DELETE BEFORE INSERTING WILL CAUSE AN   -
C           UNDERFLOW ERROR EXIT.                                 -
C           ALTERNATE RETURN 1 AND "DATA" ARE NOT USED IN THIS MODULE. -
C- - - - - - - - - - - - - - - - - - - - - - - - - - - - - -
      QUEF = 1
      QUER = 1
      DO 10 I = 1, QUESIZ
          QUEUE(I) = 0
   10 CONTINUE
      RETURN
C
C
      ENTRY QUEDMP (*, QUEUE, QUESIZ, QUEF, QUER, DATA)
C- - - - - - - - - - - - - - - - - - - - - - - - - - - - - -
C           THIS ROUTINE DUMPS THE CONTENTS OF "QUEUE" IN ORDER.   -
C           IT ALSO DISPLAYS THE VALUES OF QUEF AND QUER, THE FRONT -
C           AND REAR POINTERS, RESPECTIVELY.                      -
C           ALTERNATE RETURN 1 AND "DATA" ARE NOT USED IN THE MODULE. -
C- - - - - - - - - - - - - - - - - - - - - - - - - - - - - -
      WRITE (IOUT, 21) QUEF, QUER
      IF (QUEF .EQ. QUER) RETURN
C . . . . . . . . . . FIND TRUE REAR POINTER OF QUEUE
      TRUER = QUER-1
      IF (TRUER .EQ. 0) TRUER = QUESIZ
C . . . . . . . . . IS QUEUE CONTIGUOUS OR DOES IT OVERLAP ARRAY ENDS?
      IF (QUEF .GT. TRUER) GO TO 100
C . . . . . . . . . CONTIGUOUS
      WRITE (IOUT,22) (QUEUE(I), I=QUEF, TRUER)
      RETURN
C . . . . . . . . . QUEUE IS SPLIT IN TWO PIECES
  100 WRITE (IOUT,22) (QUEUE(I), I=QUEF,QUESIZ), (QUEUE(I), I=1,TRUER)
      RETURN
   21 FORMAT ('0QUEUE DUMP:  FRONT POINTER = ', I5, '  REAR POINTER =',
     #          I5/ ' ANY ELEMENTS FOLLOW, IN ORDER FROM FRONT TO REAR')
   22 FORMAT (1X,10I8)
      END
```

FIGURE 5-6 Queue operations.

Again we have used a fixed-sized array to represent a dynamic data structure. Although this is an easy form to represent, it does have a problem with space utilization, as we shall see in the next section.

5.4 SEQUENTIAL ALLOCATION WITH POINTERS

There are several problems with sequential allocation of lists. The first problem occurs with general sequential lists, not with stacks and queues. Suppose that a list has been sorted in ascending order and that some deletions are now to be made from the middle of the list. After each deletion, it is necessary to recompact the list, that is, to move all later elements up one position. This is necessary to preserve the sequential nature of the list. Some processes, such as the binary search of Chapter 1, rely on all elements of a list being adjacent without gaps or empty positions between two elements.

However, moving the data to recompact the list can take much time if the list contains many items and if the item to be deleted is near the top.

Similarly, a single data record may consist of many fields. It is easy to represent a list of such items as a series of parallel arrays in which the separate arrays contain the separate fields of the list; the jth record is represented by the jth element of all arrays. If the records of such a list are being sorted on some field, and if the sort technique requires interchange of elements, it is necessary to interchange elements of all of these arrays each time an interchange is made. This data movement in all arrays can be a slow process.

We can solve this problem by use of an extra array, NEXT, to relieve us from the constraints of a sequential list. Instead of each entry physically preceding its successor, elements may be placed in arbitrary positions. For the Ith element, NEXT(I) will contain the subscript of the successor of element I. One simple variable, HEAD, will indicate the location of the first element of the list; NEXT(HEAD) will point to the second element, the third element will be located by NEXT(NEXT(HEAD)), etc. When sorting this type of list, we simply interchange the contents of the NEXT array, without needing to move large amounts of data. This arrangement is pictured in Figure 5-7.

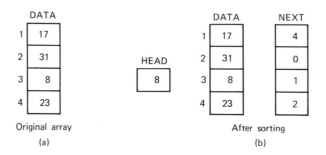

FIGURE 5-7 Sorting with NEXT array.

Notice that in the sorting process, the contents of the DATA array have not been moved. This implies that if there were ten arrays containing data, their contents would not have to be rearranged for the sorting process. The sort using a NEXT array is not appreciably more difficult than a conventional sort. In the subroutine of Figure 5-8 we show an extension of this notion. An NR by NC array is assumed to consist of NC columns of related data. The data in these columns is sorted in ascending order on the column SORTC.

Since this routine uses a bubble sort, its time complexity is of order NR**2. Because the NEXT array forces sequential processing of the list, it is not possible to use one of the better search algorithms that depend upon being able to progress through the list in an order other than from top to bottom. In the

```
      SUBROUTINE INSORT (A, NR, NC, COL, NEXT, HEAD)
      INTEGER A(NR,NC), NEXT(NR), HEAD, COL
      INTEGER NLESS2, P, K, L, I, J
      LOGICAL SWAP
C========= IN PLACE SORT - SORT TO REDUCE DATA MOVEMENT  ==============
C  THIS ROUTINE PERFORMS AN IN PLACE SORT OF ARRAY "A" BASED ON COLUMN =
C  "COL".  ON RETURN "HEAD" IS THE ROW OF THE SMALLEST VALUE,          =
C  NEXT(HEAD) IS THE ROW OF SECOND SMALLEST, NEXT(NEXT(HEAD)) IS THE   =
C  ROW OF THIRD SMALLEST, ETC.                                         =
C  PROGRAMMER: ---                        DATE: ---                    =
C=====================================================================
C                                                                      =
      HEAD = 1
      IF (NR.LE.1) GO TO 20
      NLESS2 = NR-2
C. . . . . . . . . . FIND THE SMALLEST ELEMENT; POINT "HEAD" TO IT.
C. . . . . . . . . . ALSO SET THE "NEXT" ARRAY INITIALLY
      DO 10 I=2,NR
         NEXT(I-1) = I
         IF (A(I,COL) .LT. A(HEAD,COL)) HEAD = I
   10 CONTINUE
C. . . . . . . . . . "HEAD" NOW POINTS TO SMALLEST ELEMENT
C. . . . . . . . . . MAKE (HEAD-1)TH ROW THE END OF THE LIST
      IF (HEAD.EQ.1) GO TO 20
         NEXT(HEAD-1) = 0
         NEXT(NR) = 1
      GO TO 30
   20 NEXT(NR) = 0
C. . . . . . . . . . NOW PERFORM CONVENTIONAL BUBBLE SORT,
C. . . . . . . . . . EXCHANGING "NEXT" INSTEAD OF "A"
   30 IF (NR.LE.2) RETURN
      DO 60 I = 1,NLESS2
         SWAP = .FALSE.
         P = HEAD
         DO 50 J = I,NLESS2
            K = NEXT(P)
            L = NEXT(K)
C. . . . . . . . .    _____      _____      _____
C. . . . . . . . .  --- |      | ==> |      | ==> |      |
C. . . . . . . . .    ------      ------      ------
C. . . . . . . . .    NODE P      NODE K      NODE L
C. . . . . . . . . . IF NODES K AND L ARE OUT OF ORDER, INTERCHANGE THEM
C. . . . . . . . . .
            IF (A(K,COL) .LE. A(L,COL)) GO TO 40
               NEXT(P) = L
               NEXT(K) = NEXT(L)
               NEXT(L) = K
               P = L
               SWAP = .TRUE.
               GO TO 50
   40          P = K
   50    CONTINUE
         IF (.NOT. SWAP) RETURN
   60 CONTINUE
      RETURN
      END
```

FIGURE 5-8 In-place sort.

exercises, however, a technique that uses a pointer array is described; using this technique it is possible to use some of the more efficient sorting algorithms.

5.5 LINKED ALLOCATION

The use of a NEXT field has another advantage—that of being able to use one block of space for the elements of many lists. Recall in the inventory examples that a stack or queue was used for one product; if the firm handles 10,000 products, 10,000 stacks or queues would be needed. Now suppose that the shopkeeper may have stock from as many as 50 different orders of one product, although on the average only 2 or 3 orders will be on hand for any item. If we cannot predict which queues will need 50 elements and which can operate with only a few elements, then all 10,000 queues will need to be allocated 50 positions, for a total of 500,000 storage locations. Of these 500,000 spaces, however, an average of 470,000 will be unused! This is certainly not desirable.

Think of adding an extra field to each of these records; this extra field will be used like the NEXT field of the last section. We will call the new field a LINK field, and we will use it to indicate the location of the next element in this list. Such a list is called a *linked list*, and we say that each node is *linked to* or *points to* its successor. Our logical view of the data structure differs from the physical view. The logical and physical arrangements of a small list are shown in Figure 5-9.

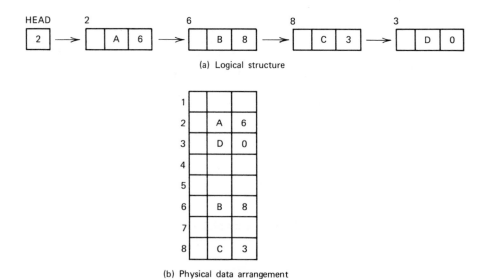

(a) Logical structure

(b) Physical data arrangement

FIGURE 5-9 Representations of linked lists.

There are unfilled positions in the sequential list shown in Figure 5-9(b), but they are not part of the linked list shown in Figure 5-9(a); the linked list consists of only four elements. The unused sequential cells could be used as a part of another list. Linked storage allocation permits two or more lists to be formed from one common pool of elements.

For example, in Figure 5-9(b), elements 1, 4, 5 and 7 might be part of a different list. For this different list we would need a new header, say, HEAD2. HEAD2 would point to the first element of the second list, perhaps element 4. LINK(4) would point to the second element of the second list, perhaps element 7; LINK(7) would point to the third element, say number 1; finally LINK(1) would point to the last element of the second list, element 5. In this way, two or more lists would share a block of common nodes.

Now recall the calculation that indicated 500,000 locations would be needed for sequential allocation of stacks containing only 30,000 items. Using the technique outlined above we can reduce that to a list of 30,000 cells for 30,000 items. In Figure 5-10 we present the code to perform insertions and deletions from a linked stack.

```
        SUBROUTINE LSTKOP (*, STKTOP, PTR, STKDBG)
        INTEGER STKDTA, STKLNK, PTR, STKTOP
        LOGICAL STKDBG
        COMMON STKDTA(1000), STKLNK(1000)
        DATA IOUT/6/
C= = = = = = = = = = = = = = = = = = = = = = = = = = = = = = = = = = = = = =
C LINKED STACK MANIPULATION ROUTINES =                                      =
C= = = = = = = = = = = = = = = = = = = = =                                   =
C                                                                           =
C     THESE ROUTINES PERFORM PUSH AND POP OPERATIONS ON STACKS THAT         =
C     ARE REPRESENTED AS LINKED LISTS.                                      =
C     EACH NODE OF THE STACK CONSISTS OF TWO FIELDS:                        =
C        A DATA FIELD, "STKDTA", AND A LINK FIELD, "STKLNK"                  =
C     THE TOP-OF-STACK POINTER IS CONTAINED IN "STKTOP"                      =
C     "STKDTA" AND "STKLNK" ARE MAINTAINED IN COMMON.                        =
C     "PTR" IS A POINTER TO THE NODE TO BE ADDED TO THE STACK, OR TO        =
C        THE NODE JUST DELETED FROM THE STACK                                =
C     ALTERNATE RETURN 1 IS USED FOR OVERFLOW OR UNDERFLOW EXIT.            =
C     NODES POPPED AND PUSHED ARE PRINTED IF DEBUGGING FLAG "STKDBG"         =
C        IS TRUE.                                                            =
C     PROGRAMMER: ---              DATE: ---                                 =
C= = = = = = = = = = = = = = = = = = = = = = = = = = = = = = = = = = = = = =
C
C
        ENTRY LSTPOP (*, STKTOP, PTR, STKDBG)
C- - - - - - - - - - - - - - - - - - - - - - - - - - - - - - - - - - - - - -
C          THIS MODULE POPS A NODE FROM A LINKED STACK.                      -
C          A POINTER TO THE POPPED NODE IS RETURNED IN "PTR" IF A            -
C          SUCCESSFUL POP OCCURS.   IF UNDERFLOW OCCURS THEN                 -
C          ALTERNATE RETURN 1 IS TAKEN.                                      -
C- - - - - - - - - - - - - - - - - - - - - - - - - - - - - - - - - - - - - -
        IF (STKTOP .LE. 0)  RETURN 1
        PTR = STKTOP
        STKTOP = STKLNK(STKTOP)
        IF (STKDBG) WRITE (IOUT,11) PTR, STKDTA(PTR), STKTOP
   11 FORMAT (1X, 'STACK POP: NODE #',I5,' POPPED. DATA IS ',
      #  I6,',  NEW TOP IS ', I5)
        RETURN
```

```
C
C
      ENTRY LSTPSH (*, STKTOP, PTR, STKDBG)
C- - - - - - - - - - - - - - - - - - - - - - - - - - - - - - - - -
C           THIS MODULE PUSHES AN ENTRY ONTO A STACK THAT IS STORED    -
C           AS A LINKED LIST.                                           -
C           THE NODE TO BE PUSHED IS POINTED TO BY "PTR".               -
C           IF PTR INVALID ON ENTRY ALTERNATE RETURN 1 IS TAKEN         -
C- - - - - - - - - - - - - - - - - - - - - - - - - - - - - - - - -
      IF (PTR.LE.0)  RETURN 1
      IF (STKDBG) WRITE (IOUT, 12)  STKDTA(PTR), STKTOP, PTR
   12 FORMAT(1X, 'STACK PUSH. DATA PUSHED IS ', I6, ',  OLD TOP IS ',
     #    I5, ',  NEW TOP IS ', I5)
      STKLNK(PTR) = STKTOP
      STKTOP = PTR
      RETURN
      END
```

FIGURE 5-10 Linked stack operations.

These routines are similar to the sequential stack manipulation modules of Section 5.2. This is not surprising since we are doing the same basic activities; only the arrangement of the data differs. Because a stack is the simplest dynamic structure to implement, stacks are commonly used to store the free nodes that are available to be joined to any list. Such a list of free nodes is often called a *list of available space*, or *LAVS.*

In Section 5.3 we introduced queues or FIFO lists in order to solve the problem of a storekeeper who needed to model the inventory of the store. The linked stacks just developed use one header node and a series of one or more data nodes, each having a link field. Linked queues are represented similarly; each linked queue requires one front pointer, one rear pointer, and a series of one or more linked data nodes. Suppose the shopkeeper has 10,000 products; this requires 10,000 front pointers and 10,000 rear pointers, which would be represented in two arrays. Each of these arrays is itself a list, and each element of those lists points to another list. The arrays thus form a *list of lists*, as pictured in Figure 5-11.

REAR			DATA	LINK
1	4		1	022	6
2	3		2	037	0
3	5		3	246	0
			4	164	2
FRONT			5	398	1
1	2		6	199	0
2	3				
3	6				

FIGURE 5-11 Arrays of list headers.

In this example, the first list has two elements, cells 4 and 2; list 2 has only one element, cell 3; and list 3 has three elements, cells 5, 1, and 6.

Working with a single list is the same as working with a list of lists. A subroutine for manipulating queues receives the front and rear pointers for one list; it does not matter if those pointers are simple variables or array elements. Figure 5-12 presents the modules for manipulating a linked list as a queue.

We conclude this section by showing how the stack and queue routines can be used together. As stated previously, a stack is commonly used to maintain the list of available space. Figure 5-13 presents a subroutine that performs a

```
      SUBROUTINE LQUEOP (*, QUEF, QUER, PTR)
      INTEGER QUEF, QUER, PTR, QUEDTA, QUELNK
      COMMON QUEDTA(1000), QUELNK(1000)
C= = = = = = = = = = = = = = = = = = = = = = = = = = = = = = = = = = = =
C LINKED QUEUE MANIPULATION ROUTINES =                                =
C= = = = = = = = = = = = = = = = = =                                   =
C     THESE ROUTINES PERFORM ADDITIONS AND DELETIONS ON LINKED QUEUES. =
C     THE FRONT AND REAR POINTERS OF THE QUEUE ARE CONTAINED IN  "QUEF"=
C     AND "QUER", RESPECTIVELY.                                        =
C     THE NODE TO BE ADDED OR THE NODE DELETED IS POINTED AT BY "PTR". =
C     THE NODES OF THE QUEUE CONTAIN TWO FIELDS, HELD IN VARIABLES     =
C     "QUEDTA" AND "QUELNK".                                           =
C     IN CASE OF QUEUE UNDERFLOW, ALTERNATE RETURN 1 IS EXECUTED.      =
C= = = = = = = = = = = = = = = = = = = = = = = = = = = = = = = = = = = =
C
C
      ENTRY QUEADD (*, QUEF, QUER, PTR)
C- - - - - - - - - - - - - - - - - - - - - - - - - - - - - - - - - - -
C         THIS ROUTINE PERFORMS ADDITIONS TO A QUEUE REPRESENTED AS  -
C         A LINKED LIST.  THE DATA TO BE ADDED IS IN THE NODE         -
C         POINTED AT BY "PTR".                                        -
C- - - - - - - - - - - - - - - - - - - - - - - - - - - - - - - - - - -
C. . . . . . . . . . MAKE SURE NODE TO BE ADDED EXISTS.
      IF (PTR .LE. 0)  RETURN 1
C. . . . . . . . . . LINK TO REAR NODE IF QUEUE IS NOT EMPTY.
      IF (QUER .NE. 0)  QUELNK(QUER) = PTR
      QUELNK(PTR) = 0
      QUER = PTR
C. . . . . . . . . . IF LIST WAS EMPTY MUST ALSO SET FRONT POINTER
      IF (QUEF.EQ.0) QUEF = PTR
      RETURN
C
C
      ENTRY QUEDEL (*, QUEF, QUER, PTR)
C- - - - - - - - - - - - - - - - - - - - - - - - - - - - - - - - - - -
C         LINKED QUEUE DELETION ROUTINE; DELETE FRONT ITEM FROM       -
C         QUEUE, PLACING POINTER TO DELETED NODE IN "PTR".            -
C         IF QUEUE EMPTY, USE ERROR RETURN 1.                         -
C- - - - - - - - - - - - - - - - - - - - - - - - - - - - - - - - - - -
      IF (QUEF .EQ. 0)  RETURN 1
C. . . . . . . . . . FIND FRONT ELEMENT, DELETE IT, AND RESET QUEF
      PTR = QUEF
      QUEF = QUELNK(PTR)
      IF (QUEF .EQ. 0) QUER = 0
      RETURN
      END
```

FIGURE 5-12 Linked queue operations.

complete allocation; it obtains a free cell from the available space list, puts a piece of data in that cell, and links the cell to a queue.

```
      SUBROUTINE INSERT (*, DATA, AVLPTR, QUEF, QUER)
      INTEGER LOC, DATA, AVLPTR, QUEF, QUER, LIST, LINK
      COMMON LIST(1000), LINK(1000)
C= = = = = = = = = = = = = = = = = = = = = = = = = = = = = = = = = = =
C INSERTION INTO LINKED QUEUE  =                                     =
C= = = = = = = = = = = = = = = =                                     =
C     THIS ROUTINE PERFORMS FULL INSERTION INTO A LINKED QUEUE.      =
C     THERE ARE THREE COMPONENTS TO THIS ROUTINE:                    =
C         1. OBTAIN A NEW CELL FROM AVAILABLE SPACE LIST             =
C         2. PLACE DATA IN THE CELL                                  =
C         3. LINK THE CELL ONTO A QUEUE.                             =
C     THE STACK OF AVAILABLE SPACE AND THE QUEUE ARE BOTH FORMED FROM =
C     NODES CONSISTING OF A "LIST" ELEMENT AND A "LINK" ELEMENT.     =
C     BOTH OF THESE VARIABLES ARE MAINTAINED IN COMMON.              =
C     THE POINTER TO THE AVAILABLE SPACE LIST, "AVLPTR" IS PASSED FROM =
C     THE MAIN PROGRAM, AS ARE THE QUEUE FRONT AND REAR POINTERS,    =
C     "QUEF" AND "QUER".                                             =
C     THE DATA TO BE INSERTED IN THE CELL IS PASSED IN "DATA".       =
C     IF THERE ARE NO FREE CELLS REMAINING, ALTERNATE RETURN 1 IS TAKEN =
C                                                                    =
C     STACK DELETION DEBUGGING IS DISABLED FOR THE AVAILABLE SPACE   =
C     STACK.                                                         =
C     PROGRAMMER: ---              DATE: ---                         =
C= = = = = = = = = = = = = = = = = = = = = = = = = = = = = = = = = = =
C
C. . . . . . . . . OBTAIN A FREE CELL FROM AVAILABLE SPACE LIST
          CALL LSTPOP (&99, AVLPTR, LOC, .FALSE.)
C. . . . . . . . . HAVE A FREE CELL AT ADDRESS "LOC"
          LIST(LOC) = DATA
C. . . . . . . . . LINK CELL TO THE QUEUE
          CALL QUEADD (&99, QUEF, QUER, LOC)
C. . . . . . . . . PROCESSING DONE
          RETURN
C. . . . . . . . . EXIT IF UNDERFLOW IN AVAILABLE SPACE LIST
       99 RETURN 1
          END
```

FIGURE 5-13 Merge of stack and queue operations.

5.6 MULTILINKED LISTS

5.6.1 Multiple Orderings of a Single List

In many applications it is necessary to process a list of data items in more than one way. Consider, for example, a hospital patient records system. Each record consists of information such as patient name, room number, and ailment. In some applications these records must be ordered by patient last names; other applications require access to all patients being treated by a particular doctor. We might choose to have one master list with all patient records in alphabetic order, and separate lists containing the patient records for all those being treated by each doctor.This solution has two obvious defects. First, it is inefficient since each record appears twice. Second, it is difficult to keep the files consistent; any change to a record in the master file requires a similar change to a record in one of the doctor lists.

In order to solve the patient records problem, it would be convenient to have just one record for each patient and to make this record a part of two independent lists: the master file and an appropriate doctor file. One approach to this is to maintain a sequential list of all patient records, ordered by last names. Each record would also contain a field to link together all patients being treated by the same doctor; one list header would be required for each doctor. While this organization solves the problems of storage waste and record inconsistency, it is a poor solution since insertions and deletions to an ordered sequential list require much data movement.

Clearly, a good solution to this problem is not possible if only one link field is used. However, with two link fields, one record can be an element of two independent linked lists. Figure 5-14 demonstrates such a solution. Here there are nine patients and three doctors. All patients are linked in alphabetic order using the list head ALFHD and the link field ALFLNK. ALFHD points to Adams; Adams points to Goldfine by the ALFLNK field for Adams; Goldfine points to Hughes; etc. There are also three doctor list heads, DOCHD(1), DOCHD(2), and DOCHD(3). DOCLNK links together patients under the same doctor's care. Thus, Goldfine, Mackey, and Rose are being treated by doctor 1; Adams, Mashey, O'Kane, and Pfleeger are being treated by doctor 2; and Hughes and Koch are being treated by doctor 3.

	NAME	ALFLNK	DOCLNK	Other fields
1	Hughes	8	8	
2	Rose	0	0	
3	O'Kane	4	4	
4	Pfleeger	2	0	
5	Adams	9	6	
6	Mashey	3	3	
7	Mackey	6	2	
8	Koch	7	0	
9	Goldfine	1	7	

ALFHD

5

DOCHD

1	9
2	5
3	1

FIGURE 5-14 Multilinked patient file.

While the solution just suggested uses two links per record, we are, of course, not limited to just two links; as many can be added as are necessary. In the patient records system, lists might be maintained by type of disease, by sex, etc. However, as the number of links increases, so does the complexity of list maintenance. For instance, in this example, when Pfleeger is discharged, his record must be deleted not only from the master list, but also from the appropriate doctor list. If Pfleeger's record was found by searching sequentially through the master list (the one headed by ALPHD), then the predecessor and successor of that record would be known, but only with regard to the master list. Pfleeger's successor in his doctor list is easily found by using the DOCLNK field. The problem is finding the predecessor of that record in the doctor list. With the above arrangement, this requires a search through each doctor list.

5.6.2 Bidirectional Lists

As just noted, our solution to the patient file problem is not appropriate when record deletions are common. In order to handle deletions easily, we introduce the technique of bidirectional lists—lists with both forward (to successor) and backward (to predecessor) pointers. Figure 5-15 demonstrates this by showing how the previous example appears when a doctor predecessor link, DOCPRD, has been added. This new solution will allow deletions to be processed more readily, but it does use one additional field in each record.

			NAME	ALFLNK	DOCLNK	DOCPRD	Others
ALFHD	5	1	Hughes	8	8	0	
		2	Rose	0	0	7	
		3	O'Kane	4	4	6	
DOCHD		4	Pfleeger	2	0	3	
		5	Adams	9	6	0	
1	9	6	Mashey	3	3	5	
2	5	7	Mackey	6	2	9	
3	1	8	Koch	7	0	1	
		9	Goldfine	1	7	0	

FIGURE 5-15 Bidirectional doctor's list.

With this structure, if we search the master list to find an entry to delete, we can determine precisely where it is in its doctor list. Hence we can delete it without processing records in any of the other doctor lists. Generally, we can delink the Nth record by executing

DOCLNK(DOCPRD(N))=DOCPRD(N).

If it happens that the head element of a doctor list is to be deleted, then more must be done. For instance, the release of Hughes is such a case, since DOCPRD(1)=0. Because there are no predecessors to Hughes in the doctor list, Hughes's successor must become the head of doctor list 3. This can be accomplished by executing DOCHD(3)=DOCLNK(1).

5.7 TREES

Another use of multilinked lists is to represent structures that are hierarchical in nature. In the hospital example, groups of patients are under the care of doctors. Suppose that the doctors are interns (say 20 total), that each group of four interns is under a senior doctor, and that all doctors are under the head surgeon of the hospital. This structure, called a tree, might appear as in Figure 5-16.

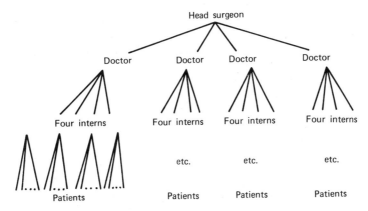

FIGURE 5-16 Tree structure.

A *tree* is a data structure consisting of elements called *nodes*. Nodes are connected to other nodes by *directed arcs*. If a node x has an arc emanating from it and entering the node y

then x is called a *predecessor* of y, and y is called a *successor* of x. Every tree has a unique node, called the *root*, which has no predecessor; all other nodes have precisely one predecessor. All nodes, including the root, have zero or more succesors. A node having no successor is called a *leaf*. Each node in a tree has an associated *level*. The level of the root is zero. All immediate successors of a level j node are at level j+1.

In the tree of Figure 5-16, the root is the head surgeon node. It is the predecessor of four doctor nodes; the doctor nodes have intern nodes as their successors; the intern nodes have patients as their successors. The leaves of this tree are the patient nodes. All leaves are at level 3, interns are at level 2, doctors are at level 1, and the head surgeon is at level 0.

5.7.1 Binary Trees

An *n-ary tree* is one in which each node has at most *n* successors. Of particular interest are *binary trees*. A binary tree is a 2-ary tree in which the successors of each node are distinguished as to which is the *left successor* and which is the *right successor*. Thus, a node in a binary tree may have no successors, a right successor, a left successor, or both a left and a right successor.

Within a binary tree, the largest subtree having the left (right) successor of some node as its root is called the *left* (*right*) *subtree* of that node. A *binary search tree* is a binary tree in which all data values in the left subtree of each node are less than the value at that node, and the data values in the right subtree are greater. Figure 5-17 is an example of such a tree.

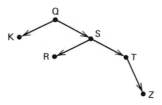

FIGURE 5-17 A binary search tree.

A binary search tree of n nodes is *balanced* if the difference between the levels of any two leaves is at most 1. The tree in Figure 5-17 is not balanced (level(Z) - level(K) = 3 > 1). However, Figure 5-18 presents all possible balanced binary search trees containing these same data values.

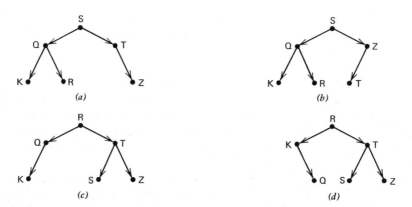

FIGURE 5-18 Balanced binary trees.

The use of binary search trees to implement table lookups introduces some storage overhead in order to represent the logical links (both left and right) between nodes. The advantage in using trees is the ease with which insertions and deletions may be handled. (Only links need to be altered.)

In FORTRAN we can represent a binary tree by using a sequential list for left links, a list for right links, and one or more lists to represent the data for each node. For example, the tree of Figure 5-17 might be stored in FORTRAN in the manner shown in Figure 5-19. (Note that in this figure we have left list positions 2 and 6 free for possible future insertions.)

ROOT

| | 3 |

	LLINK	DATA	RLINK
1	0	Z	0
2	?	?	?
3	5	Q	8
4	0	T	1
5	0	K	0
6	?	?	?
7	0	R	0
8	7	S	4

FIGURE 5-19 FORTRAN representation of a binary tree.

Once a binary search tree has been represented, as in Figure 5-19, we may now wish to determine if some data value V is contained in any node of the tree. The following algorithm accomplishes this task.

1. $N \leftarrow$ ROOT.
2. If N=0 then go to 6.
3. If DATA(N)=V then go to 8.
4. If DATA(N)>V then $N \leftarrow$ LLINK(N).
   else $N \leftarrow$ RLINK(N).
5. Go to 2.
6. Report that V is not in table.
7. Stop.
8. Report that V is at position N.
9. Stop.

This algorithm is implemented in the symbol table management routine presented in the next section.

5.7.2 A Binary Search Tree Application— Symbol Table Management

In Chapter 0, we noted that the variable names used in FORTRAN programs are stored in a symbol table. Each entry in such a table contains at least three fields.

variable name	address	mode

The address field is used to associate a variable name with one or more words of storage. The mode field is used in order to generate the correct machine commands for each statement referencing this variable. (For example, compilation of the statement A=B+C requires that the modes of B and C be checked to see whether integer or real arithmetic is to be performed.)

In order to maintain and process its symbol table, a compiler uses a symbol table lookup routine. Whenever this subprogram is entered, it is passed a symbol to be looked up. If it finds the symbol in its table, it returns a pointer to the node containing the symbol. If it cannot find the symbol, it creates a new entry in the symbol table for this variable name. It returns a pointer to this new entry and an indicator that the entry is a new one.

Since the symbol table is referenced frequently, its structure and the algorithms used to process it must be carefully designed. Hash coding, as defined in Chapter 2, is often used. Another commonly used method is to store the table entries as nodes in a binary search tree. Figure 5-20 presents a subprogram, TRETAB, that demonstrates this latter technique.

```
      SUBROUTINE TRETAB (VARNAM, NEW, P)
C ==============================================================
C= BINARY SEARCH TREE ROUTINE =                               =
C ==============================                               =
C=                                                            =
C= THIS ROUTINE SEARCHES THE TREE POINTED TO BY ROOT FOR THE OCCURRENCE=
C= OF VARNAM. IF NOT FOUND, THEN A NEW ENTRY IS FORMED. THE TREE =
C= MAY CONTAIN UP TO 100 ELEMENTS. SEQUENTIAL ALLOCATION IS USED SINCE=
C= NO DELETIONS ARE ALLOWED (FREE SHOULD BE INITIALIZED TO 1). IF AN  =
C= OVERFLOW IS DETECTED, AN ERROR MESSAGE IS PRODUCED AND EXECUTION   =
C= STOPS WITHIN THIS ROUTINE.                                 =
C=                                                            =
C=               *** COMMON VARIABLES ***                     =
C= ROOT    - INDEX OF ROOT NODE OF TREE                       =
C= LEFT    - LIST OF LEFT SUCCESSOR POINTERS                  =
C= RIGHT   - LIST OF RIGHT SUCCESSOR POINTERS                 =
C= NAME    - NAME OF VARIABLE STORED IN EACH NODE             =
C= MODE    - MODE OF VARIABLE STORED IN EACH NODE             =
C= LOC     - MEMORY LOCATION OF VARIABLE STORED IN EACH NODE  =
C= FREE    - POINTER TO FIRST AVAILABLE ELEMENT               =
C= NULL    - NULL POINTER VALUE                               =
C= OUT     - UNIT NUMBER OF PRINTER                           =
C=                                                            =
C=               *** DUMMY ARGUMENTS ***                      =
C= VARNAM - NAME OF ENTRY TO BE INSERTED                      =
C= NEW    - SET TO .TRUE. IF VARNAM DID NOT PREVIOUSLY APPEAR IN TABLE =
C=          SET TO .FALSE. IF VARNAM WAS ALREADY IN TABLE     =
C= P      - INDEX OF ELEMENT ASSIGNED TO VARNAM               =
C=                                                            =
C=  PROGRAMMER'S NAME: ---                DATE WRITTEN: ---   =
C ==============================================================
      INTEGER LEFT(100), LOC(100), MODE(100), RIGHT(100)
      INTEGER P, ROOT, FREE, PTR, OUT, NULL
      CHARACTER*6 NAME(100), VARNAM
      LOGICAL NEW
      COMMON ROOT, LEFT, RIGHT, NAME, MODE, LOC, FREE, NULL, OUT
C
C     ...EMPTY TABLE?...
      IF (ROOT .EQ. NULL) GO TO 80
      PTR = ROOT
C
```

```
C       ...COMPARE ENTRY WITH VARNAME...
10      IF (NAME(PTR) .EQ. VARNAM) GO TO 40
        IF (NAME(PTR) .LT. VARNAM) GO TO 50
C
C       ...LEFT DESCENDANT...
        IF (LEFT(PTR) .EQ. NULL) GO TO 30
        PTR = LEFT(PTR)
        GO TO 10
C       ...ADD LEFT NODE...
30      LEFT(PTR) = FREE
        GO TO 70
C
C       ...FOUND ENTRY...
40      P = PTR
        NEW = .FALSE.
        RETURN
C
C       ...RIGHT DESCENDANT...
50      IF (RIGHT(PTR) .EQ. NULL) GO TO 60
        PTR = RIGHT(PTR)
        GO TO 10

C       ...ADD RIGHT NODE...
60      RIGHT(PTR) = FREE
C
C       ...SEE IF TABLE OVERFLOW...
70      IF (FREE .LE. 100) GO TO 99
        WRITE (OUT,1000)
1000    FORMAT (5X, '** OVERFLOW IN TRETAB **')
        STOP
C
C       ...PLACE NEW ENTRY AT LOCATION P...
80      ROOT = FREE
99      P = FREE
        NAME(P) = VARNAM
        LEFT(P) = NULL
        RIGHT(P) = NULL
        FREE = FREE + 1
        NEW = .TRUE.
        RETURN
        END
```

FIGURE 5-20 Tree-structured symbol table.

The tree created by TRETAB is not necessarily balanced. In fact, if insertions of symbols are in alphabetic order, then a tree like the one in Figure
5-21(a) results; searching that tree is no faster than sequential search in a
sorted table. However, if these symbols are inserted in the order D, B, F, A,
C, E, G, then the tree in Figure 5-21(b) is produced; this tree can be searched
as fast as performing a binary search on a sorted table. The performance of
a binary search tree depends on whether or not the tree is balanced. Performing
table lookup in a balanced binary tree containing n nodes requires inspecting
at most $\log_2(n)+1$ nodes. If the tree is badly unbalanced, however, the lookup
might require the inspection of all n nodes. There exist algorithms that maintain
the balance of binary search trees during insertions and deletions, but their
descriptions are beyond the scope of this book.

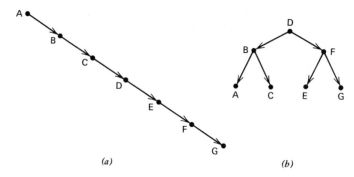

FIGURE 5-21 Unbalanced versus balanced search tree.

5.8 SIMULATION OF A GASOLINE STATION— A LIST PROCESSING EXAMPLE

5.8.1 Simulation in General

To *simulate* is to mimic some or all of the behavior of one system by a different, dissimilar system. Simulation is often performed to learn more about a system or to observe how changes affect its performance. Simulation is often used when direct experimentation is impossible (new system not yet available), uneconomical (expensive prototypes), immoral (pilot crash landing procedures), or too slow (forestry or ecology projects).

In most simulations, time may be treated as if it takes discrete steps from the time of one system event to the next. This event orientation often allows us to simulate long actual time intervals in short execution times. For example, the major events in a ten hour day at a gasoline station may be simulated in just a few seconds.

5.8.2 The System to be Simulated

We will demonstrate the use of simulation by modeling the activities at a gasoline station. The purpose of this simulation is to allow the station owner to predict profits and, possibly, to adjust policies so as to increase profits.

The gasoline station to be modeled contains a single service garage bay and two pumps. Each of these three resources has a separate service lane, and a separate employee who provides the appropriate services. The two pump attendants work from 8 A.M. to 6 P.M.; the garage mechanic works from 9 A.M. to 6 P.M.

One car arrives for mechanical service every hour, on the hour, starting at 9 A.M. On the average, cars requesting gasoline arrive every six minutes during nonpeak hours (9 A.M. to 4 P.M.) and every three minutes during peak hours (8 A.M to 9 A.M. and 4 P.M. to 6 P.M.). When a car arrives for gasoline, its driver always chooses to queue up in the lane having the fewer cars. After each arrival for gasoline, we can calculate the time of the next arrival. This interval to the next arrival is computed using the formula

$$interval = -mu * \log_2(r)$$

where the values assigned to r are randomly distributed between 0 and 1, and mu is the average time between arrivals (3 or 6 minutes). This method of generating an interval is referred to as a negative exponential arrival rate. It has the property that small values occur more frequently than large ones. (Approximately 63% of all arrivals occur in a time interval less than *mu;* less than 5% of all arrival intervals are greater than $3*mu$.)

Some additional properties of our simulated system are the following.

1. At most 25 cars can be simultaneously processed. Thus, if the total number of cars in line plus those being serviced exceeds 25, then new arrivals will choose to go to another station.

2. Cars at the gasoline pumps require between 0 and 20 gallons, in increments of 5 gallons (that is, 0, 5, 10, 15, or 20 gallons). Gasoline costs $.75 per gallon. A car may receive 0 or 1 quarts of oil at $.85 per quart. The windshield may be washed and the tires may have air pumped into them. These latter services are free.

3. Cars in the garage may purchase between 0 and 4 tires at $34 per tire, an oil change at $7.50, a lubrication at $3.50, and a tune-up at $37.95.

4. For cars at the gas pumps, it takes 2 minutes to fill each 5 gallons, 3 minutes to add a quart of oil, 2 minutes to clean the windshield, and 1 minute to put air in the tires.

5. For cars in the garage, it takes 9 minutes for mounting a new tire, 20 minutes for an oil change, 10 minutes for a lubrication, and 30 minutes for a tune-up.

6. Profits are calculated as 20% of gross receipts.

5.8.3 Event Scheduling and Processing

In our service station simulation, there are six types of events that need to be scheduled and processed.
1. A departure from service lane 1 (first gasoline pump).
2. A departure from service lane 2 (second gasoline pump).
3. A departure from service lane 3 (garage).

4. The arrival of a car needing gasoline.
5. The arrival of a car needing garage service.
6. A request to display the current status of the service station.

Type 5 events occur at 9 A.M. and hourly thereafter. Whenever an arrival occurs, the simulator schedules the next arrival for one hour later.

Events of type 4 are scheduled at mean intervals of either 3 or 6 minutes, depending upon the time of day. The first gasoline lane arrival is scheduled for one peak demand time interval from when the station opens (and thus occurs sometime shortly after 8 A.M.).

Event types 1, 2, and 3 are scheduled whenever we commence servicing a car. The departure time is based on the length of time to perform the required services.

Event type 6 does not correspond to any activity in the real system. It is used to help us analyze how effectively our service station is operating. The first of these status reports occurs at 8 A.M. and subsequent reports are given every hour until 6 P.M.

Whenever two events are to occur at the same time, the lower numbered event is processed first. Thus, departures from gasoline pump 1 occur first and status reports occur last.

A flowchart for the service station simulation program appears in Figure 5-22; the actual program is shown in Figure 5-23. This program uses a sequential

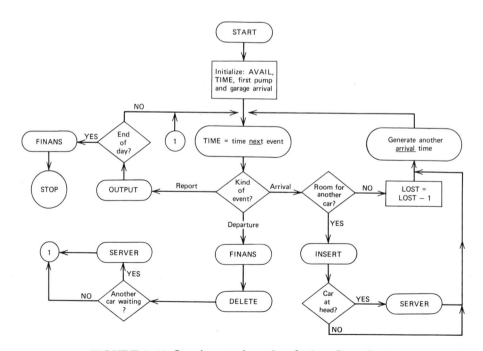

FIGURE 5-22 Service station simulation flowchart.

list, TF, to represent the times of occurrences of the next events of each type. TF consists of six elements, where TF(I) is the next time when event type I is to occur. At any given time, TIME, the event to be processed is event type I, where TF(I) is the smallest event time greater than or equal to TIME. For I ≤ 3, we assign TF(I)=TF(I)−1 after completing the departure. This disables event I until a subsequent departure time is calculated. For I=4 or 5, we assign TF(I) to the next arrival time, after completing the current arrival. For I=6, we produce a status report and then schedule the next report for one hour from then.

Output from the simulator is displayed in Figure 5-24. We have chosen to show only a portion of the status reports actually produced. Specifically, we show all activities through 9 A.M., the status report for 11 A.M., and a full trace of all activities occurring after 5:45 P.M.

```
C===================================================================
C       . . . GASOLINE STATION SIMULATION PROGRAM . . .              =
C                                                                    =
C PURPOSE: THIS PROGRAM SIMULATES A DAY OF ACTIVITY IN A GASOLINE    =
C     STATION. IT SHOWS THE USE OF ARRAYS TO REPRESENT STACKS AND QUEUES=
C     IT USES A RANDOM NUMBER GENERATOR TO EFFECT UNPREDICTABLE ARRIVALS=
C     AND CUSTOMER REQUESTS FOR SERVICES.                            =
C                                                                    =
C MAJOR VARIABLES:                                                   =
C   LANE   - LIST HEADS FOR LINKED LISTS OF CARS AWAITING SERVICES   =
C   TF     - EVENT TIMES FOR EXITS (LANES 1-3), ARRIVALS (GAS,GARAGE),=
C            AND STATUS                                              =
C   CELLS  - AVAILABLE SPACE FOR DESCRIPTION OF 25 CARS              =
C   LINK   - LINKS OF RELATED 'CELLS'. EQUIVALENCED TO COLUMN 6 OF CELLS=
C   AVAIL  - HEADER FOR LIST OF AVAILABLE 'CELLS'.                   =
C   TIME   - CURRENT SIMULATION TIME.                                =
C   LOST   - NEGATIVE OF NUMBER OF CARS WHICH WERE TURNED AWAY       =
C                                                                    =
C SUBPROGRAMS CALLED:                                                =
C   ALLOC  - FUNCTION TO GET NEXT FREE ELEMENT OF 'CELLS'            =
C   NEXT   - DETERMINE NEXT EVENT                                    =
C   DELETE - DELETE TOP OF SOME QUEUE                                =
C   INSERT - INSERT A CELL INTO SOME QUEUE                           =
C   RAND   - FUNCTION TO COMPUTE A RANDOM NUMBER                     =
C   SERVER - CALCULATE TIME FOR REQUESTED SERVICES                   =
C   DEMANS - CALCULATE SERVICE REQUESTS FOR SOME CAR                 =
C   FINANS - CALCULATE COST OF REQUESTED SERVICES; ALSO FINAL SUMMARY =
C   ARRIVE - FUNCTION TO COMPUTE NEXT ARRIVAL FOR GAS OR GARAGE      =
C   SHORT  - FUNCTION WHICH RETURNS SHORTER GAS LANE NUMBER          =
C   OUTPUT - PRINT STATUS REPORTS                                    =
C                                                                    =
C   PROGRAMMER'S NAME: ---                    DATE WRITTEN: ---      =
C===================================================================
C
        INTEGER LANE(3), TF(6), TIME, CUTOFF, PRT
        INTEGER CELLS(25,6),AVAIL,LINK(25),LOST,ALLOC,ARRIVE,SHORT
        REAL BILL
        EQUIVALENCE (CELLS(1,6),LINK(1))
        DATA LOST/0/,TIME/800/,LANE/3*0/,TF/5*759,800/,CUTOFF/1800/
        DATA AVAIL/1/,PRT/6/
C
C       . . .INITIALIZE AVAILABLE SPACE LIST. . .
        DO 1 I=1,24
            LINK(I) = I+1
      1 CONTINUE
        LINK(25) = 0
        WRITE (PRT,100)
    100 FORMAT ('1',15X,'** SERVICE STATION SIMULATION **' / )
C
```

```
C         . . . SCHEDULE FIRST PUMP AND GARAGE ARRIVALS . . .
          TF(4) = ARRIVE(TIME,4)
          I = 5
C
C         . . . SET UP NEW PUMP OR GARAGE ARRIVAL . . .
       10 TF(I) = ARRIVE(TIME,I)
C
C         . . .WHICH EVENT WILL OCCUR NEXT? . . .
       20 CALL NEXT(TIME,TF,I)
          IF(I .NE. 6) GO TO 25
C
C         . . . STATUS : PRINT IT. IF AT END, STOP. ELSE SCHEDULE NEXT ONE
          CALL OUTPUT(TIME,LANE,CELLS,LINK)
          IF(TIME .GE. CUTOFF) GO TO 60
          TF(6) = TF(6)+101
          GO TO 20
       25 IF(I .GT. 3) GO TO 30
C
C         . . . DEPARTURE:  SERVE NEXT PERSON IN LINE . . .
          CALL FINANS(LANE(I),I,CELLS,BILL)
          WRITE (PRT,101) I,CELLS(LANE(I),5),BILL,TIME
      101 FORMAT (5X,'EXIT  FROM LANE', I2,' CAR #',I3,' BILL WAS $',F6.2,
         1 ' AT TIME',I5)
          CALL DELETE(LANE(I),LINK,AVAIL)
          IF(LANE(I) .NE. 0) CALL SERVER(I,TIME,CELLS,LANE,TF)
          GO TO 20
C
C         . . .NEW ARRIVAL. . .IS THERE ROOM?
       30 K = ALLOC(AVAIL,LINK)
          IF(K .NE. 0) GO TO 40
C         . . . NO ROOM. TURN AWAY CAR . . .
          LOST=LOST-1
          GO TO 10
       40 CALL DEMANS(K,CELLS)
C         . . .PUMP OR GARAGE NEEDS?
          J = 3
          IF(I .EQ. 5) GO TO 50
C         . . .PUMP:  ENTER SHORTEST QUEUE. . .
          J = SHORT(LINK,LANE)
C         . . . ENTER NEW ARRIVAL . . .
       50 CALL INSERT(K,LANE(J),LINK)
          WRITE(PRT,102) J,CELLS(K,5),TIME
      102 FORMAT(5X,'ENTER INTO LANE',I2,' CAR #',I3,19X,'AT TIME',I5)
          IF(LINK(LANE(J)) .EQ. 0) CALL SERVER(J,TIME,CELLS,LANE,TF)
          GO TO 10
C
C         . . .END OF DAY. . .
       60 CALL FINANS(LOST,I,CELLS,BILL)
          STOP
          END

          INTEGER FUNCTION ALLOC(AVAIL,LINK)
C========================================================================
C ALLOCATE A ROW FROM THE AVAILABLE CELL SPACE                          =
C                                                                       =
C AVAIL  - POINTER TO FIRST AVAILABLE CELL                              =
C LINK   - LINK FIELD FOR AVAILABLE CELLS                               =
C                                                                       =
C THE VALUE RETURNED IS THE INDEX OF FIRST FREE ELEMENT, OR 0 IF NONE   =
C========================================================================
          INTEGER AVAIL,LINK(25),PRT
          DATA PRT/6/
C
C         . . .ALLOCATE AN EMPTY CELL ELSE REFUSE REQUEST. . .
          IF(AVAIL .NE. 0) GO TO 10
          WRITE(PRT,100)
      100 FORMAT(5X,'** FULL STATION: CUSTOMER DROVE AWAY WITHOUT SERVICE')
          ALLOC = 0
          RETURN
C
```

```
C       . . .UPDATE 'AVAIL' POINTER. . .
   10 ALLOC = AVAIL
      AVAIL = LINK(AVAIL)
      RETURN
      END

      SUBROUTINE NEXT(TIME,TF,EVTYP)
C========================================================================
C DETERMINE NEXT EVENT TIME AND TYPE                                    =
C                                                                       =
C TIME   - ON ENTRY, CURRENT TIME; ON EXIT, NEXT EVENT TIME             =
C TF     - TIMES OF NEXT EVENTS OF EACH POSSIBLE TYPE                   =
C EVTYP  - TYPE OF NEXT EVENT                                           =
C========================================================================
      INTEGER TIME,TF(6),EVTYP,EVTIME,PRT
      DATA PRT/6/
C
C       . . . FIND SMALLEST EVENT NOT LESS THAN 'TIME'. . .
      EVTYP = 0
      EVTIME = 2401
      DO 10 J = 1,6
         IF((TF(J) . GE. EVTIME) .OR. (TF(J) .LT. TIME)) GO TO 10
         EVTYP = J
         EVTIME = TF(J)
   10 CONTINUE
      IF (EVTYP .NE. 0) GO TO 20
C       . . . IF NO NEXT EVENT, WE'VE GOT PROBLEMS - QUIT
      WRITE(PRT,100)
  100 FORMAT(5X,'**ERROR: NO NEXT EVENT - STOPPING IN NEXT**')
      STOP
C
C       . . .RESET TIME AND DECREMENT TF(EVTYP) SO IT'S NOT RECHOSEN. . .
   20 TIME = TF(EVTYP)
      TF(EVTYP) = TF(EVTYP)-1
      RETURN
      END

      SUBROUTINE DELETE(LIST,LINK,AVAIL)
C========================================================================
C POP TOP ELEMENT OF LIST AND RETURN ELEMENT TO AVAIL SPACE             =
C                                                                       =
C LIST   - HEAD OF LIST FROM WHICH POP IS TO OCCUR                      =
C LINK   - LINK FIELD FOR LIST AND AVAIL SPACE                          =
C AVAIL  - LIST HEAD FOR AVAIL SPACE                                    =
C========================================================================
      INTEGER AVAIL,LINK(25),LIST,PTR,PRT
      DATA PRT/6/
C
C       . . .EMPTY LIST?. . .
      IF(LIST .GT. 0) GO TO 10
      WRITE(PRT,100)
  100 FORMAT(5X,'**ERROR: TRIED TO DELETE FROM EMPTY QUEUE**')
      STOP
C
C       . . .REMOVE LEAD CELL FROM 'LANE(I)' AND RETURN TO 'AVAIL'
   10 PTR = LINK(LIST)
      LINK(LIST) = AVAIL
      AVAIL = LIST
      LIST = PTR
      RETURN
      END

      SUBROUTINE INSERT(K,LIST,LINK)
C========================================================================
C INSERT ELEMENT AT END OF QUEUE                                        =
C                                                                       =
C K      - INDEX OF ELEMENT TO BE INSERTED                              =
C LIST   - HEAD OF LIST INTO WHICH INSERT IS TO OCCUR                   =
C LINK   - LINK FIELD OF LIST ELEMENTS                                  =
C========================================================================
      INTEGER LINK(25),LIST,K,FTR,PRT
      DATA PRT/6/
C
```

221

```
C       . . . FIND TAIL OF QUEUE . . .
        IF(LIST .EQ. 0) GO TO 30
        PTR = LIST
     10 IF(LINK(PTR) .EQ. 0) GO TO 20
        PTR = LINK(PTR)
        GO TO 10
C       . . . ADD ELEMENT 'K' AT REAR OF THIS QUEUE . . .
     20 LINK(PTR) = K
        GO TO 40
C
C       . . .START NEW LIST OF JUST THIS ELEMENT . . .
     30 LIST = K
     40 LINK(K) = 0
        RETURN
        END


        REAL FUNCTION RAND(RMAX)
C=================================================================
C       COMPUTE RANDOM REAL VALUE IN RANGE FROM 0 TO "RMAX" (NON-INCLUSIVE)=
C       AS WRITTEN THIS PROGRAM IS APPROPRIATE FOR USE ON ANY 32-BIT TWOS  =
C       COMPLEMENT MACHINE. IN PARTICULAR IT MAY BE USED ON AN IBM 360-370 =
C=================================================================
C
        REAL RMAX
        INTEGER IRAND, MULT, LARGE
        DATA IRAND/137462873/, MULT/65539/, LARGE/2147483647/
C       . . . COMPUTE A NEW RANDOM NUMBER IN THE RANGE FROM 1 TO 2**31-1 .
        IRAND = IRAND*MULT
        IF(IRAND .LT. 0) IRAND = (IRAND+LARGE)+1
C       . . . COMPUTE DESIRED REAL-VALUED NUMBER . . .
        RAND = RMAX*IRAND*.4656613E-9
        RETURN
        END


        SUBROUTINE SERVER(I,TIME,CELLS,LANE,TF)
C=================================================================
C       COMPUTES EXPECTED SERVICE TIMES FOR SERVICES IN LANE I          =
C       THIS SERVICE TIME IS USED TO COMPUTE CAR'S DEPARTURE TIME        =
C       TIMES FOR EACH SERVICE PERFORMED ARE :                          =
C       GAS LANE: 2 MIN/5 GALS.; 3 MIN/OIL; 2 MIN/WASH; 1 MIN/AIR        =
C       GARAGE: 9 MIN/TIRE; 20 MIN/OIL; 10 MIN/LUBE; 30 MIN/TUNE-UP      =
C                                                                        =
C       I     - LANE NUMBER -- 1 OR 2 FOR GAS; 3 FOR GARAGE              =
C       TIME  - CURRENT TIME                                            =
C       CELLS - ELEMENTS SPECIFY AMOUNT OF EACH SERVICE REQUIRED         =
C       LANE  - LIST HEADS FOR EACH SERVICE LANE                         =
C       TF    - TIME OF NEXT EVENTS OF EACH TYPE                         =
C=================================================================
        INTEGER TIME,CELLS(25,6),LANE(3),SRVTIM,TF(6),HR,TIMES(4,2),I
        DATA TIMES/2,3,2,1,9,20,10,30/
C
C       . . .PUMP OR GARAGE SERVICE?
        J = 1
        IF(I .EQ. 3) J = 2
C
C       . . . COMPUTE EXPECTED SERVICE TIME . . .
        SRVTIM = 0
        DO 10 K=1,4
           SRVTIM = SRVTIM+TIMES(K,J)*CELLS(LANE(I),K)
     10 CONTINUE
C
C       . . . UPDATE TIME UNTIL LANE I IS FREED . . .
        HR = TIME/100
        MIN = TIME-HR*100+SRVTIM
        HR = HR+MIN/60
        MIN = MIN-(MIN/60)*60
        TF(I) = HR*100+MIN
        RETURN
        END
```

```
      SUBROUTINE DEMANS(K,CELLS)
C===================================================================
C     COMPUTES REQUESTS FOR SERVICE OF INCOMING CAR                 =
C                                                                   =
C     REQUESTS ARE CALCULATED USING UNIFORMLY DISTRIBUTED           =
C     RANDOM NUMBERS WITH MEANS AS FOLLOWS                          =
C     GAS LANE: 0-4 5 GALLONS; YES/NO - OIL FILL, WINDSHIELD, AIR   =
C     GARAGE: 0-4 TIRES; YES/NO - OIL CHANGE, LUBE, TUNE-UP         =
C     RANDOM VALUE OF 0 OR 1  ARE USED FOR YES/NO OPTION            =
C                                                                   =
C     K     - ELEMENT OF CELLS ASSOCIATED WITH THIS CAR             =
C     CELLS - ARRAY CONTAINING SERVICE REQUIREMENTS OF EACH CAR     =
C===================================================================
      INTEGER CELLS(25,6),CARNUM,K
      REAL AMNT(4)
      DATA AMNT/5.,2.,2.,2./,CARNUM/0/
C
C         . . .COMPUTE AMOUNTS REQUESTED. . .
      DO 10 J=1,4
          CELLS(K,J) = RAND(AMNT(J))
   10 CONTINUE
      CARNUM = CARNUM+1
      CELLS(K,5) = CARNUM
      RETURN
      END
      SUBROUTINE FINANS(CAR,L,CELLS,BILL)
C===================================================================
C     COMPUTE BILLS FOR OUTGOING CARS AND FINAL SUMMARY OF PROFITS  =
C     IF CAR IS GREATER THAN ZERO THEN THIS IS A BILLING CALL       =
C        CALCULATE BILL USING THE FOLLOWING SCHEDULE                =
C     GAS LANE: 3.75/5 GAL. FILL: .85/QT. OIL                       =
C     GARAGE: 34/TIRE; 7.50/OIL CHANGE; 3.50/LUBE; 37.95/TUNE-UP    =
C     VALUE OF L INDICATES GAS LANE (L=1 OR 2), OR GARAGE (L=3)     =
C     IN CASE OF A BILLING, THE PRICE OF SERVICES IS RETURNED IN 'BILL' =
C     IF CAR IS POSITIVE, THEN IT SPECIFIES THE INDEX (WITHIN CELLS) =
C        OF THIS CAR                                                =
C     IF CAR IS LESS THAN OR EQUAL TO ZERO, THEN IT IS NEGATIVE OF  =
C     NUMBER OF CARS WHICH LEFT DUE TO OVERFLOW                     =
C===================================================================
      INTEGER CELLS(25,6),NSRVD,CAR,PRT
      REAL BILL,PROFIT,COST(4,2),AVE
      DATA NSRVD/0/,PROFIT/0./,COST/3.75,.85,0.,0.,34.,7.5,3.5,37.95/
      DATA PRT/6/
C         . . . BILLING OR FINAL PROFIT SUMMATION?  . . .
      IF(CAR .LE. 0) GO TO 30
C
C         . . .BILL FOR WHICH SERVICE?
      J = 1
      IF(L .EQ. 3) J = 2
C
C         . . .COMPUTE BILL FOR THIS CAR. . .
   10 BILL = 0
      DO 20 I=1,4
          BILL = BILL+CELLS(CAR,I)*COST(I,J)
   20 CONTINUE
      PROFIT = PROFIT+.2*BILL
      NSRVD = NSRVD+1
      RETURN
C
C         . . .FINAL PROFIT PRINTOUT. .
   30 AVE = PROFIT*5./NSRVD
      WRITE(PRT,101)
  101 FORMAT('0',T23,'**END OF DAY ACCOUNTING**')
      CAR = -CAR
      WRITE(PRT,102) NSRVD,AVE,PROFIT,CAR
  102 FORMAT(' SERVED',I4,' CARS WHO PAID $',F6.2,' ON THE AVERAGE.',
     X    ' TOTAL PROFIT = $',F8.2,/,I4,' CARS TURNED AWAY')
      RETURN
      END
```

223

```fortran
      INTEGER FUNCTION ARRIVE(TIME,EVENT)
C=====================================================================
C    COMPUTE TIME OF NEXT ARRIVAL:                                   =
C    IF EVENT=4 THEN GAS PUMP ARRIVAL- USE EXPONENTIAL               =
C    DISTRIBUTION WITH MEAN OF EVERY 3 MINUTES DURING PEAK           =
C    HOURS OF 8-9 AND 4-6. USE MEAN OF 6 MINUTES BETWEEN             =
C    SUCCESSIVE ARRIVALS DURING NON-PEAK HOURS (9-4)                 =
C    IF EVENT=5 THEN GARAGE ARRIVAL- SCHEDULE ONE NEW ARRIVAL        =
C    EVERY HOUR, ON THE HOUR                                         =
C                                                                    =
C    TIME  - CURRENT TIME                                            =
C    EVENT - EVENT TYPE                                              =
C=====================================================================
      INTEGER EVENT,TIME,MU(2),NONPEK(2),GAP,HR,MIN
      DATA MU/3,6/,NONPEK/900,1600/
C
C       ... PUMP OR GARAGE ARRIVAL? ...
      IF(EVENT .EQ. 5) GO TO 10
C
C       ...PUMP ARRIVAL:  PEAK TIME OR NOT? ...
      J = 1
      IF((TIME .GE. NONPEK(1)) .AND. (TIME .LT. NONPEK(2))) J = 2
      GAP = -MU(J)*ALOG(RAND(1.))
C
C       ...COMPUTE NEW ARRIVAL TIME(MILITARY TIME). ..
      HR = TIME/100
      MIN = TIME-HR*100+GAP
      HR = HR+MIN/60
      MIN = MIN-(MIN/60)*60
      ARRIVE = HR*100+MIN
      RETURN
C
C       ...GARAGE ARRIVAL:  ALWAYS ON THE HOUR. ..
   10 HR = TIME/100
      ARRIVE = (HR+1)*100
      RETURN
      END


      INTEGER FUNCTION SHORT(LINK,LANE)
C=====================================================================
C    RETURN LANE NUMBER OF SHORTER LANE                              =
C                                                                    =
C    LINK  - LINK FIELD FOR CARS IN EACH LANE                        =
C    LANE  - LIST HEADS FOR EACH SERVICE LANE                        =
C=====================================================================
      INTEGER LINK(25),LANE(3), LANE1, LANE2
C       ... ASSUME LANE 1 IS THE SHORTER ONE ...
      SHORT = 1
      LANE1 = LANE(1)
      LANE2 = LANE(2)
C
C       ...FOLLOW QUEUES SIMULTANEOUSLY UNTIL FIRST END FOUND. ..
   10 IF(LANE1 .EQ. 0) RETURN
      IF(LANE2 .EQ. 0) GO TO 20
      LANE1 = LINK(LANE1)
      LANE2 = LINK(LANE2)
      GO TO 10
C       ... LANE 2 WAS FOUND TO BE THE SHORTER ONE ...
   20 SHORT = 2
      RETURN
      END


      SUBROUTINE OUTPUT(TIME,LANE,CELLS,LINK)
C=====================================================================
C    PRINT OUT THE CURRENT STATUS OF GASOLINE STATION                =
C                                                                    =
C    TIME  - CURRENT TIME                                            =
C    LANE  - LIST HEADS FOR SERVICE LANES                            =
C    CELLS - EACH ROW DESCRIBES A SINGLE CAR. COLUMN 5 IS CAR #      =
C    LINK  - LINKS CARS IN EACH SERVICE LANE                         =
C=====================================================================
```

224

```
      INTEGER TIME,AGAIN,LANE(3),CAR(3),CELLS(25,6),LINK(25),NUM(3),PRT
      LOGICAL MORE
      DATA PRT/6/
C
C     . . .OUTPUT HEADER FOR STATUS REPORT
      WRITE(PRT,100) TIME
  100 FORMAT('0',14X,'SERVICE STATION STATUS CHECK:',I5,' HOURS')
      WRITE(PRT,101)
  101 FORMAT(15X, '..........', 10X, '..........', 10X, '..........' /
     1        15X, ': PUMP1 :', 10X, ': PUMP2 :', 10X, ':GARAGE :' /
     2        15X, '..........', 10X, '..........', 10X, '..........' / )
C
C     . . . OUTPUT THE QUEUES IN PARALLEL . . .
      DO 10 I=1,3
         CAR(I) = LANE(I)
   10 CONTINUE
C
C     . . .OUTPUT CAR # ELSE 0 IF AT END OF QUEUE. . .
   20 MORE = .FALSE.
      DO 40 I=1,3
         NUM(I) = 0
         IF(CAR(I) .EQ. 0) GO TO 40
         NUM(I) = CELLS(CAR(I),5)
         CAR(I) = LINK(CAR(I))
         MORE = .TRUE.
   40 CONTINUE
      WRITE(PRT,102) (NUM(I),I=1,3)
  102 FORMAT(18X,3(I3,16X))
C     . . . IF END OF ALL QUEUES NOT YET REACHED, PRINT NEW LINE . . .
      IF(MORE) GO TO 20
      WRITE(PRT,103)
  103 FORMAT('0')
      RETURN
      END
```

FIGURE 5-23 Simulation program.

```
              SERVICE STATION STATUS CHECK:   800 HOURS
              ..........         ..........         ..........
              : PUMP1 :          : PUMP2 :          :GARAGE :
              ..........         ..........         ..........

                  0                  0                  0

      ENTER INTO LANE 1 CAR #  1                    AT TIME  804
      ENTER INTO LANE 2 CAR #  2                    AT TIME  809
      ENTER INTO LANE 1 CAR #  3                    AT TIME  810
      EXIT  FROM LANE 2 CAR #  2 BILL WAS $  3.75   AT TIME  813
      EXIT  FROM LANE 1 CAR #  1 BILL WAS $ 12.10   AT TIME  815
      ENTER INTO LANE 2 CAR #  4                    AT TIME  822
      ENTER INTO LANE 1 CAR #  5                    AT TIME  826
      EXIT  FROM LANE 1 CAR #  3 BILL WAS $ 15.85   AT TIME  828
      EXIT  FROM LANE 2 CAR #  4 BILL WAS $ 11.25   AT TIME  829
      ENTER INTO LANE 2 CAR #  6                    AT TIME  834
      ENTER INTO LANE 1 CAR #  7                    AT TIME  836
      ENTER INTO LANE 2 CAR #  8                    AT TIME  836
      EXIT  FROM LANE 1 CAR #  5 BILL WAS $ 15.85   AT TIME  840
      EXIT  FROM LANE 2 CAR #  6 BILL WAS $  4.60   AT TIME  840
      EXIT  FROM LANE 2 CAR #  8 BILL WAS $  0.85   AT TIME  844
      ENTER INTO LANE 2 CAR #  9                    AT TIME  845
      ENTER INTO LANE 1 CAR # 10                    AT TIME  847
      ENTER INTO LANE 2 CAR # 11                    AT TIME  847
      ENTER INTO LANE 1 CAR # 12                    AT TIME  848
      ENTER INTO LANE 1 CAR # 13                    AT TIME  848
      EXIT  FROM LANE 1 CAR #  7 BILL WAS $ 11.25   AT TIME  849
      EXIT  FROM LANE 2 CAR #  9 BILL WAS $  7.50   AT TIME  849
      EXIT  FROM LANE 1 CAR # 10 BILL WAS $  4.60   AT TIME  855
      EXIT  FROM LANE 2 CAR # 11 BILL WAS $  0.85   AT TIME  855
      EXIT  FROM LANE 2 CAR # 13 BILL WAS $  0.00   AT TIME  858
```

```
ENTER INTO LANE 2 CAR # 14                    AT TIME   858
EXIT  FROM LANE 1 CAR # 12 BILL WAS $  3.75  AT TIME   900
EXIT  FROM LANE 2 CAR # 14 BILL WAS $  0.00  AT TIME   900
ENTER INTO LANE 3 CAR # 15                    AT TIME   900
            SERVICE STATION STATUS CHECK:  900 HOURS
        •••••••••        •••••••••         •••••••••
        : PUMP1 :        : PUMP2 :         :GARAGE :
        •••••••••        •••••••••         •••••••••

            0                0                15
            0                0                 0


        SERVICE STATION STATUS CHECK: 1100 HOURS
        •••••••••        •••••••••         •••••••••
        : PUMP1 :        : PUMP2 :         :GARAGE :
        •••••••••        •••••••••         •••••••••

           32               33                24
           34                0                35
            0                0                 0

EXIT  FROM LANE 3 CAR #143 BILL WAS $109.50  AT TIME 1747
EXIT  FROM LANE 2 CAR #140 BILL WAS $  7.50  AT TIME 1749
EXIT  FROM LANE 1 CAR #133 BILL WAS $  8.35  AT TIME 1750
ENTER INTO LANE 2 CAR #160                    AT TIME 1750
ENTER INTO LANE 1 CAR #161                    AT TIME 1753
ENTER INTO LANE 2 CAR #162                    AT TIME 1755
ENTER INTO LANE 1 CAR #163                    AT TIME 1755
** FULL STATION: CUSTOMER DROVE AWAY WITHOUT SERVICE
EXIT  FROM LANE 2 CAR #142 BILL WAS $ 15.00  AT TIME 1758
EXIT  FROM LANE 1 CAR #135 BILL WAS $  8.35  AT TIME 1800
ENTER INTO LANE 3 CAR #164                    AT TIME 1800
EXIT  FROM LANE 3 CAR #164 BILL WAS $  0.00  AT TIME 1800
            SERVICE STATION STATUS CHECK: 1800 HOURS


        •••••••••        •••••••••         •••••••••
        : PUMP1 :        : PUMP2 :         :GARAGE :
        •••••••••        •••••••••         •••••••••

          136              144                0
          139              146                0
          141              148                0
          145              149                0
          147              151                0
          150              153                0
          152              154                0
          155              156                0
          157              159                0
          158              160                0
          161              162                0
          163                0                0
            0                0                0
```

END OF DAY ACCOUNTING
SERVED 141 CARS WHO PAID $ 14.47 ON THE AVERAGE. TOTAL PROFIT = $ 407.99
4 CARS TURNED AWAY

FIGURE 5-24 Simulation output.

Exercises

5.01 Assume that you have two circularly linked lists accessed by pointers P1 and P2 as on the next page.

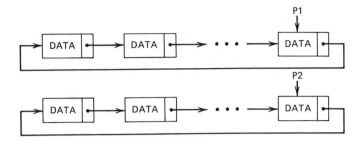

Assume further that P1=0 if the first list is empty and P2=0 if the second list is empty. The nodes of each list are formed from two integer vectors DATA and LINK, where, for example, DATA(P1) is the first element in our first list, DATA(LINK(P1)) is the second, etc.

(a) Present FORTRAN code that places the second list on the end of the first (concatenates them) and sets the second list to empty.

(b) Show how a circularly linked list as the one above may be used to simulate insertions to and deletions from a queue. Assume that available storage is in a linked list (stack) whose header is AVAIL. Thus, DATA(AVAIL) is the first available entry, DATA(LINK(AVAIL)) is the second, and so on. If AVAIL=0, then there is no available space.

5.02 The FORTRAN language requires every DO loop to be properly nested and to have a foot somewhere below the DO statement. Write a preprocessor to test any FORTRAN main or subprogram for these conditions. (*Hint.* For each DO found, "push" the foot label on a stack; for every label encountered, "pop" the stack if it matches.)

5.03 A polynomial in a single variable x may be represented by a linked list each of whose nodes are of the form

Coefficients of x
Power of x
Link

Thus, the polynomial $-3*x^6 + 4*x^3 + 6*x^2 + 9$ is stored as

where the nodes always appear in descending power order. Write subroutine INPUT that reads a value n, followed by the n+1 coefficients, an, ..., a1, a0 of some n-degree polynomial. Create a representation of this polynomial as above. Do not include nodes for zero coefficients. Write a subroutine ADD that adds together two such polynomials (zero terms must be omitted from the result). Write a subroutine OUTPUT that outputs a polynomial. Test your subprograms by reading in two polynomials, adding them, and printing the result.

5.04 A doubly linked list of the form

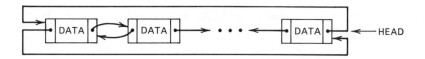

may be represented by a head pointer HEAD and three lists RIGHT, LEFT, and DATA. Given such a representation, write code to perform the following operations.
a. Return a pointer to the node whose data value is FIND. If no such node is found, return an indication of this fact.
b. Delete the element whose data value is DEL.
c. Add the node pointed to by PT to the beginning of the list.
d. Perform queue insertion and deletion.

5.05 The in-place sort of this chapter requires n² comparisons. A more efficient organization for an in-place sort is to use the list NEXT as a selector for the elements in the array A. Here, if we are sorting by column COL, we assign NEXT(I) the value J whenever A(J,COL) is the Ith smallest element in column COL. No variable HEAD is required by this method. Rewrite INSORT so that it uses the QUICKSORT algorithm described in Chapter 1 in order to assign the proper sorting values to the elements of NEXT.

5.06 Subroutine TRETAB of this chapter demonstrates how to find or insert an entry into a binary tree. Write subroutine DELTRE to delete the element of the binary tree that contains some value V.

5.07 You have been hired to model a person's family tree. Discuss the design of your tree and develop algorithms to find father, mother, aunt, cousin, brother, etc. How must the tree be organized? What will each node look like?

CHAPTER 6

Machine Representation of Data

All data types (real, integer, logical, character) are represented within computers as sequences of binary digits (called *bits*). The convention used to represent a particular data type is machine-dependent. There are, however, several basic coding forms. We first discuss these general forms and then focus our attention on the methods used by the IBM 360-370 and DEC-10 series of machines.

6.1 BINARY REPRESENTATION OF INTEGERS

The *binary number system* is similar to the more familiar decimal number system in that both are based on positional representation. For instance, the decimal number 257 is a sequence of three digits: a 7 in the units position, a 5 in the tens position, and a 2 in the hundreds position. The interpretation of this is

$$257 = 2*10^2 + 5*10^1 + 7*10^0$$

In general, a decimal number can be represented as a sequence of the digits $0,1,2,...,9$ and the base (or radix) is 10. The position of each digit indicates the power of 10 by which this digit is to be multiplied.

| d_{n-1} | d_{n-2} | $\cdots$ | d_2 | d_1 | d_0 | positional value |
| 10^{n-1} | 10^{n-2} | $\cdots$ | 10^2 | 10^1 | 10^0 | positional weight |

Value $= \Sigma_i\ 10^i d_i$

The binary number system uses only the digits 0 and 1. The radix is 2. The position of each digit indicates the power of 2 by which this digit is to be multiplied.

| b_{n-1} | b_{n-2} | $\cdots$ | b_2 | b_1 | b_0 | positional value |
| 2^{n-1} | 2^{n-2} | $\cdots$ | 2^2 | 2^1 | 2^0 | positional weight |

Value $= \Sigma_i\ 2^i b_i$

So, for example, the binary number 1101101 equals the decimal number 109, as can be seen by observing that

$$1101101 = 1*2^6 + 1*2^5 + 0*2^4 + 1*2^3 + 1*2^2 + 0*2^1 + 1*2^0$$

Although most computers represent positive integers in this binary form (called *pure binary*), differences arise in the methods used to represent negative numbers. Three such schemes are in common use: sign and magnitude, ones complement and twos complement. We now discuss each of these. For ease of presentation, we use a 10-bit word in all such discussions.

6.1.1 Sign and Magnitude

A computer that represents binary numbers in *sign and magnitude* form stores the magnitude in pure binary and reserves one bit to represent the sign. For example, the decimal number 14 has a 10-bit sign and magnitude representation of

0 0 0 0 0 0 1 1 1 0

The leftmost bit of 0 denotes a plus sign (+), the remaining bit string of 000001110 represents decimal 14. The decimal number –17 is stored as

1 0 0 0 0 1 0 0 0 1

Here, the leftmost bit of 1 denotes a minus sign (–), and 000010001 represents the decimal number 17.

Sign and magnitude representation is convenient for interpretation by humans, but has two inherent problems. First, there is no unique zero, since both 0000000000 (+0) and 1000000000 (–0) represent zero. Second, and more important, there is a difficulty in implementing the operations of addition and subtraction. This difficulty arises from the fact that, when numbers of differing signs are added, their relative magnitudes must be taken into consideration. For example, when adding 14 and –17, we cannot simply add the binary representations. If this were done, we would obtain

0000001110	+14
+1000010001	–17
1000011111	–31

which is incorrect. Instead, since the signs differ, we must subtract the smaller magnitude from the larger and then attach the proper sign.

000010001	+17
–000001110	–(+14)
1000000011	–3

This computational problem has resulted in most manufacturers designing machines that use coding schemes other than sign and magnitude.

6.1.2 Ones Complement

The *ones complement* scheme of representing negative numbers is used on many machines, including the UNIVAC 1100 series and the CDC 6000 and 7000 series. In this scheme, the leftmost bit still represents the sign, but all bits, including the sign, participate in the arithmetic operations.

Continuing with a 10-bit word, the ones complement representations of decimal +14 and -17 are

$$0\ 0\ 0\ 0\ 0\ 0\ 1\ 1\ 1\ 0\ =\ +14$$
$$1\ 1\ 1\ 1\ 1\ 0\ 1\ 1\ 1\ 0\ =\ -17$$

We arrive at the representation of -17 by first representing +17 (0000010001) and then changing every 1 to a 0 and every 0 to a 1. In effect, we are representing a number $-x$, in an n-bit word, by subtracting x from a sequence of n ones. That is, the ones complement of x is 2^n-1-x.

Now, if we add -17 to +14, the result is

0000001110	+14
+1111101110	-17
1111111100	-3

which is the correct answer. However, a correct answer is not always so easily obtained. Consider, for example, the sum of 17 and -14

0000010001	+17
+1111110001	-14
0000000010	+2

This answer is one less than the correct value. Adding the carry-out bit (the bit carried from the leftmost bit of the sum) produces the proper result.

0000010001	+17	
+1111110001	-14	
0000000010	+2	
1	+1	(carry-out bit)
0000000011	+3	

In general, the addition of ones complement numbers involves adding the numbers and then, if there is a carry out of the sign bit, adding one to this result. This points out a problem with ones complement: addition may involve two addition operations. A second problem is that the number zero does not have a unique representation: both 0000000000 (+0) and 1111111111 (-0) are valid. The -0 representation occurs every time a nonzero number x is subtracted from itself. For example,

0000000101	+5
+1111111010	-5
1111111111	-0

6.1.3 Twos Complement

The n-bit *twos complement* representation of a number $-x$ is 2^n-x. This number can be formed by first producing the ones complement of x (2^n-1-x) and then adding one $(2^n-1-x+1 = 2^n-x)$. Thus, -17 is represented by

$$1\ 1\ 1\ 1\ 1\ 0\ 1\ 1\ 1\ 1 \quad = \quad -17$$

This complementing procedure is the major drawback in the twos complement system. Unlike ones complement and sign and magnitude, changing the sign of a twos complement number requires an addition operation. On the positive side, the twos complement representation of zero is unique. In particular, observe that the twos complement of zero is

$$
\begin{array}{ll}
1111111111 & \text{(ones complement)} \\
+\qquad\quad 1 & \text{(add one)} \\
\hline
0000000000 & \text{(carry-out bit is ignored)}
\end{array}
$$

The most important advantage of the twos complement system is the fact that addition involves no special cases. As an example, the sum of +14 and -17 is

$$
\begin{array}{ll}
0000001110 & +14 \\
+1111101111 & -17 \\
\hline
1111111101 & -3
\end{array}
$$

6.2 BINARY REPRESENTATION OF REAL NUMBERS

In decimal, a number such as 12.63 is a positional representation of the sum

$$12.63 = 1*10 + 2*1 + 6*.1 + 3*.01$$

Similarly, the binary number 110.11 represents

$$110.11 = 1*4 + 1*2 + 0*1 + 1*.5 + 1*.25$$

These interpretations are based on the fact that, in a positional notation, a digit to the right of the radix point indicates a value to be multiplied times some negative power of the radix.

Computer representations of real numbers require some method to denote the position of the decimal point. Most such representations are referred to as *floating point* numbers and are based on what is called *scientific notation*. In this scheme the decimal number 12.63 is represented by $.1263*10^2$, and the binary number 110.11 is represented as $.11011*2^3$.

In each case, the number has two parts—a mantissa (or fraction) and an exponent. The fraction may be *normalized*. A normalized positive fraction is one whose leftmost digit is zero only if the entire fraction is zero. The advantage in this normalized form is that every number has a unique representation. In contrast there are many unnormalized versions of 12.63 (e.g., .01263*10^3 and 126.3*10^{-1}).

Once the scientific representation of a number has been determined, the number is generally stored in memory in the form

Sign	Characteristic	Mantissa

The characteristic represents the number's exponent. If we were representing the binary number 100.11 in a 10-bit word, we might have

0	1011	10011
	Excess 8	
Sign	Characteristic	Fraction

Here we have assigned four bits to the characteristic and five to the mantissa. The characteristic is in "excess 8" notation, which means that the value shown is 8 larger than the actual exponent. Thus, binary 1000 is an exponent of 0 = 8-8, 1011 is 3 = 11-8, 0011 is -5 = 3-8, etc.

You might wonder why this excess 8 scheme is used instead of sign and magnitude or one of the complement notations. There are two reasons. First, it makes comparison easy, the characteristic and mantissa may be treated as one sequence of bits in order to determine which of the two numbers has the larger magnitude. Second, addition is simplified, since this operation requires that we first compare exponents and then shift right the mantissa with smaller exponent until the two are properly aligned. Thus, to add 110.11 (6.75) and .01 (.25), we would progress as follows.

1. Determine the larger exponent.

$$0:1\ 0\ 1\ 1:1\ 1\ 0\ 1\ 1 \qquad (6.75) \qquad .11011 * 2^3$$
$$0:0\ 1\ 1\ 1:1\ 0\ 0\ 0\ 0 \qquad (0.25) \qquad .10000 * 2^{-1}$$
$$\text{Difference} = 4$$

2. Shift to align fractions and then add.

$$\begin{array}{l}
0:1\ 0\ 1\ 1:1\ 1\ 0\ 1\ 1 \qquad (6.75) \qquad .11011 * 2^3 \\
+0:1\ 0\ 1\ 1:0\ 0\ 0\ 0\ 1 \qquad (0.25) \qquad .00001 * 2^3 \\
\hline
0:1\ 0\ 1\ 1:1\ 1\ 1\ 0\ 0 \qquad (7.00) \qquad .11100 * 2^3
\end{array}$$

The technique just described is no different from the one that we standardly employ when adding decimal numbers. For instance, if we were to add $.675*10^1$ and $.25*10^0$, we would first align the fractions by changing $.25*10^0$ to $.025*10^1$ and then add the two fractions.

When two numbers are added together, the resultant fraction may be unnormalized. If this happens, we may perform *postnormalization*. The following demonstrates two cases where postnormalization is required.

Case 1. Too large a resultant mantissa
    1. Determine the larger exponent.

$$\begin{array}{lll}
\text{0:1 0 1 1:1 1 0 1 1} & (6.75) & .11011 * 2^3 \\
\underline{\text{0:1 0 0 1:1 1 1 0 0}} & (1.75) & .11100 * 2^1 \\
\text{Difference} = 2
\end{array}$$

    2. Shift to align fractions and then add.

$$\begin{array}{lll}
\text{0:1 0 1 1:1 1 0 1 1} & (6.75) & .11011 * 2^3 \\
\underline{\text{+0:1 0 1 1:0 0 1 1 1}} & (1.75) & .00111 * 2^3 \\
\text{0:1 1 0 0:1 0 0 0 1} & (8.50) & 1.00010 * 2^3 = .10001 * 2^4
\end{array}$$

In this case the mantissa is first calculated as 1.00010. But then we must add one to the characteristic, changing it from 1011 to 1100, and divide the mantissa by two (shifting one place to the right).

Case 2. Too small a resultant mantissa
    1. Determine the larger exponent.

$$\begin{array}{lll}
\text{0:1 0 1 1:1 1 0 1 1} & (6.75) & .11011 * 2^3 \\
\underline{\text{1:1 0 1 0:1 1 0 0 0}} & (-3.0) & .11000 * 2^2 \\
\text{Difference} = 1
\end{array}$$

    2. Shift to align fractions and then add.

```
0:1 0 1 1:1 1 0 1 1     (6.75)      .11011 * 2³
+1:1 0 1 1:0 1 1 0 0    (-3.0)     -.01100 * 2³
  0:1 0 1 0:1 1 1 1 0   (3.75)      .01111 * 2³ = .11110 * 2²
```

In the above we assumed that negative numbers are represented in sign and magnitude. The problem arose when we obtained a fraction of .01111. Postnormalization was then performed by subtracting one from the exponent and multiplying the mantissa by two (shifting one place to the left).

Negative real numbers may be represented in sign and magnitude, ones complement or twos complement. However, the number zero is always represented as a true zero (all bits zero). This zero representation guarantees that zero has the smallest possible characteristic. Thus, if it is added to another number, it will not force bits of the other fraction to be lost in the process of aligning the radix points.

6.3 ERRORS AND LOSS OF PRECISION— INTEGERS

In all our previous examples of integer arithmetic, we were able to produce a correct answer. In general, however, incorrect or imprecise answers can result. The most common cause of incorrect results is *overflow*: two numbers are added or multiplied and the result is too large to fit into a single word of memory. For example, in a 10-bit twos complement representation, we might add 71 to 445,

```
 0001000111       71
+0110111101      445
 1000000100     -508    (overflow error)
```

and get an incorrect result of -508. Usually, these types of errors are detected and your program is terminated with an appropriate error message. Unfortunately, not all machines are designed to perform such error checking.

A second common cause of error is *division by zero*. The vast majority of machines detect this error and cause your program's execution to be terminated with an appropriate message.

Even when integer division is not by zero, the result it produces is often very imprecise. Consider, for instance, evaluating the integer expressions

$$I + J/K * L$$

and

$$I + J*L / K$$

Mathematically, these are identical. But, if I=3, J=4, K=5 and L=6, the exact result is 7.8, although the first expression evaluates to 3 and the second to 7. That is,

$$I + J/K * L = 3 + (4/5)*6 = 3 + 0*6 = 3 + 0 = 3$$
$$I + J*L / K = 3 + (4*6)/5 = 3 + 24/5 = 3 + 4 = 7$$

As you can see, order of evalution has an immense impact. In general, division should be delayed as long as possible to avoid the cumulative effect (propagation) of truncation errors.

6.4 ERRORS AND LOSS OF PRECISION— REAL NUMBERS

There are three common types of errors associated with arithmetic on real values: *exponent overflow* (magnitude of number is too large), *exponent underflow* (magnitude of nonzero number is too small) and *division by zero*. As with errors in integer arithmetic, most computers detect these problems and cause your program to be terminated with an error message.

Of more serious consequence, since no machine detects them, are errors of imprecision. Imprecise results can be generated in a number of ways. First, since the mantissa is of finite length, it is not possible to represent some numbers precisely. For example, just as $\frac{1}{3}$ cannot be accurately represented by any finite length decimal fraction, the decimal .3 cannot be represented by any finite length binary fraction. Thus, execution of the statement

$$X = .3$$

introduces a small error into the results produced by a program.

Arithmetic operations such as addition and multiplication introduce further errors because of the rounding or truncation needed to store a too long fraction into a finite length computer word. Algorithms that reduce the number of arithmetic operations generally reduce the amount of accumulated (propagated) error.

One can also control the effects of rounding and truncation errors by considering the order in which operations are performed. For example, with our 10-bit word, the decimal number 64 is represented as

        0:1 1 1 1:1 0 0 0 0   +64 $.10000 * 2^7$

and 1 is represented as

        0:1 0 0 1:1 0 0 0 0   +1 $.10000 * 2^1$

Now, if we calculate (64−64)+1, we will produce the result 1. If, however, we reorder this as (64+1)−64, then we will get the incorrect result of 0. To see how this occurs, observe that 64+1 evaluates to 64.

1. Determine the larger exponent.

0:1 1 1 1:1 0 0 0 0	+64	$.10000 * 2^7$
0:1 0 0 1:1 0 0 0 0	+1	$.10000 * 2^1$
Difference = 6		

2. Shift to align fraction.

0:1 1 1 1:1 0 0 0 0	+64	$.10000$ $* 2^7$
+0:1 1 1 1:0 0 0 0 0 0 1	+1	$.0000001 * 2^7$
0:1 1 1 1:1 0 0 0 0	+64	$.10000$ $* 2^7$

The problem that arises here is caused by our adding numbers of widely differing magnitudes (given the small range of numbers representable in our 10-bit words). In actual machines the word sizes are much bigger, so that 64 is not considered to be vastly larger than 1. However, on most computer systems (i.e, those that use at most 35 bits to represent the mantissa), calculating

$$(2**35 + 2**-35) - 2**35$$

yields zero, whereas

$$(2**35 - 2**35) + 2**-35$$

evaluates to the correct answer, 2^{-35}.

An interesting example of how precision problems may be avoided arises when we consider solving a quadratic equation of the form

$$ax^2 + bx + c = 0$$

One of its solutions is

$$(-b + \sqrt{(b^2 - 4ac)})/2a$$

Now, if $a = 1$, $b = 10^5$, and $c = -1$, we would need to evaluate

$$(-10^5 + \sqrt{(10^{10} + 4)})/2$$

On a machine whose arithmetic is precise to less than 10 digits (both the IBM 360-370 and DEC-10 are such machines), $10^{10}+4$ is calculated to be 10^{10}, $\sqrt{(10^{10})}$ to be 10^5, and $(-10^5 + 10^5)/2$ to be 0. As a result, we estimate x to be 0. This is clearly imprecise, since

$$1*0^2 + 10^5*0 - 1 = -1$$

Whenever b^2 is much larger than $4ac$, a better approximation is obtained by multiplying

$$(-b + \sqrt{(b^2 - 4ac)})/2a$$

by the identity

$$(-b - \sqrt{(b^2 - 4ac)})/(-b - \sqrt{(b^2 - 4ac)})$$

This yields an equivalent solution formula

$$2c/(-b - \sqrt{(b^2 - 4ac)})$$

Although the above is algebraically equivalent to our original formula, its use causes us to evaluate

$$2/(10^5 + \sqrt{(10^{10} + 4)})$$

Assuming less than 10 digits of precision, we estimate x to be 10^{-5}. While not exact, this is a vast improvement on our original result, as can be seen by observing that

$$1*(10^{-5})^2 + 10^5 * 10^{-5} - 1 = 10^{-10}$$

An extensive discussion of the topic of precision is far beyond the scope of this book. Readers who are interested in this topic should consult one of the many computer-oriented numerical methods texts.

6.5 DOUBLE PRECISION

The number of digits of precision associated with real variables is not sufficient for many applications. To accommodate these, FORTRAN provides for a variable type called *double precision*. A variable is declared double precision by a DOUBLE PRECISION statement

DOUBLE PRECISION *list of variables*

A double precision constant is written in the same way as an E-notation real constant, except that a D is used in place of an E. For example,

2.62144000976525 D+5

represents the number 262144.000976525 . The numbers of digits of precision associated with real and double precision data types vary from machine to machine, but double precision is always at least twice as precise as real arithmetic.

A double precision variable is usually read and printed using a D-format code. Such a code is written in the same form as an E-format code, except that the letter E is replaced by a D. The interpretation of a D-format code is identical to that of an E-format code. In fact, these codes may be used interchangeably.

Two schemes are in common use for storing double precision numbers in a computer's memory. The first technique uses two words, each with a characteristic and a mantissa. The mantissa of the first word contains the most significant digits of the fraction, the least significant digits being stored in the second word. The value represented is the sum of the two words. Thus, if the mantissa is n digits long, the characteristic of the second word is n less than that of the first. Using our 10-bit words, we would represent the decimal number 8.875 (1000.111 binary) as

0:1 1 0 0:1 0 0 0 1   0:0 1 1 1:1 1 0 0 0

Here we can see that the first part represents decimal 8.5 and the second is .375, the sum being 8.875.

This first method carries with it some redundancy since the characteristic of the second part may be calculated from that of the first word. Recognizing this, some machines use all bits of the second word (or all bits except the sign bit) as an extension to the mantissa of the first word. In such a system we might represent 8.875 as

0:1 1 0 0:1 0 0 0 1   1 1 0 0 0 0 0 0 0 0

or, if the sign bit of the second word is not used, as

0:1 1 0 0:1 0 0 0 1   0:1 1 0 0 0 0 0 0 0

6.6 OCTAL AND HEXADECIMAL NUMBERS

Previously in this chapter we have limited our examples to 10-bit word sizes. These small word sizes were convenient for exposition, but unrealistic for practical applications. Actual machines like the DEC-10 and IBM 360-370 have much larger word sizes: 36 and 32 bits, respectively. In order to achieve a compact representation of such long words, it is standard practice to present the contents of DEC-10 words in the *octal numbering system* (base 8) and of IBM 360-370 words in the *hexadecimal numbering system* (base 16).

Whereas a decimal number is represented by a string of digits 0 to 9, an octal number is represented by a string of digits 0 to 7. A decimal number,

$$d_{n-1} \quad d_{n-2} \quad . \quad . \quad . \quad d_2 \quad d_1 \quad d_0$$

associates with position i (the one with digit d_i) the weight 10^i. Similarly, an octal number

$$o_{n-1} \quad o_{n-2} \quad . \quad . \quad . \quad o_2 \quad o_1 \quad o_0$$

has a weight 8^i corresponding to position i. The value of such a number is

Value $= \Sigma_i \ 8^i o_i$

Thus, for example, the octal number 324 has the value

$$3*8^2 + 2*8^1 + 4*8^0$$

which is 192+16+4, or 212.

Since $8 = 2^3$, each digit in an octal number corresponds to three binary digits. The correspondence is

OCTAL	BINARY
0	000
1	001
2	010
3	011
4	100
5	101
6	110
7	111

Thus, 324 octal is 011 010 100 binary. By memorizing the above table, you can easily convert between octal and binary numbers.

The hexadecimal (hex) numbering system uses the digits 0 to 9 and A to F, with a radix of 16. Observing that $16 = 2^4$, we arrive at the following correspondence betwen hexadecimal digits and their values in the binary and decimal systems.

HEX	BINARY	DECIMAL
0	0000	0
1	0001	1
2	0010	2
3	0011	3
4	0100	4
5	0101	5
6	0110	6
7	0111	7
8	1000	8
9	1001	9
A	1010	10
B	1011	11
C	1100	12
D	1101	13
E	1110	14
F	1111	15

Using this table, we see that the binary number 101001101111 is equivalent to the hex number A6F. This represents the sum

$$10*16^2 + 6*16^1 + 15*16^0$$

which equals the decimal number 2671.

6.7 NUMBER REPRESENTATION ON AN IBM 360-370

Within an IBM 360-370, integers and real numbers are stored in 32-bit (8 hexadecimal digit) words. Integers are represented using the twos complement scheme. Overflow is detected when it occurs as a result of an integer addition or subtraction. Division by zero is also detected. Unfortunately, if the product of two integers is not representable in 32 bits, no error is detected. Thus, an incorrect product goes unnoticed and is allowed to contaminate all further calculations.

Real numbers are represented in sign and magnitude, and are stored normalized, using the format

Sign	Characteristic		Mantissa	
0	1	− 7	8	− 31

The characteristic is an excess 64 representation of a hexadecimal (not binary) exponent. Thus, the decimal numbers 25.75 and -25.75 are stored in hexadecimal as

    4 2:1 9 C 0 0 0   25.75

and

    C 2:1 9 C 0 0 0   -25.75

Using a hexadecimal characteristic has its advantages and disadvantages. On the positive side, with just seven bits we can represent exponents from 16^{-64} to 16^{63}. The primary disadvantage is that normalized hexadecimal fractions may be unnormalized when viewed as binary fractions. For example, the fractional part of the IBM 360-370 representation of 25.75, in binary, is

    .000110011100000000000000

On the average, an IBM 360-370 maintains only 22.5 binary digits of precision, not 24 as one would first assume.

Double precision numbers are 64 bits long, with the 32 additional bits being used as an extension to the mantissa. Thus, they are of the form

Sign	Characteristic		Mantissa	
0	1	- 7	8	- 63

So, for example, the decimal number $262144.0009765625 = 2^{18} + 2^{-10}$ is stored in hexadecimal as

    4 5:4 0 0 0 0 0 0 4 0 0 0 0 0

In general, a double precision number is precise to 54.5 binary digits. The increase in decimal digits of precision is from 7 to 16. The range, in either case, is approximately from 10^{-78} to 10^{75} (16^{-65} to 16^{63}).

The small number of digits of precision on an IBM 360-370 necessitates the inclusion of a device, called the *guard digit*. This is an extra hex digit that participates in all real and double precision operations. An example most clearly shows its role.

Example   Subtract 41112217 from 4210778A.
           To align fractions we must convert 41112217 to 420112217.
           The extra mantissa digit (7) is then used as a guard digit.

       4 2:1 0 7 7 8 A   0 ← guard digit
     -4 2:0 1 1 2 2 1   7 ← guard digit
       4 2:0 F 6 5 6 8   9 ← guard digit

       4 1:F 6 5 6 8 9   Normalized

The advantage of this guard digit occurs in postnormalization. If it had not existed, the result would have been the less precise

4 1:F 6 5 6 9 0

Whenever real and double precision arithmetic operations are carried out, the IBM 360-370 detects errors due to exponent overflow and underflow and errors resulting from division by zero.

6.8 MEMORY ORGANIZATION ON THE IBM 360-370

6.8.1 Bytes, Half Words, Full Words, and Double Words

The basic unit of storage on a IBM 360-370 is an 8-bit unit called a *byte*. Each byte is associated with a unique address by which it may be referenced. The first byte in memory is addressed as byte 0, the second as byte 1, etc.

Bytes are grouped to form larger units. Any pair of consecutive bytes, where the first has an even-numbered address, is called a *half word*. Thus, bytes 0 and 1 together are a half word, and bytes 2 and 3 are a half word; but bytes 1 and 2 are not.

A *full word* is a set of four consecutive bytes, where the first has an address that is a multiple of 4. A *double word* is eight consecutive bytes, where the first has an address that is a multiple of 8. The following shows the half words, full words and double words associated with the first 16 bytes of memory.

D				D			
F		F		F		F	
H	H	H	H	H	H	H	H

Address   00' 01' 02' 03' 04' 05' 06' 07' 08' 09' 10' 11' 12' 13' 14' 15'

IBM 360's are designed so that operations on integer, real and logical variables may be performed only if these variables are stored in full words. Double precision variables must always be stored in double words. Although these restrictions do not exist on 370's, the efficiency of computation is drastically reduced if data is not stored in this manner. For these reasons, all IBM 360-370 compilers attempt to assign full words to real, integer, and logical variables, and double words to double precision variables.

As FORTRAN programmers, we need to be aware of full word and double word conventions since, through COMMON and EQUIVALENCE, we can make it impossible for a compiler to correctly assign storage to our variables. Consider, for example, the following declarations.

```
REAL R(2)
DOUBLE PRECISION D1, D2
EQUIVALENCE (D1,R(1)), (D2,R(2))
```

This requires memory to be allocated as

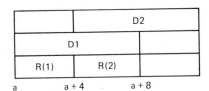

But if D1 is assigned to a double word, then D2 is not, and vice versa. On an IBM 360, this would be a fatal error (improper boundary). On a 370, this would result in a drastic increase in our execution time.

A not so obvious problem arises in the following sequence

```
REAL R
DOUBLE PRECISION D
EQUIVALENCE (R,D)
```

It appears that there is no difficulty, since all the compiler needs to do is assign D to a double word and the boundary requirements for R will be simultaneously satisfied. Unfortunately, most compilers use only the first variable in an equivalence to determine boundary requirements. Thus, the pair (R,D) implies a desire for full word alignment only. In contrast,

```
EQUIVALENCE (D,R)
```

will achieve the desired effect of double word alignment.

When equivalencing character variables with other data types, the character variables should appear last, since no boundary requirement exists for this variable type.

The problem with COMMON stems from the fact that each common area starts at a double word address. Thus, if D is double precision and R is a real variable,

```
COMMON D, R
```

will result in correct alignment, but

COMMON R,D

will not. This potential problem may be remedied by always organizing common areas so that double precision variables are placed before real, integer, and logical ones. Character variables should be placed at the end of a common area.

6.8.2 Variable Types

We have previously presented five FORTRAN variable types: DOUBLE PRECISION, REAL, INTEGER, LOGICAL, and CHARACTER*n. In addition to these, IBM 360-370 dialects allow variables to be of types REAL*8, REAL*4, INTEGER*4, INTEGER*2, LOGICAL*4, and LOGICAL*1. The numeric parts of these declarations specify the number of bytes of storage to be allocated for the variable. Thus, REAL*8 is equivalent to DOUBLE PRECISION, REAL*4 to REAL, INTEGER*4 to INTEGER, and LOGICAL*4 to LOGICAL. INTEGER*2 and LOGICAL*1 are the only two that are true extensions to the language thus far discussed.

INTEGER*2 variables are two-byte integers that are stored at half word addresses. This variable type may be used when we can expect that our integer values will not have magnitudes greater than 32767 ($2^{15}-1$). When large arrays of integers are required, the use of INTEGER*2 can result in substantial savings of memory. There are, however, several disadvantages to be considered. The primary drawback is that this variable type is nonstandard. Its use can therefore limit portability of our programs.

On some IBM 360 models, there is an efficiency problem related to the use of INTEGER*2. It takes more machine time to do half word arithmetic than it does for full word. For example, an IBM 360 model 65 takes over 28% longer to do a half word addition than it does for a full word. This apparent anomaly is explained by the fact that this machine is capable of performing only full word additions. A half word addition is performed by converting the half words to equivalent full words (sign extension to the left does this), then adding these full words and, finally, truncating the result back to a half word. If the result requires more than 16 bits, then its truncated part is incorrect. Unfortunately, the hardware of neither the 360 nor the 370 detects such half word overflow errors.

In light of the above pros and cons, INTEGER*2 should be used judiciously. In particular, frequently used counters should never be of this type.

Whenever INTEGER*2 variables are included in equivalence statements or in common areas, they should be placed after double precision, real, integer, and logical variables and before character variables. This placement will insure that they are assigned to half words.

6.8.3 LOGICAL*1 Variables and Character Manipulation

Since logical variables may assume only the values .TRUE. and .FALSE., it seems wasteful to assign them to full words (32 bits). Ideally, one would like to use only a single bit for each such variable. Unfortunately, memory is not bit addressable and thus the best we can hope for is to use only a single byte. This is, in fact, what occurs when we declare a variable to be LOGICAL*1. As with INTEGER*2 variables, the use of LOGICAL*1 variables can save a great deal of storage but destroys a program's portability.

One of the primary uses of LOGICAL*1 variables is in character manipulation on compilers that do not include the character type. Since one character requires just one byte of storage, great economy can be achieved when character strings are stored in LOGICAL*1 arrays instead of integer, real, or logical arrays. This advantage is somewhat tempered by the fact that one may not compare the values assigned to two LOGICAL*1 variables. To circumvent this problem, programmers often write short subprograms that indirectly effect the comparison of LOGICAL*1 variables. The function CHEQ demonstrated here is one such subprogram. It returns a value .TRUE. just in case the LOGICAL*1 variables L1 and L2 contain identical values.

```
      LOGICAL FUNCTION CHEQ (L1,L2)
C* * * * * * * * * * * * * * * * * * * * * * * * * * * * * * * * * * *
C* COMPARE SINGLE CHARACTERS STORED IN THE LOGICAL*1 ARGUMENTS L1, L2  *
C*                                                                     *
C* TECHNIQUE USED IS TO MOVE L1 AND L2 INTO THE RIGHTMOST BYTES OF THE *
C*  INTEGER VARIABLES L1VAL AND L2VAL, RESPECTIVELY.   THE RESULT OF   *
C*  COMPARING THESE TWO VARIABLES IS THEN RETURNED.                    *
C* * * * * * * * * * * * * * * * * * * * * * * * * * * * * * * * * * *
      LOGICAL*1 L1, L2, L1EXT(4), L2EXT(4)
      INTEGER L1VAL,L2VAL
      EQUIVALENCE (L1VAL,L1EXT(1)), (L2VAL,L2EXT(1))
C
C         ZERO L1VAL AND L2VAL.  ASSIGN L1 AND L2 TO RIGHTMOST BYTES
C            ASSIGN CHEQ THE VALUE .TRUE. IF L1VAL = L2VAL.
      L1VAL = 0
      L2VAL = 0
      L1EXT(4) = L1
      L2EXT(4) = L2
      CHEQ = (L1VAL .EQ. L2VAL)
      RETURN
      END
```

6.9 NUMBER REPRESENTATION ON A DEC-10

Within a DEC-10, integers and real numbers are stored in 36-bit (12 octal digit) words. Integers are represented using the twos complement scheme. Division by zero and all integer and real overflow errors, including those occurring as a result of integer multiplication, are detected.

Real numbers are stored normalized, using the format

Sign	Characteristic	Mantissa
0	1 - 8	9 - 35

Negative real numbers are represented in twos complement. The characteristic is an excess 128 representation of a binary exponent. Thus the decimal numbers 25.75 and -25.75 are stored in octal as

2 0 5:6 3 4 0 0 0 0 0 0

and

5 7 2:1 4 4 0 0 0 0 0 0

respectively. Note that the representation of the negative number -25.75 is formed by taking the twos complement of all bits, including the characteristic, of the representation of 25.75.

The representation scheme for double precision differs on older models (KA processors) from more recent models (KI and KL processors) of the DEC-10. On the KA processor, double precision numbers are stored in the form

Sign	Char	Mantissa 1	Sign	Char-27	Mantissa 2
0	1 - 8	9 - 35	36	37 - 44	45 - 71

So, for example, the decimal number $262144.0009765625 = 2^{18} + 2^{-10}$ is stored in octal as

2 2 3:4 0 0 0 0 0 0 0   1 7 0:2 0 0 0 0 0 0 0

The sign bit of each word is zero. The first characteristic is 223 (octal), representing a decimal exponent of 19. The second characteristic is 170 (octal), representing a decimal exponent of -8. The corresponding decimal number is

$.5*2^{19} + .25*2^{-8} = 2^{18} + 2^{-10}$

Thus, there are 9 redundant bits in the KA representation of a double precision number. In contrast, KI and KL processors use all bits, except for the sign, of the second word to extend the precision of the fraction. On these processors, 262144.0009765625 is stored as

2 2 3:4 0 0 0 0 0 0 0   1 0 0 0 0 0 0 0 0 0 0 0

Real arithmetic on a DEC-10 is precise to 8 decimal digits (27 bits). KA processors maintain 16 decimal digits (54 bits) of precision when dealing with double precision numbers. KI and KL processors improve this to 18 decimal digits (62 bits). The range, in all cases, is approximately 10^{-38} to 10^{38} (2^{-129} to 2^{127}).

6.10 MEMORY ORGANIZATION ON THE DEC-10

Unlike the IBM 360-370 machines which are "byte-oriented," DEC-10 computers are "word-oriented." That is, the smallest addressable unit of storage is a 36-bit word. Real, integer, and logical variables may be assigned to any words in memory. More importantly, a double precision variable may be assigned to any pair of consecutive words, irrespective of their addresses. Half word integer operations do not exist, nor may a logical variable be assigned less than a word of storage.

This word orientation has advantages and disadvantages. On the positive side, a programmer need not be concerned with alignment. Thus, there is no required ordering of variables in either common areas or EQUIVALENCE statements.

The disadvantage with a word orientation is its inflexibility. Integer variables must occupy 36 bits, even if their range is limited to small values. Worse yet, neither character nor the equivalent of LOGICAL*1 variables are provided by the standard FORTRAN compilers for this machine. To circumvent this latter restriction, DEC FORTRAN-10 programmers usually employ integer arithmetic and bit-masking operations in order to pack and unpack five ASCII characters (7 bits each) per word.

Exercises

6.01 Show the 10-bit representations of -21 in sign and magnitude, twos complement and ones complement.

6.02 Show all 10-bit representations of zero in sign and magnitude, twos complement and ones complement.

6.03 What decimal number is represented by the 10-bit number 1111100111 assuming sign and magnitude representation? twos complement? ones complement?

6.04 What is the result of adding the 10-bit number 1111110110 to 0000001101 in sign and magnitude? twos complement? ones complement?

6.05 What decimal numbers are represented by the eight hexadecimal digit numbers (assume twos complement)?
    000001FE
    FFFFFFE0

6.06 What decimal numbers are represented by the twelve octal digit numbers (assume ones complement)?
    777777777000
    000000001162

6.07 The following hexadecimal strings are representations of two real numbers on an IBM 360-370.
    BFC00000   41FA8000
a. What decimal numbers do these represent?
b. What is the hexadecimal representation of their sum?

6.08 The following octal strings are representations of two real numbers on a DEC-10.

 574150000000   207765600000

a. What decimal numbers do these represent?

b. What is the octal representation of their sum?

6.09 The following hexadecimal string is an IBM 360-370 double precision representation.

 46100000 C0000000

What binary number does it represent?

6.10 The following octal string is a DEC-10 KL processor double precision representation.

 217707000213 330000000000

What binary number does it represent?

6.11 Assume that we are using an IBM 360-370 and we need a common area that contains each of the variables declared below

```
DOUBLE PRECISION D
INTEGER I
INTEGER*2 K1(3), K2(4)
LOGICAL*1 L1,L2
```

In order to maintain proper boundary alignment we would normally declare common by

```
COMMON D, I, K1(3), K2(4), L1, L2
```

There are, of course, other declarations that will provide proper alignment. Show all those that are legal.

CHAPTER 7

Elementary Machine Organization

In this chapter we briefly discuss the major hardware components of computer systems and then present a description of a simple hypothetical computer. Our intention is to give you a better appreciation of how programs are executed and to lay the groundwork for our discussion of compilers and loaders in Chapter 8.

7.1 THE HARDWARE COMPONENTS OF A COMPUTER SYSTEM

Most computers may be viewed as consisting of four components: a *central processing unit* (CPU), an *arithmetic and logical unit* (ALU), *main memory* (MM), and a set of *input/output devices* (I/O). Figure 7-1 shows the primary relations among these components.

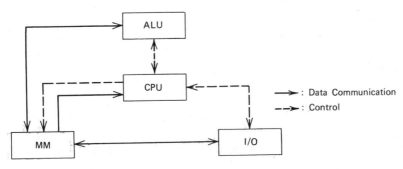

FIGURE 7-1 Interaction of the components of a digital computer.

7.1.1 Main Memory

This component is comprised of a set of locations, each of which is capable of storing a number. These numbers can represent data values or machine language instructions. No distinction is made between locations containing data and those containing instructions; it is how the number contained there is used that determines its interpretation.

Each location in a computer's main memory is assigned a unique address.

These addresses are used to reference data and to effect transfers of control between instructions.

Main memory does not itself manipulate data. The only operations that it is capable of performing are fetch and store. In order to carry out these commands, main memory has associated with it a control unit and two control words, called the *Memory Address Register* (MAR) and *Memory Data Register* (MDR). (See Figure 7-2.)

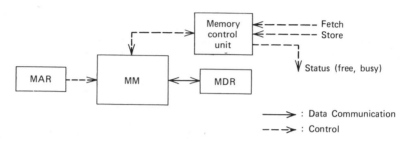

FIGURE 7-2 Main memory.

The memory control unit receives requests from the CPU, ALU or I/O to perform fetch and store operations. It can honor only one such request at a time. If a request is received while the memory is busy, the control unit queues this request until it can be carried out.

A store request requires that the memory unit be given a memory address and data to be stored at the location associated with this address. A store operation is effected by placing the address in the MAR, the data in the MDR and then signaling the memory unit to perform a store. A fetch request requires that the memory unit be given a memory address whose contents are to be fetched. A fetch operation is effected by placing the address in the MAR and signaling the memory unit to perform a fetch. The memory unit will then place the contents of that address in the MDR. Finally, the requesting unit retrieves the contents of the MDR. The following summarizes these activities.

Store: Wait until MM is not busy
MAR ← address of location to receive data
MDR ← data to be stored
Signal store request

Fetch: Wait until MM is not busy
MAR ← address of location containing data
Signal fetch request
Acquire data from MDR

7.1.2 Central Processing Unit

The primary function of the CPU is to sequence through programs and direct the execution of each of their instructions. In order to accomplish this sequencing, the CPU maintains a control word called the *Program Counter* (PC). This counter is initialized to the address of a program's first instruction and is updated as a result of each instruction execution. Thus the PC contains the address of the next instruction to be executed.

The following is a simplified step algorithm representing the process by which the CPU sequences through the instructions of a program.

Initialization: PC ← (address of first instruction)
Fetch: Wait until MM is not busy
                MAR ← PC
                Signal memory fetch request
                INSTR ← MDR
Increment: PC ← PC + 1
Decode: Determine type of INSTR; if illegal, quit
Execute: Direct the execution of INSTR
Cycle: Go back to "Fetch" step

The fact that the PC is always incremented by one after each instruction is fetched appears to indicate that no branching (transfer of control) can occur. This is not so. The performing of the "Execute" step can affect the value of the PC. In particular, if INSTR is a branch to the location, *loc*, then the result of the "Execute" step is to place the value *loc* in the register PC. Thus, nonsequential execution may be achieved.

7.1.3 Arithmetic and Logical Unit

The ALU is that portion of a computer that performs arithmetic and logical operations. This unit will normally contain hardware to perform integer arithmetic (addition, subtraction, multiplication, and division) and comparison of integer values. In addition, many computers are capable of executing the corresponding floating point operations.

In order to carry out computations and save the results obtained, the ALU has within it one or more storage locations called *registers*. These are used to store operands and the results of operations.

7.2 A SIMPLE MACHINE

7.2.1 Detailed Description of the SADSAC Machine

In order to make our description of computer components more meaningful we will now describe a simple decimal computer SADSAC (Simplified version of A Decimal Single Address Computer). The following summarizes its physical characteristics.

Main Memory. 100 locations, addressed from 00 to 99. Each location is capable of storing 3 decimal digits plus a sign.

I/O Devices. One card reader and one printer.

Arithmetic Unit. Contains a single signed 3 decimal digit register called the accumulator (abbreviated ac).

Instruction Format. Each instruction is of the form ±caa, where aa is an address in memory and ±c indicates the operation to be performed.

The instructions executed by SADSAC are

±0:	Illegal
+1:	Zero the accumulator (ac)
+2:	Load ac with contents of memory location aa
+3:	Store contents of ac into memory location aa
+4:	Add contents of aa to ac
+5:	Subtract contents of aa from ac
+6:	Multiply ac by contents of aa
+7:	Divide ac by contents of aa
+8:	Read integer value from next card into aa
+9:	Print the contents of aa
-1:	Jump to location aa. That is, set the program counter to aa
-2:	Jump to aa if ac = 0
-3:	Jump to aa if ac > 0
-4:	Jump to aa if ac < 0
-5:	Jump to aa if last arithmetic operation resulted in a number too large to be represented in the accumulator. (This situation is called *overflow*.)
-6:	Jump to aa if ac ≠ 0
-7:	Jump to aa if ac ≤ 0
-8:	Jump to aa if ac ≥ 0
-9:	Stop execution

The instruction set, although simpler than that of any real computer, is sufficient to carry out the logic of any FORTRAN program. The primary limitations are word and memory sizes and the difficulty with which floating point operations are performed. We demonstrate a SADSAC program for the following simple FORTRAN program.

```
C****          CALCULATE N FACTORIAL          ****
         INTEGER N, FACT
         READ (5,10) N
    10 FORMAT ( I12 )
         FACT = 1
         IF (N .LE. 1) GO TO 30
         DO 20 I = 2,N
            FACT = FACT * I
    20 CONTINUE
    30 WRITE (6,10) FACT
         STOP
         END
```

Memory Location	Contents	Remarks
00	+814	Read the value of N.
01	+217	If the value of N is less
01	+514	than or equal to one,
03	-812	then jump to print result of 1.
04	+216	Multiply current value of FACT
05	+615	by next factor (first time thru
06	+315	we multiply by 1, next by 2, ...)
07	+216	Compute next factor.
08	+417	Store this factor in I.
09	+316	If we are not yet done then loop
10	+514	back to multiply in this new
11	-704	factor.
12	+915	Print value of N factorial.
13	-900	Stop.
14	+000	N
15	+001	FACT (initial value 1)
16	+002	Loop index I, starts at 2.
17	+001	Constant 1
18		
.		
.	immaterial	
.		
99		

Programming in a machine language tends to be tedious and error-prone. Changes are hard to make since one small modification may make a large number of address references incorrect. For example, if we decide to print the value of N as soon as it is read, then we would insert

+914

at location 01. This insertion causes all further instructions and data to be shifted down one location. Such shifting causes our jump and data addresses to change. In particular the location of N is no longer at 14 but, instead, at 15. In order to make coding and modification easier, programmers usually write machine-oriented programs in *assembler language*, not machine language.

7.2.2 Assembler Language Programming for SADSAC

An assembler language allows us to reference memory addresses symbolically and to use mnemonics for our operation codes. For SADSAC, we might devise a language where each instruction appears in the following format.

Columns	1 - 8	10 - 13	15 - 22	25 - 72
Contents	*label*	*opcode*	*operand*	*comments*

where

        label is a 1 to 8 character, left-justified string

        opcode is a 1 to 4 character mnemonic for one of our machine operations, or is the mnemonic CON or END

        operand is dependent on the opcode

        comments is any textual description

Legal assembler opcode mnemonics and their meanings are:

mnemonic	Equivalent Machine Instruction Code	Operand
ZERO	+1	None
LOAD	+2	Label
STOR	+3	Label
ADD	+4	Label
SUB	+5	Label
MUL	+6	Label
DIV	+7	Label
READ	+8	Label
PRNT	+9	Label
BR	-1	Label
BRZ	-2	Label
BRP	-3	Label
BRM	-4	Label
BRO	-5	Label
BRNZ	-6	Label
BRNP	-7	Label
BRNM	-8	Label
STOP	-9	None
CON	Defines an initial data value	Integer
END	Marks the physical end of program	None

An assembler language program equivalent to our N factorial machine language program is

```
        READ N          READ IN VALUE OF N
        LOAD ONE        IF N IS LESS THAN OR EQUAL TO 1,
        SUB  N            THEN WE ARE DONE
        BRNM DONE
NEXT    LOAD I          MULTIPLY CURRENT VALUE OF FACT BY NEXT TERM
        MUL  FACT         IN SERIES THAT COMPUTES N FACTORIAL
        STOR FACT
        LOAD I          CALCULATE NEW TERM.
        ADD  ONE
        STOR I
        SUB  N          IF IT EXCEEDS N, THEN WE ARE DONE
        BRNP NEXT       OTHERWISE, CONTINUE CALCULATION
DONE    PRNT FACT       DONE - PRINT RESULT
        STOP
N       CON  0          N STORED HERE
FACT    CON  1          FACTORIAL IS PLACED HERE
I       CON  2          FIRST TERM IN FACTORIAL
ONE     CON  1          USEFUL CONSTANT OF 1
        END
```

Notice how much easier it is to modify and understand assembler language. For example, if we wished to print the value of N after reading it, we would simply insert the statement PRNT N after the READ. No other statements need to be modified to accomodate this change.

In studying SADSAC you may be wondering how array operations are carried out. Since no subscripts are allowed, it might first appear that we are restricted to processing simple variables. This is not so. The essence of our ability to process arrays lies in the fact that memory locations containing instructions are no different in appearance from those containing data. Thus an instruction may be treated as data and hence may be modified. We demonstrate this in Figure 7-3 by writing a SADSAC program equivalent to a FORTRAN program that reads data and prints it in reverse order.

```
C****          REVERSE PRINTING ORDER OF INPUT DATA        ****
        INTEGER LIST(10), N
        READ (5,10) N
   10 FORMAT ( I12 )
        DO 20 I = 1, N
          READ (5,10) LIST(I)
   20 CONTINUE
        DO 30 I = 1, N
          K = N+1 - I
          WRITE (6,10) LIST(K)
   30 CONTINUE
        STOP
        END
```

(a) FORTRAN Program to Print Input Data in Reverse Order

```
             READ  N        NUMBER OF ADDITIONAL CARDS TO BE READ
NEXTRD       LOAD  I        MODIFY READ TO REFERENCE NEXT ELEMENT
             ADD   RD1       OF ARRAY LIST
             STOR  RD2
RD2          READ  LIST     **THIS READ IS MODIFIED**
             LOAD  I        INCREMENT CARD COUNTER AND SEE
             ADD   ONE       IF THERE ARE ANY MORE
             STOR  I
             SUB   N        IF SO, GO BACK TO READ NEXT CARD
             BRM   NEXTRD
NEXTWR       LOAD  I        ALL CARDS READ, ANY MORE TO PRINT?
             SUB   ONE
             BRM   DONE
             STOR  I        IF SO, MODIFY PRINT TO REFERENCE NEXT
             ADD   WR1       ELEMENT, PROGRESSING BACKWARDS.
             STOR  WR2
WR2          PRNT  LIST     **THIS INSTRUCTION IS MODIFIED**
             BR    NEXTWR   TRY NEXT VALUE
DONE         STOP           COME HERE WHEN DONE
RD1          READ  LIST     USE TO CREATE READ
WR1          PRNT  LIST     USE TO CREATE PRINT
N            CON   0        NUMBER OF CARDS TO BE READ
I            CON   0        COUNTER FOR LOOPS
ONE          CON   1        USEFUL CONSTANT
LIST         CON   0        ARRAY FOR CARD VALUES
             CON   0
             CON   0
             CON   0
             CON   0
             CON   0
             CON   0
             CON   0
             CON   0
             END
```

(b) Equivalent SADSAC Program

FIGURE 7-3 Array processing in SADSAC.

7.2.3 Simulation of SADSAC Machine

One of the interesting features of digital computers is their ability to simulate the operations of other computers. We will demonstrate this by presenting a FORTRAN program (Figure 7-4) that takes as input a SADSAC machine language program and its data. The output produced is a dump of the SADSAC machine's memory before the program is executed, any lines produced by prints within the SADSAC program and, finally, a dump of memory after execution. Termination of the SADSAC program may occur for any of the following reasons.

1. A STOP is executed.
2. An invalid operation code (+0 or −0) is detected.
3. A divide by zero is attempted.

4. An attempt is made to execute an instruction at the nonexistent location 100.
5. An attempt is made to read beyond the end of all data (end-of-file).

The input of a sADSAC program to our simulator must take the following form.

Columns 2,3   An integer between 0 and 99 representing the address associated with this card.

Columns 6-9   A signed or unsigned integer between -999 and +999 representing the value to be loaded into memory. If this value is out of range then an error message is produced and no execution occurs.

The end of the sADSAC program is denoted by a card containing a * in column 1. All other columns on this card are ignored. Any data items to be read by the sADSAC program follow this * delimiter card.

```
C* * * * * * * * * * * * * * * * * * * * * * * * * * * * * * * * * * * *
C* SADSAC SIMULATION PROGRAM                                           *
C*   THIS PROGRAM READS IN A SET OF CARDS SPECIFYING THE INITIAL        *
C*   CONTENTS OF THE MACHINE'S MEMORY. EACH INPUT CARD IS IN THE FORM   *
C*                                                                      *
C*        COLUMNS 2-3 : LOCATION NUMBER OF THIS WORD                    *
C*        COLUMNS 6-9 : CONTENTS OF THIS WORD                           *
C*                                                                      *
C*   THE END OF ALL SUCH CARDS IS DENOTED BY A CARD WITH AN * IN COLUMN *
C*   ONE. NO DATA IS RECORDED ON THIS CARD. FOLLOWING THE * CARD IS THE *
C*   SET OF CARDS TO BE READ BY THE USER'S SADSAC PROGRAM.              *
C*                                                                      *
C*   OUTPUT PRODUCED:                                                   *
C*        DUMP OF MEMORY AFTER INITIAL PROGRAM LOAD                     *
C*        TRACE OF ALL INSTRUCTION EXECUTIONS (IF TRACE=.TRUE.)         *
C*        OUTPUT OF EACH PRNT ISSUED BY USER PROGRAM                    *
C*        DUMP OF FINAL CONTENTS OF MEMORY                              *
C*        ERROR MESSAGES, WHENEVER APPROPRIATE                          *
C*                                                                      *
C*   COMMON VARIABLES:                                                  *
C*        MEM    - LIST OF CURRENT MEMORY CONTENTS                      *
C*        PC     - PROGRAM COUNTER                                      *
C*        AC     - ACCUMULATOR                                          *
C*        PRT    - UNIT NUMBER FOR PRINTER                              *
C*        RDR    - UNIT NUMBER FOR READER                               *
C*        TRC    - UNIT NUMBER FOR TRACE OUTPUT                         *
C*        OVFLOW - IF TRUE, THEN LAST ARITH. OP. CAUSED OVERFLOW        *
C*        TRACE  - SET TO TRUE IF TRACE REQUESTED                       *
C*                                                                      *
C*   SUBPROGRAMS CALLED:                                                *
C*        DUMP   - DUMPS CONTENTS OF MEMORY                             *
C*        INTERP - INTERPRETS SADSAC PROGRAM                            *
C*                                                                      *
C*   PROGRAMMER'S NAME: ---              DATE WRITTEN: ---              *
C* * * * * * * * * * * * * * * * * * * * * * * * * * * * * * * * * * * *
        INTEGER LOC, STMT, DELIM, DEL
        LOGICAL EXEC
        LOGICAL OVFLOW, TRACE
        INTEGER MEM(100), PC, AC, PRT, RDR, TRC
        COMMON/SADSAC/ MEM, PC, AC, PRT, RDR, TRC, OVFLOW, TRACE
        DATA    DEL/'*'/, EXEC/.TRUE./
C
```

```
C               READ NEXT CARD IN SADSAC PROGRAM
10    READ (RDR,11,END=30) DELIM, LOC, STMT
11    FORMAT ( A1, I2, 2X, I4 )
C
C               SEE IF THIS IS END OF USER PROGRAM
      IF ( DELIM .EQ. DEL ) GO TO 40
C
C               SEE THAT MACHINE INSTRUCTION IS VALID
      IF ( IABS(STMT) .LT. 1000 ) GO TO 20
C
C               ERROR, MARK PROGRAM AS NON-EXECUTABLE
      EXEC = .FALSE.
      WRITE (PRT,15) STMT, LOC
15    FORMAT ('0** ERROR ** INVALID COMMAND - ', I4, 'AT LOCATION', I2)
      GO TO 10
C
C               LEGAL INSTRUCTION - STORE IT
20    MEM(LOC+1) = STMT
C
C               GO BACK TO READ NEXT CARD
      GO TO 10
C
C               ERROR, UNEXPECTED END-FILE
30    WRITE (PRT,31)
31    FORMAT ('0** ERROR ** UNEXPECTED END-OF-FILE')
      STOP
C
C               END OF PROGRAM - IF ERROR IN PROGRAM, QUIT NOW
40    IF ( EXEC ) GO TO 50
      WRITE (PRT,45)
45    FORMAT ('0** NO EXECUTION DUE TO ERROR IN PROGRAM **')
      STOP
C
C               EXECUTION BEGINS - DUMP MEMORY, INTERPRET PROGRAM
50    CALL DUMP
      CALL INTERP
C
C               TERMINATE WITH A DUMP
      CALL DUMP
      STOP
      END

      SUBROUTINE INTERP
C* * * * * * * * * * * * * * * * * * * * * * * * * * * * * * * * * *
C* INTERPRET USER PROGRAM UNTIL A STOP IS EXECUTED OR AN ERROR IS    *
C* DETECTED. TRACE OF EACH INSTRUCTION IS PRODUCED IF 'TRACE' IS TRUE *
C* * * * * * * * * * * * * * * * * * * * * * * * * * * * * * * * * *
      INTEGER ADDR, INSTR, OPCODE, MM, OPTYP, VALUE
      LOGICAL OVFLOW, TRACE
      INTEGER MEM(100), PC, AC, PRT, RDR, TRC
      COMMON/SADSAC/ MEM, PC, AC, PRT, RDR, TRC, OVFLOW, TRACE
C
C*******************************************************************
C****                EXECUTE NEXT COMMAND                        ****
C               IF WE HAVE GONE BEYOND END OF MEMORY, QUIT
40    IF ( PC .GT. 99 ) GO TO 666
C
C               DECODE NEXT COMMAND
80    INSTR = MEM(PC+1)
      OPCODE = INSTR/100
      ADDR = IABS(INSTR - OPCODE*100)
      MM = MEM(ADDR+1)
      IF ( TRACE ) WRITE (TRC,90) PC, INSTR, MM, AC
90    FORMAT (' ** TRACE ** PC=', I2, ':IN=', I4, ':MM=', I4, ':AC=',I4)
      PC = PC + 1
C
C               SELECT CODE NECESSARY TO INTERPRET THIS COMMAND
      OPTYP = OPCODE + 10
      GO TO (444,208,207,206,205,204,203,202,201,555,
     X       101,102,103,104,105,106,107,108,109),OPTYP
C
```

258

```
C
C              OPCODE = 1  --  ZERO ACCUMULATOR
101   AC = 0
      GO TO 40
C              OPCODE = 2  --  LOAD
102   AC = MM
      GO TO 40
C              OPCODE = 3  --  STOR
103   MEM(ADDR+1) = AC
      GO TO 40
C              OPCODE = 4  --  ADD
104   AC = AC + MM
      GO TO 150
C              OPCODE = 5  --  SUB
105   AC = AC - MM
      GO TO 150
C              OPCODE = 6  --  MUL
106   AC = AC * MM
      GO TO 150
C              OPCODE = 7  --  DIV
C              CHECK FOR ILLEGAL DIVISION BY ZERO
107   IF ( MM .EQ. 0 ) GO TO 777
      AC = AC / MM
      GO TO 40
C              OPCODE = 8  --  READ
C              WE USE A WATFIV FREE-FORMAT READ HERE. IF YOUR COMPILER
C              DOES NOT SUPPORT FREE READS, THEN SUBROUTINE EDCHIN,
C              AS DESCRIBED IN CHAPTER 3, MAY BE USED.
108   READ (RDR,*,END=888) VALUE
      MEM(ADDR+1) = MOD(VALUE,1000)
      GO TO 40
C              OPCODE = 9  --  PRNT
109   WRITE (PRT,110) ADDR, MM
110   FORMAT (' CONTENTS OF LOCATION ', I2, ' ARE ', I4)
      GO TO 40
C
C              IF OVERFLOW OCCURRED, SET OVERFLOW FLAG
150   OVFLOW = .FALSE.
      IF (IABS(AC) .LE. 999) GO TO 40
      AC = MOD(AC,1000)
      OVFLOW = .TRUE.
      GO TO 40
C
C              OPCODE = -1  --  BR
201   PC = ADDR
      GO TO 80
C              OPCODE = -2  --  BRZ
202   IF ( AC .EQ. 0 ) PC = ADDR
      GO TO 80
C              OPCODE = -3  --  BRP
203   IF ( AC .GT. 0 ) PC = ADDR
      GO TO 80
C              OPCODE = -4  --  BRM
204   IF ( AC .LT. 0 ) PC = ADDR
      GO TO 80
C              OPCODE = -5  --  BRO
205   IF ( OVFLOW ) PC = ADDR
      GO TO 80
C              OPCODE = -6  --  BRNZ
206   IF ( AC .NE. 0 ) PC = ADDR
      GO TO 80
C              OPCODE = -7  --  BRNP
207   IF ( AC .LE. 0 ) PC = ADDR
      GO TO 80
C              OPCODE = -8  --  BRNM
208   IF ( AC .GE. 0 ) PC = ADDR
      GO TO 80
C              OPCODE = -9  --  STOP
444   WRITE (PRT,445)
445   FORMAT ('0** NORMAL TERMINATION BY EXECUTION OF STOP **')
      GO TO 999
```

```
C
C              ERROR TERMINATIONS
C
C              ATTEMPT TO EXECUTE OPCODE = 0
555   WRITE (PRT,556)
556   FORMAT ('0** ERROR ** INVALID OPERATION CODE')
      GO TO 999
C              PC ATTAINED A VALUE GREATER THAN 99
666   WRITE (PRT,667)
667   FORMAT ('0** ERROR ** PC VALUE GREATER THAN 99')
      GO TO 999
C              ATTEMPT TO DIVIDE BY ZERO
777   WRITE (PRT,778)
778   FORMAT ('0** ERROR ** DIVIDE BY ZERO')
      GO TO 999
C              UNEXPECTED END-OF-FILE
888   WRITE (PRT,889)
889   FORMAT ('0** ERROR ** UNEXPECTED END-OF-FILE')
999   RETURN
      END


      SUBROUTINE DUMP
C* * * * * * * * * * * * * * * * * * * * * * * * * * * * * * * * * * *
C* DUMP - DUMP CONTENTS OF SADSAC MEMORY. ALSO SHOW CURRENT PC AND AC  *
C* * * * * * * * * * * * * * * * * * * * * * * * * * * * * * * * * * *
      INTEGER LOC1, LOC2
      LOGICAL OVFLOW, TRACE
      INTEGER MEM(100), PC, AC, PRT, RDR, TRC
      COMMON/SADSAC/ MEM, PC, AC, PRT, RDR, TRC, OVFLOW, TRACE
C
C              DUMP SYSTEM STATUS
      WRITE (PRT,10) PC, AC
10    FORMAT (///, T40, '** SADSAC SYSTEM DUMP **' //
     1        T16, 'PROGRAM COUNTER=', I3, T68, 'ACCUMULATOR=', I4 //
     2        T45, 'MEMORY CONTENTS' //)
C
C              DUMP MEMORY
      DO 20 I = 1, 91, 10
         J = I + 9
         LOC1 = I - 1
         LOC2 = LOC1 + 9
         WRITE (PRT,15) LOC1, LOC2, (MEM(K), K=I, J)
15       FORMAT (T13, 'LOCATIONS ', I2, '-', I2, 10I6)
20    CONTINUE
      RETURN
      END


      BLOCK DATA
C* * * * * * * * * * * * * * * * * * * * * * * * * * * * * * * * * * *
C* INITIALIZE COMMON AREAS AS FOLLOWS:                                 *
C*      MEM    = 0   :ALL MEMORY LOCATIONS ARE INITIALLY ZERO          *
C*      PC     = 0   :START PROGRAM AT FIRST MEMORY LOCATION           *
C*      AC     = 0   :ACCUMULATOR STARTS AT ZERO                       *
C*      PRT    = 6   :IBM 360-370 PRINTER UNIT NUMBER                  *
C*      RDR    = 5   :IBM 360-370 READER UNIT NUMBER                   *
C*      TRC    = 6   :IBM 360-370 PRINTER UNIT NUMBER                  *
C*      OVFLOW =FALSE:ASSUME NO OVERFLOW TO START WITH                 *
C*      TRACE  = TRUE:INCLUDE DEBUGGING TRACE                          *
C* * * * * * * * * * * * * * * * * * * * * * * * * * * * * * * * * * *
      LOGICAL OVFLOW, TRACE
      INTEGER MEM(100), PC, AC, PRT, RDR, TRC
      COMMON/SADSAC/ MEM, PC, AC, PRT, RDR, TRC, OVFLOW, TRACE
      DATA MEM/100*0/, PC/0/, AC/0/
      DATA PRT/6/, RDR/5/, TRC/6/, TRACE/.TRUE./, OVFLOW/.FALSE./
      END
```

Figure 7-4 SADSAC Simulator

Exercises

7.01 Write a sadsac assembler language program that reads values A, B and C, and then calculates and outputs the result of the fortran statement

$$A = ((B-C) * (A-C))/(B+C)$$

7.02 Assume that we have an inexpensive model of the sadsac machine. In this version, the only arithmetic operation implemented is subtract (assembler SUB, machine +5). The ZERO, ADD, MUL, and DIV operations are not legal. The STOR is still acceptable but the LOAD is not. Operations such as LOAD may be implemented by a sequence such as

```
STOR    TEMP
SUB     TEMP        ZERO ACCUMULATOR
SUB     X           HAVE -X
STOR    TEMP
SUB     TEMP        NOW HAVE ZERO
SUB     TEMP        FINALLY LOADED X
```

Using only STOR and SUB, calculate

$$E = A + 2*B - C$$

Hint. Before doing this calculation, design the programs required to perform + and *.

7.03 Our sadsac machine has instructions that reference only one word of memory. Some machines include two operand instructions. These instructions do not involve any explicit references to an accumulator. Consider such a machine having the following operations.

ADD	A,B -	Add A to B storing result in A
SUB	A,B -	Subtract B from A storing result in A
MUL	A,B -	Multiply A by B storing result in A
DIV	A,B -	Divide A by B storing result in A
MOV	A,B -	Copy value of B into A

Using these instructions, write code to calculate

$$X = ((Y-Z) * (X-Z))/(Y+Z)$$

You may assume that X, Y, and Z are already defined. If you need temporary storage areas, select names T1, T2, ...

7.04 Write sequences of sadsac assembler language programs that "simulate" each of the 5 instructions given in problem 7.03.

7.05 Write a sadsac assembler language program that calculates the greatest common divisor of two input values A and B.

CHAPTER 8

Effective Programming—Using Operating System Facilities

In previous chapters we presented advanced programming techniques and advanced features of the FORTRAN language. More recently we have focused on the computer itself and on how its structure affects the FORTRAN programmer. In this chapter we will examine the steps between the input of a source program and the end of its execution.

8.1 OPERATING SYSTEMS

The first computers, produced in the late 1940s and early 1950s, were, by today's standards, slow, small, and difficult to program and run. As a result, they were used by a very limited number of people. Typical machines resembled the SADSAC computer of Chapter 7, and users programmed in machine or in assembler language. Each user was responsible for setting up, monitoring execution of, and gathering results from a program's execution. Generally only one person used a machine at a time.

Three important developments of the mid-1950s changed this single-user relationship. First was the development of higher level languages, such as FORTRAN and COBOL, and of compilers for these languages. Use of compilers increased the ease of programming so that more people saw the computer as a helpful tool for the solution of problems. Second, because of advances in computer hardware, computer speeds increased by a factor of 1000. With this increased speed, larger problems became amenable to computer solution. The third change was the introduction of libraries of computer programs and subprograms that could be shared among all users. Shared code meant that a user did not have to be an expert in mathematics just to use a square root or sine routine; one person could code such a routine and place it in a shared library, so that all users could call it. These three developments caused an increase in computer accessability, and hence also an increase in computer demand.

Because of greater demand for computer time, it became wasteful to have each job manually set up and run. Often the manual setup time exceeded the execution time of the program. The difference in speeds between humans and computers led to the development of supervisory programs that could do some of the setup for execution of a computer program. These programs were called *monitors*. A monitor read in one or more user programs; invoked compilers, loaders, and utility routines on demand; and turned control over to each user program in succession, receiving control back after execution terminated. The monitor was available to provide services to users as requested. The sequence of jobs processed by a monitor was called a *batch*.

Further developments in technology allowed the overlapping of I/O activity with computation. Input and output operations, particularly reading cards and printing lines, involve physical motion, such as moving a card past a read station. The speeds at which cards can move are quite slow compared to the electronic speed at which the CPU operates. Because a program can seldom continue with meaningful computation while awaiting the results of an I/O operation, the CPU was idle for a long time during I/O operations. This situation resulted in the development of *multiprogramming*, in which more than one program was loaded into memory at a time. Since there was only one CPU, only one program could be actively computing at a time; others could, however, be ready to use the CPU any time the first had to wait for an I/O event to be completed. Thus two or more programs could progress simultaneously, each overlapping the I/O wait time of the others. In this way, the idle time of the CPU was reduced.

As multiprogramming developed, the supervisory program changed from a passive monitor to a more active routine. With multiple users being served simultaneously, resources needed to be controlled; the supervisor kept track of who possessed which resources and allocated the available ones to requesting programs. The supervisor, now called an *operating system*, became responsible for providing to the users sharable and non-sharable resources, including compilers, memory, and I/O devices. A natural extension was to have the operating system schedule user programs for execution in an order that increased utilization of the system resources; a job that would make few requests for I/O but that required much use of the CPU might be scheduled along with one that performed much I/O. The operating system became the controller of execution for a group of programs, as opposed to a provider of services to a single program on request.

In the transition from a single user of a system to multiprogrammed batch execution, personal interaction was lost. A user originally was able to program the computer to accept certain inputs from the console and to use these inputs to alter the course of execution. As computer speeds increased and multiprogramming evolved, it was too costly to have the computer waiting for a human to type in some values. It was also wasteful of human time, since the time at which a job would be scheduled for execution was not easily predictable.

Human interaction with computation is desirable in many tasks. The use of *timesharing* permits such human interaction without excessive cost. Timesharing is a system in which many users are simultaneously interacting with a machine, all of them feeling they have its exclusive use. Because the computer operates faster than humans, it can service several other requests in the time it takes a person to input one request. The normal media for communication are terminals, generally typewriters or video screens with keyboards attached. Some computers provide both batch and timesharing services simultaneously.

8.2   COMPILERS

A large portion of programming on modern computers is done in higher level languages; thus a variety of compilers have been developed to meet the needs of different programmers. There are several possible goals for a compiler. These goals include:

1. Small compiler size—for use on a machine having a limited memory.
2. Fast compilation—for use where the demand for computer use or the number of programs to be compiled is high.
3. Extensive error checking and intelligible diagnostic messages—useful in environments where many users will be unfamiliar with the source language (such as students in a beginning programming class).
4. Fast execution or small size of compiled code—useful if the compiled program is to be executed frequently or if each execution requires a long period of time.

Some of these goals conflict with others, and so a given compiler may emphasize some at the expense of others. The IBM FORTRAN H compiler can produce a program that is small and executes rapidly; the compiler itself, however, is large and slow. Such compilers, that produce "optimized" output, are often used for compilation of so-called "production" programs that will be executed many times. The WATFIV compiler, on the other hand, produces relatively inefficient programs, but it compiles quickly. It is appropriate in student environments where many short programs are executed only once each.

8.3   OBJECT CODE

A compiler takes a source program and converts it into a sequence of machine instructions to effect the intent of the source code. Code produced by a compiler is called *object code*. This code is often placed on an auxiliary storage device where it can be retained for later execution. For programs that will be reused, the object code from one compilation can be executed an unlimited number of times. If the program size or execution time is substantial, then the use of optimized object code may effect a considerable savings in time or memory space.

FORTRAN subprograms are separately compiled modules. The code of a subprogram is placed in memory separate from that for all other subprograms. Under most computing systems it is possible to combine the code of a newly compiled subprogram with that of other previously compiled ones. By this technique, a change in the source code often requires recompilation of only one subprogram. This is another justification for modular program development using subprograms.

The object code for a program can be retained on an auxiliary storage device, or it can be punched on cards. This latter form is called an *object deck*. An object deck can be submitted for execution, perhaps along with other source code. Punched cards make an inexpensive medium on which to retain object code for long term storage.

8.4 RELOCATION

The programs for the SADSAC computer of Chapter 7 are always placed in memory with the first instruction at location 0 of the machine. Since only one user makes use of that machine at a time, this is a reasonable restriction. However, most major computers are multiprogrammed, and two different programs cannot both be placed at location 0.

We also want the ability to use subprograms from a library shared by all users. If there are a substantial number of shared subprograms, we will not be able to allocate a unique set of memory locations for each library routine. But if two subprograms are assigned to overlapping memory locations, the two would be mutually exclusive and could not both be called by one program.

The solution to these problems is *relocatable* code, which means that the code can be placed in any available block of memory locations.

Consider, for example, the instruction

```
RD2      READ      LIST
```

in the second sample SADSAC program of Chapter 7. This is the fifth instruction of the program. If each instruction occupies one word, then this is the fifth word of the machine code program. Assume that the program is being relocated in a machine with a larger memory. If the program now begins at memory location 1001, the READ instruction will be at word 1005. If, however, the program begins at location 7491, this instruction is contained in word 7495. This means that the instruction

```
STOR      RD2
```

needs to reference location 1005 or 7495 in the two cases presented (or other locations, depending on where the program begins). The beginning address of a program is called its *load point*. The process of updating references that vary with the load point of a program is called *relocation*.

Most computers have hardware facilities to assist in relocation. Frequently there is an internal storage location called a "relocation register." The compiler generates object code in which all references within the program are computed as if the program begins at location 0. When the program is placed in memory, the load point address is placed in the relocation register. Any time a reference within the program occurs during execution, the contents of the relocation register are added to the relocatable address computed by the compiler.

External references—references to points outside a program or subprogram—are handled differently. Recall that each subprogram is separately compiled. Let us consider the example of subprogram SUB1 that calls another, SUB2. As SUB1 is being compiled, it is impossible to know where the code for SUB2 will be located during execution; it might immediately precede the code for SUB1, immediately follow it, or be located in some completely separate part of memory. The compiler must note those instructions within SUB1 that refer to SUB2, so that when both subprograms are loaded in memory, these instructions can be updated to contain the proper address.

The relocation of SUB1 and SUB2 can be handled in several ways. One is that each time SUB2 is called, the relocation register is changed to contain the address of SUB2; when SUB2 returns to SUB1, the relocation register must be reset to the address of SUB1. Another approach is to do partial relocation as a main program and its subprograms are bound together to create a combination called a "load module." Partial relocation requires computing the displacement of SUB2 from the start of the load module and adding that displacement to any references to routine SUB2. During execution, the relocation register contains the address at which the load module begins, and this is added to any references within the load module. These techniques permit separate relocation of subprograms prior to execution.

The two processes described here are loading and linking. *Loading* is the process of taking an object program, placing it in memory, and relocating it. *Linking* is the process of taking an object program and binding it with those other program modules that it calls.

8.5   OVERLAY STRUCTURES

As mentioned in the last section, subprograms are separately relocatable modules. Because they are separately compiled, a change to one subprogram or main program requires recompilation of only that one module, not of the entire program. Another important advantage of separate relocatability is that subprograms can be loaded into any available memory locations. We will now see how this property can be useful when dealing with large programs.

Consider a program, the main activities of which can be divided into three phases: (1) initialize work areas and read a set of initial data; (2) read and process a series of transactions that affect the initial data; (3) reorganize and output the revised data for future runs. Each phase is independent from the other two. The program can be constructed as a main "driver" program and three subprograms that fetch, update, and save the data. Thus the program can be represented by the tree of Figure 8-1.

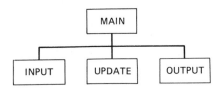

FIGURE 8-1 Three-phase program

If the tasks are complicated, we may need a considerable amount of memory to contain the entire program. In fact, the size of such a program might exceed the size of available memory. Even if this program would fit in main memory, it might be desirable to minimize its storage requirements because, under many operating systems, a job's execution priority is inversely proportional to its memory demands.

Notice that once routine INPUT has returned, it is no longer needed in memory. In fact, UPDATE and INPUT, being mutually exclusive, could share the same memory area, as could UPDATE and OUTPUT. An *overlay structure* permits these modules to share memory. What is needed is auxiliary storage space such as a disk to store copies of all three modules, main memory to contain the largest of the three, and a supervisory routine to move the modules in and out of main memory on demand. A program design such as this is called an overlay structure because one module overlays the space previously occupied by another.

Suppose that the sizes of the routines had been as follows. (K is an abbreviation for 1024, and is commonly used as a measure of computer memory. The approximation of 1000 units = 1K is usually a good estimate of a program's size.)

MAIN 30K

INPUT 30K   UPDATE 48K   OUTPUT 32K

Then, instead of requiring 140K words (30+30+48+32) of main memory for this program, by using a simple overlay, we can execute it in only 78K (30K for main + 48K for the largest of its subordinate routines). We speak of this sort of overlay as being "tree structured." The main program is the root, and all routines it calls directly are immediate descendants of it. There is a unique path from the root to any other node in the tree. Any time a routine is in memory, all routines along the path from the root to it are also in memory.

An overlay structure can be more complex than the one pictured above. For example it might have the form of Figure 8-2. (Sizes of the modules are shown after them.)

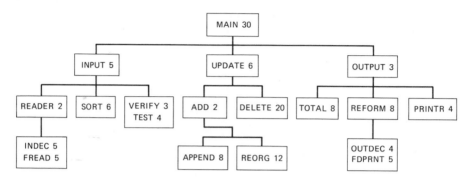

FIGURE 8-2 A Complex Program Structure

In this diagram, READER and its descendants INDEC and FREAD are mutually exclusive with SORT, which is mutually exclusive with VERIFY and TEST. An amount of memory is reserved for these three sections, large enough for the largest of the three (READER and its descendants). One space similarly serves for the two descendants of UPDATE. Notice that part of that space is shared by routines APPEND and REORG. Thus we see that an overlay area may itself contain one or more overlay areas. We calculate the amount of memory required to contain an overlay structure from the bottom up. First determine the size of each terminal node (each node having no successors) in the tree. Then, to the size of each predecessor of a terminal, add the size of its largest successor. Continue this process until the size of the entire structure is computed. In the preceding figure, for example, the sizes of all individual modules are shown. Space for READER is 12K, the size of its one successor node, plus the size of READER itself. Space for UPDATE is 26K, since it is of size 6K and the spaces for its two successors are 14K and 20K, respectively. Continuing this process, we see that the total space required for this program structure is 56K.

Overlay structures do entail some overhead. First, additional time is needed to put an object program into overlay form prior to execution. Additional auxiliary storage space may be needed during execution, since an entire copy of the program must be kept on some direct access device. Because calls may cause different portions of the structure to be brought into main memory, there will be additional time required to effect these calls. Finally, the supervisory routine that monitors calls in a overlay structure occupies space both for itself and for tables that it must maintain.

Of these sources of overhead, the time to create an overlay structure is usually not severe, since it occurs only once. The auxiliary space requirement is also not a major concern, since the amount of available auxiliary space at most installations is generally far greater than the amount of available main memory. The final one is likewise normally unimportant, since the tables are relatively small and in some systems, the overlay supervisor does not reside in a user's memory area, but is written so that one copy may be shared among all users.

The added time that is required to process calls among overlay routines is not trivial, however. A programmer seeks to plan an overlay structure that minimizes this time. If a routine SUB1 will call both routines SUB2A and SUB2B frequently, it is wise to have SUB2A and SUB2B located along the same path, so that calls to these can be effected with little change to memory. Another technique of overlay planning is to place a routine used by several others close to the root of the overlay tree, so that it will be in memory at the time it is called.

Another consideration with overlay structures is that, depending on circumstances in the program's execution, certain segments may or may not be overlaid. Suppose that one segment contains a subprogram with the statements

```
DATA I/1/
      :
      :
I = 5
```

In some dialects, once I receives the value 5, it retains it in subsequent calls. But in an overlay structure, if this segment is ever overlaid and later recalled, a fresh copy may be brought from disk, and that copy might have I reinitialized to 1. Programmers using overlay structures should be careful that any values to be retained are in common blocks, and that these common blocks are located in such a position that they will be overlaid only when no values in them are ever needed again.

8.6   CASE STUDY: DEC-10

LINK-10 is the program that creates overlay structures for the DEC-10. For LINK-10, the overlay must be structured in tree form, as we have described above. If execution is in progress in a routine at one point in the tree, all routines represented along the path from the root to that node are also required to be in memory. The root always remains in memory.

Switches that are used for an overlay are:

/OVERLAY that indicates an overlay structure is being created.

/LINK that indicates the completion of a particular node of the overlay tree. This switch may optionally be followed by :*name*, where *name* is any name by which the programmer wishes to refer to this node later (for positioning of descendant nodes).

/NODE to reposition the editor to a particular node of the tree, in order to define another subordinate of that node. This switch may be followed by one of three position indicators. These are   :0 that repositions to the root of the tree, :-*n* for some integer *n* that repositions to the *n*th predecessor of the present node, or :*name*, for some name *name* that repositions to node *name* for preparation of a descendant of node *name*.

The user lists names of subprograms that are to appear in each node and then supplies the /LINK command. When this command is interpreted, it completes a particular node of the overlay structure, and begins processing of the first subnode of that node. For example the tree

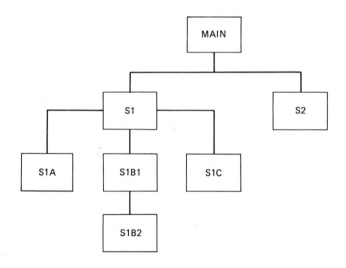

could be prepared by the following sequence of commands.

```
/OVERLAY,MAIN/LINK
 S1/LINK:CNE
 S1A/LINK
 /NODE:-1 S1B1/LINK
 S1B2/LINK
 /NODE:ONE S1C/LINK
 /NODE:0 S2/LINK/GO
```

8.7   CASE STUDY: IBM 360-370

Overlay structures under the DEC-10 have the disadvantage that a routine needed by two different nodes must be located higher in the tree than the two nodes, or each node must contain a copy of the routine. If there are many such independent routines, a tree that is top-heavy or highly redundant can result.

IBM has resolved this difficulty by the multiregion overlay. Each region is the equivalent of a separate overlay structure. In the structure of Figure 8-3, MAIN and SUB1 or MAIN and SUB2 can be in memory simultaneously with either SUBA or SUBB or SUBC.

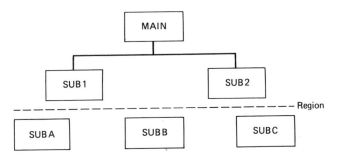

FIGURE 8-3   Multiple Region Overlay Structure.

SUBA, SUBB, and SUBC may have descendants just as if they had been descended from either SUB1 or SUB2. However, since SUBA, SUBB, and SUBC constitute a separate region, they are effectively descendants of both SUB1 and SUB2.

The linkage editor is the IBM processor to create an overlay structure. Statements to the linkage editor are:

INSERT to position one or more object modules as part of an overlay node. This statement is followed by the names of one or more subroutines that are to be a part of the current node.

OVERLAY to reposition the linkage editor to a particular level in the overlay structure. This statement names a node to be begun; when the name is used on subsequent OVERLAY statements, those statements define other nodes at the same level as the node first identified by the name. The OVERLAY statement may also identify a node as a region. When used this way, the OVERLAY statement has the form OVERLAY *name*(REGION) .

NAME to name an entire load module as a program.

Suppose you want to create an overlay structure corresponding to the tree shown in Figure 8-4.

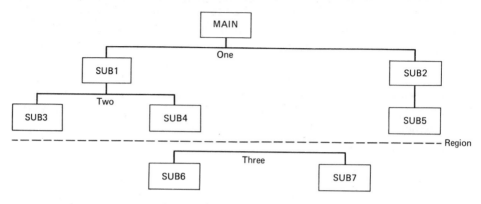

FIGURE 8-4   Overlay Tree

This structure could be created by the following overlay statements.

```
INSERT MAIN
OVERLAY ONE
INSERT SUB1
OVERLAY TWO
INSERT SUB3
OVERLAY TWO
INSERT SUB4
OVERLAY ONE
INSERT SUB2,SUB5
OVERLAY THREE(REGION)
INSERT SUB6
OVERLAY THREE
INSERT SUB7
NAME OVERSTR
```

This sequence of code produces the overlay structure identified in the above picture.

Common Built-In Function Subprograms

Function	Name	Definition	Arguments Num-ber	Arguments Type	Result Type
Maximum/ minimum of argu- ments	MAX0 MAX1 AMAX0 AMAX1 MIN0 MIN1 AMIN0 AMIN1	$y = \max(x_1, \ldots, x_n)$ $y = \min(x_1, \ldots, x_n)$	$\geqq 2$ $\geqq 2$ $\geqq 2$ $\geqq 2$ $\geqq 2$ $\geqq 2$ $\geqq 2$ $\geqq 2$	INTEGER REAL INTEGER REAL INTEGER REAL INTEGER REAL	INTEGER INTEGER REAL REAL INTEGER INTEGER REAL REAL
Truncation	AINT INT	$y = (\text{sign } x) \cdot n$ where n is the largest integer $\leq \mid x \mid$	1 1	REAL REAL	REAL INTEGER
Modulo	MOD AMOD	$y = $ remainder $x_1 \div x_2$ (i.e., $y = x_1 \bmod x_2$)	2 2	INTEGER REAL	INTEGER REAL
Float	FLOAT	$y = $ real equivalent to x	1	INTEGER	REAL
Fix	IFIX	$y = $ integer equiva- lent to x	1	REAL	INTEGER
Transfer of sign	ISIGN SIGN	$y = (\text{sign } x_2) \cdot x_1$	2 2	INTEGER REAL	INTEGER REAL
Positive difference	IDIM DIM	$y = x_1 - \min(x_1, x_2)$ (i.e., $y = x_1 - x_2$ if $(x_1 - x_2) > 0$, $= 0$ otherwise)	2 2	INTEGER REAL	INTEGER REAL

Function	Name	Definition	Arguments Number	Arguments Type	Result Type
Logarithm	ALOG	$y = \ln x$	1	REAL	REAL
	ALOG10	$y = \log_{10} x$	1	REAL	REAL
Exponential	EXP	$y = e^x$	1	REAL	REAL
Square root	SQRT	$y = \sqrt{x}$	1	REAL	REAL
Sine	SIN	$y = \sin x$	1	REAL	REAL
Cosine	COS	$y = \cos x$	1	REAL	REAL
Arc tangent	ATAN	$y = \arctan x$	1	REAL	REAL
Absolute value	IABS	$y = \lvert x \rvert$	1	INTEGER	INTEGER
	ABS		1	REAL	REAL

APPENDIX 2

Summary of Changes between FORTRAN IV and FORTRAN 77

This appendix indicates changes in the FORTRAN language included in the FORTRAN 77 revision. It is not intended as a complete description of FORTRAN 77, but as an announcement of changes to material included in Chapter 0. We do not introduce new statements here but, instead, we note how the syntax or meaning of existing statements has been changed. There is one exception, however. FORTRAN 77 contains an IF-THEN-ELSE construct; since a number of FORTRAN compilers already permit something of this form as an extension to FORTRAN IV, we will describe the form of the new IF.

The items in this appendix are arranged in the same order as the original topics were presented in Chapter 0 of this book. Section numbers in this appendix are the same as those for the relevant sections from Chapter 0. This is so that you can easily find the appropriate note in the appendix each time you find a vertical mark in the margin for a section of Chapter 0.

0.2.1 Statement format

Completely blank lines are now permitted, and are treated as comments. (That is, they are ignored.) Comments, furthermore, may begin with either the letter "C" or with the symbol "*", asterisk.

0.2.2 Data items

Character constants in H form *(n H string)* are now permitted only in FORMAT statements. Character constants represented in apostrophe form *('string')* are the current permitted form. However, many processors will probably continue to allow H-type character constants in CALL and DATA statements for compatibility.

A subscript may be any legal arithmetic expression; if it is not of integer mode, it will be truncated for use as a subscript.

0.2.3 Operators

Two new logical operators have been included. These are .EQV. and .NEQV., which stand for "equivalent to" and "not equivalent to," respectively. If L1 and L2 are two logical expressions, (L1.EQV.L2) will be true if both L1 and

L2 are true or if both L1 and L2 are false. That is, .EQV. is true just in case its two arguments have the same true/false value. The expression (L1.NEQV.L2) is the same as (.NOT.(L1.EQV.L2)); that is, (L1.NEQV.L2) will be true just in case L1 and L2 have different true/false values.

For character operations a new operator, //, has been added, as well as a new notation. The // operator stands for concatenation, or joining together of two strings. If S1 has value 'DOG' and S2 has the value 'HOUSE,' S1// S2 has the value 'DOGHOUSE'. Similarly, it is possible to break a string apart by means of a substring operation. To indicate a substring, a pair of parentheses encloses two expressions, representing the positions of the first and last character to be included in the substring. For example, if S3 has the value 'DOG-HOUSE', S3(1,3) is 'DOG' and S3(4,5) is 'HO'. If the array reference and substring reference are specified for the same variable, the array subscripts appear first; that is, A(I,J)(K,L) is the substring of the Kth through the Lth characters of array element A(I,J).

0.3.1 Declarations

Variables of type CHARACTER are now permitted. The syntax of the CHARACTER statement is the same as that described in Section 3.8. The type CHARACTER may also be specified on an IMPLICIT statement or on a FUNCTION statement. In these three contexts, CHARACTER may be qualified as CHARACTER*n where n is an integer constant denoting the length of the characer string.

Dimensions may be specified as A(d_1:d_2) where d_1 and d_2 are the lower and upper limits on subscript values, respectively. For example, DIMENSION A(3:10) declares an eight element array, having elements A(3), A(4),...,A(10).

0.3.1 Data statement

A *value* need not be the same type as the *variable* that it is to initialize; conversion will occur just as if the *variable* and the *value* were in an assignment statement. It is also possible to initialize portions of any array by specifying A(i_1):A(i_2) in the *variable* list. This notation means that values are to be supplied for all elements of array A beginning with that one having subscript i_1 through that one having subscript i_2.

0.5.2 Free format input (also called "list-directed input")

A form of the read statement READ (*indev*, *) *list* is now permitted.

0.5.3 Free-format output (also called "list directed output")

A form of the write statement WRITE (*outdev*, *) *list* is now permitted.

0.5.3, 0.5.6 Free-format output, formatted WRITE

The list of variables being written may also include constants and expressions.

0.6.2 Computed GOTO

The index of the computed GOTO may be any integer expression. If the value of the expression is greater than the number of statement labels listed, or if the value is not positive, execution continues with the statement following the GOTO.

0.6.3 IF statement

Four new statements have been added to the language.

IF *(exp)* THEN   END IF
ELSE IF *(exp)* THEN   ELSE

Each IF-THEN must be matched with a corresponding END IF statement. Between IF-THEN and its associated END IF, there may be any number of ELSE IF-THEN statements, and at most one ELSE statement. These groups must be properly nested. That is, if one IF group is contained within another IF group, all statements of the first IF group must be between the IF-THEN and the END IF of the second (containing) IF group. Branching into an IF group from outside the group is not permitted.
The meaning of the statements is similar to that described for the IF-THEN-ELSE construct in Section 1.3.2.

0.6.4 DO statement

The parameters (*initial, final,* and *increment*) may now be any integer expression. An "iteration count" is established before the DO loop is commenced. This count is MAX0((*(final-initial+increment)* / *increment*), 0). The value of the iteration count is the number of times the loop will be performed; notice that the iteration count may have a value of 0, in which case no statements in the loop are performed. This increment of the loop may be negative. It is possible to change the values of the loop parameters during execution of the loop. However, this does not affect the number of times the loop will be repeated, since this is determined by the iteration count, which is computed before the loop is executed the first time. It is not permitted to transfer from outside a DO loop into the range of the loop.

INDEX